Reviews for Larry P. English's
Improving Data Warehouse and Busi[ness]
Information Quality

"The Information Quality Bible for the Information Age!

"Practical and useful. . . this book has it all in one package: 'concept book, textbook, reference book, practitioner's guide.'

"English's sense of humor is reflected throughout. The rewards from the implementation of his methods should be as enjoyable as the reading"

> *Masaaki Imai, Founder, Kaizen Institute*
> *Bud H. Cox, Managing Director, Kaizen Institute of Japan*
> (*Kaizen* is a Japanese word that connotes "continuous improvement involving everyone in the organization")

"Very lively reading. The book belongs on the bookshelf of every manager and technician."

> *Bill Inmon, Pine Cone Systems*
> *"Father of Data Warehousing"*

"This book is a must for every business bookshelf. Larry English has been on the forefront of the Data Quality issue from the outset. . . [and] has some real wisdom on this vital issue."

> *John Zachman, Zachman International*
> *Creator of the Framework for Enterprise Architecture*

"This book is long overdue. As a leading expert on Quality in the world today, Larry English shows the impact that data and information quality directly have on costs and on profitability—not just for data warehouses but also for business information. His examples are clear, and vital for management to read.

"This book will maximize your chances for success. No Data Warehousing project and no IT Department should be without it. I predict that it will become the 'Bible' of Quality success."

> *Clive Finkelstein, Information Engineering Services Pty Ltd.*
> *"Father of Information Engineering"*

"Everywhere we go. . . we see the results of data quality problems. In this book, Larry English not only turns up the heat by discussing the sources and nature of data quality problems, he also sheds real light through a practical approach to addressing data quality improvement. Time spent understanding and applying the principles and tips Larry offers will be well worth the investment."

> *Vaughan Merlyn, The Concours Group*

"Excellent reading for those taking the holistic approach to database design, in which a good database considers where the information comes from, how it is used, and what results come from that use."

> *David Wall, Amazon.com*

"A superior work. A tremendous addition to the field of business intelligence. Pragmatic, experience and reality based, but most important, focused on tangible, measurable benefits to the business."

Doug Hackney, Enterprise Group, Ltd.
Data Warehouse and Business Intelligence Expert

"A practical approach to using information quality as a business management tool to reduce the business and systems costs resulting from poor information quality. Argues that information quality is not an isolated function, but an inherent and integral part of the business management and that everyone in the enterprise has a stewardship role in it."

Booknews, Inc.

"Larry's book is simply brilliant. . . it wrestles with a sometimes elusive but extremely costly business problem in a most clear and pragmatic manner. The book is extremely timely because the Y2k challenge has embarrassingly exposed the world's data quality problem. . . Armed with yesterday's Y2k tools and Larry's visionary book, an organization can get closer to cleaning up the rest of the enterprise's data. Such an endeavor may mean the difference between business success and business failure."

Barbara von Halle, Founder of Knowledge Partners, Inc.
and editor of Handbook of Data Management

"Larry English's new book has terrific value. While English's new book has "Data Warehouse" in its title, the concepts and step-by-step instructions can be applied to any information system project. . . . The author gets right to the point through an excellent and organized writing style which is a pleasure to read.

"English states he will personally refund the purchase price if the reader doesn't achieve value worth multiple times the cost of the book. After spending a few weeks with this text, I'm sure the author will process very few, if any, refunds."

Andy Matthiesen, Director of Technology, Rx Remedy, Inc.
in a TDAN book review

"Larry provides a clear, easy-to-follow roadmap for identifying and solving information quality problems and ensuring that they don't' come back. The methods and techniques in this book are a cornerstone for any successful data warehouse project. I use his techniques on all of my projects and strongly recommend his book to anyone who really wants to improve their business performance."

Earl Hadden, co-author of the Hadden-Kelly Data Warehouse Method
Principal, Hadden & Company Management Consultants

"Comprehensive, well-written and well-organized.

"An in-depth manual that can be used by both managers and information technology specialists.

"One of the best manuals on information quality that you can find."

Soundview Executive Book Summaries, 11/99

"As we enter the age of eBusiness, companies can no longer hide their information quality problems from their customers. . . . Successful eBusiness companies will be those who recognise and manage information as their key strategic asset. This book is essential reading for all who are serious about profitable survival in the information age."

Nigel Turner, British Telecommunications

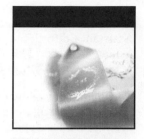

Improving Data Warehouse and Business Information Quality

Methods for Reducing Costs and Increasing Profits

Larry P. English

Wiley Computer Publishing

John Wiley & Sons, Inc.

NEW YORK • CHICHESTER • WEINHEIM • BRISBANE • SINGAPORE • TORONTO

Publisher: Robert Ipsen
Editor: Robert M. Elliott
Assistant Editor: Pam Sobotka
Managing Editor: Marnie Wielage
Text Design & Composition: Benchmark Productions, Inc.

Designations used by companies to distinguish their products are often claimed as trademarks. In all instances where John Wiley & Sons, Inc., is aware of a claim, the product names appear in initial capital or ALL CAPITAL LETTERS. Readers, however, should contact the appropriate companies for more complete information regarding trademarks and registration.

TQdM® is a registered trademark of INFORMATION IMPACT International, Inc.

This publication is designed to provide accurate and authoritative information in regard to the subject matter covered. It is sold with the understanding that the publisher is not engaged in professional services. If professional advice or other expert assistance is required, the services of a competent professional person should be sought.

Library of Congress Cataloging-in-Publication Data:

English, Larry, 1947–
  Improving data warehouse and business information quality :
methods for reducing costs and increasing profits / Larry English.
    p. cm.
  Includes bibliographical references and index.
  ISBN 0-471-25383-9 (pbk. : alk. paper)
  1. Industrial management--Data processing.   2. Business--Data
processing.   3. Data warehousing.   I. Title.
HD30.2.E54   1999
658.4'038'0285574--dc21   98-33167
                                    CIP

Printed in the United States of America.
10 9 8 7 6 5

Contents

Acknowledgments

First and foremost to Diane, my partner in business and in life, without whose encouragement, support, and patience, this book would never have become a reality.

To Beth and Bill, my Mom and Dad, who taught me about life, faith, and personal integrity. Isn't this the basis for any kind of improvement?

To Ashley and Chancellor, my children, whom I have seen mature, taking both backwards and forward steps, and from whom I have learned about the challenges of change.

To Clay Steakley, our administrative assistant, who diligently read every word of this book and provided valuable insights.

To Frank Dennis, an associate, who has provided insights on statistical methods and for proofing the section on random sampling.

And especially to the dozens of information professionals whose organizations have allowed me the privilege of providing guidance in their journey toward information quality maturity, and from whom I have learned much.

Introduction

*"The best effect of any book is that it excites the
reader to self activity."*

–THOMAS CARLYLE

The state of information quality today is worse than it was five years ago, and it is getting worse day by day. In fact, the quality of information in many organizations is enterprise-threatening. Consider some of my recent experiences:

Having just returned from chairing my fourth Data Quality conference, the first in London in November 1998, my renewed excitement about information quality improvement as a trend was brought back to reality. The next week I keynoted conferences in Phoenix, Arizona, and Orlando, Florida. When I checked into the Sheraton Mesa Hotel in Phoenix, the registration clerk asked if I was checking in. I replied, "Yes, my name is English." She entered that into the computer, and asked if my first name was Ron. "No," I replied, "it is Larry." "I'm sorry, but we have no reservation for a Larry English," was her reply. "But that is okay, we have rooms." My confirmation number validated that the reservation was indeed for me, but under the name "Ron." The clerk replied, "that's no big deal, we can change it." "It *is* a big deal," I contended. "No it isn't," she insisted, probably thinking about the ease of making the change in the database, but not about the customer service aspect of the event. Seeing the history of the record, she asked if the last time I had stayed there was the 22nd of last month. No, I had not. When she gave me the printed copy of the registration form to sign, I discovered Arizona State University had just been "relocated" to my address in Brentwood, Tennessee!

I flew from there to Orlando, where registration went smoothly. I had a letter and fax waiting for me at the mail desk at the Omni Rosen hotel. I was pleased with the information that allowed me to pick them up then, rather than having to return after getting to my room and finding I had to go back to the mail desk. After I got to the room, I opened the fax, noting that only 8 of the 10 sent pages were stapled together and sealed in an envelope to protect its privacy. The sealing was good; the quality control was not. There is an important reason why you document page counts on faxes: to assure all pages go through. Customer service is more than taking the pages and stuffing them in an envelope. Customer service is what The Hyatt in Phoenix did a month later when they received only 6 pages of an 11 page fax. They called my office, allowing them to re-send the missing pages immediately. This is information quality, comparing the information to reality and taking action to assure information customers have what they need when they are supposed to without having to chase it down. In Orlando, I had checked in after my office had closed, causing me to have to wait for the last 2 (most important) pages until the next day.

This book is not about information quality from an esoteric or theoretical standpoint. It is a practical book about using information quality as a business management tool for reducing the business and systems costs resulting from poor information quality. More importantly, this book is about increasing business profits and business effectiveness as a result of having higher-quality information and the customer satisfaction it generates.

The world is now experiencing a phenomenon that future historians may classify as The Golden Age of Information. The Oxford Dictionary defines *golden age* as a period during which commerce, the arts, and so forth, flourish. "Flourish" means that something is successful, very active, or widespread. With this litmus test, we are indeed living in the Golden Age of Information. Data warehouses that now contain multiple terabytes of data have forever altered the information processing landscape. The explosion of information on the Internet over the past few years confirms the importance and value of accessible information.[1]

With this proliferation of information, the challenge of managing data and providing quality information has never been more important or more complex.

The premise of this book is that:

- Information and data are strategic enterprise resources.

- Quality information enables competitive advantage and business effectiveness.

- Information quality is not an isolated "function"; it is an inherent and integral part of business management.

- Everyone in the organization has a stewardship role for information quality.

- Without information the enterprise will fail, even process-driven organizations. For example, Coca-Cola has its formulas (information) required to produce its products. For the manufacturing firm Optical Fibres, "the

---

[1] L. P. English, "The Golden Age of Information," *DM Review*, January 1997, p. 20.

key is in the chemicals and the formula for turning sand (silicon di-oxide) into optical fiber capable of transmitting laser signals for thousands of miles without losing information."

- Without *quality* information the enterprise will be suboptimized. Some organizations will fail. In fact, some already have.

- The costs of poor-quality information are high. Poor-quality information causes process failure and information scrap and rework that wastes people, money, materials, and facilities resources. The most significant problems caused by poor-quality information, however, is that it frustrates the most important resources of the enterprise—its people resources—keeping them from effectively performing their jobs, and it alienates its customer resources through wrong information about them and to them. Because there is a direct correlation between customer complaints and customer defection, the real cost of poor-quality information is in lost customer lifetime value, profits, and shareholder value.

- Information quality is free. When people ask, "what is the business case for making an investment in information quality improvement?" the answer is, "what is the business case for all the information scrap and rework caused by *not* having quality information?" It is the poor-quality information that costs money. The investment in improving both information product and information process quality is recouped multiple times in decreased costs and increased value of information to accomplish strategic business objectives.

QUALITY IS FREE

"Quality is free. It's not a gift, but it is free. What costs money are the unquality things— all the actions that involve not doing jobs right the first time.

"Quality is not only free, it is an honest-to-everything profit maker. Every penny you don't spend on doing things wrong, over, or instead, becomes half a penny right on the bottom line. If you concentrate on making quality certain you can probably increase your profit by an amount equal to 5 to 10 percent of your sales. That is a lot of money for free."[2]

Who Should Read This Book

This book is not for everyone. It is for people who care about their customers and their information customers. This book is for people who do not like to see people and money resources wasted on information scrap and rework when they could be doing things that add value. This book is for people who seriously

[2]Philip B. Crosby, *Quality Is Free*, New York: Penguin Group, 1979, p. 1.

want to see shareholder value increase on a long-term basis, not merely from quarterly statement to quarterly statement.

If you do not want to rock the boat, make waves, or change your own behavior, please do not buy this book. This book is for people who are discontent with the status quo of their organization's practices in information management. If you are *reactive*, not *proactive*, this book is not for you. This book is for people ready to be change agents. If you are looking for a silver bullet or a magic panacea to solve your information quality problems, skip this book. It is for people ready to roll up their sleeves and make information quality happen.

This book is not just for companies in the private sector that face competitive pressures just to survive. It is for government and other not-for-profit organizations that desire to truly serve their constituents—or customers—and accomplish their mission. This book is for those who desire to provide quality services at the lowest cost.

You are a candidate to receive value from this book if:

- You recognize that information is an important business resource and you want to maximize its value.

- You care about your customers, both internal and external, and desire to maintain accurate information about them and for them.

- You are fed up with the high costs of low-quality information and the resulting problems, and are asking, "is there a better way?"

- You are a business person who requires quality information or who creates information and you don't just want to do your job, you want to do the *right* job, efficiently and effectively.

- You are an information systems professional and you don't just want to build applications or databases, you want to build applications and databases that *add value* to the business and to the end customers.

Who should read this book:

- Information quality managers and staff responsible for information quality processes.

- Data resource managers and staff, and those responsible for developing data models and databases that represent and house the enterprise knowledge resources.

- Data warehouse managers and staff responsible for data architecture, data acquisition, and cleansing, transforming and loading data into the enterprise's strategic knowledge base.

- CIOs and information systems managers responsible for application development processes who are responsible for creating and managing the *information* infrastructure—not just the information *technology* infrastructure—for the enterprise.

- Systems analysts and designers who desire to add value to the business— not just create technology "solutions."

- Business information stewards who are responsible for care taking of parts of the information resources for the enterprise.

- Business managers who are owners of processes that create information used by others outside of their business area. This book will be of special value to business managers of information-intensive business areas such as customer relationship management, marketing, sales, order entry, claims processing, customer service, accounting, accounts receivable, human resources, account management.

- Business personnel, such as business analysts, actuaries, and other knowledge workers who are intensive information customers.

- Senior management who are concerned about the high costs and low success of IT and who desire to deliver shareholder value. It is senior management who must understand the absolutes of quality as a management tool and who must establish a management environment that enables information quality to increase business performance.

Why *You* Should Read This Book

In the *Harvard Business Review*, Schaffe and Thompson cite a survey showing 63 percent of companies that had embarked on TQM-based programs had failed to improve quality defects in products by even as little as 10 percent.[3] This book aims to help you understand how to avoid the pitfalls when conducting information quality improvements and when implementing an effective information quality environment.

The Gartner Group states that most reengineering initiatives will fail because of lack of attention to information quality. Experience is revealing that more than half of data warehouses built fail to meet expectations because of poor information quality. This book seeks to help you be successful in all information-related projects by addressing and solving the real problems and causes of poor quality information.

Making any kind of change to the status quo requires effort and work. Information quality is neither automatic nor easy. If it was, there would be minimal information quality problems today. Most of us need guidance in applying new skills. This book seeks to provide that guidance to minimize your risk in making information quality happen.

---

[3] *Harvard Business Review*, 1/92 volume.

Organization of This Book

This book is organized into four sections:

Part One, "Principles of Information Quality Improvement," deals with the fundamental principles of quality and of improving information quality.

Part Two, "Processes for Improving Information Quality," describes how to measure and improve information quality.

Part Three, "Establishing the Information Quality Environment," outlines how to implement an information quality environment.

Part Four, "Appendixes," provides an extensive glossary, recommended reading, and bibliography.

Part One: Principles of Information Quality Improvement

Part One describes the fundamental principles of information quality. They are not theory—they are very real and practical principles, even though they are foreign to many organizations. They provide the basis for understanding the background to information quality improvement as a management tool. Without understanding the principles of quality improvement, implementing the processes may be a hollow and empty exercise that performs the actions but lacks the soul. This may result in loss of motivation for any information improvement initiative, no matter how well intentioned.

Chapter 1, "The High Costs of Low-Quality Data," outlines the business case for information quality improvement. It describes why data that appears to be of satisfactory quality is, in fact, not. Examples highlight the high costs of low-quality data. Failure to solve information quality problems can be fatal to organizations.

Chapter 2, "Defining Information Quality," defines information quality, what it is and is not. Information quality is not a soft measure. It in fact can be quantified in bottom-line terms.

Chapter 3, "Applying Quality Management Principles to Information," describes the principles of quality in general: customer focus, continuous process improvement, and the use of scientific methods. It describes the concept of information as a product, and knowledge workers as information customers. We outline who has accountability for information quality. The answer may surprise you.

Part Two: Processes for Improving Information Quality

Part Two is the guide and road map of the processes to assess and improve information quality. It defines the processes of information quality improvement as a management tool for business performance excellence.

Chapter 4, "An Overview of Total Quality data Management (TQdM)," provides an overview of the TQdM (Total Quality data Management) methodology. It provides a thumbnail sketch of information measurement, assessment, and improvement processes. It further outlines a methodology for guidance in the data warehouse context.

Chapter 5, "Assessing Data Definition and Information Architecture Quality," outlines how to measure and assess the quality of data definition and information architecture. This represents the product "specification" of the information product. Without quality of information architectures that store the enterprise's knowledge resources, information quality will be much more difficult to achieve.

Chapter 6, "Information Quality Assessment," describes how to measure, analyze, and report information quality in databases, data warehouses, or produced by the business processes.

Chapter 7, "Measuring Nonquality Information Costs," describes the process of analyzing and quantifying the costs of poor information quality in business terms. It provides a road map for measuring the devastating impact poor-quality information has on business operations, mission accomplishment, customer satisfaction, and profits.

Chapter 8, "Information *Product* Improvement: Data Reengineering and Cleansing," describes the process of information product improvement; that is, reengineering and cleansing. It describes how to audit and control the extract, transformation and cleansing, and load processes for data warehousing.

Chapter 9, "Improving Information *Process* Quality: Data Defect Prevention," outlines how to improve the quality of the information product through business process improvement. It describes how to identify root causes of information quality problems, and how to plan and implement permanent information quality improvements.

Chapter 10, "Information Quality Tools and Techniques," describes the various categories of information quality tools and techniques that support the processes described in this section.

Part Three: Establishing the Information Quality Environment

Information quality improvement is not simply "scrubbing" data to put it into the data warehouse. Information quality is not simply auditing data to measure it. Information quality improvement *means* fundamental changes in how the information systems organization defines, develops, and delivers its products and services, and fundamental changes in how the enterprise plans, organizes, manages, and performs its business processes, and measures its business performance.

Sustainable information quality improvement will be accompanied by a change in the way people think about their information products and information "customers." Part Three describes the culture shift required to create a sustainable information quality environment.

Chapter 11, "The 14 Points of Information Quality," outlines Deming's 14 Points of Quality along with their direct ramifications for information quality improvement.

Chapter 12, "Information Stewardship: Accountability for Information Quality," describes Information Stewardship, the people roles and accountabilities for information products.

Chapter 13, "Implementing an Information Quality Improvement Environment," describes the steps to implement an information quality environment. It begins with how to conduct an information quality management maturity gap analysis and describes a set of steps to take from where you are.

Chapter 14, "Epilogue: Reaping the Benefits of Quality Information," concludes with an epilogue rather than a conclusion. The information quality journey will never bring you to a final destination. Rather, it will bring you incredible adventures and joys as you bring your organization into the *realized* Information Age.

Part Four: Appendixes

Appendix A is an extensive glossary that defines terms from the information management information, general quality, and statistical analysis domains.

Appendix B contains an extensive bibliography for further reading, beginning with a recommended starter set.

Internet Resources Available in Conjunction with This Book

Because of currency of information and space limitations, there are resources about information quality products, techniques, and information quality best practice case studies available for book holders at www.infoimpact.com under *Information Quality Resources*.

How to Use This Book

This book is a concept book, a textbook, a reference book, and a practitioner's guide. Depending on your work and interests, your use of this book may vary.

Do not assume that you must implement every step described in this book to implement information quality. There are many steps and activities that could be performed. You must identify your priority needs and concentrate on those processes and process steps (see Table I.1). Be eclectic and pragmatic.

There are many ways to use this book; however, shelfware is not one of them.

Table I.1 How to Use This Book

AREA OF INTEREST:	SEE BOOK SECTION:
What is information quality?	Part One
Principles of information quality.	Chapter 3 and Chapter 11
Cost justification for information quality.	Chapter 1, states it; Chapter 7 describes how to justify it
How to determine what level of maturity your enterprise has in information quality practices.	Chapter 13, with an example information quality management maturity grid, along with guidance in how to conduct a maturity assessment
How much is poor quality information is costing your enterprise?	Chapter 7
Developing a data warehouse with focus on identifying authoritative source databases, and cleansing and transforming data.	Chapter 8
How to perform an information quality assessment.	Chapter 6
You know you have information quality problems, but need to know how to eliminate them once and for all.	Chapter 9
What tools are available to assist in information quality and how to evaluate them.	Chapter 10, and Internet at www.infoimpact.com: *Information Quality Resources*
Developing a data model and creating a quality model.	Chapter 5
How to set up an information or data stewardship program.	Chapter 12
Best practices in information quality.	Chapter 9, last section
How to implement an environment for sustainable information quality.	Part Three
Case studies or organizations making information quality happen.	Throughout the book, especially in Chapter 9, Chapter 13, and on the Internet at www.infoimpact.com: *Information Quality Resources*

The Maturing of the Information Age

Every economic era, from the Agricultural Age, to the Industrial Age, to the Information Age, has its paradigms and principles, along with its technologies. The Agricultural Age had a paradigm of "managed" land and crops with principles of cultivation. Its technology was cultivation tools. The Industrial Age paradigm was "managed" work with principles of mass production and specialized labor. Its technology was power and machines applied to work. The Information Age paradigm is one of "managed" information with principles of resource management and collaborative work. The full power of information technology cannot be fully realized until business and information systems management comprehend and *apply* principles of resource management and collaborative work to information.

Every economic era sees maturation of its processes through experimentation, trial and error, and then formalized process improvement. Data warehousing has focused new attention on information quality. This signals the beginning of a new phase of the Information Age: the Awakening. It is in this phase that organizations will challenge the Industrial Age paradigms and replace them with Information Age paradigms and principles. Business process reengineering initiatives are now replacing the vertical, functional management paradigm with horizontal, process, or value-chain management principles. The notion of data as a byproduct of business processes is giving way to the eureka of information as a direct product that has value beyond its immediate processes. Organizations that fail to recognize and manage information as a strategic business resource will fail in the realized Information Age.

As a product, information has processes that create and maintain it. Information has processes that use it. Information has customers, those knowledge workers who use information to perform their work. Information likewise has suppliers, those information producers who originate and add value to data through their work processes.

Information quality problems occur when data as supplied by the information producers does not meet the expectations of the knowledge workers as "information customers" or "information consumers."

Data warehousing has exposed horrific information quality problems that become apparent when an organization attempts to integrate disparate data. Its quality *may* satisfy operational knowledge workers and functional processes, but fail miserably to satisfy the downstream knowledge workers and enterprise processes. The fact that these information quality problems have not surfaced until now is not because information quality has suddenly gone downhill. Information quality problems have been masked by bad business and systems practices over the years. To be fair, the earliest computing technology did not enable data sharing. As a result, all early application development methodologies were created around that technology limitation. That limitation resulted in building isolated applications and islands of information independent of or only loosely interfaced with other applications and databases.

Information quality problems have been masked by layer upon layer of interface programs in which inconsistent data of one application is "transformed" into usable data structure and values required by another application area. Organizations have accepted this as necessary. However, the validity of this approach is seriously challenged as the weight of those layers of interfaces consume the time and resources of information systems organizations to maintain them. One organization discovered that the equivalent of 120 to 160 of its 250 highly skilled application developers spend their careers maintaining programs that simply copy data from one database, transform it, and put it into another database. Is this a valuable use of developer skills? Hardly, especially considering the people are a *consumable* resource and data is a *reusable* source.

Any new process takes time and experimentation to mature. Agricultural processes continue to be improved to provide greater quality of crops. For example, genetic alteration in foods like tomatoes have extended shelf life and increased taste. The Japanese began improving manufacturing process quality in the early 1950s when Dr. W. Edwards Deming introduced Statistical Quality Control techniques. This led to the dramatic turnaround of the postwar Japanese economy and the quality revolution and maturing of the Industrial Age manufacturing processes. It was not until the 1980s and the Japanese quality invasion of America that American business began transforming and improving American industry's manufacturing processes.

Fifty years into the Information Age we are now seeing the same quality improvement techniques being applied to information as the product of business processes. We are now seeing the maturation of the information management processes and the dawn of the *realized* Information Age. In the Realized Information Age, quality information indeed becomes the new economic currency and the competitive differentiator.

Information Quality Improvement: Beyond Data Cleansing

This entire book addresses not just the techniques for cleansing data for the data warehouse. It addresses a complete set of processes to attack information quality *problems*. Before an organization can significantly improve its information quality, it must understand the paradigms of information as a business resource and as a product. Information quality improvement seeks to measure information quality, both data definition (data specification) and data content; analyze and identify root cause of data defects; and improve processes to prevent defective data. The sole reason for improving information quality is to improve business efficiency and effectiveness and end-customer satisfaction by eliminating the problems caused by nonquality data. This book addresses the components of mature information management processes and organization culture that embody a customer satisfaction mind set to provide quality information. We will also identify the fundamental changes that are required to move an organization from data as a neglected and proprietary resource to information as a strategic and open business resource for competitive advantage and to achieve information maturity.

The information quality movement signals the beginning of the maturing of the Information Age. A word of warning is due the reader: Information quality improvement does not mean "more of the same" way of doing business. After all, we have been successful in the past. It does not mean building the same kinds of systems faster. It does not mean building bigger databases faster. Information quality improvement will force management to rethink the way it builds (or buys) applications and databases. It will force management to rethink the relationship of business processes and information. It will force management to rethink how it performs work. It will finally force management to rethink its performance measures and accountabilities for the resources of the enterprise.

Author's Warranty

If you are not able to apply ideas contained in this book to achieve value to your organization worth multiple times the cost of the book, I will personally refund to you the purchase price you paid for this book. Simply contact me at Larry.English@infoimpact.com for refund instructions as to where to send the book. All I ask is for you to give me a copy of your sales receipt along with a statement of what you tried that did not work, as well as your assessment of why it failed to result in value. No further questions asked.

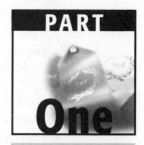

PART

One

Principles of Information Quality Improvement

"Back of every noble life there are principles that have fashioned it."
—GEORGE HORACE LORIMER

The three chapters of Part One describe the fundamental principles of information quality. This is not theory. These are very real and practical principles, even though they are foreign to many organizations. They provide the basis for understanding the background to information quality improvement as a management tool. They are the basis for the processes of information quality improvement described in Part Two, "Processes for Improving Information Quality." Without understanding the principles of quality improvement, implementing the processes may be a hollow and empty exercise that performs the actions but lacks the soul. This may result in loss of motivation for any information improvement initiative, no matter how well intentioned.

Chapter 1 describes the business case for information quality improvement. The bottom line is that poor data quality is just too expensive for organizations in a competitive or tight economy. It describes why information initiatives, such as data warehouses, so often fail.

Information systems organizations are in crisis today, a crisis caused by using information technology in ways that add complexity to information processing and information management based on industrial-age paradigms. This compounds information quality problems by creating redundant databases.

Chapter 1 presents many examples of the high cost of low-quality data. The result is that failure to solve information problems can be fatal to organizations.

Chapter 2 defines information quality. It first defines what quality is and is not. In order to understand information quality, *data* and *information* must be defined. The chapter then defines knowledge and wisdom, which is where information impacts business performance.

In defining information quality, we differentiate between *inherent* and *pragmatic* information quality. Essentially, inherent quality is the correctness of facts, and pragmatic quality is the correctness of the *right* facts. Chapter 2 defines the three components required for information quality: data definition and information architecture quality, data content quality, and data presentation quality.

Chapter 3 describes the principles of quality in general: customer focus, continuous process improvement, and use of scientific methods. It briefly outlines several quality approaches to illustrate the common themes of quality principles. Included in this discussion are encapsulations of Deming's 14 Points of Quality, the Juran Trilogy, Ishikawa's quality control as a movement, Kaizen, Quality Function Deployment, Crosby's 14 Steps, ISO 9000 quality management system standards, and the Baldrige Framework of Seven Categories for Business Performance Excellence.

Chapter 3 then describes how these quality principles apply to information as a product, and knowledge workers as information customers. The stewardship roles in information quality are discussed briefly. Everyone in the enterprise has accountability for quality of information. Chapter 3 then describes the notion of "customer service" of information products in the information value chain, and concludes with a list of the fundamental principles of information quality.

The High Costs
of Low-Quality Data

*"Quality is Free. . . . What costs money are the unquality things—all
the actions that involve not doing jobs right the first time."*

–PHILIP CROSBY

In this chapter I describe the reason why an organization is—or should be—interested in information quality. It can be summed up in one word: *profit*. Profit, however, is only a byproduct. Profits come when we know and focus on customers' needs and provide quality products that meet those needs. When information products fail to meet customers' needs, profits go down. Information systems and data warehouses fail, squandering the investments.

We describe why data that appears to be of satisfactory quality is, in fact, not. We illustrate the huge costs incurred as a result of low-quality data. We illustrate examples of the costs, including enterprise failure.

There is and must be only one purpose for improving information quality: to improve customer and stakeholder satisfaction by increasing the effectiveness and efficiency of the business processes. Information quality is a business concern, and information quality improvement is a business issue. Information quality improvement actually reduces business costs by eliminating costly scrap and rework caused by defective data. It increases business profits by providing more reliable information products that result in more usage, better decisions, and increased exploitation of business opportunities.

Unfortunately, the state of information quality in most organizations' databases is so abominable that if the same level of quality existed in their products and services, they would go out of business. "Justify that statement!" you say. You can do it yourself by answering two questions:

How many private, proprietary databases and files that reside on personal computers (in spreadsheets, PC databases, and even in word processor files) in your enterprise include information contained in corporate databases or files that are not integrated with and synchronized to those corporate databases?

If the data in those corporate databases is high quality, why is there a need for those redundant, private databases? After all, data is the only business resource that is completely reusable without being used up.

Why Data Warehouses Fail

Many see data warehousing as the silver bullet out of the operational data abyss. Not! If data warehousing is approached with the same information and (mis)management principles that have produced the disintegrated islands of automation legacy environment, it will fail. It will fail spectacularly. In fact it will deserve to fail.

Data warehousing projects fail for many reasons, all of which can be traced to a single cause: *nonquality*. Poor data architecture, inconsistently defined departmental data, inability to relate data from different data sources, missing and inaccurate data values, inconsistent use of data fields, unacceptable query performance (timeliness of information), lack of business sponsor (no data warehouse customer), and so forth, are all components of nonquality.

With all of the emphasis on data warehousing *technologies*, it will serve you well to remember two things:

The *product* of the data warehouse is *information*.

The *customers* of the data warehouse are the *knowledge workers* who must make increasingly important decisions faster than ever before.

If the data warehouse does not deliver *reliable* information that supports the customers' decisions and strategic processes *to their satisfaction*, history will repeat itself.

The Information Quality Crisis

If the state of quality of your company's products and services was the same level of quality as the data in its databases, would your company survive or go out of business? One insurance company had a list of 12 "sacred data elements" that were considered so important that if the data was wrong, the company could fail. When it did a data inventory, it discovered that this data element was maintained in 43 separate databases by 43 independent applications, with data entered by 43 different information producers.

One manufacturing firm had 92 Part files, many defined with different primary identifiers so that the same part in different files could not even be cross-referenced.

A major bank had 256 different Customer files that it had to analyze just to answer the question, "Who is our best customer?"

A consumer goods company discovered it had over 400 Brand files containing product information.

Topping the list, however, a Telecommunications provider has the highest known information chaos with over 800 Customer files.

If the data in those corporate databases is high quality, why is there a need for the redundant, disparate databases that seem to multiply like rabbits? Data is the *only* business resource that is completely reusable. All other resources, when used, are used up; for example, money can be spent once, employees can perform only one task at a time, raw materials can be used once in the production of a finished good, and facilities can be used for only one purpose at a given point in time.

Yet data, the only nonconsumable resource, is the only resource where high redundancy is accepted as a "legitimate" cost of doing business. The insurance company with 43 different databases and applications capturing the same facts is the information equivalent of accounts payable paying a single invoice 43 times, or Human Resources hiring 43 people to perform the same task 43 different times, or building 43 buildings when only one is needed. Is this the legacy that Information Systems (IS) should provide its enterprise?

The dark side of the business case for data warehousing is the failure of Information Systems to provide for effective data management of the business-critical information resource across its operational applications—and the enterprise is paying for this dearly.

But Our Information Quality Is Not So Bad . . .

After all, the operational processes are running well. That may be, with an emphasis on *may*. The truth of the matter is that the tactical and strategic process requirements of data warehouse data are completely different from the operational process requirements of data. Consider the following scenario.

An insurance company downloaded claims data to its data warehouse to analyze its risks based upon Medical Diagnosis Code for which claims were paid. The data revealed that 80 percent of the claims paid out of one claims processing center were paid for a diagnosis of "broken leg." "What is happening here?" was the concern. "Are we in a really rough neighborhood?" No. The claims processors were paid for how fast they paid claims, so they let the system default to "broken leg." The information quality was good enough to pay a claim because all the claims payment system needed was a *valid* diagnosis code. However, that same data was totally useless for risk analysis.

But worse than this is the fact that over the years, the archaic legacy data structures have failed to keep up with the information requirements of even the operational knowledge workers. As a result, because they require more and more information to do their jobs, knowledge workers have been forced to create their own data workarounds and store the data they need in creative ways that differ from the original file structure. The cause of this problem is simple. The Information Systems staff is busy maintaining, on average, a ten-fold redundant databases and the redundant applications or interface programs that recreate or move data. They don't have time to keep a *single sharable* database current to meet knowledge workers' needs. This represents only the beginning of the information quality challenges facing the data warehouse team.

Why have these issues not been seriously addressed until now? Two reasons: First, information quality is not a sexy topic. After all, who wants to work at the sewage treatment plant when they could be building factories (that create pollution!)? The second reason is insidious: Management has either deemed the costs of the status quo and the current level of low-quality data as acceptable and normal costs of doing business or they are unaware of the real costs of nonquality data.

The Incredible Costs of Nonquality Data

Most organizations have come to accept the level of nonquality data as normal and usual or they are totally unaware of its costs—after all, we are profitable, aren't we? As long as the level of information quality is relatively the same among the competition, the competitive battle lines are drawn in other areas. However, when someone redefines the role of information quality, as the Japanese did with automobile quality, the rules of the game change. The U.S. auto industry's Big Three (GM, Ford, and Chrysler) have been losing ground over the past decade. Their domestic car market share fell from 76 percent in 1984 to 62.5 percent in 1996, an all-time annual low. January 1997 started out worse with the Big Three's domestic auto market share dipping to 59.3 percent, according to industry tracker Autodata.[1]

General Motors lost a whopping $4.5 billion in 1991 and followed that with an incomprehensible $23.5 billion loss the next year before it got its act together. While GM has regained profitability, with a record $6.9 billion in 1995, its combined profits from the four years 1993–1996 have not erased the loss of 1992, and its market share in the United States continued to slide, from 34 percent in 1992 to 31.6 percent in 1996.[2]

[1]Micheline Maynard, "Buyers taking a pass on Detroit's passenger cars," *USA Today*, February 2, 1997, p. 1B.

[2]Micheline Maynard, "GM's report card barely surpasses expectations," *USA Today*, November 11, 1996, p. 17B.

GM stockholders can only speculate what their stock value might be today if the American auto manufacturers had not been oblivious to the quality revolution.

The quality revolution has redefined quality from an optional characteristic to a basic requirement for both goods and services. It is no longer sufficient to compete on price alone. Customer satisfaction is the key driver for long-term financial and organizational success today. GM's new CEO, Jack Smith, admonished employees in October 1996, "We cannot afford the luxury of complacency. Continuous improvement is the name of the game if we want to assure our jobs and the future of this great company."[3]

The same kind of revolution *will* happen with information quality, and it *will* change the economic landscape. Continuous improvement of information products and services will become the name of the game if information professionals want to assure their jobs and the futures of their organizations. Those oblivious to its imminence will suffer; the only question is, "How much?"

Management can no longer afford the luxury of the excessive costs of non-quality data. In the Information Age a quality, shared knowledge resource will differentiate the successful enterprise. Information quality is to the next decade what product quality was to the 1980s.

THE HIGH COSTS OF LOW-QUALITY DATA

The high costs of low-quality data are ubiquitous. They negatively impact all areas of our lives, personally as well as in our work. Anyone could fill a book with their own personal experiences in which nonquality data has cost them time, money, or bodily injury. Some are dramatic. Consider the following:

- Some Metro Nashville city pensioners were overpaid $2.3 million from 1987 to 1995, while another set of pensioners was underpaid $2.6 million as a result of incorrect pension calculations, according to *The Tennessean*, March 21, 1998.
- "Two 20-year-old 'calculation errors' . . . socked Los Angeles County's . . . pension systems with $1.2 billion in unforeseen liabilities, and will probably force cash-strapped county officials to spend an additional $25 million a year to make up for insufficient contributions to the fund," according to the *Los Angeles Times*, April 8, 1998.
- Trans Union Corp. was ordered by a jury to pay $25 million because of a clerical error that released names of several hundred First National Bank of Omaha customers to other credit card issuers, in breach of a confidentiality agreement (*Washington Post*, March 10, 1998).
- Ninety-two percent of claims Medicare paid to community health centers over one year's time were "improper or highly questionable," according to an investigation conducted by the inspector general of the Department of Health and Human Services (*Washington Post* story reported in *The Tennessean*, October 7, 1998).

Continues

---

[3]Micheline Maynard, "GM's report card barely surpasses expectations," *USA Today*, November 11, 1996, p. 17B.

THE HIGH COSTS OF LOW-QUALITY DATA *(CONTINUED)*

- Wrong price data in retail databases may cost American consumers as much as $2.5 billion in overcharges annually. Data audits showed four out of five errors in database prices read by bar-code scanners are overcharges from the published price of goods.[4]
- Four years later, information quality had not significantly improved, with 1 out of 20 items scanned incorrectly according to a Federal Trade Commission study of 17,000 items. As a result, some state and local governments have passed laws requiring stores to put price stickers on items, or face substantial fines (up to $25,000 in Michigan). One Michigan retailer spends $2.4 million a year—11 percent of its payroll—to affix price tags on items.[5]
- The U.S. Attorney General's office has stated that "approximately $23 billion, or 14 percent of the health care dollar, is wasted in fraud or inaccurate billing."[6]
- According to *The Financial Times,* information quality problems were a factor in a $770-million pretax loss suffered by an investment firm in 1994, causing the company to write off $217 million in 1994 as a result of "bookkeeping errors."[7]
- Inaccurate data about one constituent cost a municipality a $2.5 million lawsuit.
- A suspect in a kidnapping/homicide incident was accidentally released after posting a low bond for misdemeanor charges, because it was not known he was wanted for the kidnapping and shooting death of an 18-year-old. For whatever reason, only the hold order for the lesser charge followed the suspect in transferring from one jurisdiction to another. The sheriff's department, police department, and warrants officials are now working together "to improve the computer database system and communications with other jurisdictions" (*The Tennessean,* June 19, 1998).
- A physician in Florida amputated the wrong leg of a patient. The original order had been changed as to which leg was to be amputated, but the doctor, while following standard procedures before performing an amputation, followed the old order. The nurse who was aware of the changed order had left the operating room before the amputation, but assumed the doctor was aware of the change. Three years later, the same doctor failed to verify the name on a patient's wrist-band and performed a risky procedure on the intended patient's roommate! His license was suspended (*The Tennessean,* July 12, 1998, p. 7A).
- A European company discovered through a data audit that it was not invoicing 4 percent of its orders. For a company with $2 billion in revenues, this meant that $80 million in orders went unpaid.
- A petroleum exploration company drilling a new well in the North Sea drilled through the well shaft of a neighboring well because of flawed data that misidentified the well shaft's exact location. Fortunately, the well was no longer producing oil. Had it

[4] D. Bartholomew, "The Price Is Wrong," *Information Week,* September 14, 1992, pp. 26–36.

[5] R. Beck, "Item-pricing nice, but not for retailers," *The Tennessean,* August 24, 1997.

[6] Tara Eck, "Health care companies renew compliance focus," *Nashville Business Journal,* September 1–5, 1997, p. 24.

[7] Maggie Urry, "Book errors figure in Salomon $770m pretax loss," *The Financial Times,* February 3, 1995. As cited in Madhavan K. Nayar, "Framework for Achieving Information Integrity," *IS Audit & Control Journal,* Vol. II, 1996, p. 31.

been, the pressure from the oil in the ruptured pipe would have gushed up the drilling well's shaft, blowing the $500-million drilling investment to smithereens, and surely causing fatality to the crew.

- In 1992, 96,000 IRS tax refund checks were returned as undeliverable due to bad addresses.
- No fewer than one out of six U.S. registered voters on voter registration lists have either moved or are deceased, according to an audit comparing voter registration lists with the U.S. Post Office change-of-address list.
- Until January 1998, when new information quality processes were put in place, the State of Tennessee Department of Safety routinely sent out 200,000–300,000 motor vehicle registration renewal notices, with 20 percent (40,000–60,000) not getting to the intended owner because of incorrect addresses (*The Tennessean*, January 1998).
- Electronic data audits reveal that invalid data values in the typical customer database averages around 15 to 20 percent. Physical data audits suggest that actual data errors, even though the values may be valid, may be 25 to 30 percent or more in those same databases. The cost of this nonquality data takes its toll on the business' bottom line in the form of wasted communication costs to its customers. The most significant real cost, however, is lost *customer lifetime value* as a result of missed or late communication or the *aggravation factor*. The aggravation factor is the nuisance caused to customers as a result of nonquality information such as incorrect invoices or having to change address information multiple times. Lost or missed customer lifetime value as the result of poor information quality can be significantly greater than the money wasted on duplicate and wrong address mailings.[8] Wasted mailout costs of $10,000 may actually result in millions of dollars in lost customer lifetime value.
- A U.S. manufacturing company stock lost 20 percent of its value (dropping 4.5 points to 20) due to a discrepancy in actual inventory and automated inventory reports in December 1995.
- A U.K. engineering company stock lost 13 percent of its value in April 1997 because a data error caused profits to be overstated. Some costs that had been written off as they were incurred continued to be carried in the balance sheet.
- Barbra Streisand pulled her investment account from her investment bank because it misspelled her name as "Barbara."
- When we wrote an $8,000 check against our home equity loan, the money was paid from someone else's account because the printer had printed the wrong account number on the checks. The bank branch manager called us personally to inform us about the mistake, told us to destroy those checks, and new checks were printed for us.
- A $29,000 wire transfer due to me in Brentwood, Tennessee, ended up in someone else's bank account in Seattle, Washington. The $3,000 wire transfer that was supposed to be deposited to that Seattle account ended up in my account. The payer's reply, "Oops!" The Seattle account owner's reply, "Wow!" My reply, unprintable.

Continues

[8]Customer lifetime value is the net present value of the profit and/or revenue of a typical customer over the life of their relationship with the organization. Chapter 7, "Measuring Nonquality Information Costs," describes how to calculate customer lifetime value.

THE HIGH COSTS OF LOW-QUALITY DATA *(CONTINUED)*

- In 1994, an American bank employee transposed some digits on a bid for a bond from an Italian bank that resulted in a $4-million loss to the bank. The Italian bank refused to return the money.
- In March 1997, a U.K. bank discovered it lost around £90 million ($145 million) due to data errors in a computer model that caused inaccurate valuation of a risk manager's investment positions.
- A Catholic school sent out invitations to 5-year-old children to come for consideration to attend their elite school's kindergarten. In attendance was a woman born in 1888, age 105.

Information Quality and the Bottom Line

Information quality problems hamper virtually every area of a business, from the mailroom to the executive office. Every hour the business spends hunting for missing data, correcting inaccurate data, working around data problems, scrambling to assemble information across disintegrated databases, resolving data-related customer complaints, and so on, is an hour of *cost only*, passed on in higher prices to the customer. That hour is not available for value-adding work. Senior executives at one large mail-order company personally spend the equivalent of one full-time employee (senior executive) in reconciling conflicting departmental reports before submitting them to the Chief Executive Officer. This means there is the equivalent of one senior executive's time is wasted because of redundant and inconsistent (nonquality) data!

Bill Inmon observes that 80 to 90 percent of the human efforts in building a data warehouse are expended handling the interface between operational and data warehouse environments.[9]

This effort is caused by not having an integrated data environment. This requires data warehouse professionals to have to map undefined and unintegrated data from many disparate and redundant databases and files, standardize, remove redundant occurrences of data both within single files and across redundant files, and integrate and consolidate data and format it into an integrated data warehouse data architecture. Well over half of these costs are attributable directly to nonquality data and nonquality data management and systems development practices.

Even worse, because of the complexity and content, the temptation is great to quickly produce "90-day wonder" data marts, thrown together quickly without addressing the data integration issues. This only exacerbates the already huge problem of nonquality data and increases the costs of solving the right

[9] B. Inmon, "Data Warehouse—Into the '90's," presentation given at the *All About IRM '92* conference, Beaver Creek, CO, July 21, 1992, p. 6.

ONE HUGE INFORMATION QUALITY PROBLEM THAT CAN'T BE LATE

The Gartner Group estimates the worldwide costs to modify the software and change databases to fix the Year 2000 problem to be from U.S. $400–$600 billion. T. Capers Jones says this estimate is low. He expects the costs to "fix" the Year 2000 problem to be around U.S. $1.5 trillion, including lawsuits that will arise.

To restate the Year 2000 problem, the costs to fix this single, pervasive information quality problem represents an amount equivalent to nearly one-third of the U.S. federal deficit. Yes, this is an information quality problem. When the systems analysts and data analysts designed these databases with only two digits because of processing speed, reducing data storage costs, or because of ignorance, they inadvertently condemned their organizations, or customers, to an expensive fix.

To look at the Year 2000 information quality problem from another perspective, the 50 most profitable companies in the world earned a combined $178 billion in profits in 1996. If the entire 1996 profits of these companies were dedicated only to the Year 2000 problem, the companies would cover only 12 percent of the total costs.

Fixing the Year 2000 problem will hurt the U.S. economy, reducing the growth rate by 0.3 percentage points in 1999 and 0.5 percentage points in the years 2000 and early 2001, according to a study by Standard & Poor's DRI.[10]

An even worse tragedy exists for many unenlightened organizations that are "solving" this problem the wrong way. Treating the Year 2000 as a programming problem rather than a data problem, they are attempting to change the date comparison algorithm rather than convert the fields to support a four-digit year value. This *programming* "solution" allows one to define a new century breakpoint such as the year '35. Two digit dates of 35 and above are considered to have a "19" century prefix. Dates 00–34 are considered to be dates with a "20" century prefix. This merely postpones when the Year 2000 problem affects the business and requires the problem to be solved—and *paid* for—again.

problem later on. For data warehousing projects to be successful, the organization must address the problem of nonintegrated data head on.

The bottom line is that information quality problems hurt the bottom line.

Quality experts agree that the costs of nonquality are significant. Quality consultant Philip Crosby, author of *Quality Is Free*, identifies the cost of nonquality to manufacturing as 15 to 20 percent of revenue.[11]

Joseph M. Juran is one of the world's pioneering experts in quality. He is the recipient of the "Second Class of the Order of the Sacred Treasure," the highest decoration presented to a non-Japanese citizen. Juran pegs the costs of poor quality at 20 to 40 percent of sales, including costs of "customer complaints, product liability lawsuits, redoing defective work, [and] products scrapped."[12]

A.T. Kearney CEO Fred Steingraber confirms that "we have learned the hard way that the cost of poor quality is extremely high. We have learned that in

---

[10]Michael J. Mandel, P. Coy, and P.C. Judge, "ZAP! How the Year 2000 Bug Will Hurt the Economy (It's worse than you think)," *Business Week*, March 2, 1998, p. 47.

[11]Philip B. Crosby, *Quality Is Free*, New York: Penguin Group, 1979, p. 15.

[12]J. M. Juran, *Juran on Planning for Quality*, New York: The Free Press, 1988, p. 1.

manufacturing it is 25 to 30 percent of sales dollars and as much as 40 percent in the worst companies. Moreover, the service industry is not immune, as poor quality can amount to an increase of 40 percent of operating costs."[13]

But what about the costs of nonquality data? If early data assessments are an indicator, the business costs of nonquality data, including irrecoverable costs, rework of products and services, workarounds, and lost and missed revenue may be as high as 10 to 25 percent of revenue or total budget of an organization. Furthermore, as much as 40 to 50 percent or more of the typical IT budget may actually be spent in "information scrap and rework," a concept well known in manufacturing. Chapter 7, "Measuring Nonquality Information Costs," describes in detail how to analyze the costs of information and the costs of poor-quality data.

POOR INFORMATION QUALITY CAUSES BUSINESS FAILURE

Oxford Health Plans Inc.: In 1997, Oxford Health Plans disclosed that computer snafus in trying to convert to a new computer system and resulting inaccurate data caused it to overestimate revenues and underestimate medical costs. Other information quality problems caused overbilling of its customers at the same time. Estimating a third-quarter loss of up to $69.3 million, its stock dropped 62 percent—the actual loss was even greater. The New York State Insurance Department fined Oxford $3 million for violations of insurance laws and regulations and ordered Oxford to pay $500,000 to customers that it had overcharged, according to the *Wall Street Journal*, December 24, 1997. Oxford is struggling for survival. Its stock price as of October 8, 1998 was around $8—only 9 percent of its all-time high value of around $89. Oxford will lose money in 1998, and the consensus of stock market analysts is that it will lose money in 1999 as well.

Hudson Foods: In August 1997, Hudson Foods lost its largest customer, Burger King, due to E. coli bacteria contamination that caused several illnesses. While the plant was one of the most modern, and was clean and generally well run, it had two problematic practices: "poor record-keeping and the mixing of one day's leftover hamburger into the next day's production."[14]

The information quality problem of not knowing which batches were mixed caused the largest meat recall in U. S. history: 25 million pounds. Accurate information would have probably limited the size of recall significantly. Without its largest customer, Hudson Foods was not able to be profitable, and not only was that plant subsequently sold to IPB Inc., but the rest of Hudson Foods was acquired by Tyson Foods.

National Westminster Bank: The British bank had to dispose of its equities businesses in February 1998, taking a pretax loss of around $1.77 billion (£1.01 billion), according to *The Financial Times*, February 25, 1998. The failure stemmed out of losses of over $150 million (£90 million) caused by incorrectly pricing its derivatives over a two-year period according to *The Times*, March 14, 1997.

---

[13]Samuel Boyle, *Quality, Speed, Customer Involvement & the New Look of Organizations* seminar, Excel, 1992, p. 17.

[14]"Burger King Dropping Beef Supplier," *New York Times* News Service, reported in *The Tennessean*, August, 24, 1997.

Why Care about Information Quality?

Because the high costs of low-quality data threatens the enterprise.

There is and must be only one purpose for improving information quality: to improve customer and stakeholder satisfaction by increasing the efficiency and effectiveness of the business processes. This in turn increases profits and shareholder value. Information quality is a business issue, and information quality improvement is a business necessity.

For organizations in a competitive environment, information quality is a matter of survival, and then of competitive advantage. For organizations in the public and not-for-profit sectors, information quality is a matter of survival, and then of stewardship of stakeholder (taxpayer or contributor) resources.

Defining Information Quality

"Beauty is in the eye of the beholder."
–MARGARET HUNGERFORD IN *MOLLY BAUN*

Before one can measure and improve information quality, one must be able to define it in ways that are both meaningful and measurable.

Information quality is defined in this chapter—what it is and what it is not. In order to understand *information quality*, *data* and *information* and their key concepts must be defined. Knowledge and wisdom are also defined, because this is where information impacts business performance, and where nonquality information can harm that performance.

In defining information quality, we differentiate between *inherent* and *pragmatic* information quality. Essentially, inherent quality is the correctness of facts; pragmatic quality is the correctness of the *right* facts presented correctly. Chapter 2 concludes with defining the three components required for information quality: data definition and information architecture quality, data content quality, and data presentation quality.

What Is Quality?

The best way to look at information quality is to look at what quality means in the general marketplace and then translate what quality means for information. As consumers, human beings consciously or subconsciously judge the "quality" of things in their experience. A conscious application of quality measurement is when a person compares products in a store and chooses one of them as the "right" product. "Right" here means selecting the product that best meets one's overall needs, not necessarily the best features in every category. After purchase, people determine quality based on whether that product for its price met their expectations for its intended use.

An unconscious application of quality measurement is the frustration one gets with a nonquality product or a service. Waiting in a long line at a store checkout while store clerks who are capable of coming to a checkout stand idly by, is an experience in nonquality service. It communicates that the store is not concerned about their customers' time.

Quality Is Not . . .

First, let us define what quality is *not*. Quality is *not* luxury or superiority, nor is it "best" in class. Quality exists solely in the eyes of the customers based on the value they perceive on how something meets their needs. What is quality to one customer may be totally defective to another.

Take, for example, the diagnosis code of "broken leg" in 80 percent of the claims mentioned earlier. That was acceptable quality to the claims processors, because the only requirement to pay a claim was that it had a valid diagnosis code. But to the actuary, as a data warehouse customer and the ultimate "customer" of that data, it was nonquality and completely unusable for risk analysis. The second or so saved in the claim processor's time was more than offset by the inability of the actuary to analyze the company's risk or understand its own customer's needs.

A far worse scenario exists. What if the medical diagnosis codes were indiscriminately applied to the claims? What if those incorrect codes resulted in no unusual pattern that called attention to itself that something might be askew? Then, what if the actuary determined risks based on that inaccurate data? What if insurance policies were then priced based on those (questionable) risks? What if the customer service group sent out form letters to find out how well their customers were recovering from their "medical diagnosis"? What if. . .

Quality is *not* fitness for purpose. The diagnosis code of "broken leg" was "fit for purpose" to pay a claim. But it was *not* fit to analyze risk. Quality is fitness for *all* purposes made of the data, including the *likely* future uses. Quality information will be used in many new ways in the intelligent learning organization. Information fit for one purpose but lacking inherent quality will stunt the intellectual growth of the learning organization.

Quality is not subjective or intangible. It can be measured with the most fundamental business measures—impact on the bottom line. The business measures of information quality are described in Chapter 7, "Measuring Nonquality Information Costs."

Quality Is . . .

What, then, is quality? Total Quality Management provides a useful definition of quality: "consistently meeting customer's expectations."[1]

When quality expert Philip Crosby defines quality as "conformance to requirements,"[2] he does not imply simply conformation to written specifications.

Customers' requirements may be formal and written, or informal mental expectations of meeting their purpose or satisfying their needs. If a product meets formally defined "requirement specifications," yet fails to be a quality product from the customers' perspective, the requirements are defective.

If an application is designed and built to *meet* the functional requirements signed off by the business sponsors, and during final testing the business sponsors reject the application as not meeting their needs, what does that say? Either the requirements specification or the analysis and design process is defective.

Quality also means meeting customers' needs, not necessarily exceeding them. The luxury automobile producer Rolls Royce went bankrupt in the early 1980s. Analysis revealed that, among other things, Rolls Royce was improving components that the luxury automobile customers felt were irrelevant and polishing parts they did not care about. This drove the price beyond what the luxury-automobile customer felt was value for money. Quality means improving the things customers *care about* and that make their lives easier and more worthwhile. On the other hand, when Lexus sought to make its first major redesign of its highly rated LS 400 luxury automobile, representatives of the company sought out their existing customers. They even visited the homes of a variety of LS 400 owners to observe home furnishings, what kind of leather they had on their attaché cases, and other minute details to get a sense of their customers' subconscious expectations.

What Is Data?

Before we can describe information or data quality, we must understand what *data* is, what *information* is, and why information quality is required. To define *information quality*, we must define *data* and *information*. And because the ultimate objective of business is to achieve profit or to accomplish its mission, we must define what we mean by *knowledge* and *wisdom*. For it is in wisdom, or applied knowledge, that information is exploited, and its value is realized.

---

[1] Larry English, *Information Quality Improvement: Principles, Methods, and Management*, Seminar 5th Ed., Brentwood, TN: INFORMATION IMPACT International, Inc., 1996, p. 1.2.
[2] Philip B. Crosby, *Quality Is Free*, New York: Penguin Group, 1979, p. 15.

Data

Data is the plural form of the Latin word *datum*, which means "something given." It comes from the neuter past participle of the Latin word *dare*, "to give." In the context of classical computer science the term *data* has come to mean numeric or other information represented in ways that computers can process. However, we define data from a business perspective and independent of information technology. The *Oxford English Dictionary* defines *fact* as something "that is known to have happened or to be true or to exist." Simply stated, data is the representation of facts about things.

Data as Things or Entities

Data represents things or entities in the real world. *Webster's Dictionary* defines *entity* as "something that has separate and distinct existence and objective or conceptual reality." My son, Chancellor, is at the time of this writing a student at Middle Tennessee State University (MTSU). Chancellor and MTSU are entities; that is, they exist. When modeling data we represent the *classification* of entities that have similar characteristics as an *entity type*. For example, Student is an entity type that classifies the role that a Person such as Chancellor plays in his relationship to MTSU. MTSU is also an entity. MTSU is one occurrence of a classification of Organizations in a role called an Academic Institution.

The statement "Chancellor is a student at MTSU" is a statement of fact, or, in other words, data. This can be represented graphically in an entity relationship diagram as shown in Figure 2.1.

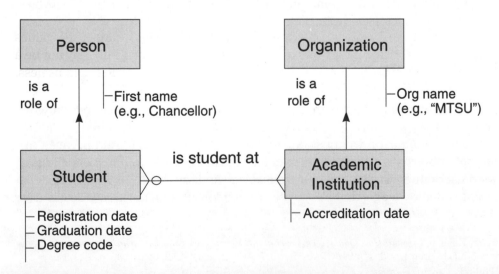

Figure 2.1   An entity relationship diagram example.

Data as Facts or Attributes

Data is a symbol or other representation of some fact about some thing. My son's name is Chancellor. That is a fact. The type of fact, `first-name`, is an attribute type. "Chancellor" is the actual value of the attribute type `first-name` for my son and is not to be confused with the value "Chancellor" of a different attribute type `Title` of an entity type `Employee` of `Academic Institution`.

Data is the raw material from which information is derived and is the basis for intelligent actions and decisions. As an example, `16155551212` represents a fact that is true. While it represents something real in the world, this data without a descriptive definition or a context is meaningless. Data is only the raw material from which information may be produced.

Information

If data is the raw material, information is a finished product. Information is *data in context*. Information is usable data. Information is the *meaning* of data, so facts become understandable. The previous example of data becomes understandable information when one knows that `+1 (615)555-1212` is the telephone number of information directory service for Nashville, Tennessee, and surrounding areas. It includes country code `1`, area code `615`, and telephone exchange `555` and number within exchange `1212`.

Information quality requires quality of three components: clear definition or meaning of data, correct value(s), and understandable presentation (the format represented to a knowledge worker). Nonquality of any of these three components can cause a business process to fail or a wrong decision to be made. Information is applied data and may be represented as a formula:

Information = f(Data + Definition + Presentation)

From a business perspective, information may be well defined, the values may be accurate, and it may be presented meaningfully, but it still may not be a valuable enterprise resource. Quality information, in and of itself, is useless. But quality information understood by people *can* lead to value.

Knowledge

Quality information becomes a powerful resource that can be assimilated by people. Knowledge workers plus quality information provide the potential for information to have value. A database without knowledge workers using it produces as much value as a product warehouse without ordering customers.

Knowledge is not just information known, it is *information in context*. Knowledge means understanding the *significance* of the information. Knowledge is applied information and may be represented as a formula:

Knowledge = f(People + Information + Significance)

Knowledge is the value added to information by people who have the experience and acumen to understand its real potential. With the continuing evolution of information technology, organizations are now able to capture knowledge electronically, organize its storage, and make it sharable across the enterprise. The advances in Internet, intranet, the World Wide Web, and data mining are expanding the horizons of sharable data in both data warehouses and in operational databases.

It is possible, however, to have a wealth of enterprise knowledge but still see an enterprise fail. Knowledge has value only to the extent that people are empowered to act based on that knowledge. In other words, knowledge has value only when acted on.

Wisdom

The penultimate goal in any organization is to maximize the value of its resources to accomplish its mission. The information resource is maximized when it is managed in a way that it has quality *and* when it is easily available to those who need it. People resources are maximized when they are trained, provided resources, including information, and *empowered* to act, carry out the work of the enterprise, and satisfy the end customers. Wisdom is applied knowledge and may be expressed in the formula:

Wisdom = f(People + Knowledge + Action)

The goal of information quality is to equip the knowledge workers with a strategic resource to enable the intelligent learning organization. Peter Senge defines the learning organization as one that "is continually expanding its capacity to create its future" through learning and shared learning.[3]

The intelligent learning organization is one that maximizes both its experience and its information resources in the learning process. The intelligent learning organization shares information openly across the enterprise in a way that maximizes the entire organization (see Figure 2.2).

In the Information Age, the dysfunctional learning organization is at a distinct disadvantage. The term *dysfunctional* means "impaired or abnormal functioning." Dysfunctional organizations try to operate with inconsistently defined islands of proprietary data "owned" by business areas, whose quality serves to meet only "my" business area's needs (see Figure 2.3). Dysfunctional organizations are hampered by nonquality information that prevents them from sharing information and knowledge. Nonquality information keeps these organizations from being effective and competitive because "it hinders knowledge of markets, customers, technologies, and processes that help any organization

---

[3]Peter Senge, *The Fifth Discipline*, New York: Doubleday, 1990, p. 14.

High-quality information is an *open, shared* resource with *value-adding* processes.

Figure 2.2 The intelligent learning organization.

grow. Knowledge gains added power when it is the primary ingredient of a business" to facilitate learning as a competitive weapon.[4]

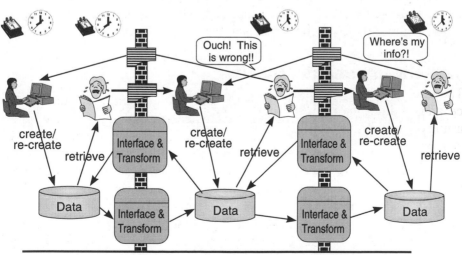

Low-quality data is a *proprietary* resource with *cost-adding* processes.

Figure 2.3 The dysfunctional learning organization.

[4]Thomas A. Stewart, *Intellectual Capital*, New York: Doubleday, 1997, p. 179.

Since the end result of data is to perform work successfully, the quality of that data will either hamper or facilitate correct business actions.

What Is Information Quality?

There are two significant definitions of information quality. One is its *inherent* quality, and the other is its *pragmatic* quality. Inherent information quality is the correctness or accuracy of data. Pragmatic information quality is the value that accurate data has in supporting the work of the enterprise. Data that does not help enable the enterprise accomplish its mission has no quality, no matter how accurate it is.

Inherent Information Quality

Inherent information quality is, simply stated, data accuracy. Inherent information quality is the degree to which data accurately reflects the real-world object that the data represents. All data is an abstraction or a representation of something real. Jean Baudrillard, the French semiologist,[5] observes that "the very definition of the real becomes: that of which it is possible to give an equivalent reproduction."[6]

Data is an *equivalent reproduction* of something real. If all facts that an organization needs to know about an entity are *accurate*, that data has inherent quality—it is an electronic reproduction of reality. For example, if someone has a data value of "October 24, 1976" for my daughter Ashley's "Birth Date," that data has inherent quality. Inherent information quality means that data is correct.

Pragmatic Information Quality

Pragmatic information quality is the degree of usefulness and value data has to support the enterprise processes that enable accomplishing enterprise objectives. In essence, pragmatic information quality is the degree of customer satisfaction derived by the knowledge workers who use it to do their jobs.

Data in a database or data warehouse has no actual value; it only has *potential* value. Data has *realized* value only when someone uses it to do something useful; for example, to ship an order to a customer, or to determine the correct location to drill a well shaft. Pragmatic information quality is the degree to which data enables knowledge workers to meet enterprise objectives efficiently and effectively.

---

[5] Semiology is the science dealing with signs or sign language.
[6] *The Columbia Dictionary of Quotations* is licensed from Columbia University Press. Copyright © 1993 by Columbia University Press.

Information quality lies in its ability to satisfy its customers, those who use the data in their work. For example, if a college has recorded a data value of "27" for my son Chancellor's senior high school year "Composite ACT Score," that data has inherent quality; it is correct. If that college uses "Composite ACT Score" values of 26 or higher as a means of automatic acceptance, and sends letters to those prospective students having a "Composite ACT Score" meeting that criteria, that data has *pragmatic* information quality. Having a correct data value and using it enabled Middle Tennessee State University to meet an objective of increasing its entering student average ACT scores for fall 1997.

It is possible to have *inherent* information quality without having *pragmatic* information quality. Data not required to support any business processes, or required to make any decision, or useful in trend analysis, is irrelevant. Even if the values are correct, and therefore have inherent quality, that data is useless, and has no value to the enterprise. In fact, it is actually nonquality information because it costs the enterprise money and resources to acquire and maintain but adds no value. It has a negative net worth. If my insurance company knows that the interior upholstery of my automobile is black, but that fact is not useful in any of its business processes, it lacks quality. In fact, it increases the company's cost of doing business, and is passed on to me in higher insurance premiums.

Pragmatic information quality prevents people from:

- Performing work incorrectly or making a wrong decision
- Performing work over again because it was previously performed incorrectly
- Recovering from the impact of making a wrong decision
- Taking unnecessary time to investigate the integrity of the data before using it
- Performing calculations or reformatting the data before it can be used
- Hunting for additional information in order to use the data
- Losing customers because it caused work to be performed incorrectly
- Causing unrecoverable damage
- Missing business opportunities
- Miscommunicating within the business or with end customers and other information stakeholders

Information Quality Defined

The same premise of quality of consumer products holds true for information quality. To define *information quality*, one must identify the "customers" of data, the "knowledge workers" who require data to perform their jobs. Information quality is "consistently meeting knowledge worker and end-customer expectations" through information and information services,[7] enabling them to perform their jobs efficiently and effectively. Information quality describes "the attributes of the information that result in user (customer) satisfaction."[8]

Information quality exists when information enables knowledge workers to accomplish their "enterprise" objectives. Information quality is measured not just by the immediate beneficiaries, but also by the downstream knowledge workers. Quality information eliminates the need for transforming interface programs, because specific facts are defined and represented in the same way across the enterprise.

Let us now examine the elements of information quality:

"Consistently meeting knowledge worker and end-customer expectations."

"Consistently"

When knowledge workers get information about a given entity or event, they expect consistent quality. They know ahead of time the level of quality of the data with which they work. For some decision support processes, knowledge workers can tolerate some degree of error and omission if they are aware of the degree and nature of error. If there are wide swings in the reliability of data in the data warehouse, knowledge workers may resort to gut feel as their decision support system, rather than trust what they perceive as unreliable data in an untrustworthy electronic decision support system.

Consistently means the information quality meets *all* knowledge worker needs, not just some. If one set of knowledge workers requires 95 percent accuracy and another 99 percent accuracy, then a 99 percent accuracy is required to consistently meet expectations.

Consistently also means that if knowledge workers have to use data about the same thing from two different databases, whether two operational databases or an operational database and the data warehouse, they expect the data to agree. If I get information about John Smith from our central database, from the marketing database, from the accounting database, and from the data warehouse, I expect consistency of the attributes that are supposed to be the same in all four data databases.

[7]Larry English, *Information Quality Improvement: Principles, Methods, and Management*, Seminar 5th Ed., Brentwood, TN: INFORMATION IMPACT International, Inc., 1996, p. 1.5.

[8]Madhavan K. Nayar, "A Framework for Achieving Information Integrity," *IS Audit & Control Journal*, Vol. II, 1996, p. 30.

Failure to maintain consistency in redundant databases remains one of the most prevalent information quality problems. If there is a business case for building (and buying) redundant databases, there is a business case for maintaining its consistency.

"Meeting"

Some data is required to be zero-defect data. Domain reference data such as medical diagnosis codes and product prices must have 100 percent accuracy if medical claims and product sales are to be accurate. Zero-defect data is required when the consequences of nonquality cause major process failure or catastrophic consequences. Consider the consequences of an inaccurate temperature value to be set in a monitor of a steel blast furnace. The result may cause the furnace to overheat, resulting in a breakout of molten steel from its container.

However, not all data is required to be complete, or even to be precisely accurate. Many decisions may be made from warehouse data that is incomplete. Correct decisions may be made from data that contains some degree of error, when this is factored into the decisions.

Some data, especially data about business events, may not be able to be captured after the initial business event opportunity without extensive investigation and event re-creation. For example, variables in a scientific experiment not captured during the point of contact with the event, may not be able to be re-created at any expense. Even conditions that led to a customer inquiry about a product or service may be lost forever if not captured during that inquiry.

"Knowledge Worker and End Customer"

Who is able to discern quality information? Knowledge workers who require the data to do their jobs. The term *knowledge worker* as used in this book means the role in which one requires or uses data in any form as part of their job function or in the course of performing a process. Hence, a knowledge worker is a *customer of information*. Knowledge workers, as information customers, determine whether data is quality or not based upon how well that data supports their ability to do their jobs.

Virtually all employees are knowledge workers. Executives who make decisions are obviously knowledge workers. Business analysts who require accurate trend data are major customers of the data warehouse. Warehouse clerks who fill orders and builders who use architectural plans to build houses are knowledge workers. Even the order entry clerk who creates orders is a knowledge worker of product information.

Any function that calls itself a *quality* initiative must have the customer as its sole focus. A quality function that does not focus on the needs and requirements of its customers will ultimately fail.

Data warehouse architecture cannot be developed without understanding the needs of the warehouse customers. Who are the customers of the data warehouse? What questions do they need answered? What decisions do they make, and what information is required? To assume one simply needs to load data from the operational databases into the data warehouse guarantees a nonquality information product.

Immediate Information Customers

Immediate information customers are those knowledge workers who are in the same department or business area as the producer of the data. For example, order entry personnel are both producers and knowledge workers of customer data. One clerk may create John Smith's customer record when he first calls in an order. For subsequent orders, the clerk receiving John Smith's call becomes a knowledge worker, retrieving John's customer record in order to create a new order for him. Because the producers of the customer data also use the information, there is a high stake in getting correct data needed to take an order.

Downstream Information Customers

The departmental knowledge workers are not the only customers of data. Not only does the order entry department need Customer data, so does order fulfillment, customer service, accounts receivable, marketing, and possibly product research and development. These downstream knowledge workers also expect quality customer information to perform their processes of filling orders, invoicing and applying payments, marketing efficiently and effectively, and developing new products. Data in one database about a given entity is nonquality if it cannot be used by other knowledge workers who have a stake in that data.

A systemic problem has been caused by the past practices of developing applications from a myopic functional or departmental view of data requirements. The fact of the matter is that data created in one department by one application may have many more knowledge workers outside the originating department who depend on that information.

Quality information is data that satisfies not only the immediate customers, but also satisfies the downstream information customers without major transformation. If common data required in many different business areas, such as name and address, must be transformed by interface programs into different formats for different applications to use, an information quality problem exists. The cost of transformation interfaces diminishes the value of the data by reducing the profit derived from the use of that data. The interface programs also introduce another point of potential error into the process.

"Expectations"

The bottom line is that conscientious employees want to do their jobs well, and they expect to have the necessary resources available to carry out their work in exchange for fair pay. Knowledge workers who require information to perform their work expect and deserve to have the necessary information (resource) with the right quality available to perform that work efficiently and effectively.

The real goal of information quality is to increase customer and stakeholder satisfaction. In fact, information quality can be seen in and measured by end-customer satisfaction. Suppose a customer who orders three widgets but receives only two because the order taker entered "2" instead of "3." The customer, expecting three black widgets, will be an unhappy customer because of nonquality information.

Information Quality Components

Earlier we indicated that information can be represented by the formula:

Information = f(Data + Definition + Presentation)

The three components that make up the finished product of information are separate and distinct components that must each have quality to have information quality. If we do not know the meaning (definition) of a fact (data), any value will be meaningless and we have nonquality. If we know the meaning (definition) of a fact, but the value (data) is incorrect, we have nonquality. If we have a correct value (data) for a known (defined) fact, but its presentation (whether in a written report, on a computer screen, or in a computer-generated report) lacks quality, the knowledge worker may misinterpret the data, and again we have nonquality.

Data *Definition* and Information *Architecture* Quality

Data *definition* refers to the specification of data; that is, the definition, domain value set, and business rules that govern data. Data definition quality is the degree to which data definition: accurately describes the meaning of the real-world entity type or fact type the data represents *and* meets the needs of *all* information customers to understand the data they use. Information customers include both business and information systems personnel:

- Knowledge workers must know the meaning of information in order to perform their work.

- Information producers must know the meaning of information along with valid values and business rules in order to create it or keep it updated.

- Data administration staff must know the meaning of information along with valid values and business rules in order to develop accurate data models.

- Database administration staff must know the meaning of information along with valid values and business rules in order to design high-integrity databases and code triggers correctly.

- Systems analysts must know the meaning of information along with valid values and business rules in order to design high-integrity application models.

- Application developers must know the meaning of information along with valid values and business rules in order to develop high-integrity application logic.

Information architecture quality is the degree to which the data structure:

- Implements the inherent and real relationships of data to represent the real-world objects and events.

- Is stable, enabling new applications to reuse the original data without modification and only require new, non-redundant entity types (and files) to be created, and new attributes (and fields) to be added to existing data models or databases. Database stability means new applications can use data in existing databases without changes in the *structure* of the data model or database, only adding new data.

- Is flexible, supporting changes in how the enterprise performs its processes without significant change to the data model or database. Database flexibility means two lines of business can merge to eliminate duplicate overhead and to maximize cross-selling with minimal change to the database design. Database flexibility means businesses can reengineer processes with minimal change to the database design.

Clear, precise data definition is required to assure clear communication among all handlers of information. Data definition is to data (content) what *Oxford* or *Webster's Dictionary* definition is to an English-language word. Without knowing the meaning of words, how can people understand and use them correctly? Without knowing the precise meaning of data, how can anyone understand and use it correctly?

You cannot *assume* that others in the organization understand the meaning of business terms and data without having a definition. People in general must use a dictionary from time to time. Just as a language requires lexicographers to identify and define the meaning of words, so an enterprise requires business lexicographers to define the precise meaning of business terms and facts.

Business terms can mean different things in different contexts, so each definition and context must be maintained in an enterprise business glossary.

Data definition quality applies to concepts. Does the enterprise have a clear understanding of the *customer* or *order*? Does it have a clear understanding of *customer first service date* or *order date*? Without it, information producers will not know the correct values, and knowledge workers will not know the meaning of the data. And without that, business communication will fail and business performance will suffer.

Data definition quality is a characteristic and measure of data models produced by the application and data development processes. The measures of data definition quality are described in Chapter 5, "Assessing Data Definition and Information Architecture Quality."

Data *Content* Quality

Information quality requires both data definition and data content quality. Data content quality is the degree to which data values accurately represent the characteristics of the real-world entity or fact, and meet the needs of the information customers to perform their jobs effectively.

Data content quality applies to actual occurrences of things. Does the enterprise have an accurate representation of Customer "John Smith" in order to maintain an effective customer relationship with John Smith? Does the enterprise have the accurate values for John Smith's Order, number 12345, in order to fill it properly and identify the trends of product sales and customer needs?

Data content quality is a characteristic and measure of data created and updated by business processes and the applications that implement them. The measures of data content quality are described in Chapter 6, "Information Quality Assessment."

Data *Presentation* Quality

Business processes can still fail even when data is accurate, complete, and conforms to a clear precise definition. Processes can fail if:

- Data is inaccessible.
- Data is not available on a timely basis.
- Data is presented in an ambiguous way or with a label inconsistent with the data name or definition, causing misinterpretation.
- Data is presented in a way that requires excessive work to interpret it, thereby introducing potential errors in the additional processes required to make the data usable.
- Data is combined with other data incorrectly, producing incorrect derived or calculated data.

Data presentation quality applies to information-bearing documents and media, such as a report or window presenting the results of a query of data from a database. Does the order filler have an accurate *presentation* of Customer "John Smith's Order, number "12345", in a format to efficiently and correctly fill the order?

Two microwave ovens flash a message to signal the conclusion of their heating processes. One message flashes "End," and the other message flashes "Ready." When I first saw each message I had different responses. With the "Ready" message I said, "Great, my food is done." When I saw the "End" message my first thought was, "End of what?" The message "End" is a message presented from the view of the oven itself: "This is the end of my process." The "Ready" message is presented from the customer's perspective: "The food is ready for you." Data presentation must focus on the needs of the knowledge workers and their purpose for knowing the information. Data presentation quality means knowledge workers can quickly and easily understand both the meaning and the significance of the information and apply it correctly to their work.

Because information is used for many different purposes, it will have different presentation formats. Quality of presentation means the format presented is intuitive for the use to be made of the information.

Data presentation quality is a characteristic and measure of data access by and presentation to business personnel for their use in performing their work. The measures of data presentation quality are described in Chapter 6, "Information Quality Assessment."

Conclusion

Information quality is not an esoteric notion; it directly affects the effectiveness and efficiency of business processes. Information quality also plays a major role in customer satisfaction.

Information quality is not a subjective characteristic that cannot be measured. It is measurable in the most fundamental of business measures: the bottom line of the business.

Inherent information quality is the measure of how accurately data represents the real-world facts that the enterprise should know. Pragmatic information quality is the measure of how well information enables knowledge workers (the information customers) to accomplish business objectives effectively and efficiently, *and* to satisfy end customers.

To put it another way, information quality is:

QUALITY CHARACTERISTIC	KNOWLEDGE WORKER BENEFIT
The *right* data	The data I *need*
With the right *completeness*	*All* the data I need
In the right *context*	Whose *meaning* I know
With the right *accuracy*	I can *trust* and rely on it
In the right *format*	I can *use* it *easily*
At the right *time*	*When* I need it
At the right *place*	*Where* I need it
For the right *purpose*	*I can accomplish our objectives and delight our customers*

Applying Quality Management Principles to Information

"From the errors of others, a wise man corrects his own."
–PUBLILIUS SYRUS (CIRCA FIRST CENTURY B.C.)

Because information is, in fact, a product of business processes that create and maintain it, we can learn quality principles others have used to improve manufactured product quality and apply them directly to improve the quality of "information" products. If we do so we can bypass the significant learning curve, gaining significant benefits faster.

In this chapter we explore the fundamental principles of quality. These principles are not new. They are the same principles that quality pioneers such as Deming, Juran, Crosby, Ishikawa, Shewhart, Imai, and others have applied to manufacturing and service quality.

We explore their approaches and concepts, as well as the concepts of Kaizen and quality function deployment (QFD), and how they can be applied to information quality. This includes taking a strong customer focus and customer involvement in product requirements and design, applying continuous process improvement to all kinds of business processes that produce products (Kaizen), whether tangible or informational, and using statistical methods for process management and control.

In this chapter, we introduce ISO 9000 standards for quality management systems, and describe the seven categories of performance excellence used in the Malcolm Baldrige National Quality Award assessment as a framework for quality. In the section *Applying Quality Principles to Information*, we illustrate how quality principles apply directly to information as the product of a business process. This chapter concludes with a statement of the fundamental principles of information quality, including:

- The information product
- The information customer
- Planning for information quality
- Controlling information quality
- Leadership for information quality
- Stewardship for information quality
- Application development for quality information products
- Funding application development and systems operations for quality reuse and information sharing

First, though, we discuss the fundamental components of quality and business excellence:

- Customer focus
- Continuous process improvement
- Application of scientific methods to process management, control, and improvement

Over the next several pages, we will describe each component in detail.

Customer Focus

In the end, the customer determines quality. Wise suppliers will understand their market, know their customers, and be ahead of the curve in knowing their customers' needs for their products and services. They will also develop a partnership mind set and relationship with their customers. Suppliers are successful when they meet their customers' needs and help them be successful.

Understanding the Market

To provide a customer focus, you must understand your market in general. Customers come from specific markets that tend to have general needs in common. If we understand the needs of a representative sample of customers from a market, we can develop a fairly accurate understanding of the general needs of a customer group.

There are two categories of information customers or markets: *external customers and stakeholders*, and *internal knowledge workers*.

External customers and stakeholders are those outside the enterprise who require or use information from or about the enterprise. Internal knowledge workers are those business persons who require or use information to perform their jobs.

External Customers and Stakeholders

External customers are those who buy or receive products and services from the enterprise. They need accurate information about an organization's products and services, and expect accurate information about their relationship with the enterprise. For example, all customers expect accurate billing. Likewise, customers of stock brokerage firms expect timely and accurate information about the performance of the equities in their portfolios. As recipients of government services, citizens are information customers who expect accurate information about themselves and the services provided, such as accurate history of contributions to Social Security.

External stakeholders include shareholders, regulatory bodies, and the communities in which an organization exists. These entities also need accurate and timely information. Shareholders need information to assure their investment decisions, and regulatory bodies require accurate and timely information to assure that organizations are operating in accordance with policies and to protect the public trust.

Internal Knowledge Workers

The term *user* should not be used to refer to business people, whether in relationship to information technology or not. *User* connotes "one who uses something," or "one who has an addiction." Missing from that definition is the concept of a customer focus or a partnership relationship. Implied in the term is the notion that the *user* has no choice in the relationship to the thing that is used. The reality is that knowledge workers are information customers—they do in fact have a choice. If knowledge workers' information needs are not met by the information systems or from the "authoritative" production databases, they will go elsewhere to satisfy their information needs, such as their own privately maintained database.

Everyone in the organization who uses information in any form is a knowledge worker, or an information customer. Both business personnel and information systems personnel must understand their markets. They need to know their customers of the information products and services they provide, both inside and outside the enterprise. A major problem in information quality is that information producers and information systems personnel tend to have too narrow a focus on their respective marketplaces. Information producers who create data only see their immediate departmental knowledge workers or first-line recipients of their data as their market. In reality, the market for the data they create may be the entire enterprise, extending to the external customers and end consumers. Order takers may only see the distribution personnel as their market for their information products and not consider the needs of marketing or procurement.

Information systems staff frequently have too narrow a focus on their markets. The application developers may perceive their market to be solely the delivery of applications to business areas. If so, they may simply *automate* manual processes, missing the bigger market of reengineering business processes and transforming the way work is performed. Data resource management staff may see their market as developing data models or developing databases to support application developers by providing data definition and database design. If so, they will miss the much more powerful market of downstream knowledge workers across the enterprise.

The most significant benefit of information technology is when it is used to *informate* knowledge workers. Shoshana Zuboff has coined the term *informate* to describe the fundamental duality of information technology.[1]

On the one hand, information technology can be used to *automate* processes. However, if one only uses technology for automation, the result is merely an automated nineteenth-century machine system. The more powerful benefit is when information is captured about the business processes and events in a way to *informate* knowledge workers. Personnel in other departments can gain from the knowledge gained in one area without having to re-create or recapture the knowledge learned elsewhere in the enterprise.

Every organization and role within the enterprise produces information products and services. They must discover their customers and understand the markets they really serve. Key questions are:

Who are the customers of your information products?

Do you know all categories of information customers, including downstream and end customers?

Do you understand their needs from your information products?

Are you providing the right information products and services?

We answer these questions in this and other chapters.

Customer Satisfaction

Having defined its market, the quality enterprise will seek to discover who its customers are, understand its customers' needs, and relentlessly strive to "consistently meet customer expectations." No enterprise can survive in an increasingly competitive global economy if it fails to know and understand its

[1] Shoshana Zuboff, *In the Age of the Smart Machine*, New York: Basic Books, 1988, p. 10.

customers and their needs, and both its traditional and nontraditional competitors. The enterprise can only know this through quality information from both inside and outside the organization.

A key to customer satisfaction is capturing and maintaining information about customer contacts and communication, especially complaints. Capturing and maintaining this information in a managed, accessible database is key to analyzing existing customer satisfaction and emerging needs. The customer contact database must be accessible to all employees who are a point of contact with specific customers, both for updating the data and for intelligence about customers as they prepare for communication with them. This information must not be the exclusive database of sales representatives or customer satisfaction staff. It must be accessible by accounts receivable, product development staff, and anyone else who adds value to customers. Figure 3.1 illustrates a typical data model of customer complaint data.

For information quality purposes, customer complaint types include information-related codes to identify nonquality information complaints. Such codes may be big-picture classifications, such as direct information quality problems in customer interaction (for example, incorrect billing amount sent to

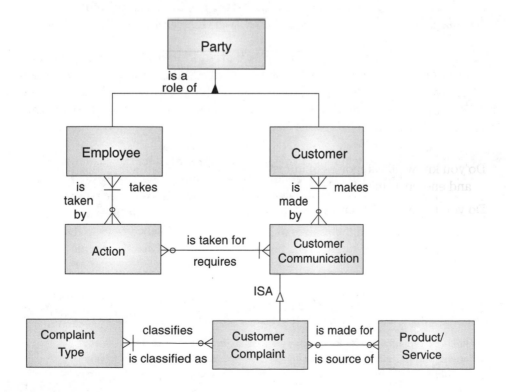

Figure 3.1   An essential part of the customer data model.

a customer, or a misspelled name), and indirect information quality problems (like inaccurate inventory quantities causing ordered items to not be sent to customers in a timely fashion). Or the information quality complaint codes may be specific, such as the following:

- Name misspelling
- Address error
- Duplicate data (multiple catalogs or mailings, etc.)
- Billing error
- Product misinformation
- Shipment miscommunication

Analyze this information over time to identify whether the organization is improving customer satisfaction and to identify improvements of customer satisfaction due to increased information quality.

> **TIP** *Know Thy Customer.* **The customer-complaint database must not be perceived as a mechanism for finding fault with people. It must be perceived as a learning tool for sharing knowledge and for measuring the health of the enterprise. Customer complaint data is one of the key business indicators. Organizations must capture and maintain it—and study and *act* on it.**

The message for information quality is that you must discover the internal knowledge workers' complaints in the same way. Make it easy for knowledge workers to let you know their information problems. How can you improve your services if you do not know, or choose to ignore, the real problems in the information value chains?

> **TIP** **An *unquality* way to reduce complaints: Make it hard for the customer to complain. Two of the largest U.S. airlines, American and Delta, seeing their customer complaints increase, decided that an easy and inexpensive way to reduce complaints was to take the customer comment forms off the planes! By so doing, they deprived themselves of one of the most effective ways to learn about their customers' expectations and how well they are meeting them.**

BRITISH TELECOMMUNICATIONS USES INTRANET FOR INFORMATION QUALITY ISSUES AND RESOLUTION

Putting a system into use for knowledge workers to document information quality problems, and to track solutions, has enabled British Telecommunications to improve information quality and increase communication among knowledge workers.

Customer-Supplier Partnership

The customer relationship value chain begins and ends with the customer. The customer requests products and services, and the enterprise delivers (it had better) value to the customer. The quality enterprise views its customers as partners in its business success and, as a result, will treat its customers with trust and respect. Unquality enterprises treat customers as targets for making money. This may work in the short haul, but will fail in the long run.

The ramification for information quality is that information producers and process owners (information producer management) must seek to discover all of their customers and partner with them for enterprise success, not just departmental success.

Continuous Process Improvement

Continuous process improvement, or Kaizen, is all about a passion for being the best we can be for our own health and well being as well as that of the enterprise. Defective products and services are merely symptoms of the underlying problem: defective processes. To improve products and services to meet customer expectations requires improving the processes to remove the *cause* of defects. To improve processes one must:

- Create customer-focused product specifications
- Define processes across their value chain
- Establish effective feedback loops throughout the value chain
- Encourage teamwork
- Establish a process improvement process

Create Customer-Focused Product Specifications

Product specification is the definition of the requirement for a product. When defined well, the definition in fact reflects requirements that meet the needs of the customers. Product specifications are the mechanism for documenting all components of the product being produced, or service to be provided to meet customer needs.

Information products must likewise be defined. Data definition serves as the product specification of the information product. Data definition must describe data so that it meets the requirements of *all* knowledge workers who depend on and use that information to perform their work. Data definition is the mechanism to enable quality information to be understood by application developers and database designers, who build the applications and databases, as well as the information producers who create the information and the knowledge workers who use it.

Furthermore, data definition must name, define, and represent information to the external customers and stakeholders. The goals are clear communication and intuitive, easy use of all products and services to those stakeholders.

Define Processes Across Their Value Chain

Process definition is the specification of a process to perform some task that produces some result. The result is the product of the process. Process definition includes:

Process definition. *What* should be done.

Process objectives. *Why* it should be done and the goals it is to accomplish.

Location. *Where* it should be performed, and *where* the input comes from and the output goes. Location is relative in the virtual enterprise.

Roles. *Who* should do it.

Triggers or dependence. *When* it should be performed.

Procedures or steps. *How* it should be performed.

Quality measures. *How* to know it was performed successfully.

Processes must be defined consistently across the *business value chain*. A business value chain is an end-to-end set of activities initiated by a *request* from a customer (external or internal) and results in a delivered *benefit* to that customer. James Martin calls this a "value stream,"[2] and Michael Hammer uses the term *business process* to refer to the same concept in business reengineering.[3]

A value chain generally consists of activities that cross functional or organizational boundaries. The most effective way to define data is to define it consistently across its primary value chain to support the needs of all information customers in the value chain.

Encourage Teamwork

A principle of process and product quality is that all players in the value chain operate as a team and not as independent operators disinterested in the results of the complete value chain. All players must share a common vision and know the objectives for the *end result* of the customer of the value chain. They should know

[2]James Martin, *Enterprise Engineering*, Vol. 1, Savant Institute, 1994, p. 67.
[3]Michael Hammer and S. A. Stanton, *The Reengineering Revolution*, New York: HarperBusiness, 1995, p. 4.

all information within the value chain and their information quality requirements. They must each provide feedback on a timely basis.

Establish Process-Improvement Processes

There are two broad categories of process improvement:

Incremental process improvement. These are illustrated in continuous process improvement (CPI) methods, or Kaizen.

Radical process improvement. These are illustrated in business process reengineering (BPR) methods.

These two sets of improvement methods share the same ultimate goals and are complementary. They differ in the urgency with which improvements must be made. The fact that an organization undertakes a business process reengineering project does not mean it does not need continuous process improvement. The fact that a business value chain is radically altered does not mean it is completely optimized. Experience demonstrates that radically altered processes create new problems that require refinement and improvement.

ORGANIZATIONAL RESTRUCTURING IS *NOT* PROCESS IMPROVEMENT

There is a false notion that restructuring and reorganizing is a way to improve the processes and outcomes. If an organization attempts to restructure itself without analyzing and discovering the root causes of the problems it wants to solve, it will fail. That attempt will result in continued failure while giving a false sense of accomplishment. Organizational restructuring will continue to fail until top management understands:

- Managing an organization in the Information Age is different than in the Industrial Age.
- Information, the resource of the Information Age, is a strategic business resource that requires business management principles such as are applied to other business resources like capital, the Industrial Age resource. These principles are outlined and defined in this chapter in the section entitled *Information Quality Principles*.

Process improvement requires teamwork and participation by all involved in the value chain. Those closest to the work understand the problems and already know how to improve the process given a chance. The quality enterprise will empower those workers to make those improvements.

Many of today's information quality problems illustrate the need for major business process engineering for maximum benefit. However, significant benefits can be gained by applying incremental CPI improvements to defective processes.

Scientific Methods

Business processes, like manufacturing as well as application development and data development processes, are not merely random activities. They are processes that can be managed, improved, and controlled to produce consistent quality results.

Ishikawa, Shewhart, Deming, and Juran pioneered and applied scientific methods to process management, control, and improvement. These methods are fact-based, applying measurements to the outputs of processes to determine consistency of the processes, and improving them where necessary.

Statistical Quality Control

Statistical quality control, sometimes called *statistical process control*, consists of the set of techniques for measuring process performance, identifying unacceptable variance, and applying corrective actions. Getting processes into control requires:

Process management. Management includes process and product definition or specification in order to assure processes perform properly. Process management also requires training to assure the producers know how to perform the process properly.

Process measurement. Measurement tests whether the processes perform and produce products as specified and within the acceptable degree of variability.

Process improvement. Improvement assures processes perform and produce products as specified with minimal variance to meet customer expectations. Quality control seeks to assure consistency of results to within acceptable limits. Process improvement seeks to reduce the variability of output.

Shewhart Cycle

The Shewhart cycle is the basic technique for improving processes. Created by Walter Shewhart, Deming adopted it and introduced it in Japan, where it is known as the *Deming Cycle*. The technique, popularly known as PDCA, or *Plan-Do-Check-Act*, consists of four steps of process improvement:

1. **Plan.** Plan an improvement of a known and unacceptable problem, using such techniques as Cause-and-Effect diagrams to analyze and identify the root cause of the problem.

2. **Do.** Implement the planned improvement in a controlled manner.

3. **Check.** Measure the improved process to test if it achieves the desired level of quality.

4. **Act.** Standardize the effective improvement to eliminate the defective products and the costs of defective products and process failure.

The Shewhart cycle is an effective technique for improving processes in all kinds of contexts. It is useful as a tool for information quality improvement.

DEMING AND INFORMATION QUALITY

Most readers know that Deming brought the statistical control principles to the Japanese after World War II, resulting in one of the world's most remarkable economic turnarounds. But few probably know that before Deming went to Japan, he actually applied his statistical control principles to *information quality*. Deming was recruited to help with the 1940 U.S. census, where he developed the sampling techniques that were used for the first time for the census. He demonstrated that statistical controls could be applied to "information production" as well as industrial production. With training and expertise, the error rate of card punchers (the state of information technology at the time) dropped significantly, requiring the inspection of only one-third of their work.[4]

Quality Approaches

There are many lessons learned in quality improvement that can be applied directly to information quality improvement. I am indebted to the quality pioneers who have led the way. I have mentioned them previously, but in the next several sections, I will describe their concepts and techniques briefly along with their ramifications for an information quality management system.

Deming's 14 Points of Quality

W. Edwards Deming is credited with creating the quality revolution in Japan when he took his principals to help Japan in the reconstruction following its devastation during World War II. His 14 Points of management transformation were not just adopted by Japanese management; they were embraced as the *only* way of managing business for success. These points are not just points for a quality team; they are fundamental principles of management transformation for fundamental business change. They are the principles required to move from a mentality of "do it *fast*" to a mentality of "do it *right*." These principles are described in detail in Chapter 11, "The 14 Points of Information Quality."

---

[4]Mary Walton, *The Deming Management Method*, New York: The Putnam Publishing Group, 1986, p. 70.

The fundamental essence of Deming's points is that management must adopt quality as it would a religion and cease the counterproductive measures and management practices that drive up costs while driving down quality.

The Juran Trilogy[5]

Dr. Joseph M. Juran defines quality as a combination of product performance and freedom from product deficiencies.[6]

Product performance means product satisfaction as determined by external customers. Freedom from deficiencies means freedom from product dissatisfaction or customer complaints. The focus of quality is meeting customer needs.

Juran identifies a trilogy of "managerial" processes required for quality. They are:

Quality planning. The objective is to provide the operational staff with the means of producing products that can meet customers' needs. If a process produces a 20 percent level of waste consistently, it indicates that the process was *designed* to produce waste. Chronic information quality problems are an indication of poor information quality planning and design.

Quality control. Quality control seeks to maintain a specified level of quality within acceptable limits of variability or at least to keep quality from getting worse. It calls for putting out fires caused by processes out of control.

Quality improvement. The purpose of quality improvement is to improve the processes to eliminate scrap and rework and increase the ability of the product to meet customer needs more effectively.

Juran's principles of quality mean knowing the customers and their needs, and providing products and services that meet those needs. Juran cites as an example of internal suppliers and customers, "employees in department A supply data to employees in department B."[7]

Juran's message for information quality is clear: Information producers and process owners must discover *all* downstream customers of their information products and seek to satisfy their information needs.

Ishikawa: Quality Control as a Movement

Kaoru Ishikawa, the president of Musashi Institute of Technology, was a central figure in creating the quality revolution in Japan. He characterizes the quality control "movement" in Japan as having six features:

---

[5] J. M. Juran, *Juran on Planning for Quality*, New York: The Free Press, 1988, p. 12.
[6] Ibid., pp. 4–5.
[7] Ibid., p. 9.

- Companywide total quality control in which *all* employees participate
- Strong emphasis on training and education
- Quality circle activities for process improvement
- Total quality control assessments, illustrated by the Deming Prize and Baldrige award
- Use of statistical methods
- Nationwide promotion of total quality control

Some important messages for information quality improvement include the fact that information quality is an enterprisewide concern, with data created in one part of the business required in other parts of the business. Ishikawa sees quality not as an enterprise domain problem, but as a contribution to the *national* economy.

Information quality is also a national economic concern. According to a study conducted by Standard & Poor's DRI, the Year 2000 information quality problem alone will have a significant impact on the U.S. economy, reducing GNP by 0.3 percent in 1999 and 0.5 in 2000 alone.[8]

The Year 2000 information quality problem is only the most visible and publicized of the information quality problems that insidiously reduce business output and productivity.

Kaizen: The Art of Continuous Improvement

Masaaki Imai, founder of the Kaizen Institute of Europe, describes Kaizen as the Japanese word for continuous process improvement. "Kaizen simply means continuous improvement involving everybody in the organization. I think the two key words, one is improvement and the other is continuous. And it is possible for people to make improvement once, but to keep people making improvements year after year is another challenge."[9]

The objectives of Kaizen are to continually improve everything in the organization by encouraging everyone to take responsibility for the process. Kaizen and Gemba Kaizen concepts described in Imai's books *Kaizen* and *Gemba Kaizen* (McGraw-Hill, 1987 and 1997, respectively) include:

Kaizen and management. Management has two major functions in Kaizen: maintenance of current management and operating standards for quality, including training and discipline; and improvement, meaning elevating quality standards, including innovation.

Process versus result. Kaizen focuses on human effort, and therefore fosters process-oriented thinking.

---

[8] Michael J. Mandel, P. Coy, and P. C. Judge, "ZAP! How The Year 2000 Bug Will Hurt the Economy (It's worse than you think)," *BusinessWeek*, March 2, 1998, pp. 46–51.

[9] Masaaki Imai, *Quality in Practice: BS 5750 and Kaizen*, BBC Training Videos, London, 1993, 36.

Following the Plan-Do-Check-Act/Standardize-Do-Check-Act cycles. Before you can improve a process you must stabilize and *standardize* it.

Putting quality first. The temptation to sacrifice quality for attractive price and delivery terms risks the life of the business.

Speak with data. Kaizen is a problem-solving process. To solve a problem, you must understand the facts of the problem using gathered, verified, and analyzed data, not hunches or feelings.

The next process is the customer. Every process has a supplier and a customer. Knowing that one has internal customers should lead to a "commitment never to pass on defective parts or inaccurate pieces of information to those in the next process" (*Gemba Kaizen*, page 7).

Major Kaizen systems include:

Total quality control/total quality management. Total quality has evolved to encompass all aspects of management.

Just-in-time production system. The goal is to eliminate all kinds of non-value-adding activities and create a lean, flexible production system.

Total productive maintenance. This focuses on improving equipment quality through preventive maintenance.

Policy deployment. Management must create clearly-defined targets, provide leadership, and perform Kaizen to reach targets.

Quality suggestion system. The goal is to increase quality-minded and self-disciplined employees and increased morale through employee participation.

Small-group activities. Informal activities, such as quality circles, carry out specific tasks in a workshop setting.

Gemba Kaizen emphasizes the *gemba* ("real place") where work is performed:

Standardization. To manage resources such as people, equipment, materials, and *information* requires standards. This is essential for daily improvement.

Good housekeeping. The five S's (English equivalents of *sort, straighten, scrub, systematize,* and *standardize*) are required to increase order, efficiency, and discipline in the workplace.

Muda elimination. Muda is the Japanese word for waste. The goal is to eliminate non-value-adding activities with processes.

Quality Function Deployment

Quality function deployment (QFD) is a systematic approach for involving customers directly in the design and development process for new products and services. First employed in the Kobe Shipyards in the early 1970s, QFD has been a powerful tool for product innovation.[10]

QFD goes beyond the notion of improving processes by reducing variability in the product to incorporate customer involvement and active input into every phase of the manufacturing process.

By involving customers in product and service design in a methodical way, you discover their needs early and increase the likelihood of consistently meeting their expectations when the products first reach the customers. The experiences learned from applying QFD include eliminating waste and improved customer satisfaction early in the design process, leading to increased sales, profits, and market share.[11]

The ramification of this for information quality is significant. To deliver quality information, you must actively involve the information customers in the data modeling and design phase prior to implementing information systems. While many organizations involve business representatives in the application requirement specifications, they may do so in ways that suboptimize the output. Two critical ingredients for involving information customers in the design process are:

Knowledge workers must actively define the information they need to perform their work efficiently.

Involvement in the data definition and design process must include representatives of all stakeholders in the information products being designed. The classic failure of traditional "user" involvement is to include only the immediate beneficiaries of the application being built. Sharable (quality) databases must satisfy all information customers' needs.

Crosby's Quality Is Free

Philip Crosby founded Philip Crosby Associates in 1979 and built it into a large quality-management consulting firm before he retired in 1991. Crosby has outlined a 14-step quality program. The steps are:[12]

Step 1: Management Commitment. "To make it clear where management stands on quality.

Step 2: The Quality Improvement Team. "To run the quality improvement program.

Step 3: Quality Measurement. "To provide a display of current and potential nonconformance problems in a manner that permits objective evaluation and corrective action.

---

[10]Jeremy Main, *Quality Wars*, New York: The Free Press, 1994, p. 96.
[11]John Terninko, *Step-By-Step QFD*, 2nd Ed., Boca Raton: St. Lucie Press. pp. 2–11.
[12]Philip B.Crosby, *Quality Is Free*, New York: Penguin Group, 1979, pp. 149–222.

Step 4: The Cost of Quality. "To define the ingredients of the cost of quality, and explain its use as a management tool.

Step 5: Quality Awareness. "To provide a method of raising the personal concern felt by all personnel in the company toward the conformance of the product or service and the quality reputation of the company.

Step 6: Corrective Action. "To provide a systematic method of resolving forever the problems that are identified through previous action steps.

Step 7: Zero Defects Planning. "To examine the various activities that must be conducted in preparation for formally launching the Zero Defects program.

Step 8: Supervisor Training. "To define the type of training that supervisors need in order to actively carry out their part of the quality improvement program.

Step 9: ZD Day. "To create an event that will let all employees realize through a personal experience that there has been a change.

Step 10: Goal Setting. "To turn pledges and commitments into action by encouraging individuals to establish improvement goals for themselves and their groups.

Step 11: Error-Cause Removal. "To give the individual employee a method of communicating to management the situations that make it difficult for the employee to meet the pledge to improve.

Step 12: Recognition. "To appreciate those who participate.

Step 13: Quality Councils. "To bring together the professional quality people for planned communication on a regular basis.

Step 14: Do It Over Again. "To emphasize that the quality improvement program never ends."

ISO 9000 and Repeatable Quality

ISO 9000 is an international set of quality management system standards that provides guidelines for an organization's quality management systems. ISO 9000 registration is a process whereby an accredited third party assesses whether an organization's quality management system meets an agreed-upon set of requirements for managing the quality of its products or services. The intention of ISO 9000 registration is to eliminate the need for an individual customer organization to have to assess the quality management systems of its suppliers.

The ISO 9000 standards structure appears in Figure 3.2.[13]

---

[13] H. James Harrington and Dwayne D. Mathers, *ISO 9000 and Beyond*, New York: McGraw-Hill, 1997, p. 11.

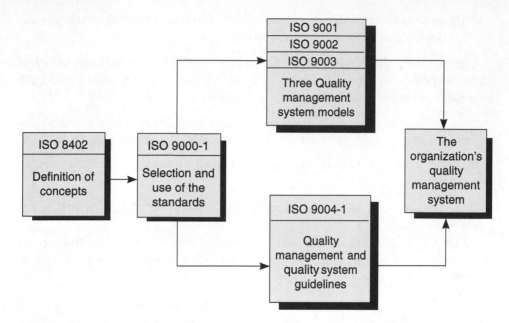

Figure 3.2   The ISO 9000 quality standards structure.

Source: Harrington & Mathers, *ISO 9000 & Beyond*, New York: McGraw-Hill, 1997, p.11.

According to Harrington and Mathers in *ISO 9000 and Beyond*, the ISO 9000 standards consist of five primary documents.[14]

ISO 9000-1: Quality Management and Quality Assurance Standards—Guidelines for Selection and Use. The key message here is that work should be treated as a process that should be defined, with procedures well documented. The process should be controlled as documented, and records must be maintained to verify the procedures are followed.

ISO 9001: Quality Systems—Model for Quality Assurance in Design, Development, Production, Installation, and Servicing. ISOs 9001, 9002, and 9003 are standards used to demonstrate the organization's ability to supply products that meet customer expectations.

ISO 9002: Quality Systems—Model for Quality Assurance in Production, Installation, and Servicing.

ISO 9003: Quality Systems—Model for Quality Assurance in Final Inspection and Test.

ISO 9004-1: Quality Management and Quality System Elements—Guidelines. This document provides further information about the preceding

---

[14]Harrington and Mathers, *ISO 9000 and Beyond*, p. 10.

three standards. It also addresses components that should be included in an overall quality management system.

Organizations that have attempted to adopt the ISO 9000 standards have had varied experiences. There seems to be a correlation in organizations that have achieved real and sustainable quality improvements with:

A movement beyond the documentation and procedural aspects of the standards with management commitment to quality—not just standards.

Changes in the environment that incents quality rather than treating quality as a "necessary evil."

ISO 9000 should be seen as a *tool* to achieve repeatability levels of quality, not as an *end* in itself.

ISO 9000 ramification for information quality means processes that create data models, databases, applications, and processes that create or update information should be documented to achieve repeatable quality.

The Baldrige Quality Award

The Malcolm Baldrige National Quality Award was created in 1987 by law as the highest level of national recognition a U.S. for-profit organization can receive for performance excellence. The seven Categories of Performance Excellence represent a balanced, results-oriented *framework* for assessing both the management systems and results of an organization. The categories are interrelated and interdependent, as illustrated in Figure 3.3.

The first three categories represent the Leadership Triad, which represents how well the organization plans for quality. The fourth category, Information and Analysis, is a foundation category that supports and enables the other six. The last three categories represent the Results Triad, which indicates how well the organization implements quality, including a balanced set of business results. The seven categories are:

Leadership. "The Leadership Category examines the company's leadership system and senior leaders' personal leadership. It examines how senior leaders and the leadership system address values, company directions, performance expectations, focus on customers and other stakeholders, learning, and innovation. Also examined is how the company addresses its societal responsibilities and provides support to key communities.

Strategic Planning. "The Strategic Planning Category examines how the company sets strategic directions, and how it develops the critical strategies and action plans to support the directions. Also examined are how plans are deployed and how performance is tracked.

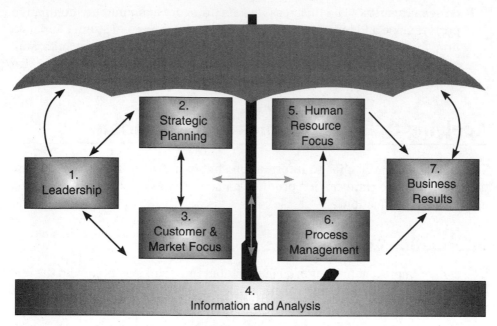

Figure 3.3 The Baldrige performance excellence criteria framework.
Source: H. Hertz, NIST National Quality Program.

Customer and Market Focus. "The Customer and Market Focus Category examines how the company determines requirements, expectations, and preferences of customers and markets. Also examined is how the company builds relationships with customers and determines their satisfaction.

Information and Analysis. "The Information and Analysis Category examines the selection, management, and effectiveness of use of information and data to support key company processes and action plans, and the company's performance management system.

Human Resource Development and Management. "The Human Resource Development and Management Category examines how the company enables employees to develop and utilize their full potential, aligned with the company's objectives. Also examined are the company's efforts to build and maintain a work environment and work climate conducive to performance excellence, full participation, and personal and organizational growth.

Process Management. "The Process Management Category examines the key aspects of process management, including customer-focused design, product and service delivery, support, and supplier and partnering processes involving all work units. This category examines how key processes are designed, implemented, managed, and improved to achieve better performance.

Business Results. "The Business Results Category examines the company's performance and improvement in key business areas—customer satisfaction, financial and marketplace performance, human resource results, supplier and partner performance, and operational performance. Also examined are performance levels relative to competitors."[15]

Applying Quality Principles to Information

To apply quality principles to information simply means to focus on information customers, the information product, and the processes that create, update, and present information.

Information Customer Focus

One cannot improve information quality without first thinking about who the real information customers are and what their needs are in their information products. Information customers include:

End customers. Organizations do not just provide products and services to their customers. They also provide information products in the form of product information, whether in catalogs, advertisements, Web sites, correspondence, or voice-mail messages they receive when they call. Invoices and account statements are information products. Verbal or written information, such as promises an employee communicates to customers during a point of contact, is in fact an information product.

Internal knowledge workers. All employees who require information to do their jobs are information customers.

External stakeholders. These include shareholders who need information to know about their investment, regulators who need information to assure the enterprise is in compliance, and communities who need to know if the enterprise is a good steward within their communities, among others.

Data as the Raw Material and Information as the Finished Product

Data is the *raw material* produced by one or more business processes that create and update it. Created and maintained data becomes the materials, or input, for many other business processes. The supply chain of information as a product is illustrated in Figure 3.4.[16]

---

[15] "Malcolm Baldrige National Quality Award: 1998 Criteria for Performance Excellence." www.quality.nist.gov. National Institute of Standards and Technology, Gaithersburg, 1998, pp. 5–21.

[16] Larry P. English, This was first published in "Data Quality: Meeting Customer Needs," *DM Review*, November, 1996, p 46.

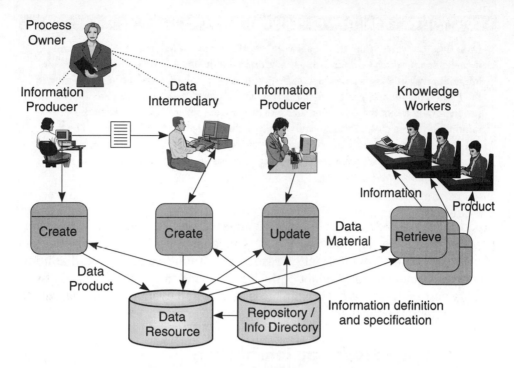

Figure 3.4   The information product in the information supply chain.

This implies business roles of supplier and customer. The information customer is any knowledge worker who uses information to perform their job. The person who originates or causes the creation or updating of data is a "supplier" of data, or "information producer."

As the product of a process, the same principles of quality improvement that are applied to manufacturing processes to improve manufactured product quality can be applied to business processes to improve information product quality.

It is important to distinguish between the actual information *producer* and a data *intermediary*. A data intermediary is someone who takes data in one form and transcribes it into another form adding minimal value. For example, the internal information producer may receive a telephone call from a claimant and capture claim information on a form. That form may be passed to a data entry clerk (data intermediary) who enters the information into a database from the form. The data intermediary is an extra point of data handling. Data intermediation introduces information *float* (delay in potential data accessibility) and can decrease information quality through the introduction of transcription errors such as omissions, transposition of characters, or loss of the document itself.

A fundamental flaw in process definition today is that most processes are defined in terms of their physical or tangible outputs, and the information

"OH, YOU'RE FROM THE 'PAPERWORK' PROJECT".

I saw this "Oh, you're from the 'Paperwork' Project" mind-set in a major manufacturing organization in which I was assisting the information quality initiative. One of the major information producers, a sales representative, that we were interviewing kept referring to the information quality project as the "paperwork project." It was no surprise that the review revealed that the sales area was one of the most severe bottlenecks in the information value chain. This role consistently failed to capture the data needed by the downstream order takers, causing the order takers to spend up to 50 percent of their time in information scrap and rework, having to chase down missing information needed to take a simple order.

products are treated as byproducts or documentation of the real work, or simply paperwork. In the Information Age, this myopia is fatal. No enterprise can exploit the value of its information resources without a clear vision that information is a fundamental product of the business and manufacturing processes. Quality data collected about the business objects and events can be analyzed to discover trends and insights impossible to discover in any feasible way.

Planning and Producing Information Quality

Quality information requires careful planning and controlled execution. Planning for information quality includes determining what information is required to effectively run the business and perform its essential processes to fulfill its mission. This is performed both in business planning and in the planning and development of application systems, databases, and data warehouse of the enterprise.

Figure 3.5 illustrates the context of information *definition* and *information architecture* quality. The roles represented here facilitate or define information, information requirements, and information architecture. Figure 3.6 illustrates the context of information *product* quality. These roles participate in the creation, maintenance, and use of information.

The information production processes are simply the business processes including manufacturing, in which information becomes created, collected, captured, or updated, whether manually or electronically. Every process includes personnel who are responsible for the actual work and/or who are responsible for the process and its outputs, including information products.

The roles in information quality, described shortly, include:

- Strategic and tactical knowledge workers
- Operational knowledge workers
- Information producers
- Data intermediaries

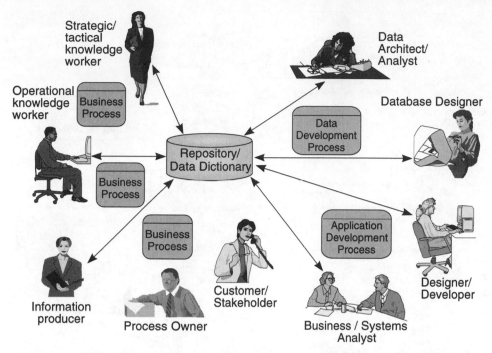

Figure 3.5 Planning for information quality: Components of data definition and information architecture quality.

- Information managers, architects, modelers, and analysts
- Database designers and administrators
- Business and systems analysts
- Application designers and developers
- Data warehouse architects and designers

Strategic and Tactical Knowledge Workers

This is the absolute starting point for data definition and information quality. If the organization does not start here in planning and developing its data warehouse, the project will fail. The data warehouse must support the knowledge workers who perform the strategic and tactical processes of the enterprise. The data warehouse information must be defined to support both the base (detail) data requirements, as well as the key derived and summarized information needs.

Strategic and tactical knowledge workers and information managers must also be included in the data definition and information quality in planning and developing the *operational* applications and databases. If not, the resulting applications and databases will fail to achieve maximum value. The reason?

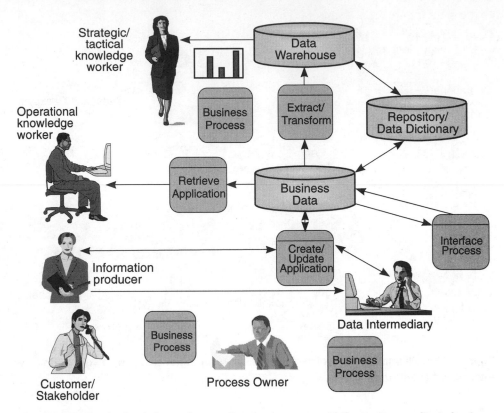

Figure 3.6   Producing information quality: Components of information quality in business processes.

Not considering strategic information requirements may cause the analysis and design processes to not define key facts about business objects and events that are essential to perform strategic or trend-analysis processes, but not needed to perform the operational process.

> **TIP**   When analyzing information requirements for any operational application, always include information views (e.g., key queries, decisions, and key business indicators) required to support strategic and tactical processes. This information may not be needed to support the immediate operational processes, but may be needed for decision support. This minimizes overlooking key attributes that should be captured by processes being automated.

Operational Knowledge Workers

Because knowledge workers perform the business processes of the enterprise, every application and database designed must be designed to capture information to meet their needs. This includes both downstream knowledge workers as well as the immediate or departmental knowledge workers.

For quality information design, data must be defined consistently *across* the business value chain. Defining information consistently across the value chain reduces the work required to automate subsequent downstream processes. Furthermore, it increases the value of the immediate application by capturing information that downstream knowledge workers can use immediately.

TIP When defining information requirements for an application, identify downstream knowledge workers who have a stake in the data of the application. Actively involve them in the data definition process. Consider all processes—or a representative sample—and their required information views to validate the stability of the information models.

Information Producers

Information producers are the keys to the information supply chain. As the actual originators of information, they are key to information quality. They must be involved in the definition of information being automated along with the knowledge workers so that data definition is consistent and agreed upon by both the information producers and information consumers.

TIP Actively involve both information producers and knowledge workers in the data definition processes *together*. Producers must know who their customers are and their needs. Knowledge workers must know their information suppliers and the complexities they may have in capturing the required information. By involving both groups together, they can become a supportive team, rather than competing adversaries.

Data Intermediaries

Data intermediaries are those whose role it is to transcribe data from one form into another. The data entry clerk who enters data into a database from a paper form plays an intermediary role. While intermediaries do not define the requirements of the data they transcribe from one form to another, they are actually knowledge workers themselves. They will use other information in the data entry processes, and therefore must also have representation in the data definition processes to the extent of defining what they need to know in order to perform their jobs efficiently.

Data intermediaries must also have representation in the application design process to provide input as to the human factors required to facilitate efficient and effective data transcription. Many kinds of data entry quality problems can be minimized by collaborative design of application human interfaces with information producers and intermediaries.

TIP Seek to eliminate *unnecessary* data intermediation. Quality is enhanced when data is captured electronically or by the originating information producers. Because data intermediaries are not at the point of information creation, they may not be able to "correct" data errors discovered by the automated business rule tests. As a result, the information may have to be written to an exception file and require subsequent handling in order to discover the correct values.

Information Managers, Architects, Modelers, and Analysts

Those who create information and data models are the facilitators of data definition. While they cannot, and should not, attempt to define the meaning of data alone, they must facilitate data definition to meet all information stakeholder needs.

Information managers, or data administrators, and data architects are accountable for the integrity of the *structure* of the information and data models. They facilitate the definition of data with business subject matter experts, including clear, robust definition, accurate data relationships, and complete domain value specifications and business rules. Their accountability is to design accurate, stable, flexible, and reusable data structures. The purpose of data models, as the blueprints of information requirements, is to improve business and systems communication and productivity and to guide physical database design to produce stable and flexible physical data structures.

Database Designers and Administrators

Database designers are those who transform conceptual or "logical" data models into physical database designs and physical databases that house the electronic data. They, like a builder with an architectural blueprint, "build" databases from architected data models.

Their accountability is for the integrity of the physical design of databases to balance performance speed and conceptual integrity of the physical data structures, and may include assuring physical integrity of the electronic data such as recoverability and physical security.

Business and Systems Analysts

Business analysts are those who analyze and define requirements and specifications for applications. Generally, people with functional specialties fill these roles, but the role is evolving to include cross-functional requirement definition across entire business value chains. No process can be defined without a specification of the product produced. No application specification is complete without a robust specification of the information products produced.

Their accountability is for facilitating the definition of the business processes and capturing the real business process requirements in ways that can be translated into effective business process definition, and requirements that can be designed into automated application designs.

TIP Define processes across their business value chain. Ask, "Who are all the customers of the final product?" They will be internal knowledge workers and external customers. "What are the customers' *real* expectations for the outcome of this process?" "What must the process do to meet these expectations?" Business and systems analysts must be able to read between the lines and differentiate the "stated" requirements of those who perform the processes and the "real" requirements of those who are the customers who use those processes.

Applications Designers and Developers

Applications designers and developers are those who design and develop computer or automated applications implementing all or part of a business process. Of special importance is the design of the information presentation. Human factors must be included in screen design and report layouts, as well as in other information presentation forms, such as graphics to visualize data.

Their accountability is to assure the designed and implemented application systems and programs accomplish the defined requirements and specifications.

TIP Involve both the process performers and downstream knowledge workers who are the ultimate customers of the information products produced. Proactively include them in prototyping the designs and developed applications so that testing comes *during* development, not *after*.

Data Warehouse Architects and Designers

This includes those who plan and design data warehouses, data marts, or executive information systems. The chief difference between data warehouse architects and (operational) data architects is the nature of the processes supported. Data warehouse databases must be modeled and designed to support the strategic and tactical processes. Operational databases must be modeled and designed to support first the operational processes and then strategic and tactical processes. Operational data stores must be designed with an enterprise consensus definition of operational data. It may evolve into the enterprise operational record-of-reference database as legacy applications are reengineered. The fact that strategic and tactical processes must be addressed as a secondary requirement for operational databases and processes is that certain business event facts are only known during the business event transaction. These facts may never become known after the event has taken place. If a database does not have fields for those facts, and the process does not capture them, those facts will be lost forever.

TIP Data warehouse architects and operational data architects and analysts must work together. The base data facts in the data warehouse must be a part of the enterprise information architecture with a common definition.

Base facts required by the data warehouse for trend analysis must be defined and included in the appropriate operational database and origination application.

These are the major roles in information planning and production. There will, of course, be other roles, such as webmasters, who have important roles. They will have one or more of the accountabilities similar to those already described.

Information Quality as Customer Service

Information as a product leads to the concept of information quality as customer service. Because knowledge workers require quality information to do their jobs, they depend on the information suppliers. Information customer service requires defining data across the business value chain to support all knowledge workers rather than from a vertical stovepipe or organizational perspective.

If information is a product and knowledge workers are customers, then providing quality information means providing customer service to those knowledge workers. Information creation and production is not some clerical task. Information creation is the "manufacturing" process for the data materials required to perform both the physical work and the knowledge work of the enterprise. In a quality organization, process owners and information producers take on a customer service mind set toward those downstream knowledge workers who depend on their information.

The Information Value Chain

The information value chain is the entire collection of processes and computer applications that create, update, extract, interface, transform data, and present information from its original inception or knowledge creation, whether in electronic or other form, to its final retrieval and information presentation to its ultimate knowledge workers. The information value chain also includes all information stakeholders, including information producers who create the knowledge, data intermediaries who translate information from one form to another, and knowledge workers who use information. The information value chain finally includes all databases and files, whether computerized or manual, such as filing cabinets or report libraries, in which the data is stored, from origination to final storage, including archives if information needs to be kept for potential future use.

The information value chain documents the information customer-supplier relationships. This tool enables the organization to understand who the information customers are of what information created by which information suppliers. For a description of how to document an information value chain, refer to Figure 6.4 in Chapter 6, "Information Quality Assessment."

Customer Satisfaction of the Information Products

Consumers rate the quality of products and services they buy based on how well they satisfy their needs or purposes. Knowledge workers will also characterize information quality based on how well it meets their needs for the information, whether to perform a process, support a decision, or answer a question.

Business Performance Excellence through Information Quality

Data is not simply a necessary documentation of business transactions; it is the basis for effective and efficient business performance. Quality information is a necessary component of *business* quality. For a breakdown of quality principles, see Table 3.1.

Table 3.1   Information Quality Principles

The information product	Information is a *strategic* enterprise resource held and used by the enterprise and "owned" by the stakeholders.
	Information is the *product* of one of more business processes and has many customers (knowledge workers).
The information customer	Knowledge workers, including downstream knowledge workers.

Continues

Table 3.1   Information Quality Principles *(Continued)*

The information customer	As information customers, knowledge workers specify information requirements, including quality expectations.
	Customer satisfaction in the information product by end customers and knowledge workers is the true measure of information quality.
	The ultimate target level for information quality is the requirement of the most rigorous process and the knowledge worker. Suppose five processes use one data group. Suppose four of the processes require 98 percent accuracy, while the fifth process requires a 99.99 percent accuracy level. To consistently meet customer expectations, the information quality target for accuracy level requires 99.99 percent accuracy.
Planning for information quality	Drive strategic information plans by enterprise business vision and strategic (not tactical) plans.
	Effective information policy is required to communicate shared values, guidelines, and accountabilities for information products.
	Model, name, and define information consistently among *all* knowledge workers and information producers.
	Model *all* information types for an integrated information resource.
	Cross-functional enterprise information architecture to enable data sharing and maximize reuse.
	Use enterprise information model to *evaluate application software packages*.
	Reengineer business processes across the value chain *before* "automation" to eliminate cost-adding, error-introducing intermediary steps and interfaces.
Controlling information quality	*Automate* information collection where possible.
	Minimize unnecessary intermediary processes such as passing paper forms from the real information producer to a data intermediary for keying.
	Capture information electronically only once, at the business event of its origin.

Table 3.1   *(Continued)*

Controlling information quality	Capture *all* information required for *all* downstream processes.
	Develop processes that empower anyone who comes to know correct facts to update the data directly, or communicate easily with an information producer who can and will update it.
	Access data from a single database or tightly controlled set of databases.
	Eliminate unnecessary transforming interface programs where transform errors can be introduced.
	Distribute data in the form of *replication* and maintain common definition and domain values across distributed databases.
	Tightly *control* any transforming interfaces if data *cannot* be replicated (such as for software packages or data warehouses).
	Measure information quality to identify, correct, and control defective processes to improve customer satisfaction.
Leadership for information quality	Develop effective information quality improvement processes.
	Empower employees to suggest improvements and recognize them.
	Train information producers adequately.
	Provide information producers access to data definition and business rules.
	Develop performance measures that *incent process owners* and *information producers* to capture quality information for downstream knowledge workers.
	Train knowledge workers adequately.
	Provide knowledge workers access to data definition and business rules.
Stewardship of information quality	Process owners are *accountable* for information quality (first). This must be written into their job descriptions as accountabilities for financial and people resources.

Continues

Table 3.1 Information Quality Principles *(Continued)*

Stewardship of information quality *(Continued)*	Then information producers may be held *accountable* for information quality.
	If I retrieve/receive downloaded data, I am accountable for how I use it. If I come to know correct facts, I will not just update "my" database, I will get it updated in the source database.
	Define information quality targets and measure and report information quality (feedback) for improvement—not fault-finding.
Value-Centric Application development for quality information products	Develop applications from a full customer service and resource perspective. The customer service perspective means applications must be developed as an integrated component of the business value chain to meet the needs of downstream knowledge workers, not just the immediate beneficiaries. The resource perspective means applications are not the product themselves; rather, they are the automation part of a process that produces one or more information products. Applications are to their information products what manufacturing equipment is to the manufactured product.
	Single create programs (resource acquisition) for each entity type with extensions for each subtype and entity life cycle state.
	Applications create and update data into an authoritative record-of-reference database or an authoritative record-of-origin database with controlled replication to the record-of-reference database.
	Data create programs capture data required for all downstream processes, not just the immediate beneficiary.
	Minimize interface programs that transform data (reacquisition of information resources). Use replications instead.
	Eliminate redundant create programs (reacquisition of information resources). This makes data consistency uncontrollable.
	Maximize retrieval programs (applying the information resource), where the information value is derived.

Table 3.1   *(Continued)*

Fund application development and systems operations for quality reuse and information sharing	Authoritative, single data create and update programs and information architecture (*infrastructure development*). The information infrastructure development should be paid in the same way other capital expenditures are made. This capital *investment* should be allocated equitably across the enterprise.
	Information retrieval programs (*value delivery*): Retrieving and using information is where information's value is derived. The cost of retrieval and presentation of information should be charged back to the beneficiary process or organization unit.
	Redundant data create/update programs and interfaces (cost-adding only). Development that results in redundancy, in proprietary databases and applications must be dis-incented. Redundant development includes developing new data models of data types that already exist, building new databases of data of a similar type that already exists in an authoritative and sharable infrastructure database, and application programs that redundantly create and maintain data that is already being created and maintained. This type of development needs to have a business case as to why it is needed outside the authoritative databases. The cost of development needs to be charged back to the "sponsor" at a premium. In addition, the sponsor of this redundant development should be charged all expenses associated with monitoring and controlling the data consistency between the redundant databases and the authoritative databases.

Conclusion

The principles of quality and business excellence are well known, if not practiced well. Information is the differentiating resource in the Information Age.

If the principles of quality are known, why have those principles not been applied vigorously to information quality? Two reasons: First, senior management has not fully understood the ramifications of data and information as strategic enterprise resources, nor have they understood the principles for managing the information resources like they understand the principles for managing the other enterprise resources. Unfortunately, most CIOs do not understand the ramifications or the principles, either. The typical CIO believes the charter is to manage the information *technology*. To do so condemns the organization to manage the wrong resource: the tools and not the *results*. Second, senior management is unaware of the real costs of nonquality information, both in the form of irrecoverable costs of materials, computing resources, and time, and in lost and missed opportunity of increased revenue.

The principles of information quality are clear:

1. Focus on the customer of the information products. This means the end customer, whom we serve and to whom we communicate through information, and the knowledge worker who requires information to serve them.

2. Adopt a mind-set of continuous improvement of the processes that create, update, and present information so as to eliminate the costs of nonquality information and improve business performance.

3. Apply proven scientific methods to measure and improve the right things, such as customer satisfaction, and use the results to improve business processes, not punish scapegoats who may not have been given the resources necessary to create information products properly to begin with.

The business justification for an information quality initiative is not "How much will the information quality initiative save in money." Management cannot abdicate its responsibility or delegate information quality improvement. Rather, the business justification is, "This is how much the status quo is costing the enterprise unnecessarily, including direct costs and lost and missed opportunity."

PART

Two

Processes for Improving Information Quality

"It takes less time to do a thing right than it does to explain why you did it wrong."

–HENRY WADSWORTH LONGFELLOW

How can one improve without guidance? How can one get to where one is going without a road map? Part Two is the guide and road map for information quality improvement. It defines the processes of information quality improvement as a management tool for business performance excellence.

Chapter 4 provides an overview of the TQdM (Total Quality data Management) methodology. It provides a thumbnail sketch of information measurement, assessment, and improvement processes. Chapter 4 further outlines a methodology for guidance in the data warehouse context. It also provides an overview of the ingredients required for a healthy environment for a culture of information quality as a management tool for business performance excellence. See Part Three.

The first three TQdM processes of quality improvement are assessment processes. These processes address how to assess data definition and data content quality, analyze the costs of poor information quality, and are the subjects of the next three chapters, respectively.

Chapter 5 describes the characteristics of data definition and information architecture quality and outlines how to measure and gauge quality. Without quality of information architectures that store the enterprise's knowledge resources, information quality will be much more difficult to achieve.

Chapter 6 describes the characteristics of information quality and outlines how to measure, analyze, and report information quality in databases, data warehouses, or output from the business processes.

Chapter 7 describes the process of analyzing and quantifying the costs of poor information quality in business terms. It provides a road map for identifying the devastating impact poor-quality information has on business operations, mission accomplishment, and customer satisfaction.

The next two TQdM processes are improvement processes. The first of these is improvement of the *information product* itself, as discussed in Chapter 8. The second process is improvement of the *processes* to prevent data defects, outlined in Chapter 9.

Chapter 8 describes the process of information cleansing and reengineering. This process defines how to improve the information product itself; that is, bring data up to an acceptable level of quality. This process is used for improving the information products within an existing database by converting data from legacy files to new database architectures or software package files and by reengineering and cleansing data for a data warehouse or data mart.

Chapter 9 outlines how to improve the quality of the information product through business process improvement. It describes how to identify the root cause of information quality problems and how to plan and implement improvements that are permanent, not just stopgap.

Part Three addresses how to establish the information quality environment.

An Overview of Total Quality data Management (TQdM)

"The best way to escape from a problem is to solve it."

—ANONYMOUS

Total Quality data Management (TQdM) is not a *program*, and it is not simply a *process* of data measurement or data cleansing. Rather, TQdM is:

- A *mind set* that acknowledges that everyone in the enterprise is interdependent on each other for information.

- A *belief system* that quality information has value to the enterprise—in fact, is required—in order for the enterprise processes to perform properly and optimally.

- A *value system* of customer satisfaction through quality information products.

- A *culture* in which everyone takes responsibility for continually improving processes to increase customer satisfaction and drive down costs.

TQdM is the *habit* of continual information process improvement of two categories of processes:

Information systems development processes that define information, develop and implement business processes, information systems, and information architecture and databases.

Business and manufacturing processes that create, update, and delete data, distribute or disseminate information, and retrieve or present information to information producers and knowledge workers.

TQdM seeks to accomplish this by integrating *quality* management *beliefs*, *principles*, and *methods* into the *culture* of the enterprise.

This chapter provides a big-picture view of the TQdM methodology. It will help you understand the context for information quality improvement, so that as you read about a specific process, you have an understanding of how it fits into the overall methodology.

Here we introduce you to the TQdM processes of information quality improvement. Information quality improvement is not an end in itself; rather, it is a means for improving business performance and customer satisfaction. This chapter provides an overview of the assessment and measurement processes, and further outlines a methodology for improving information quality of data in existing source databases as well as in data warehouses. It describes the basics of information process improvement to eliminate the causes of data errors. It provides a basic approach to beginning an information quality environment when the immediate project at hand is to develop a data warehouse. It also provides an overview of the systemic changes required to create a culture of information quality for excellence in business performance and customer satisfaction.

The TQdM processes are illustrated in Figure 4.1.

Processes for Information Quality Improvement

Information quality management consists of five processes of measuring and improving information quality, and an umbrella process for bringing about cultural and environmental changes to sustain information quality improvement

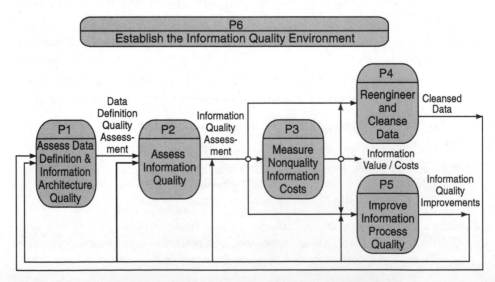

Figure 4.1   Total Quality data Management methodology overview.

as a management tool and a habit. Process 6 is described first because this represents the framework for transforming the enterprise to a culture of information quality. Even though you may begin your information quality initiatives with quality assessment and cleanup, you must plan for the cultural transformation outlined here and described in Part Three, "Establishing the Information Quality Environment."

Process 6: Establishing the Information Quality Environment

Process 6 is more than a single process. It represents the systemic, management, and cultural requirements for a sustainable information quality improvement environment. Without these cultural characteristics, an information quality initiative may achieve some short-term benefits, but those benefits are not likely to continue.

This process is treated first because it is foundational for long-term information quality improvement. In reality, you will have to perform activities from the other five processes, in order to change the strongly held paradigms of the status quo. The first paradigm change is from information as a byproduct and data creation as clerical work to information as a direct product and information creation as knowledge production. The second paradigm change is from acceptance of the costs of unquality information as a normal "cost of doing business" to acceptance that unquality information costs are unnecessary, unacceptable, and survival threatening.

If poor information quality exists in an organization, the environment and culture invariably will have encouraged and incented that level of poor information quality. Organizational and cultural barriers will have been placed in the way. Management will reward speed over quality, either because they do not recognize the value of quality information, or because they and other information producers are measured for how fast they perform a process and not how the information products produced meet the needs of downstream knowledge workers (information customers). A final cause of poor-quality information is a lack of understanding that improved information quality actually reduces the costs of business operations and increases customer satisfaction and profit.

This process assesses the cultural readiness of organization, using the Information Quality Management Maturity Grid. This is a required starting point to understanding the next steps in effecting a culture change for information quality.

A key to sustainable information quality is that everyone in the organization is accountable and responsible for their processes and information products. To effect this requires:

- Understanding the information value chains and the fact that every employee is interdependent on information products from other employees to successfully accomplish their objectives.

- Finding out who your information customers are and what they expect in their information products.

- Education, education, and more education. How do I do my job correctly? How can I develop myself to the fullest extent possible? How can I improve my day-to-day processes for my own efficiency and effectiveness and for the good of our end customers?

- Changing the performance measures and incentives to include customer satisfaction incentives both internally among the knowledge workers and externally among our end customers.

See Part Three, "Establishing the Information Quality Environment," for how to institute a culture for information quality.

We now introduce the five key processes for information quality assessment and improvement.

Process 1: Assess Data Definition and Information Architecture Quality

The process of measuring data definition and information architecture quality is a precursor to measuring information quality. One cannot measure the quality of a product without knowing that the product specifications themselves are accurate and are what they *should* be. In order to measure information quality in a database or out of a process, analyze the definition of the data as documented and communicated first. This process is illustrated in Figure 4.2 and is described in depth in Chapter 5, "Assessing Data Definition and Information Architecture Quality."

The baseline step (step 1.1) for this process defines the essential and critical characteristics of data definition and information architecture. These are the minimum requirements for the naming and definition of data that must be in place for communication among information producers and knowledge workers, and among data resource management and application development personnel. At a minimum, these requirements include data names, definitions, valid value sets, and pertinent business rules. These data definition requirements should be clearly described in the enterprise data or information standards.

These definition requirements constitute the *technical* "measures" of data definition quality. One caution must be raised here. Any technical measure of data definition quality must be coupled with a customer satisfaction measure or assessment of data definition quality, as described in step 1.6. Data definition must serve to facilitate communication among knowledge workers and improve business productivity. The following are the steps to assessing data definition and information architecture quality.

Step 1.2 identifies an important group of information to assess; in other words, a group of information where poor quality results in high costs or other unacceptable consequences.

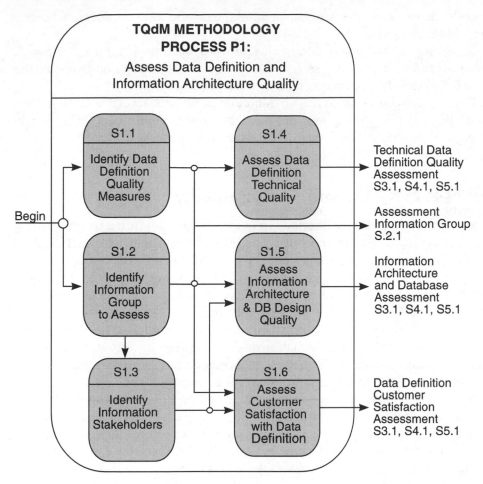

Figure 4.2 Assess data definition and information architecture quality process steps.

Step 1.3 identifies the categories of information stakeholders in the selected group of information. These include the information producers who create and maintain the information, the knowledge workers who use it, as well as the external customers and external stakeholders who require it.

Step 1.4 performs a technical assessment of the data definition for conformance to data standards and guidelines. This step assesses whether the data documentation conforms to the minimum established standards.

Step 1.5 is another technical assessment. This step assesses the quality of the information architecture and database design and implementation against data design and implementation best practices. It measures the degree of capability of the enterprise to communicate through shared learning, using an information chaos quotient.

Step 1.6 is the most important step in this process. It measures customer satisfaction with the definition of the information products as determined by the knowledge workers who use the data and the information producers who create and maintain it.

Deficiencies discovered during this process become input to *Process 5: Improve Information Process Quality*. The processes to be improved are the data definition and application development processes.

If the data to be assessed has no definition or unsatisfactory definition, then it should be defined by representations of the various groups of stakeholders in that group of information. This becomes input to *Process 2: Assess Information Quality*.

Process 2: Assess Information Quality

The process of measuring information quality is like measuring manufacturing product quality. There are technical measures of conformance to specification and reduced variability of the products produced. Then there are ways to measure the degree of customer satisfaction against customer expectations. Figure 4.3 illustrates the steps in the information quality assessment process described in Chapter 6, "Information Quality Assessment."

Step 2.1 identifies or reconfirms the group of information to be measured.

Step 2.2 establishes the information quality characteristics to be measured in that collection of data. Information quality includes such characteristics as completeness, conformation to business rules, accuracy, and timeliness.

Step 2.3 documents the information value and cost chain for the information group. This includes an identification of all databases that house the data; all processes and applications that create, update, interface, and transform or extract the data; as well as the processes and applications that retrieve and use the information. This step identifies the various categories of stakeholder in the information group.

Step 2.4 identifies which databases or processes are to be measured. Important databases include the record-of-origin database, record-of-reference database, and other databases where consistency is required. The record-of-origin database is the first database where data of a given type is electronically captured and stored. The record-of-reference database is, or should be, the most authoritative source of data of a given type. Because the record-of-reference database is the source for distributing data if access cannot be centralized, it must contain high-quality data.

Step 2.5 identifies the data validation sources against which the accuracy of data is measured. The validation source may actually be a surrogate source—a source document of data about a real-world object or event—or may be the actual real-world object itself, or a recording of an event. For example, the authoritative sources to validate customer data are the customers themselves. To validate product dimension attributes you measure samples of the products themselves. To confirm correctness of telephone stock trade or order, you

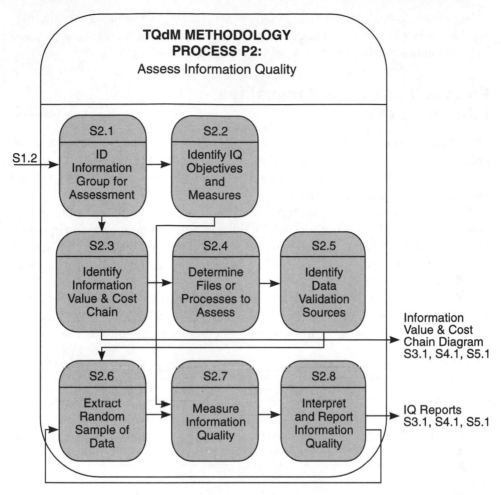

Figure 4.3   Assess information quality process steps.

observe or record the business transaction for comparison to the actual trade or order data.

Step 2.6 is the step in which data is randomly sampled from the selected databases or processes for assessment. The use of statistical sampling techniques here reduces the cost of the assessment while still providing an accurate picture of the reliability of the data being assessed.

Step 2.7 is the activity of actual measurement of the data sampled. There are two kinds of assessments. Automated assessments use query tools or quality analysis software to measure completeness and conformance to business rules. Physical assessments use physical comparison of the sampled data to the real-world objects, events, or their surrogates to determine accuracy.

Step 2.8 determines the best way to present the findings of the assessments for communicating to the appropriate stakeholders.

Now we know the state of information quality. This is the basis for quantifying its costs (Process 3), cleansing it (Process 4), or implementing process improvements to eliminate the defects (Process 5).

Process 3: Measure Nonquality Information Costs

One of the myths of information quality improvement is that the costs of poor-quality information cannot be measured. On the contrary, these costs can be *precisely* measured in terms of reduced profit and revenue; in other words, the bottom line of the organization.

The process outlined in this step describes how to measure and quantify the costs of poor-quality information. It establishes the business case for information management and information quality improvement. Figure 4.4 illustrates these steps. This process is described at length in Chapter 7, "Measuring Nonquality Information Costs."

Information quality costs must be measured against the business drivers, both formal and informal. The baseline step (3.1) is to identify those business drivers such as increase profits, increase customer satisfaction, or reduce

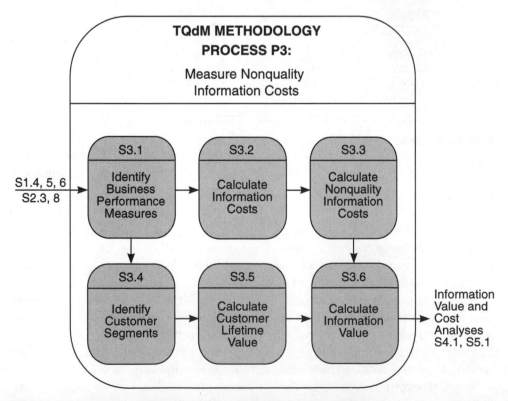

Figure 4.4   Measure nonquality information costs process steps.

costs. Any attempt to quantify nonquality information costs must do so against these measures.

Poor-quality information and its resulting impact on service and product quality drives customers away. Customer lifetime value is a tool for assessing lost and missed business opportunity.

Step 3.2 analyzes the cost of information. It identifies the degree of redundancy of data. Here you determine how much of the Information Systems effort is invested in:

Infrastructure development. The basis for capturing and maintaining information.

Value delivery development. The development of applications that retrieve and use information to add value.

Cost-adding development. Redundant database development, redundant applications capturing the same data that is captured elsewhere, and development of interfaces that copy and transform data from one database to another.

The purpose of this is to measure the effectiveness of the processes of application and database development or acquisition.

Step 3.3 determines categories of cost to the enterprise, resulting from missing and inaccurate data. It also calculates the measurable costs incurred as a result of process failure due to nonquality information.

Steps 3.4 and 3.5 identify customer segmentation and establish customer lifetime value, used to measure missed and lost opportunity as a result of poor information quality.

Step 3.6 establishes the value of quality information by measuring the missed and lost opportunity that results from not having quality of information products.

This now gives you not just an understanding of the state of information quality, but of the actual costs of that poor quality. It provides the business case for making investments in the next two processes of data cleanup and information process improvement.

Process 4: Reengineer and Cleanse Data

The information reengineering and cleansing process is the process for information *product* improvement. It serves to take existing data that is defective and correct the deficiencies to bring it to an acceptable level of quality. This process is one of information scrap and rework and is identical in nature to the process of manufacturing scrap and rework. Data that is cleansed is *reworked*. Data that cannot be cleansed is *scrapped* and thrown out, or identified as not correctable.

This process defines how to bring data up to an acceptable level of quality for any of the following:

- Information quality within specific source databases or files

- Data being converted to a new system or software package database

- Data to be transformed, cleansed, and propagated to a data warehouse or data mart

Figure 4.5 illustrates the steps in the general reengineering and cleansing process of source data, and Figure 4.6 illustrates the steps in the reengineering and cleansing process for conversion, data warehouse, and data mart data. These processes are described in depth in Chapter 8, "Information *Product* Improvement: Data Reengineering and Cleansing."

The following steps provide the basis for general data cleansing.

Step 4.1 identifies the data sources that require reengineering and cleansing of the source data. If data is being used from these sources, the principle is to cleanse it *here*, and not just in transit to a data warehouse.

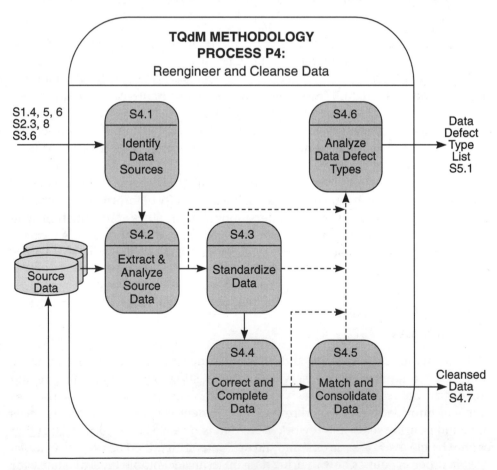

Figure 4.5 Reengineer and cleanse data process steps.

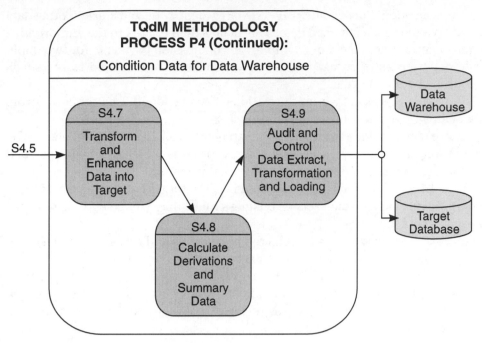

Figure 4.6   Condition data for data warehouse process steps.

Step 4.2 extracts and analyzes the source data to identify anomalies and patterns in the data. If databases have not been robustly defined or maintained to incorporate new knowledge requirements, they will tend to have significant anomalies when compared with the data structure definition. The analysis performed here seeks to identify the semantic meaning, patterns, and business rules in the actual data so that it can be standardized across different redundant databases storing similar information.

Step 4.3 standardizes the data based on its semantic meaning, so that it can be compared, merged, duplicates identified, and standardized for consistency of use.

Step 4.4 fills in missing data values, where known, and corrects data values known to have changed since it was last updated or incorrectly updated. This step has two categories of correction:

Automated correction. Where correct values are electronically known or can be derived using software.

Physical, **or human correction.** Where correct values cannot be ascertained electronically.

Step 4.5 matches potentially duplicate data from within a single database or across multiple databases. The duplicate data is electronically consolidated according to a defined set of algorithms. Cases where the algorithm may not be able to determine the most likely accurate value will require human intervention for consolidation. Consolidation also requires identifying and consolidating data that is related to the matched data. This data is then related to the authoritative occurrence of reference. For example, the commission payments for two duplicate occurrences of an agent must be consolidated and related to the single occurrence for that agent.

Step 4.6 extracts data from the various steps to identify patterns of errors that can be used for process improvement.

These steps provide for the activities required to correct data in place. The next three steps continue the reengineering process for data to be propagated to a target conversion database or to a data warehouse.

Step 4.7 maps the cleansed base data into the target data structure. If there are different domain value sets or business rules, they will be applied to transform the data properly.

Step 4.8 summarizes data by selected dimensions and calculates derived and summarized data to be stored in the data warehouse or data mart.

Step 4.9 provides the audits and controls to assure that data extraction, transformation, summarization, and loading are performed according to specification. This is the control process to verify that required data is not omitted, or data applied multiple times.

Process 5: Improve Information Process Quality

This process is the habit of the High IQ organization. High IQ stands for *High Information Quality*, meaning an intelligent learning organization.

The process of "process improvement for information quality" should be the most used of the information quality processes. It takes known problems, analyzes root causes, and plans and implements process improvements that prevent data defects. This improvement process is illustrated in Figure 4.7 and is described further in Chapter 9, "Improving Information *Process* Quality."

This process may be performed formally or informally. It may encompass resolving information problems as small as within one individual's work activities, or as large as across enterprises, such as the supply chain. This process utilizes the Shewhart cycle of PDCA, the Plan-Do-Check-Act that we reviewed in Chapter 3, "Applying Quality Management Principles to Information," and is described in detail in Chapter 9.

Step 5.1 establishes a process improvement initiative. This activity may be initiated anytime and anywhere there is an information problem brought to light. This step defines the problem to be solved, identifies the pertinent processes, and establishes the information quality improvement team.

Step 5.2 develops the plan for the improvement. Root cause analysis is used to sort through the symptoms and get to the true cause. The plan includes identifying the specific changes to be made in a controlled environment.

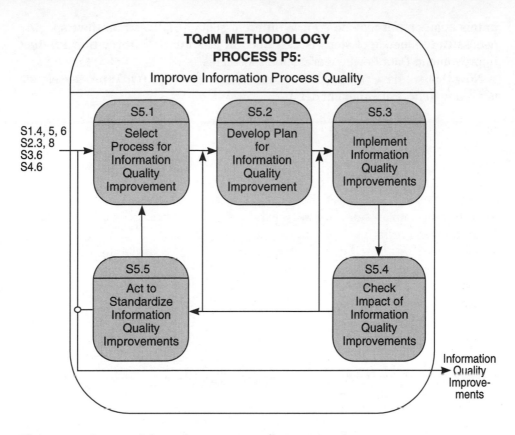

Figure 4.7   Improve information process quality process steps.

Step 5.3 implements the corrective changes in a controlled mode, so the improvements can be tested.

Step 5.4 assesses the effectiveness of the improvement changes made. If the desired improvement is not achieved, the improvements are reimplemented or replanned.

Step 5.5 takes the effective improvements and implements them across the enterprise and standardizes them, so they are controlled to produce consistent quality results.

Performing this process eliminates or minimizes the need for cleansing unquality data, as well as the costs incurred.

Processes for Information Quality in the Data Warehouse

Organizations embarking on data warehouse initiatives and that do not yet have an information quality function must conduct many of the steps we just covered in this chapter, but may do so in a different sequence, based on their specific needs. The sequence of steps is described in Chapter 8, "Information *Product* Improvement: Data Reengineering and Cleansing."

Now that we have provided a thumbnail sketch of the TQdM processes, we are ready to describe them in detail.

CHAPTER 5

Assessing Data Definition and Information Architecture Quality

"You cannot measure what is not defined."

—PAUL STRASSMAN

Business information is the language of the enterprise. Failure to robustly define the business language can cripple the enterprise's ability to communicate. Poorly defined data can lead to misunderstanding, making information quality uncertain, thereby creating a dysfunctional learning organization. Dysfunctional learning organizations cannot perform efficiently, let alone effectively.

In this chapter we define what data definition is and why it is essential to information quality of internal data marts and databases or application software package databases. We identify the components of data definition and describe the data definition components whose quality is essential for business performance.

We also define a process for measuring data definition and information architecture quality of data models and databases or application software package databases. The process includes how to define measures for data definition quality, how to identify information for quality assessment, and how to identify the information stakeholders who are the information customers. Then we describe how to conduct the two kinds of data definition quality assessments: a technical assessment of information architecture and database design quality, and a customer satisfaction assessment with data definition quality.

This chapter is *not* a treatise on data resource management, data standards, or data modeling conventions or methods. Rather, it defines the definition quality measures and explains how to assess the quality of data definition and information architecture.

Data Definition Quality

Data definition refers to the set of information that describes and defines the meaning of the "things" and events, called entity types, the enterprise should know about and what facts, called attributes, it should know about them to accomplish its mission. The term *data definition* as used here refers to all of the descriptive information about the name, meaning, valid values, and business rules that govern its integrity and correctness, as well as the characteristics of data design that govern the physical databases.

Data Definition as Information Product Specification

Data definition and information architecture are to data what a product specification is to a manufactured product. Product specs describe clearly the "requirements" along with acceptable variation for product manufacturing. Those characteristics for product quality must be clearly and unambiguously defined so that the manufacturing processes consistently produce products of acceptable quality; in other words, within the limits of variability.

To produce consistently high-quality information you must have a quality "information product specification." This specification includes robust and precise definition of the meaning, domain values, and business rules for the business information the enterprise needs to know, along with a well-designed information architecture to house the information efficiently and effectively. Business information includes the entities (for example, persons, organizations, places, objects, and events) the enterprise needs to know about and the facts the enterprise needs to know about those entities. Information architecture includes both the data models of this information, along with its physical database design.

INFORMATION PRODUCT SPECIFICATION

Product Specifications (n) 1: A detailed, exact statement of particulars, especially a statement prescribing materials, dimensions, and quality of work for something to be built, installed, or manufactured. 2: An exact written description [of something]. (*American Heritage Dictionary*)

Specify (v) 1: State or name clearly and definitely (details, materials, etc.). (*Oxford English Dictionary*)

Data Definition as Meaning

Data definition *quality* is, first of all, a measure of how well data definition captures and communicates the actual meaning of the real-world "things" people must know about to perform their jobs. Second, data definition quality is a measure of how well the data architecture and database design implement the information requirements of the enterprise, and how well applications capture and present information to meet knowledge workers' needs.

DATA DEFINITION IS *NOT* DATA DOCUMENTATION

Definition 1: The act or process of stating a precise meaning. 3: The act of making clear and distinct. (*American Heritage Dictionary*)

Definition (n) 1: (a) Stating the exact meaning (or words, etc.): (b) statement that gives the exact meaning (of words, etc.): Definitions should not be more difficult to understand than the words. (*Oxford English Dictionary*)

Define (v) 1: State precisely the meaning of (e.g., words). 2: State clearly; explain. (*Oxford English Dictionary*)

The term *data definition* as used here is synonymous with the technical term *metadata*, which means "data that describes and characterizes other data." Metadata is a technical term that has not yet made its way into the *Webster's Unabridged Dictionary* or Oxford's unabridged dictionary as a recognized English language word. Because information is a business resource, I shall use the term *data definition* in discussing quality of the description and defined meaning of data.

Data definition begins with the quality of data standards used to guide the process of data definition and design. Data definition includes name, definition, and relationship aspects, as well as business rules that govern business actions and data integrity.

Data Definition as Information Architecture

Data definition is to data what a blueprint is to a constructed building (see Figure 5.1). One can build a simple building, such as a doghouse or tree house, without a blueprint. But to build a Sears Tower, World Trade Center, or Kuala Lumpur's Petronas Towers (now the world's tallest buildings at 1483 feet) without a robust blueprint would be impossible and foolishly dangerous to attempt.

In 1993 the World Trade Center withstood a devastating terrorist explosion without structural failure. That there were only 6 fatalities, and over 1000 injuries out of the more than 50,000 workers in the twin towers, is something of a miracle. What would the consequences have been if the bomb had caused the tower to collapse? The fact of the matter is that quality architecture and a sound foundation saved tens of thousands of lives and unimaginable economic catastrophe.

But two years later the six-year-old, and only five-story-tall, Sampoong Department Store complex in Seoul, South Korea, collapsed in 1995, killing 501

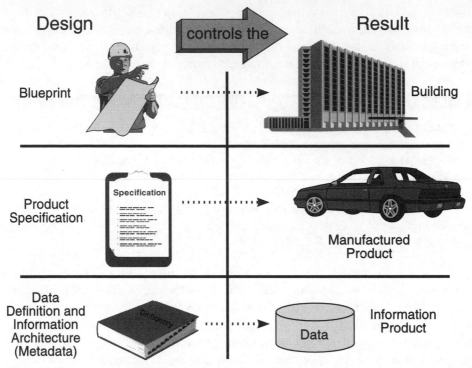

Figure 5.1 Data definition and information architecture are like blueprints and product specifications.

people and injuring nearly 1000. The cause? Faulty design and construction. The Sampoong officials built the building well beyond the approved blueprint, adding an entire floor on top and twice as much floor space as allowed. Substandard steel reinforcing rods and substandard concrete materials were apparently used in the construction, so the structural support was insufficient for the additional weight. The owner and the president of the shopping mall have since been convicted for negligence in the disaster.

Building databases for complex systems and business value chains without an information architecture is likewise foolishly dangerous. Yet databases today are predominantly designed based upon functional and application data requirements. This puts the survival of the enterprise at risk. Designing databases on an application basis alone is tantamount to designing the architecture of the World Trade Center one floor at a time, as one might design the room layout for the office spaces on the floor. Databases so designed have structural failure when additional applications are added on top of the existing application for which the data was originally and exclusively designed. Information must be modeled and databases must be designed across the enterprise and business value chains if they are to support the business.

Information Product Specification Quality

There are three aspects of information product-specification quality:

Data standards quality. Data standards govern the definition of data, to enable consistent and quality information definition. Data standards quality measures the degree to which data is defined consistently, accurately, clearly, and understandably.

Data definition quality. Quality here is the quality of the defined *meaning* of the information required by the business. Are the definition, set of valid values, and business rules meaningful to and understandable by the information customers?

Information architecture quality. This quality includes the quality of the *design* of the data models and databases that house the information resources to support all knowledge worker requirements in a way that information is sharable and reusable. Information architecture quality measures the reuse, stability, and flexibility of data model and database design.

Specific characteristics of information product specification quality include the following. They are listed here and described in greater detail in the following sections.

Data standards quality. The data standards enable people to easily define data completely, consistently, accurately, clearly, and understandably.

Data name quality. Data is named in a way that clearly communicates the meaning of the objects named.

Business term clarity. The business term name or phrase is appropriate and is consistently understood across all interested knowledge workers.

Entity type name clarity. The name of the "things" or entity types the enterprise needs to know about is consistent with the real-world classification of those objects.

Attribute name clarity. The names of business "facts" are consistent with the real-world data represented.

Domain type consistency. Domain type is also referred to as a "class word." The name of the attribute indicates the nature of the data being represented, such as a "date," "amount," or "name," and the valid values for the attribute are consistent with the type of data.

Business term abbreviation and acronym clarity. There is a single enterprise abbreviation for each business term that is universally accepted among the knowledge workers. Alias abbreviations serve as a cross-reference to abbreviations not able to be standardized in legacy files or software packages.

Data name or label consistency. The data names or labels representing entity types and facts are consistent across all presentation media, such as field names, screens, and reports.

Definition quality. How well data definition completely and accurately describes the meaning of the data the enterprise needs to know.

Business term definition completeness, accuracy, and clarity. The definition of business term clearly and accurately communicates the *meaning* of the concept being described.

Entity type definition completeness, accuracy, and clarity. The definition of entity type clearly and accurately communicates the *meaning* of the object being described.

Attribute definition completeness, accuracy, and clarity. The definition of business and attribute clearly and accurately communicates the *meaning* of the type of fact being described.

Data name and definition consistency. The name of the attribute and its definition communicate the same *meaning*.

Domain (valid set of values) value definition completeness and clarity. The specification of the set of valid values for a given attribute is complete and consistent with the domain type of the attribute. If the attribute is a code domain type, all code values are clearly defined, and the codes are consistent with the definition of the attribute.

Business rule quality. How well the business rules specify the policies that govern business behavior and constraints.

Business rule completeness and accuracy. The business rules that describe policies governing business actions and, as a result, specify data integrity requirements, and are complete, accurate, and clear.

Information and data architecture quality. How well information and data models are reused, stable, and flexible and how well they depict the information requirements of the enterprise; and how well the databases implement those requirements and enable capture, maintenance, and dissemination of the data among the knowledge workers.

Data relationship correctness. The specification of relationships among entities and attributes in data models accurately reflects the correct nature of relationships among the real-world objects and facts.

Business information model clarity. The high-level information model represents and communicates the fundamental business resources or subjects, and fundamental business entity types the enterprise must know about completely and clearly. The business information model is understandable by and approved by senior management as representing at a high level what the enterprise must know about to perform its processes and accomplish its mission.

Data model completeness and correctness for operational data. The data model of operational data reflects completely all fact types required to be known by the enterprise to support *all* business processes and all business or functional areas. This detailed model correctly illustrates the relationships among entity types and between entity types and their descriptive attributes. The model has no redundancy of entity types or of attributes except for attributes used to relate occurrences of one entity type to another. All "view" models that support information requirements are derivable from the conceptual data model *without alteration* of the conceptual model. These local, or information view, models represent data to support a single view of information, such as for one business area or function, one organization unit, one application or system, or one business process.

Data warehouse model completeness and correctness to support strategic and decision processes. The data model of strategic or tactical information (for data warehouses or data marts) completely and accurately reflects the information requirements to support key decisions, trend analysis, and risk analysis required to support the planning and strategic management of the enterprise. All view models, such as used to design a data mart, are derivable from a single strategic information model. This model contains the base data required to calculate key business indicators and key aggregations and summaries of data, as well as the derived data reflected in the model. The model has a *minimum* number of redundant or overlapping derived attributes, maximizing the sharing of information.

Database design to support operational processes. The physical database design accurately implements the data as defined in the conceptual model with minimum compromises. Design trade-offs that compromise the structure in the conceptual data model have data integrity plans accompanying them that provide controls to minimize data integrity problems.

Distributed database architecture and design. Data that is implemented redundantly in separate or distributed databases have consistent definition and domain value sets. Data distribution is managed by replication or controlled distribution processes that assure consistency of data values in the redundant data stores. There is minimal information chaos. The count of uncontrolled redundant database files is a measure of the "information chaos" of the enterprise.

Database design to support strategic and decision processes. Data warehouse and data mart physical designs accurately implement the information requirements as defined in the strategic data model. Processes that extract, cleanse, transform, aggregate, summarize, and load data are specified correctly and operate correctly.

Data Standards Quality

To define data, you must have clear *specification standards* and *guidelines* that enable different teams to produce consistent quality of data definition and information architecture. The role of data standards, however, has often been misunderstood and misused. As a result, the real benefits of data standards frequently have not been achieved.

The objectives of data standards are twofold: to increase communication, and to increase productivity across business value chains. That's it.

COMMUNICATION AND PRODUCTIVITY

Communication (n) 1: A process by which information is exchanged between individuals through a common system of symbols, signs, or behavior.
Communicate (v) 1: To transmit information, thought, or feeling so that it is satisfactorily received or understood. (*Webster's Dictionary*)
Productivity (n) 1: Efficiency, esp. in industry, measured by comparing the amount produced with the time taken or the resources used to produce it. (*Oxford English Dictionary*)

Data standards are not an end in and of themselves; they are a means to achieve consistency in the definition and specification of the information resources of the enterprise. Their purpose is achieved when data is defined in ways that increase communication and productivity among business areas across the enterprise that have a stake in a common type of information, and between business and information systems personnel, and between data resource management and application development personnel.

Well-defined data standards become the mechanism for the *technical* assessment of data definition and information architecture quality.

Data definition quality requires quality information standards. Data standards are to data definition what the lexicographic guidelines are for dictionary producers, such as *Oxford* or *Webster's*.

Consider the usefulness of the dictionary if the lexicographers for each letter or functional groups of words chose their own standard format for definition, pronunciation, derivation of the word, and so forth. The result would be inconsistency making it difficult to use for dictionary customers.

The real benefit of quality data standards is to increase the effectiveness of business communication and productivity.

Data Standards Quality Checklist

The following checklist can be used to assess the quality of your organization's data standards. It provides a complete set of standards and guidelines to create complete documentation and specification of data requirements that can be used for understanding and communicating the meaning of data, and for developing reusable and sharable databases and applications.

❑ The data standards encompass the enterprise. That is, they cover data definition and database design over the scope of the enterprise or the breadth of stakeholder interest in a *subject* of information.

❑ The data standards provide standards and guidelines for *all*-important information objects the enterprise requires to conduct business.

❑ The data standards have examples and tips for what is good and what is bad, so those using them know when they have "complied" with the standards.

❑ The data standards are developed by or reviewed and *approved* by a group of business information stewards or business personnel who represent the entire scope of the enterprise. Because data standards affect business communication, they should be developed with business representation.

❑ The data standards have a review and appeal process that encourages improvement of the standards process itself.

❑ The data standards are followed for *all* new application development. There is no such thing as data "standards" that are not universally followed.

❑ The data standards are used to evaluate *all* new application software packages. The purpose here is not to expect application packages to conform to your data standards, but to know how well the package data is defined, and what language communication problems the organization will have in using the package.

❑ The result of following data standards over time has resulted in increased communication and productivity. This means that productivity is increased in the subsequent projects after the learning curve, and in which the data defined earlier is being reused.

Using the data standards results in both increased database design productivity as well as increased application development and maintenance productivity. This can be measured in terms of the percent of data objects reused in database design and in the percent of redundancy in database design. The process step is defined in step 4, *Assess Data Definition Technical Quality*.

It also results in increased cross-functional business area communication productivity. This can be measured in terms of increased business productivity across business areas.

Data Definition Quality

Before you can build a quality database, you must have a clear, precise, and robust definition of the data required for the business processes to perform correctly. Because data is of interest to multiple sets of knowledge workers across multiple business units, data must be defined consistently across the stake-holder business areas.

Data Name Quality

Data name quality is a characteristic of how well data and business term names clearly communicate the meaning of the objects represented.

Figure 5.2   What does this have in common with data standards?

Source: Amsco Music Sales Co., New York, 1984.

> ### MUSIC NOTATION AND DATA STANDARDS
>
> Let us take an example from music. Since the sixteenth and seventeenth centuries, the world has had a fairly stable and standard set of notation and terminology for representing music (see Figure 5.2). Out of more than 600 groups to which I have shown this figure, fewer than 10 groups (less than 2 percent) did not have someone who could identify Beethoven's *Für Elise* by name. Beethoven, who composed this in 1810, spoke German. How is it that any trained musician, regardless of native language, can "translate" the composition illustrated in Figure 5.2 into this most beautiful melody? Well-defined standards and universally adopted notation for musical composition.
>
> What would our musical heritage be like today if every composer adopted their own musical notation for their compositions? Suppose they could choose their own shapes and meanings of note representations, the clefs representing the relative pitches of notes, key signatures, and dynamic markings. The result would be chaos. Musicians would have to learn multiple notation standards to play different composers' music, decreasing their productivity. Much music would not be played as frequently, if at all, because people would not be willing to learn different notations. The value of the music would be diminished, and the world would be much poorer culturally.
>
> Now consider the communication and productivity in business and information systems if there were comparable universally adopted data standards.

Business Term Clarity

A *business term* is a word, phrase, or expression that has a particular meaning to the enterprise. It may or may not be an entity type or an attribute. It may be a particular way that an entity type may be used within the enterprise or within a specific business area. Business term names should be standardized when the concept requires consistent meaning *across* the enterprise or a group of business areas. Document all significant business terms in an enterprisewide glossary.

Entity Type Name Clarity

An *entity type* is a representation or classification of a set of entities or real-world objects that have common characteristics. Entity types represent the things the enterprise needs to know about. Name clarity means that the name of an entity type is intuitively understandable to the knowledge workers as to the classification of objects represented. Given a set of occurrences of an entity type, a knowledgeable business person would intuitively associate the set of occurrences with this name.

Characteristics of entity type name quality include:

❑ The name is a classification of things that have common characteristics. In other words, all occurrences have or can have values for all attributes describing the entity type.

❏ The name consists of business terms that are defined.

❏ The name is a noun or noun phrase. Examples include `Customer` and `Retail Customer`.

❏ The name is a *singular* noun or noun phrase that represents a *classification* of things, not the collection of things. For example, `Customer` is preferred over `Customers`.

❏ The name is understandable and intuitive to the knowledge workers.

Attribute Name Clarity

An *attribute* is a type of fact that describes an entity or object. The fact has the same format, interpretation, and domain value set for all occurrences of the entity type it describes. Attribute name clarity means the name is intuitively understandable to the knowledge workers as to what kind of fact is represented. Given a value for this attribute for a specific occurrence of an entity type, a knowledgeable business person would intuitively associate the fact for this occurrence with the attribute name.

Characteristics of attribute name quality include:

❏ The name is a type of fact that may contain a single value.

❏ The name consists of business terms or entity type names that are defined.

❏ The name is easily associated with the entity type it describes.

❏ The name is understandable and intuitive to the knowledge workers.

Domain Type Consistency

Also called *class word* consistency, the domain type or class word in an attribute name represents the kind of values the knowledge worker expects to see for the attribute. Domain type consistency means that the domain, or set of valid values for an attribute, is from the category of values of its specified domain type. For example, the attribute `person-birth-date` has a domain type of "date." The domain or set of valid values for `person-birth-date` is a subset of all possible dates. One expects to see valid birth dates as values of the attribute. If the valid values for `person-birth-date` were the days of the week ("Monday," "Tuesday," etc.) the domain type is actually "day of week" and the attribute name `person-birth-date` lacks domain type consistency. The attribute name should be `person-birth-day`.

Domain types or class words should be clearly defined for those who name and define data. `Date` [domain type]: "An attribute type whose set of values represent valid Gregorian calendar days, including day, month, year, and century."

Typical domain types include `Date`, `Time`, `[Currency] Amount`, `Code`, `Name`, `Quantity`, `Description`, for example.

Business Term Abbreviation and Acronym Clarity

Every business term that is longer than a few letters should have a single, enterprise-standard abbreviation. This abbreviation should be used in all data names where abbreviations are required. Because of legacy applications and software packages, a business term may have been abbreviated differently. These alternate and nonstandard abbreviations should be documented as unofficial, alias abbreviations for the term, and are documented only so knowledge workers using data from those sources are aware of their existence.

The following are guidelines for effective abbreviations and acronyms:

- Use abbreviations that are as short as possible without loss of meaning in other words, `Quantity` = "`Qty`" as opposed to "`Quant.`"

- Use universally accepted abbreviations as the best choice rather than industry-specific or creative abbreviations. Universal abbreviations usually communicate better to a wider, more general audience. Technical, industry-specific abbreviations and acronyms may be generally known by experts in the industry, but may be less clear to cross-functional business areas.

- Use industry-standard abbreviations when there is not a universal abbreviation available.

- Use enterprise-standard abbreviations when there is not an industry-standard abbreviation.

- Always use the first letter of the term as the first letter of the abbreviation. Avoid such shortcuts as "`Xref`" for "cross reference." "`Cross-ref`" is preferred.

Your guidelines for creating new abbreviations should provide consistency in abbreviations. You may adopt a first-letter approach ("`Cust`" for `Customer`) or a consonant approach ("`Cstmr`"). Either way is fine, as long as it is consistently applied and the abbreviation is intuitive among the knowledge workers. They should also assure understanding in context. For example, "`Rev`" might be the abbreviation for both "`Revenue`" and "`Revision`." The attributes `Prod-Spec-Rev-Num` (`Product specification` *revision* `number`) and `Prod-Rev-Amt` (`Product` *revenue* `amount`) should be clearly distinguishable.

Acronyms usually are not used in data names unless they are more accepted than the phrase itself, generally recognized as standard, and generally understood by the stakeholder knowledge workers, or unless the attribute name would be excessively long without it, and the stakeholder knowledge workers can adapt to the acronym easily. For example, VIN for "vehicle identification number."

Data Name or Label Consistency

Attribute names for a single fact type should be consistent across the different formats of presentation and storage formats. The business name for a fact, the database name of the fact in a database file, the field name of the fact on a display screen, and the column name for the fact in a printed report, should be consistent.

The names do not have to be equivalent, but the names should be consistent so that a knowledge worker familiar with the subject matter will know that facts in different context are the same. For example, the attribute `Customer-Identifier` might have the following name formats as listed in Table 5.1.

There will, of course, be a requirement for deviating from the standard data names, due to limitations of space on a screen or disparity in the length of a field and the column header name. These should be the exception and should be documented when they occur.

Data Definition Quality

Because data is the language of the business, it must be defined precisely and clearly. This includes defining the meaning of business terms, entity types, and attributes.

Lexicography, or the process of writing a dictionary, uses a formal format for definition. The format is:

Term = general class + differentia.

"[A(n) _____ (term, entity type, or attribute being defined) is] a(n) _____ (general class from which it belongs) that _____ (what differentiates this term, type, or attribute from all others)."

Example: Lexicon. [A lexicon [term being defined] is] "a book [the general class] containing an alphabetical arrangement of the words in a language and their definitions [what differentiates a lexicon from other books]" (*Webster's Dictionary*). Note that the phrase "A lexicon is" is implicit in the definition and does not have to be explicitly written in the definition.

Defining information should follow this format. Definition quality is characterized by:

❏ Accuracy of definition to express the meaning of the real-world object, fact, or term being defined

Table 5.1   Data Name Consistency

CONTEXT	DATA NAME
Business term	Customer Identifier
Repository or data dictionary name	Cust-Id
Database and program name	Cust-Id
Short name (for files that do not allow long names)	Custid
Screen layout name or label	Cust Id
Report name	Customer Identifier

❑ Precision of the definition to differentiate the defined term from all others

❑ Clarity of definition to communicate to the intended audience, as measured through customer satisfaction surveys among information stakeholders

Business Term Definition Quality

Business terms should be precisely defined in an *enterprisewide* glossary. Most organizations have glossaries of business terms germane to their line of work. For example, the Accounting Department will have glossaries of financial terminology, while Marketing will have its own glossary. Because business terms, like regular words, have homonyms and synonyms, an enterprise glossary that identifies the definition and the context for that definition can increase cross-functional communication. Figure 5.3 represents a business term defined and used differently in different contexts.

Business terms must be precisely defined, because these terms may be used in the definition of entity types and attributes. Without robust definition of the words used to define data, the data definition will be compromised.

There should be a business glossary steward in the enterprise who is responsible for keeping it current, along with a process for adding business terms and for changing their definition as needed. Each business term definition should be associated with a business information steward or subject matter expert who is responsible for assuring the contextual definition of the term is complete, accurate, and clear.

Term	Definition Number	Definition	Context	Business Steward	Rev. Date
Volume	1	The amount of space, expressed in cubic or volume units, that a substance or material occupies	Material Handling	J. B. Bloggs	10/04/1983
Volume	2	A specific book of the 5-volume multi-book or multiple document series	Information Center	B. R. Schmidt	06/10/1997
Volume	3	An estimated length of copper wire as calculated from the weight of the spool of wire	Wire Production	A. J. Jones	02/03/1999

Figure 5.3 Business glossary example.

Entity Type Definition Quality

An entity type represents a classification of real-world objects or events, not simply a file of data. As such, the definition defines the real-world object or event the entity type represents.

Characteristics of quality entity type definition include:

❏ A classification of persons, organizations, places, things, concepts, events, or relationships that is of interest to the enterprise.

❏ The definition of all business terms and other entity names used in the definition.

❏ The definition of a nonredundant, unique type or subtype of things the enterprise should know about to accomplish its objectives and fulfill its mission.

❏ An example or occurrence can be illustrated, visualized, and described. Entity type definition should include listing one or more example occurrences.

❏ Each occurrence can be uniquely identified with one or more (identifying) attributes known to and controlled by the enterprise.

❏ It defines a type of thing that can be described with specific types of facts or attributes.

❏ All occurrences or potential occurrences are examples of the classification described by the entity type's name and definition.

❏ The definition is understandable and acceptable to the knowledge workers.

Examples of definition of `Customer`:

■ Poor: "[A customer is] a person who has a record in the customer table."

■ Poor: "Information about a customer."

■ Better: "[A customer is] a person who has purchased, or expressed active interest in purchasing ACME's products and/or services. This includes prospects, current customers, and previous but now inactive customers. Examples: Jane J. Jones and Joe Bloggs."

Attribute Definition Quality

Attributes are the types of facts that should be known by the enterprise. Attributes do not exist in a vacuum. They are facts that describe something; that something is an entity type.

A quality attribute definition includes:

❏ The description of a *specific kind of fact* that can be used to add value to the enterprise.

❏ The description of *only one* type of fact.

❏ The attribute is an *inherent* characteristic of the entity type it describes.

❏ The business terms, entity names, or other attribute names used in the definition have already been defined.

❏ The description of *one and only* one entity type or subtype of things.

❏ The illustration of example values. Attribute definition should include listing one or more example values. Ultimately, all domain values should be documented for attributes with a finite value set such as codes, or the business rules identifying the integrity requirements for infinite value sets such as ranges of values.

Examples of definition of `Item-Reorder-Point-Qty`:

■ Poor: "Tells when to reorder an item."

■ Poor: "An indicator of when to reorder an item."

■ Better: "The quantity value for an `Inventory-Item` that automatically triggers a reorder of an `Item` from the `Supplier` when the `Item-Inventory-On-Hand-Quantity` falls below this value."

Data Name and Definition Consistency

This characteristic measures how well the name connotes its definition, and how well the definition describes what is communicated by the name. In other words, how well the name and its definition are understood by representative knowledge workers to refer to the same concept, classification of things, or type of fact.

Examples of name and definition consistency for `Product-Effective-Date`:

■ Poor: `Product-Effective-Date` (name) is "the date a new product was conceived."

■ Better: `Product-Effective-Date` (name) is "the date a product is first available for customers to purchase." The attribute defined in the first bullet is better named `Product-Concept-Date`.

Domain Value Correctness

The domain is a set of valid values for an attribute. The nature of the definition depends on the type of data (domain type) being represented. Some domains, such as the domain for `Product-Description`, will simply be textual description and will come from the domain type of all text data. Other domains will be specific ranges of values, such as the domain for `Product-Price`, that will have a logical lowest-price value and a logical highest-price value. These kinds of domains will be defined by business rules that identify the reasonability tests for upper and lower values.

Other domains, such as Product-Line (a list of names), Standard-Industry-Code, or Customer-Classification-Code, will have a finite set of values. The values for these codes or lists must have a definition as to the meaning. The purpose of having code definitions is twofold: first, to assure communication among those reading and using the code values; and second, to verify that the codes or lists represent a single type of fact.

Domain chaos is an information quality problem caused when one attribute or field is used to store more than one kind of fact. The example in Table 5.2 illustrates the problem of a single attribute representing two types of facts.

This is the actual submitted domain for the attribute Product-Status-Code in a publishing firm. It was defined as "the production status of a product"; in other words, printed literature. This domain, however, represents two types of facts. The code values IN and OS are not production states, they are inventory states. The problems of domain chaos are twofold:

Complex logic is required to use this field. To have an accurate picture of all products that have stock in inventory, one has to look for products where the Product-Status-Code was either IN or GOP. The code GOP, or Going Out of Print, implies there is inventory on hand; else the status would be OP (Out of Print). The answer to a query looking for only products that had a status of IN (In Stock) would yield an incorrect answer.

If the occurrence can have values of both fact types, the field will not be able to hold values for both facts, causing some information to be missing. For example, a product can be IN and GOP at the same time.

Another problem in this example is that the codes are not defined, only the business term is named along with the abbreviated value. What is the difference between "Forth Coming" and "Not Yet Published"? Code values must be defined so information producers know how to create correct values and knowledge workers know how to interpret them. A better domain specification is found in Table 5.3.

Table 5.2   Domain Chaos in the Attribute Product-Status-Code

CODE VALUE	CODE DEFINITION
IN	In stock
OS	Out of Stock
OP	Out of Print
GOP	Going Out of Print
FC	Forth Coming
NYP	Not Yet Published

Table 5.3 Domain Singularity in the Attribute Product-Production-Status-Code

CODE VALUE	BUSINESS TERM	CODE DEFINITION
IP	In Print	The product is currently available.
OP	Out of Print	The product has been discontinued with no stock available.
GOP	Going Out of Print	The product is being discontinued when no stock is available.
FC	Forth Coming	The complete manuscript has not yet been submitted.
NYP	Not Yet Published	The complete manuscript is being edited but not yet available.

Note that the attribute name more accurately reflects the meaning of the attribute as to its development and production state.

Business Rule Quality

Business rules are policies governing business actions. They involve actions, objects of those actions and the policies, constraints, or qualifiers of the actions. Policies may be internally set or they may be externally imposed policies such as regulatory rules governing financial institutions or codes governing building construction. Business rules generally result in constraints or integrity parameters on data relationships or values.

Because business rules tend to be volatile or subject to frequent change, there must be a single source where business rules are documented and distribution is controlled. This is important for quality control, so that data management, application development, and all business areas have access to the authoritative definitions of business rules. This prevents different business areas or different application development teams from creating inconsistent business rules governing the same activity.

Business rule quality includes the following:

❏ It defines or governs an aspect of business action. In other words, it can be understood and applied on specific actions. For example, "treat customers right" is not a business rule; it is too broad and vague. "Treat customers right" is a value statement that may translate to several business rules. "Provide a prompt refund if a customer returns merchandise for any reason within 30 days of purchase" is a business rule. It is specific, atomic, and understandable.

❑ It is expressed in business terms, not technical terms. "If customer code is 'preferred,' call the 'pref-cust' stored procedure" is not an acceptable business rule.

❑ All business terms, entity names, or attribute names used in the definition have been previously defined.

❑ It defines the "what" and "when" of the rule. It describes what the policy is, and when (the conditions under which) it is applied. It does not describe the "how." The physical implementation may vary and change from human assurance to electronic assurance.

❑ It is complete and specific.

❑ It supports likely future direction, not simply today's policies.

❑ The rule's requirement is not due to a technical or existing system limitation. One insurance company had a "business rule" of not insuring more than five vehicles on a single auto insurance policy because the policy file was designed with only five fields to hold automobile vehicle identification numbers!

❑ It identifies any exceptions, along with the guidelines for handling the exceptions. For example, there may be business rules governing credit limits for customers under normal conditions. Special conditions may call for "overriding" that business rule. The rule may allow for an exception with supervisor approval. Data must be designed so that these exceptions can be captured along with some means of indicating the approval or condition that allowed the exception. Otherwise, electronically implemented business rules will reject the correctly overridden data. Also, data assessments may show the data to be invalid because of nonconformance to the business rules, when in fact it is a correct value.

❑ It is associated with a business information steward who is responsible for maintaining the currency of the business rule.

Information and Data Architecture

Information architecture quality consists of how well information and data models depict the information requirements of the enterprise, and how well the databases implement those requirements and enable capture, maintenance, and dissemination of the data among the knowledge workers.

There are three information architecture measures that matter: stability, flexibility, and reliability.

Before we can describe the quality characteristics of information architecture, we must define what is meant by information architecture. Information architecture must have different levels of abstraction that support different purposes, including planning for data development (conceptual business modeling), designing databases (physical database design), and creating and using information products (business operations). There is no such thing as a single enterprise data model diagram that represents the entire set of information requirements for the organization. There is, however, a single conceptual aggregation of enterprise information requirements. Rather, there will be high-level, detailed levels, information view models, and physical database designs of the enterprise information requirements.

Probably more than anyone, John Zachman has called attention to the fundamental requirement to have an enterprise architecture with different abstractions or representations of a working enterprise. The information resource requires an architecture in the same way there are different representations required to build a complex building or manufacture a complex product.[1, 2]

The framework is evolving beyond a framework for "information *systems*" architecture to a framework for "Enterprise Architecture."[3]

This significant transition correctly communicates that the framework is a business model framework for managing the enterprise and not simply a tool for Information Systems personnel for developing applications.

Figure 5.4 represents the Zachman framework views and dimension categories. The rows represent different abstractions or views of the modeled product. The different views have different purposes in moving from idea to implemented result. The rows are important to assure the requirements or purposes of complex products are communicated to all involved from concept to implementation.

The dimensions identify the different categories of model. The dimensions are based on the six interrogatives: What, How, Where, Who, When, and Why. They provide the basis for a holistic set of models of the business.

Figures 5.5 and 5.6 represents four rows (2, 3, 4, 6) of the framework with the various representations or models in each cell.

The model in each cell contains objects that are related to other objects horizontally across the various dimensions. For example, a process modeled in the Process (How) dimension will create, update, retrieve, or delete data represented in the Data (What) dimension. The models also must be integrated vertically across the different rows or views. For example, a business entity type modeled in the Enterprise Business Model (row 2) will directly relate to one or more data entities in the Conceptual Business Model (row 3). A data entity in row 3 will directly relate to one or more files or tables represented in the Technical Model (row 4).

---

[1]J. A. Zachman, "A Framework for Information Systems Architecture," *IBM Systems Journal*, Vol. 26, No. 3, 1987, pp. 276–292.

[2]J. F. Sowa and J. A. Zachman, "Extending and Formalizing the Framework for Information Systems Architecture," *IBM Systems Journal*, Vol. 31, No. 3, 1992, pp. 590–616.

[3]J. A. Zachman, "Enterprise Architecture: The Issue of the Century," *Database Programming and Design*, March 1997, pp. 44–53.

Dimension / View	What (Data)	How (Process)	Where (Location)	Who (Person)	When (Time)	Why (Motivation)
Objectives / Scope (Contextual) *Planner View*						
Enterprise Model (Business) *Owner View*						
Business Model (Conceptual) *Designer View*						
Technical Model (Physical) *Builder View*						
Detailed Representations *Out of context View*						
Working Enterprise (Real) *Visible Result*						

Figure 5.4   Enterprise architecture framework.

Source: John Zachman.

While the columns or dimensions of architecture have no implied order, the Motivation Dimension that represents "why" the enterprise exists, and contains

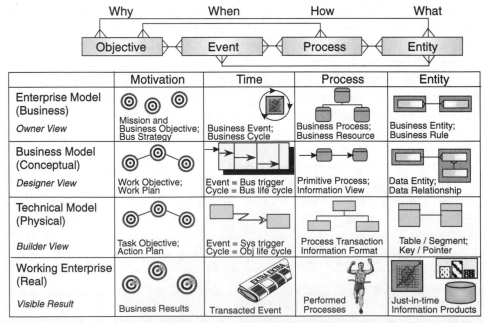

Figure 5.5   Enterprise architecture framework *(continued)*.

Source: Adapted from John Zachman's Enterprise Architecture Framework.

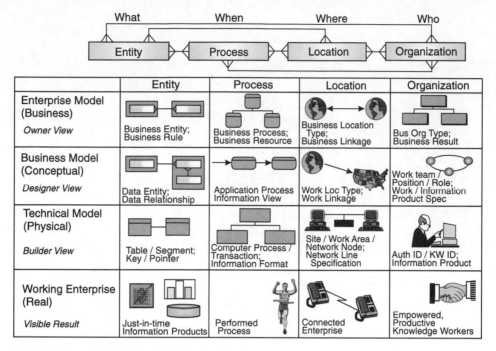

Figure 5.6 Enterprise architecture framework (continued).

a model of the business mission, objective, and accomplished results, must be the logical beginning point for any quality architecture. This is, and must be, the basis for modeling the other aspects of the enterprise. Failure to begin with the enterprise mission and objectives will cause most business process and data models to be deficient (omitting critical components) or excessive (including components that do not add value).

One caveat about the Motivation Dimension should be noted here. Some interpret rows 3 through 6 of this dimension to represent business rules. I interpret this dimension to represent the raison d'être, or purpose, of the enterprise (rows 1 and 2) down the accomplished results (row 6). Row 6 of motivation, I believe, represents the attainment of the business goals and objectives, as Zachman suggests in his original discussion.[4] Did we accomplish our goals? Did we fulfill our purpose?

Where do business rules fit in the framework? As policies governing business actions and the objects of those actions, business rules are actually objects that constrain the relationship of objects in the Process dimension to objects in the Data dimension (see Figure 5.7).

[4] J. A. Zachman, "A Framework for Information Systems Architecture," *IBM Systems Journal*, Vol. 26, No. 3, 1987, p. 292.

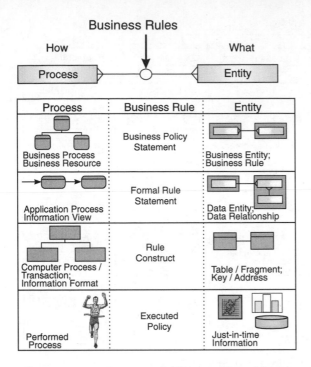

Figure 5.7   Business model framework and business rules.

Source: Adapted from John Zachman's Enterprise Architecture Framework.

Information Architecture Quality Measures

Quality of information architecture requires data name and definition quality described earlier. Without accurate and complete definition of entity types and attributes, you cannot build an accurate model of the enterprise information requirements.

Data Relationship Correctness

Creating quality information models is dependent upon correctly identifying the relationships in the data. To do this, one must correctly identify the relationships among the real-world objects the data represents. There are four sets of relationships important in data models:

Entity-type-to-entity-type relationship quality

Attribute-to-entity-type relationship quality

Entity-type-to-entity-subtype relationship quality

Entity life-cycle quality

Entity-Type-to-Entity-Type Relationship Quality

The objective here is to assure the correctness of *relationships* of the things and events in the real world that the enterprise must know about. Many organizations suffer "information myopia," a disease that occurs when knowledge workers can see *only part* of the information they need. The first cause of information myopia is not defining the correct relationships among data. For example, if Address is defined as a one-to-one relationship with Customer, but in fact a Customer may have more than one Address, the database will not be designed correctly. The organization will not be able to capture the second Address. The second cause is not having access to data that is logically related, but is inaccessible to a knowledge worker. This occurs if Shipping Address exists in the distribution database and Billing Address exists in the Accounts Receivable database, each of which is not integrated or accessible by the other applications.

Entity-type-to-entity-type relationship quality characteristics include:

❏ Both entity types represent real-world objects or events that the enterprise must know about.

❏ Both entity types are defined clearly.

❏ The relationship(s) between them is (are) defined clearly.

❏ The relationships expressed in the model are the same that exist between the real-world objects represented.

Attribute-to-Entity-Type Relationship Quality

Attributes describe occurrences of entity types. Because attributes are inherent characteristics of a classification of things, the quality measure is simple. Do the attributes associated with entity types represent the same relationship as the relationship of the characteristics of the real-world objects and events? For example, person-name is an inherent characteristic of the entity type Person. A Person may play the role of Customer who places an Order. If the attributes order-identifier, person-name, and order-date are modeled as attributes of the entity type Order, then the attribute person-name is modeled incorrectly. Person-name is not inherent to the Order itself, but to the Person placing the Order.

Attribute-to-entity-type relationship-quality characteristics include:

❏ The attribute is an inherent characteristic of this type.

❏ All occurrences of this type (or subtype) may contain a value for this attribute.

❏ An occurrence of this type never needs more than one value for this attribute for any process requiring this fact.

❑ If processes need to know historical values of attributes that may change over time, such as name or address or product-price, these attributes are documented or modeled to illustrate the time requirement.

❑ The attribute does not contain more than one kind of fact to describe this entity.

❑ The attribute describes only one entity type or subtype. (Inheritance of attributes by subtypes is described in the next section.)

❑ An attribute that is derivable or calculable from other known facts is documented as derived. The formula or calculation of the attribute is in the derived attribute definition. All base data used to calculate the derived data is defined in the model.

Entity-Type-to-Entity-Subtype Relationship Quality

A major breakthrough in information modeling has occurred with the understanding of types and subtypes. The real world has general classifications of things that have some attributes in common. For example, all Buildings have such attributes in common as Total-Area, Height, Construction-Cost, and so forth. But the general type Buildings may have different subsets or subtypes of attributes common to the subtypes, but different from the other subtypes. A House, Apartment, Office Building, or Manufacturing Building is a specialized kind of Building, and each has all the attributes that are characteristic of Buildings in general. This is called *inheritance*. An occurrence of an entity subtype *inherits* all attributes of its *supertype*. Houses will have attributes in common with each other, such as relationship to School District or Resident, that are not characteristic with Office Buildings or Manufacturing Buildings. The entity type Building is a more general type, sometimes called a supertype, while the entity type House and the others are more specialized types (subtypes) of Building.

Figure 5.8 illustrates an entity type hierarchy of Party that models both persons and organization as one type hierarchy and roles a Party may play. The "type" of Party is a structural classification. The "role" of Party is a functional classification.

Modeling types and subtypes allows one to differentiate between similar groups of things and model them more robustly. The concept of inheritance enables models to more accurately capture the information requirements simply and nonredundantly. Inheritance is the capacity of an entity subtype to inherit or acquire the attributes of a more general entity type of which it is a specialized subset.

Take for example the types Person, Customer, and Employee. Customer and Employee are specialized subtypes of Party based on the role each plays. They inherit the common attributes of birth-date and person-name that are inherent characteristics of Person. By defining birth-date and per-

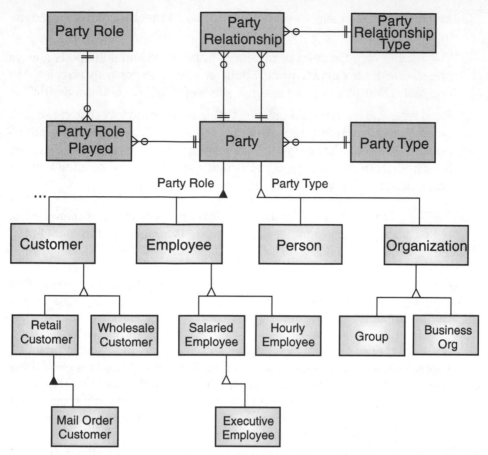

Figure 5.8 Entity type hierarchy of `Party` illustrating both type and role subtypes.

son-name as attributes of `Person`, one does not need to define them over and over for `Customer` and `Employee`, or for other roles played by `Persons`. These attributes are permanent characteristics of `Person` and do not change based on role. `Hire-date`, however, is an attribute inherent to `Employee`, but not all `Persons` in general. `First-sale-date` is an attribute inherent to `Customer`, but not to `Employees` or other `Persons` in general. They would be defined as attributes of their respective entity subtypes.

Entity-type-to-entity-subtype relationship quality characteristics include:

❏ Each type and subtype is a meaningful object classification to the enterprise. At the topmost level, the generalized type may not be *perceived* by the business as a *business* classification of things. However, experience shows that business people involved in modeling of information can easily see the value and have no trouble modeling information by subtypes, or in reading subtype model hierarchies.

❑ An occurrence or member of a subtype is also a member of any supertype in its hierarchy.

❑ The relationship between occurrences of the type and subtype is always one-to-one. For example, a John Smith as a `Person` can only be related to one "John Smith" as a `Customer` or the one `Employee` "John Smith."

❑ Each type and subtype has unique attributes or behaviors that cause it to be unique and therefore represented in the model. There are some exceptions to this in that the only attributes some subtypes may have are those inherited from the more general supertype. They may be modeled for communication purposes and balance.

❑ Each subtype is in fact a more specialized classification of members of the entity type. For example, an `Employee` is a more specialized kind of `Party` who must also be a `Person`.

❑ All attributes are inherent characteristics of the type or subtype with which they are first associated. `Birth-date` is inherent to `Person`, not to the role of a `Party` as an `Employee`.

❑ An occurrence of a subtype inherits all attributes of all its ancestor supertypes. This is a very important rule. The hierarchy is not precise if there are exceptions to inheritance. It should be noted, however, that for a given process not all attributes of a supertype are necessarily required for subtype occurrences. For example, `Birth-date` is an inherent characteristic of `Person`. It is a fact required for `Customer` and `Employee` subtypes, but does not need to be known about a `Supplier Contact`.

Entity Life-Cycle Quality

Entity life cycles are another extension to classical data modeling that significantly increase precision and robustness in information architectures and business rule specification. Entity life cycles are like state transition diagrams and are used to capture the different (important) states that an occurrence of an entity type may exist in over the life that the enterprise needs to know about it. Things in the real world have states of existence in which certain attributes become known, and during which certain business rules apply that may not apply to that same occurrence in another state.

Examples of entity life-cycle states include:

```
Employee: Applicant -> Candidate -> Employee (Active or On-Leave) ->
Retiree or Former Employee.
```

Figure 5.9 illustrates an example of an entity life cycle for `Order`. It shows the business events triggering a change in state, the resulting state, and the attributes that become known within that state.

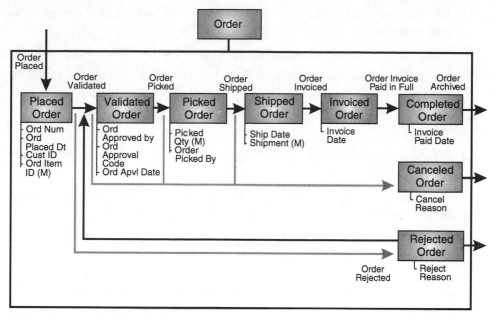

Figure 5.9   Entity life cycle for Order.

The boxes represent distinct states of existence for an Order. The names in the boxes represent the order state. The lines with arrows represent state transitions. An occurrence of an Order may change states from a "placed" Order to a "validated" Order , but may not change states from a "placed" Order to a "shipped" Order . The names on the lines represent events that cause the state change.

Entity life cycles are also called entity life histories. Object technology and real-time applications call these state transition diagrams.

From an information quality standpoint, entity life cycles provide for a more robust mechanism for defining business rules that govern the integrity of data. For example, in the Order life cycle, it becomes clear that the business rule for canceling an order is if the Order is in the state of "placed," "validated," or "picked." Once the Order is shipped, however, the Order may not be "canceled," because it is out the door. It may be "returned," but not "canceled."

Entity life-cycle quality characteristics include:

❏ The life cycle identifies the creation, or existence event, and the deletion, or archiving event.

❏ All events that may affect or cause significant change to an occurrence of this type are identified. Significant change means that new attributes are known and some different business rules apply. For example, change of name or address is not a significant state change event unless new rules apply, such as in insurance policy coverage.

❏ The life cycle is defined in a way that a specific occurrence can exist in only one state at a point in time, as in the real world.

❏ Every state change is triggered by an identifiable business event.

❏ Every state change is associated with a process invoked by the business event.

❏ Each state lists all attributes whose values are created or may be modified upon change to that state.

❏ Business rules governing the behavior of an occurrence in a given state are identified.

❏ The attributes required to have valid values in a state will be assured before the state transition event has been completed.

Business Information Model Clarity

The business information model is the high-level view of the enterprise's information requirements. Its purpose is twofold: to *facilitate communication and understanding* of the fundamental information requirements of the enterprise, and to *control the development* of detailed data models and databases.

The business information model is the Zachman Row 2 model, or the Enterprise Business View. As a communication mechanism, this level or abstraction must be understandable to the executive office or executive management as well as to knowledge workers in general and all information systems personnel.

The model is used by senior management responsible for planning and managing the information and information technology resources. This is a planning and control tool for the design and control of the information resource. Its use is similar to:

- Financial management's use of the chart of account and budget (financial resource models) for financial planning and control

- Business management's use of organization charts (human resource models) for planning and managing the people resources

- Facilities management's use of building layout diagrams (facilities models) for building management

The business information model will be used to control the planning and development of detailed data models and applications.

Business information model quality characteristics include:

❏ The model is expressed in business terms.

❏ All data names and definitions conform to the name and definition quality characteristics described earlier.

❑ The model is modeled by business resource or subject area, not department or functional business area. Business resources include both internal and external resources:

- People
- Financial resources
- Materials and supply
- Product or services resources
- Facilities and physical assets
- Information resources
- "Parties" or customers, suppliers, and other external stakeholders
- Accounts or customer to product or service relationships; such as, `Insurance Policy`, `Financial Account`, `Order` and `Sale`
- External factors, such as regulation, economic condition, news

❑ The business resource or subject areas are *nonoverlapping* business classifications of information. Entity types should be able to be classified in only one business resource or subject area. If an entity type is listed in more than one business resource area, the areas may be functional classifications; in other words, data required by a function or business area. The problems caused by a functional classification of "subjects" include:

- Entity types may be defined functionally, such as `Supplier` and `Vendor`, `Customer` versus `Account` (Payable).
- The same entity type may be inconsistently defined across different functional views.
- Loss of, or overlapping, business information stewardship roles; e.g., one steward for `Supplier` and one steward for `Vendor`.

❑ The model identifies and defines the most fundamental entity types, sometimes referred to as *business* entity types.

❑ The fundamental entity types are documented with sample attributes (not an exhaustive list) and occurrences and may include highly derived attributes as key business indicators, such as `customer-lifetime-value`, `employee-attrition-rate` or `daily-product-sales-amount`.

❑ The sample attributes should include key business indicators that are associated with the most fundamental entity types to document strategic information requirements. For example, `market-share-percent` and total `daily-product-sales-amount` are derived attributes that describe `Product`.

❑ The model is understandable by executive management.

Operational Data Model Quality

This level model is a detailed conceptual model of enterprise information requirements, independent of any technology considerations.[5]

This level model represents the Zachman row 3, the conceptual business model or designer's view.

Operational data model quality characteristics include:

❑ The model is modeled by business resource or subject area as expressed in the Business Information Model, not a department or functional business area nor an application area.

❑ Various application models or business area models can be derived without change from the enterprise detailed conceptual model.

❑ The model contains all base data required to calculate derived data that needs to be documented in the model.

❑ All data names and definitions conform to the name and definition quality characteristics described earlier.

❑ All data relationships conform to the data relationship quality characteristics described earlier.

❑ The model is *clear*. The stakeholders, knowledge workers, and information producers *understand* the pertinent portions of the model or views of the model with a brief introduction to the data modeling concepts and conventions.

❑ The model is *stable*. Model stability means that new applications may be developed and the model undergoes minimal structural change. New entity types may be discovered and new attributes may be defined, but they are simply added to the model without changing the structure of the existing entity types. If adding new applications causes attributes to have to be removed from one existing entity type to another new or existing entity type, then it was incorrectly modeled in the first place.

❑ The model is *flexible*. Model flexibility means the business may change how it performs its business processes, but those changes cause minimal change to the data model structure. If business process reengineering or process improvement changes cause more than minor change to the data model, then it was incorrectly modeled in the first place.

❑ The model is *reusable*. Applications that need the information contained here can and do derive their views from this model.

---

[5] Some differentiate between conceptual and logical model. When they do, they tend to use the term *conceptual data model* to be completely independent from the technology, and the term *logical data model* to reflect a model that includes primary and foreign key attributes, but without any compromises for physical design.

Physical Database Design to Support Operational Processes

Physical database design is the process of developing the structure of physical database files that will house the enterprise's electronic knowledge resources.

Physical database design accurately implements the data as defined in the conceptual model with minimum compromises. Design tradeoffs that compromise the structure in the conceptual data model have data integrity plans accompanying them that provide controls to minimize data integrity violations.

INFORMATION CHAOS

Information chaos is a state of the dysfunctional learning organization. Having unmanaged, inconsistent, and redundant databases that contain data about a single type of things or facts causes information chaos. The information chaos quotient is the count of the number of redundant databases that are not controlled by replication and that may have inconsistently defined domains containing data about a single type of things or facts.

Physical database design quality has the following characteristics:

❑ A conceptual data model was developed *prior to* and *independent* of physical database design.

❑ The data model was developed with knowledge workers from *outside* the sponsoring project team who have an interest in the data, not just project team members.

❑ If there were compromises in the physical design from the conceptual data model, a data integrity plan was developed to manage potential integrity problems.

❑ Other applications are using the database.

❑ The database design is stable. That means new applications can access the database by only adding attributes, entity types, and relationships.

❑ The database design is flexible. That means new attributes can be added with minimal modification of database structure.

❑ The database is reusable. Other applications are using the database without changing the structure (only adding tables and columns).

❑ The database design is atomic. That means one field (other than true descriptive text fields and single complex objects) contains only one distinct type of fact.

Distributed Database Architecture and Design Quality

Because data will not always be maintained in and accessed from one single physical database by all knowledge workers, it will need to be distributed. The processes that distribute data must be controlled to assure successful distribution and required transformation of data, if any.

Data that is implemented redundantly in separate or distributed databases have consistent definition and domain value sets. Replication or controlled distribution processes that assure consistency of data values in the redundant data stores are used for all data distribution.

Physical database design quality has the following characteristics:

❏ A business case was established for creating a distributed or redundantly implemented database. All avenues for data sharing from the authoritative record-of-reference database were explored.

❏ The database design is minimally redundant with other existing databases.

❏ Data is being distributed from the authoritative record-of-reference database.

❏ There are minimal transformations of data while distributing it from the record-of-reference database to the target. Only cases in which data is distributed to legacy systems where reengineering is unfeasible or to software packages that have been evaluated on the basis of data model requirements (not just functional requirements) are legitimate transformations.

❏ All transformation processes have audit processes defined that assure the transformations are happening properly.

❏ There are processes to maintain consistency of redundant or replicated data where redundancy exists.

Data Warehouse Design Quality

Data warehouse design differs from operational database design. While operational databases must support operational processes and some ad hoc queries, data warehouses and data marts must support strategic and tactical processes, as well as key decisions and trend analysis. Table 5.4 highlights some of the key differences.

Table 5.4 Operational and Data Warehouse Data Model Differences

OPERATIONAL DATA MODEL	DATA WAREHOUSE DATA MODEL
Data supports operational processes and base data for ad hoc queries and decision support	Data supports historical query, decision (DSS) and strategic (EIS) processes, and trend analysis

Table 5.4   *(Continued)*

OPERATIONAL DATA MODEL	DATA WAREHOUSE DATA MODEL
Subject or application oriented	Subject oriented
May have disparately defined data and domains due to legacy databases and application software packages	Has singular, enterprise consensus data definition and common domain value sets
Fully normalized for effective integrity management	Controlled denormalization for efficient retrieval
Current data values	Historical data values
Minimal derived data	Base and summarized data
Contains all operational data currently required	Contains data that has value over time
Contains mostly data generated within the enterprise	Contains internally generated data along with externally generated data that adds value and enables trend analysis; e.g., profile, demographic, economic indicators
Validated with information views of operational processes and operational queries and reports, plus key business indicators and key decisions	Validated with information views of historical queries, trend analyses, key business indicators, and key decisions

Data warehouse model quality characteristics are:

❏ The model is developed from an enterprise perspective with enterprise consensus models and data definitions, not merely a departmental or business area perspective. The data warehouse may be the last opportunity to develop a true enterprisewide information model. Not developing an enterprise data warehouse model will exacerbate the disparate information chaos, fail to accomplish the most important strategic benefits of the data warehouse, and increase the likelihood of having to redevelop or abandon the data warehouse.

❏ The model is created by business resource or subject area, not department or functional area.

❏ The model includes base data as well as derived data required for strategic and tactical business processes. Base data from which aggregate and derived data is calculated must be maintained for at least a period of time to audit the transformation processes to assure they are successfully accomplished. The base data may be maintained in the data warehouse itself, in an operational data store (ODS), or in a controlled staging area or operational database.

❑ The model includes data that supports not only known queries, but also data mining analysis to answer questions the enterprise did not know it should ask. Many valuable patterns discovered by data mining will be "Eureka" patterns that are not even looked for.

❑ The model includes important data that has been "discovered" in legacy data files, but has not been formally documented. See the discussion of business rule discovery in Chapter 8, "Information *Product* Improvement."

❑ The model includes the time dimension for historical data. The time dimensions for time-variant data will include the lowest-level granularity required among the knowledge workers; for example, daily sales versus monthly sales. You can always derive a higher-level granularity from lower-level granularity, but you cannot recover a lower-level granularity if only the higher-level granularity is stored.

❑ The base entity types and attributes in the data warehouse model are mapped to their counterparts in the enterprise detailed conceptual model for operational data. Changes to one will require changes to the other. There is a procedure defined to maintain consistency of the operational data model and strategic (data warehouse) data model.

❑ Business rule transformations are mapped from the operational data sources and the warehouse database files. See the discussion of data transformation mapping in Chapter 8, "Information *Product* Improvement," step 7, *Transform and Enhance Data into Target*.

❑ If there is no enterprise information architecture, the base data model for the data warehouse becomes the de facto enterprise data model and is actively used to control physical database design for operational systems and to reengineer legacy databases when they come up for redeployment. This maximizes the value of the model. It simplifies the extract and propagation processes for the data warehouse by eliminating the need for transforming the base data. It increases the quality of the data source and data warehouse data because it has defined the data integrity rules and eliminates the data transformation process.

Assess Data Definition and Information Architecture Quality: Process Steps

Assessing data definition quality seeks to measure the quality of the "information product specification"; in other words, data definition and information architecture.

Figure 5.10 identifies the process steps along with their dependencies and major outputs.

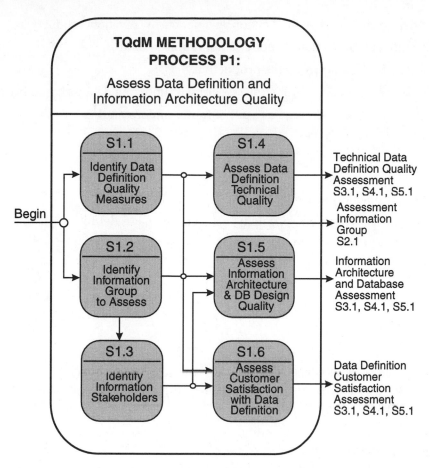

Figure 5.10   Assess data definition and information architecture process steps.

Each step outlines the objective, step inputs and outputs, along with useful tools and techniques that can be used to perform the step. A general discussion of the tools and techniques can be found in Chapter 10, "Information Quality Tools and Techniques." Specific uses of tools and techniques will be described in the specific steps.

Step 1: Identify Data Definition Quality Measures

This step is a planning step. Perform this step once, revisit it, and refine your measures as necessary to assure quality information models and database designs. The objective is to establish the important components of data definition required for effective business and information systems communication and productivity. Absence of quality in these areas can cause:

- Misunderstanding, miscommunication, and decreased business productivity
- Inadequate databases that do not contain required data
- Decreased information systems productivity
- Nonquality information production (creating or updating data incorrectly)
- Incorrect business actions as a result of faulty understanding

Inputs

- Business problems caused by information quality problems
- Application development problems caused by data definition quality problems
- Data standards manuals

Outputs

- Data standards conformance measures
- Data definition quality measures
- Information architecture quality measures for conceptual models and physical design

Techniques and Tools

- Facilitated brainstorming
- Root cause analysis and prioritization

A description of these and other techniques and tools is found in Chapter 10 and on the Internet at www.infoimpact.com: select the *Information Quality Resources* button for descriptions of quality products, techniques, and best practice case studies.

Process Description

This step establishes the measures to be used to assess the quality of data definition and information architecture. There are two kinds of quality measures:

Conformance to effective data standards. This step assumes the organization has adopted data standards in place. If not, perform a prerequisite activity to develop a draft data standards document. This step will, in fact, cause an organization to reevaluate its existing data standards and improve them as necessary.

Data object stability, flexibility, and reuse. Because data is a nonconsumable resource, reuse is a major indicator of quality of data definition, information architecture, and physical database design.

Conformance to Effective Data Standards

First, identify all stakeholders in data standards. Stakeholders include anyone whose work is affected by the standards. They include information systems *and* business personnel. Stakeholders also include those who work with the information products, such as information producers, data intermediaries, and knowledge workers, as well as external customers, suppliers, distribution channels, and regulators.

Select a team that represents all stakeholders to identify the measures for assessing definition and architecture quality. The team serves to achieve a majority view on the important quality measures for the *technical* assessment of definition quality. Do not let the process get bogged down.

Review major problems in development caused by data definition and data architecture quality problems and identify root cause. See Chapter 9, "Improving Information *Process* Quality," for a discussion of root cause analysis. Also review business problems stemming from misunderstandings, especially across business areas.

Analyze problems to identify which aspects of definition and architecture are most important to improve business and information systems communication and productivity. Use the quality characteristics described earlier in the section, *Information Product Specification Quality* as a template and baseline.

Analyze the data standards documentation to assure its effectiveness. Multiple teams should be able to use it to develop consistent quality information product specification. Augment data standards as necessary to define the most important standards clearly.

Identify the highest priority data standards, as measures for data development. A short list of critical data standards includes:

- ❏ Data names
    - ❏ Business name appropriate
    - ❏ Standard, single abbreviations
    - ❏ Domain type (class word) appropriate
    - ❏ Complete code values with descriptions
- ❏ Data definition
    - ❏ Clear, noncircular
    - ❏ Singular definition (defines one type of things or one type of fact)
    - ❏ Defines the real-world object itself, independently of how it may be used
    - ❏ Inclusive of all occurrences

❑ Business rules

   ❑ Existence and state change

   ❑ Dependency relationships

   ❑ Derivation formula or calculation definition

   ❑ Security class

   ❑ Retention requirements

❑ Presentation

   ❑ Consistency of names in different contexts, such as screens and reports

   ❑ Presentation format for formatted data such as dates, currency values

Once you have selected the appropriate measures for technical assessment of definition quality, conduct a pilot to test the workability and to get a general sense of how well data standards are followed.

Data Object Stability, Flexibility, and Reuse

If data is defined to meet all knowledge workers' needs, the model will be reused. If information architecture represents the inherent nature of data relationships, it will be stable. If information architecture and database design are developed from an enterprise, cross-functional, business-process perspective, they will be flexible to meet changes in how business processes are performed. If data is created and maintained according to its definition and business rules, and with quality to meet all knowledge workers' needs, it *will* be reused.

There are four simple measures of data definition and information architecture reuse on a project-by-project basis. They apply to both conceptual models and to physical database designs:

Count and percent of entity types and attributes *reused* as defined and implemented. This measure should go up over time as new, well-defined data becomes available.

Count and percent of *new and architected* entity types and attributes defined and implemented *nonredundantly*. This should go down over time. The more base facts defined, the fewer that remain to be defined. Data, such as `telephone-number`, or `person-last-name`, or `product-identifier`, if well defined, requires defining only once.

Count and percent of *new but redundant* entity types and attributes defined and implemented. Redundant data represents nonquality information, and incidences should approach zero. Discover and document the cause. Causes include the definition team did not have access to the repository, they did not know the data was already defined, or the architected and supposedly reusable data definition did not meet the needs of all knowledge workers. All are quality problems, and are caused by processes that need improvement.

Count and percent of entity types and attributes *modified* and reused. This may also represent information quality problems, and incidences should approach zero. Discover and document the reason. Valid examples include the fact that the business has expanded or changed strategic direction in ways not anticipated, and the definition required broadening, such as when two companies merge. It should be noted here that *flexible* data models of reference data, such as Party, or Customer should be minimally affected. Business event data such as Order, Sale, Policy, or Account may require more change.

These measures are assessed in step 4, *Assess Data Definition Technical Quality*. Well-defined and reusable data facilitates improved communication among all stakeholders, whether building applications and databases or in operating the business. Reusable data increases productivity by preventing the need to redefine it.

ULTIMATE PROCRASTINATION

Don't put off until tomorrow...
   ...what you can get out of all together.
   (Because data was already defined well and reusable, we did not have to spend money and time defining it again, and again, and again . . .)

Step 2: Identify Information Group to Assess

This step selects a collection of information for information quality assessment, or for data definition and information architecture quality assessment. The objective is to determine information where assessment and improvement could yield significant tangible benefits.

Inputs

- Repository, data dictionary, or case tool
- Business problems involving information quality
- Application problems involving data definition or information architecture quality

Outputs

- Information Group for quality assessment

Techniques and Tools

- Facilitated brainstorming

Process Description

This process selects information for quality assessment. There are three purposes for this:

To assess quality of the data itself. To measure data content quality requires assessing its definition to know how to measure the data itself.

To assess information development productivity and assess how well data is being defined on a project-by-project basis.

To assess the overall state of quality of data definition and information architecture within the enterprise.

For the third purpose, simply select a random sample of important data, including business terms, entity types, and attributes. The sample should include data from different business areas and across different projects.

For the first two purposes, identify a group of data for assessment where low quality can cause significant negative consequences. First identify significant business problems, and examine those problems where information quality is a contributing factor. Examine existing customer complaints, or conduct a customer satisfaction survey. Examine report logs. Examine business processes where cross-functional communications problems exist.

Select a small sample of important data, including 5 to 10 entity types and 20 to 50 attributes. This will consist of one or more Information Group. An Information Group is a cohesive group of information (business terms, entity types, and attributes) about a single subject or a subset of a subject. The assessment Information Groups should include both the most significant and most shared data from a business perspective, and then a random sample of other data. Select the significant data because poor definition has greater consequences. Select a random sample of data to assure consistency of definition quality while minimizing assessment costs.

> **TIP** For most efficient assessment, select information that is of general interest to the same kinds of knowledge workers. For example, if Product data is the broad Information Group, be sure to include several general attributes about Product that is of interest to all Product stakeholders. This will expedite the customer satisfaction sessions described in step 5.

Step 3: Identify the Information Stakeholders

This step identifies all roles that have an interest in the Information Group. The objective is to identify the "customers" and "suppliers" of information who may be negatively affected by a lack of quality of that information or its definition.

Inputs

- Information Group for definition quality assessment

Outputs

- Information stakeholder to Information Group matrix

Techniques and Tools

- CASE with matrix facility
- Repository or data dictionary
- Sharable, accessible spreadsheet or database

Process Description

Identify any existing documentation of relationships of stakeholders and information in existing repositories. Obtain a list of the various job titles or roles from Human Resources.

Identify subject matter experts (SME) or personnel who have broad experience in the organization. Brainstorm with the SMEs to identify all roles of persons who have an interest in the Information Groups. Include both internal and external information stakeholders. A checklist of stakeholder categories includes:

- ❑ Information producers
- ❑ Data intermediaries
- ❑ Knowledge workers
- ❑ Process owners
- ❑ Business information stewards
- ❑ Internal and external auditors
- ❑ External customers (immediate customers)

❑ End customers (ultimate end consumers)

❑ Third-party information providers who may collect and sell information, (e.g., credit agencies, research organizations)

❑ Distribution channels

❑ Regulatory bodies

❑ Communities

You may send out a questionnaire to business area managers to identify stakeholders in the data.

> **TIP**   Identify roles or job titles for documentation purposes. This will tend to be stable over time. As more data is reused, this matrix of stakeholders to an information group will grow.

Document this in an authoritative repository or reusable database. This can be used for subsequent assessments. This is also a valuable tool for change management to know who is impacted by changes to a given set of data.

From this list of general titles or roles, identify a few *people* in each of the internal information stakeholder categories; for example, information producer, knowledge worker, and so on. This will become the assessment team for the definition quality assessment conducted in step 5, *Assess Information Architecture and Database Design Quality*.

Step 4: Assess Data Definition Technical Quality

The assessment of the technical quality of data definition is quality assurance that the information specification conforms to (good) quality information standards and guidelines. This step requires effective data standards to result in improved communication and productivity. Any technical assessment must be coupled with step 6, *Assess Customer Satisfaction with Data Definition Quality*. The objective is to assure the data meets meaningful data naming and definition standards to create a common, consistent business language.

Inputs

- Data for definition quality assessment
- Data dictionary/repository/definitions
- Data standards manuals
- Data definition quality metrics

Outputs

- Technical data definition quality assessment
- Data reuse assessment

Techniques and Tools

- Quality assurance review

Process Description

This process has two parts: review of data definition for conformance to data standards and guidelines and reuse assessment.

Review of data definition for conformance to data standards and guidelines. Take the random sample of data from a data model or application software package and review it for conformance to the data definition standards and guidelines. Conduct this quality assessment to assure data definition process quality. Do not use this to find fault or to blame the people in the process. The goal is to improve overall working relationships among all development team members, including business, applications, and data management personnel. Provide immediate feedback to the data definition team.

Be open to feedback and suggestions from the team to improve the documentation of data standards and guidelines.

TIP The quality assurance team must be independent of the team that developed the data definition.

Reuse assessment. This assessment measures the quality of previously defined data. Data definition quality *will* result in reuse of data by subsequent projects. Count all entity types and attributes defined or used within the data modeling or application project. Use the "Development Quality" template shown in Figure 5.11.

Classify and count the reuse of conceptually defined data (entity types and attributes) in the four categories as defined in the section, *Data Object Stability, Flexibility, and Reuse*, in step 1 of this chapter:

Count and percent of entity types and attributes *reused* as defined and implemented.

Count and percent of *new, architected* entity types and attributes defined and implemented *nonredundantly*.

Project Number _____ Project Name _____		Completion Date: _____ Project Manager: _____						
Application metrics (reuse over time)		Entity/File Count		%		Attribute/ Field Count		%
	Ent	Fil/R	E%	F%	Attr	Field	A%	F%
Objects reused as defined and implemented (should go up)								
New architected objects (should go down)								
New but redundant objects (should approach zero [0%])								
Objects modified (list reason) (should approach zero [0%])								
Total Information Product Units			100%	100%			100%	100%
"Obsolete" legacy objects deleted (should increase, then decrease as objects are replaced)			N/A	N/A			N/A	N/A

Figure 5.11 Development quality assessment template.

Count and percent of *new but redundant* entity types and attributes defined and implemented.

Count and percent of entity types and attributes *modified* and reused.

Classify and count the reuse of database files and fields in the same four categories. Note that if you model data by business resource or subject area, and an application project only uses some of the data modeled, there will be fewer files and fields implemented than modeled. Subsequent applications will require the data defined but not yet implemented.

Count and percent of files and fields *reused* as implemented in shared files or in controlled (not interfaced and transformed) or replicated database files.

Count and percent of *new, architected* files and fields implemented *nonredundantly.*

Count and percent of *new but redundant* files and fields implemented.

Count and percent of files and fields *modified* and reused in shared files or in controlled (not interfaced and transformed) or replicated database files.

Track the reuse quality over time in a control chart. Figure 5.12 is an example, with reuse statistics compiled from project 5 documented in Figure 5.13. Maintain a copy of these Development Quality and Information Reuse Measures in the application development and maintenance areas.

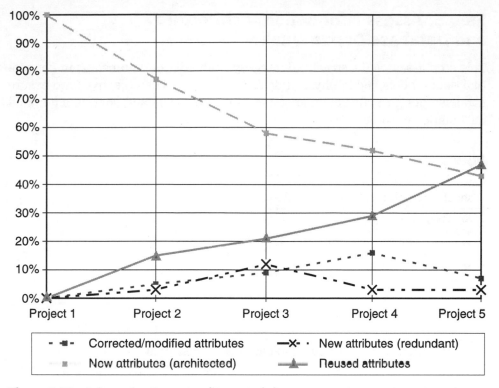

Figure 5.12 Information Reuse quality control chart.

Project Number: **P0117**		Completion Date: **9/4**						
Project Name: **Database Marketing**		Project Manager: **KB**						

Application metrics (reuse over time)	Entity / File Count		%		Attribute / Field Count		%	
	Ent	File	E%	F%	Attr	Field	A%	F%
Objects reused as defined and implemented (should go up)	87		54%		293		47%	
New architected objects (should go down)	68		42%		268		43%	
New but redundant objects (should approach zero [0%])	2		1%		19		3%	
Objects modified (list reason) (should approach zero [0%])	5		3%		44		7%	
Total Information Product Units	162		100%	100%	624		100%	100%
"Obsolete" legacy objects deleted (should increase, then decrease as objects are replaced)			N/A	N/A			N/A	N/A

Figure 5.13 Development quality measures example.

Step 5: Assess Information Architecture and Database Design Quality

This step assesses the structural integrity of the data relationships in conceptual data models and in physical database designs. The objective is to assure database design is flexible and stable to enable reuse and sharing among all information customers.

Inputs

- Information and data models
- Data definitions
- Data standards manual
- Information views

Outputs

- Information architecture and database assessment

Techniques and Tools

- Quality assurance review
- Structured information view walkthroughs
- Metadata management quality control software

Process Description

This process step has three parts: information architecture completeness, information architecture correctness, and information chaos (data redundancy).

Information Architecture Completeness Assessment

Here you assess whether the data model has all required entity types and attributes to support the business processes.

1. Select a data model or application software package database for assessment. This assessment has optimum value when conducted early in the application analysis and prior to physical database design or package selection.

2. Identify all processes that create, update, retrieve, or delete the data represented in the model. This includes not only processes to be automated

by the application in the sponsoring project, but also processes outside the scope of the immediate application.

3. Identify all types of information stakeholders in the data represented in the model.

4. Select representative subject matter experts from the information stakeholder types.

5. Develop information views for the most important processes, both inside and outside the immediate application project scope using the Pareto principle or 80/20 rule. Have the information stakeholders develop two or three information views of their most important queries, reports, and decisions made from the data.

6. For data warehouse walkthroughs, the information views must include the key business indicators and key decisions to be supported.

7. Perform walkthroughs of the information views against the model. Test for the following:

   All base data required to support the processes or information views exist in the model.

   All data required to support the processes or information views are related. In other words, all the data required is accessible to the view or process.

8. Count the number of entity types and attributes added to the model and the number of changes made to the model, and present them as a percent of total objects.

INFORMATION ARCHITECTURE COMPLETENESS CASE STUDY

A large pharmaceutical company developed a complete, detailed data model of its human resource subject area. The data model was developed by 20 subject matter experts that spanned five management levels and different business areas. I had the privilege to facilitate the data modeling sessions that consisted of two five-day modeling sessions over a five-week period. The completed model consisted of 110 entity types and 512 attributes, including consensus of data names and definitions.

A subsequent workshop was facilitated by another consultant and a business team developed about 300 information views of various processes, queries, reports, and decisions. They walked all information views through the model. One new entity type was discovered, 30 new attributes were discovered, and two data relationships were changed. The completeness of the initial model:

Entity type completeness:	99.1 percent (110 out of 111)
Attribute completeness:	94.5 percent (512 out of 542)

The business team concluded that the final model was in the high end of the 90 to 100 percent completeness percentile.

Information Architecture Correctness Assessment

The information view walkthrough just described also assesses the correctness of the model. The question asked is, "Does the model contain all attributes required for me to perform this process, answer this query, or support a decision?"

The correctness assessment tests the architectural stability as described earlier in the section entitled *Information Architecture Quality Measures*. Test for the following:

Entity-type-to-entity-type relationships. All related entity types reflect accurately the relationships of the objects and events in the real world.

Attribute-to-entity-type relationships. All attributes associated with an entity type are inherent characteristics of that entity type.

Entity-type-to-entity-subtype relationships. All subtypes are more specialized classifications of their supertypes. All attributes are inherent to the entity type and are inherited by all subtypes below that level.

Entity life-cycle states. All major states of existence are identified. The transitions reflect accurately the transitions experienced by the real world objects and events.

Information Chaos (Data Redundancy) Assessment

For the most critical information groups or entity groups, such as `Customer`, `Product`, and `Sales`, maintain a count of redundant files in controlled replication, uncontrolled redundancy, application software package files, or independent and proprietary files. "Disparate data are highly redundant; data often are repeated 10 or more times within the organization. It is often unclear which of these redundant data sources contains the most appropriate data, which most accurately reflects the real world, and which is most current."[6]

INFORMATION CHAOS CASE STUDIES

One division of a large insurance company found they had one critical fact maintained independently in *43* different databases.

A large manufacturing firm discovered *92* `Part` files (in one of its plants). Different Part IDs in the different databases prevented the company from knowing its real inventory.

A large bank had *256* `Customer` files. It took six people four months to answer the simple question, "Who is our best customer?"

One consumer goods company maintains over *400* `Brand` files.

A major telecom company discovered over 800 `Customer` files.

---

[6]Michael Brackett, *The Data Warehouse Challenge: Taming Data Chaos*, New York: John Wiley & Sons, p. 21.

Develop a questionnaire to identify private departmental databases or personal databases in which information about the same information group is maintained.

Step 6: Assess Customer Satisfaction with Data Definition Quality

This step assesses the degree to which the definition of data communicates the meaning of the data accurately and completely to the information stakeholders. This assessment is far more important than the technical assessment in step 4, *Assess Data Definition Technical Quality*. The objective is to verify that the name(s), definition, values, and business rules meet the needs of information producers and knowledge workers, and that there is a clear and common understanding among all information stakeholders.

Inputs

- Information Group for quality assessment
- Information producers/knowledge workers list

Outputs

- Data definition customer satisfaction assessment

Techniques and Tools

- Customer satisfaction survey questionnaire
- Information quality analysis software
- Pareto diagram
- Spreadsheet and bar charts

Process Description

1. Select five or so entity types and 15 to 25 important attributes for a customer satisfaction assessment.
2. Compile the data names, including business names and abbreviated names, definitions, domain values and definitions, and business rules into a survey for individual assessment. A sample assessment form is shown in Figure 5.14.

134

Data definition quality and value	Unsatis-factory	Fair	Satis-factory	Excel-lent	Don't Know (N/A)
1	Business name(s) are understandable and appropriate	☐	☐	☐	☐	☐
2	The abbreviated names are understandable and consistent	☐	☐	☐	☐	☐
3	The definitions accurate and complete	☐	☐	☐	☐	☐
4	The name and definition are consistent	☐	☐	☐	☐	☐
5	List of valid values, or codes is complete	☐	☐	☐	☐	☐
6	The code definitions, if any, are accurate/understandable	☐	☐	☐	☐	☐
7	The business rules are complete and correct	☐	☐	☐	☐	☐
8	Business rules are useful and effective	☐	☐	☐	☐	☐
9	This data has value to me in my area of responsibility	☐	☐	☐	☐	☐
10	This data has value to the business	☐	☐	☐	☐	☐

Entity / Attribute Business Name: _____ Ver: _____ State: _____ Date: _____

Abbreviated Name: _____ Reviewer Name / Business Area: _____

Please check the best description in the following:

If unsatisfactory, please list reasons and/or recommendations for improvement: _____

Figure 5.14 Data definition quality and usefulness assessment form.

3. Select representative individuals from all different business areas that have an interest in the information groups to be assessed. Be sure to include information producers and data intermediaries, as well as knowledge workers who use the data.

4. Assemble the group or send out the survey questionnaire with instructions.

TIP Perform a trial run of your questionnaire internally, before using it with actual information customers.

This is best conducted in a facilitated session, to address questions that will arise.

If the survey participants are geographically close, hold the session over a working lunch hour to improve participation.

5. Compile and report the results. See Figure 5.15.

6. Identify areas that need improvement, and follow Process 5 (described in Chapter 9) to improve the application and data development processes.

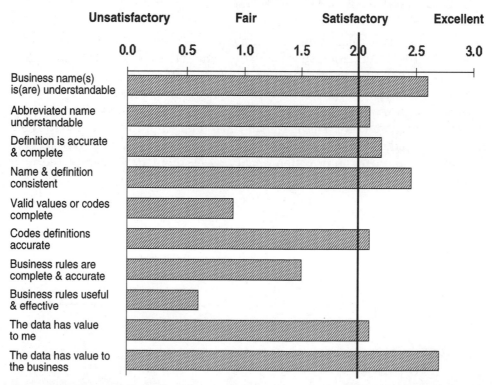

Figure 5.15 Data definition quality/usefulness assessment results example.

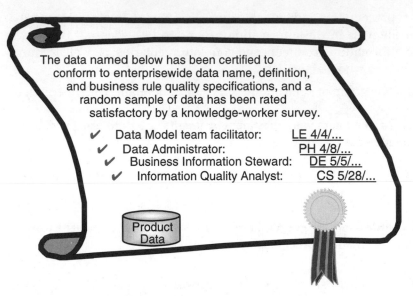

The data named below has been certified to conform to enterprisewide data name, definition, and business rule quality specifications, and a random sample of data has been rated satisfactory by a knowledge-worker survey.

✔ Data Model team facilitator: LE 4/4/...
✔ Data Administrator: PH 4/8/...
✔ Business Information Steward: DE 5/5/...
✔ Information Quality Analyst: CS 5/28/...

Product Data

Figure 5.16 Data definition certification guarantee.

Data Definition Certification

Data that meets technical definition standards, technical information architecture standards, information view validation, and customer satisfaction of definition, is now certifiable (see Figure 5.16). Information stakeholders can trust the data definition and can use it with reliability in their work.

Now you have a level of understanding of the quality of data definition and information architecture. This may lead you to make improvements to the data definition and data modeling processes. It also provides you with the expected definition of data for information quality assessment described in the next chapter.

Information Quality Assessment

"One accurate measurement is worth a thousand expert opinions."
—GRACE HOPPER (1906–1992), ADMIRAL, U.S. NAVY

Measuring or assessing information quality is the process of inspecting business information to assure it meets the needs of the knowledge workers who depend on it.

In this chapter, I describe the objectives for measuring information quality along with guidelines and tips for how to avoid pitfalls. Measure things that will add value to the enterprise and improve customer satisfaction.

I describe several kinds of information quality characteristics and measures that knowledge workers may deem important in the quality of their information. I differentiate between inherent information quality characteristics, such as whether the data is accurate to the real-world objects the data describes, and pragmatic quality characteristics, such as the degree to which information quality helps knowledge workers accomplish enterprise objectives.

I then outline a step-by-step process for information quality assessment, again providing guidelines for how to perform this successfully.

The ultimate result of improving information quality will be your ability to report and certify information quality that consistently meet all knowledge worker and end-customer expectations.

Objectives of Information Quality Assessment

There are three reasons to measure information quality. The first is to assure that the data production processes are providing consistently reliable data for all knowledge workers and information stakeholders. Unsatisfactory quality becomes the basis for process improvement. Information quality assessment is the measurement technique required for applying statistical process control to information production processes. Measurement tells us how we are doing and where process improvement is needed.

Information quality assessment represents part of the inspection costs of quality. Inspection costs must be offset by process improvement to reduce the costs of failure caused be the data defects discovered.

> **TIP** What data should be assessed? For the initial information quality assessment, identify an information group in which the costs of failure are high. For example, oil-well location data is a priority information group for a major offshore petroleum exploration company where information quality problems can cause the explosion of a drilling rig. A drilling accident in the North Sea caused it to drill through the well shaft of a neighboring nonproducing well because the data identifying the well shaft's location was inaccurate. Had the well been a producing well, the pressure from the oil in the ruptured pipe would have blown up the $500-million drilling investment and caused fatalities to the crew.

The second reason for information quality assessment is to provide an understanding of the reliability of the data resource. Without a clear understanding of the quality of data output of a process, one does not know the data reliability without some validation by downstream knowledge workers. This downstream data validation requires time and cost, and it may prevent some knowledge workers from using data based upon what could be a misconception of its reliability. Or the reverse may happen. Knowledge workers using the data warehouse or database may do so expecting reliable data. Knowledge workers will test a new data source with data they know. If they discover errors, credibility is lost. Credibility lost this way is most difficult to regain.

Not all data will be able to be cleaned to an acceptable level. If data warehouse customers know the level of data completeness and accuracy, they can factor the data's reliability in their decisions.

The third reason for information quality assessment is to discover information quality problems that will have to be addressed in a cleanup effort. That cleanup may be within the source or record-of-reference database files, or for data reengineering and cleanup before propagation to the data warehouse. The effort to clean the data may be, and most likely will be, far greater than any estimate prior to the assessment.

ASSESSMENT VERSUS AUDIT

The term *information quality assessment* is preferred to *information* or *data quality audit*. The word *audit*, while accurate, has unfortunate negative connotations. Assessments provide the basis for assuring that processes are performing correctly, communicating to knowledge workers the reliability of the data they work with, and become the basis for improvement. Data assessment must never be used to find guilty "culprits" "responsible" for bad data. If, in fact, poor information quality is discovered, it indicates broken processes, not broken people. The ultimate goal of data assessment is to improve information quality and improve substandard processes.

Pitfalls of Data Measurement Systems

To achieve the benefits of information quality measurement, care must be exercised to establish an effective information-quality assessment process. Measurement influences behavior; therefore, measure the right things, the things that have a positive impact on knowledge workers and customer satisfaction.

Measure the Right *Things*

While it may be tempting to measure people's performance, one should refrain from the information quality assessment as a behavioral performance measure. Deming's eleventh point of quality implies that measuring people against some arbitrary quota is one of the most harmful detriments to quality than anything else.[1] When people characterize the quality of consumer goods, they are not interested in who produced the goods; they only care that they meet their needs. The same is true for data. Knowledge workers are concerned with the quality and reliability of the data they depend on, not who created it.

Measure the information product. Then focus on the causes of nonquality in the processes involved.

People do play a role in the process. If, information quality is not acceptable, the process must be improved. Information producers and, ultimately, the process owner are accountable for the quality of the information products produced by the business process. They are accountable to the downstream knowledge workers who depend on that data. Assessment must measure the quality of the information product, not the quality of the people.

---

[1]W. Edwards Deming, *Quality, Productivity, and Competitive Position*, Cambridge, Mass: MIT Center for Advanced Engineering Study, 1982, p. 40. See Chapter 11 of this book for a detailed discussion of Deming's 14 points of quality and their ramification for information quality.

Measure with the Right *Measures*

One I/S organization that prided itself on its service promised its "customers" a service level measure of subsecond response time for operational transactions. They consistently designed systems that did deliver that "quality" response time. Were the information producers who received that subsecond response time happy? In a word, no. No one had really bothered to find out from them their expectations. In order to achieve this response time, the order taker had to enter the order header information separately, and then enter each order line separately, wait for a response, and then enter the next order line. They actually complained at their subsecond response time. They responded that they could tolerate 10-second response time if they were able to enter the entire order without interruption.

Measure the characteristics of information quality that matter to the business.

This example teaches two lessons. The first is that the only information quality criteria that matter are those of the information producers and knowledge workers. The information quality team must have the actual information producers and customers define their quality expectations. The second lesson is that the measures must assess aspects of quality that make a difference to the business and end-customer satisfaction. In this example, the measure of transaction response time (a system event) was the wrong measure. Rather than measure the artificial response from hit-the-enter-key to screen-refresh, the correct measure was the business event time that consisted of initiation of customer call (second telephone ring) to the successful completion of the customer order capture.

Measure at the Right *Place*

If data is measured at the wrong place, the organization may not get a true picture. Data cannot be measured just within the data warehouse.

Measure information quality in the record-of-origin database to determine the effectiveness of the data creation processes. The record-of-origin database is the point of first electronic data capture within the information value and cost chain.

Measure information quality in the record-of-reference database to determine the effectiveness of the data update and propagate processes. The record-of-reference database represents the authoritative source of data for the major operational processes. The more data is shared across functional boundaries, the more value the data has. At the same time, it is more important for that data to have quality to support all knowledge workers.

Measure information quality in the data warehouse to determine the effectiveness of the data transformation and propagation processes.

Measure at the Right *Time*

Information quality assessment must produce a reliable measure of the state of quality within the database or process being measured. It must be conducted as an independent and unbiased assessment. Conduct assessments independently of knowledge and control of information producers to measure the current process. If the information producers are aware that information quality will be assessed the last Friday of the month, they will rise to the occasion and pay special attention to quality—on that day. The following Monday, it will be business as usual. Information quality means "*consistently* meeting knowledge worker expectations."

TIP When should data be assessed?

- The schedule for information quality assessments should be varied to prevent intentional skewing and to account for variables in such things as day-of-week pattern changes, personnel changes, and workload variations.

- Information quality assessment of current processes should also take place before subsequent inspection and correction processes alter the data.

When measuring the effectiveness of current processes, information quality should be measured close to the time the data is created and before any potentially unnecessary data correction processes take place.

MEASURING AT THE *WRONG* TIME

A utility company was pleasantly surprised when an information quality assessment revealed 99.4 percent information quality level (only 0.76 percent defects) of some key work-order data. Investigation of why the quality was unexpectedly high revealed that the processes that generated work-order data were "review-intensive." It was estimated that about 10 percent of the process effort and cost occurred in initial data creation, and that approximately 90 percent of the effort was bound up in review and in manipulating the data to assure its correctness. Unanswered questions from this data assessment were, "What was the level of information quality of the original work-order data at its point of capture?" "Was the 90 percent effort of the process to review and update the data really required, or did it include a lot of information 'rework' that could have been captured at the original data create point?"

Information Quality Characteristics and Measures

Information quality *characteristics*, such as accuracy and timeliness, are the aspects or dimensions of information quality important to knowledge workers. Accuracy may be more important to one knowledge worker, while timeliness may be more important to another. Information quality *measures* are the information quality characteristics assessed.

Before you can measure information quality, you must define the quality characteristics knowledge workers expect of their information products. To "consistently meet knowledge worker and end-customer expectations," find out from them what their requirements and needs are. Knowledge workers who depend on information to do their jobs are quite capable of identifying what they need from the data on which they depend. Those characteristics are the "qualities" the data must possess for the knowledge workers to do their jobs and accomplish their business objectives. It is important that these quality characteristics be tied to the knowledge workers' ability to satisfy the end customer. Information quality measures should support good business objectives that result in increased customer satisfaction and loyalty.

Information quality includes a number of aspects. Some of these will be significant to the knowledge workers, and will therefore be characteristics to be measured in an information quality assessment. Focus on the quality characteristics that are most significant to the knowledge workers.

There are two basic categories of information quality characteristics and their related measures. The first is the inherent quality of the data. In a database, data has certain *static* quality characteristics. The second category are pragmatic quality characteristics. These include how intuitive the information is in its presented format and how well it enables knowledge workers to accomplish their objectives. *Inherent* information quality characteristics are listed here and discussed later in the chapter.

Definition conformance. The consistency of the meaning of the actual data values with its data definition.

Completeness (of values). The characteristic of having values for the data fields.

Validity or business rule conformance. A measure of the degree of conformance of data to its domain values and business rules.

Accuracy to surrogate source. A measure of the degree to which data agrees with an original source of data, such as a form, document, or unaltered electronic data received from outside the control of the organization that is acknowledged to be an authoritative source.

Accuracy (to reality). The degree to which data accurately reflects the real-world object or event being described. Accuracy is the highest degree of inherent information quality possible.

Precision. The characteristic of having the right level of granularity in the data values.

Nonduplication. The degree to which there is a one-to-one correlation between records and the real-world object or events being represented.

Equivalence of redundant or distributed data. The degree to which data in one data collection or database is semantically equivalent to data about the same object or event in another data collection or database.

Concurrency of redundant or distributed data. The information float or lag time between when data is knowable (created or changed) in one database is also knowable in a redundant or distributed database.

The second category of information quality characteristics is the pragmatic quality, including intuitiveness of its presentation and its value to enable knowledge workers to effectively perform their jobs. Here, data has certain *dynamic* quality characteristics. Static quality characteristics are independent of the processes that use the data. Presentation quality characteristics are associated with the human-machine interface; that is, presentation quality characteristics are pertinent only to the interaction of people and data. *Pragmatic* information quality characteristics include:

Accessibility. The characteristic of being able to access data when it is required.

Timeliness. The relative availability of data to support a given process within the timetable required to perform the process.

Contextual clarity. The relative degree to which data presentation enables the knowledge worker to understand the meaning of the data and avoid misinterpretation.

Derivation integrity. The correctness with which derived or calculated data is calculated from its base data.

Usability. The degree to which the information presentation is directly and efficiently usable for its purpose.

"Rightness," or fact completeness. The characteristic of having the right kind of data with the right quality to support a given process, such as to perform a process or support a decision.

TIP To determine information quality characteristics, conduct a survey of knowledge workers' information quality expectations of the data with which they work. Include the widest range of knowledge workers, both at an operational level and as current and prospective data warehouse consumers. Bring knowledge workers from different parts of the business together in a focus group to determine general categories of information quality characteristics. Facilitate the session to gain consensus and the names and definitions of the information quality characteristics. Note that this is not to determine the *level* of quality of each characteristic, but to establish the kinds of measures required.

Inherent Information Quality Characteristics and Measures

Inherent information quality characteristics are those that are independent of the way data is used. These characteristics are measures of the data itself, regardless of how it might be presented to knowledge workers. They are differentiated from the pragmatic characteristics that are aspects of the way in which information is presented to knowledge workers and the ease with which they can understand and use it.

Definition Conformance

Definition conformance is the consistency of the meaning of the actual data values and the definition of the data. Do the data values represent facts of the type indicated in the data definition? For example, the attribute "order date" may be defined as "the date the order was *received* from the customer." The application may automatically propagate the attribute with the system date. If orders may be received one day and entered into the system the next day, the date would be incorrect. The value would actually represent the data-entry date.

Definition conformance is a characteristic of communication. People may "assume" they know the meaning of an attribute or field and provide a value based upon their understanding. Definition conformance is the degree of agreement between the "meaning" people assign to data and its "official" definition. This underscores the importance of the data definition process, education, and the ability for knowledge workers and information producers alike to have access to data definition.

The measures of data definition quality described in the previous chapter and the measures of validity and accuracy defined later in the chapter are used to assess definition conformance.

Completeness
(of Values)

Completeness is the characteristic of having all required values for the data fields. The *measure* completeness is an assessment of the percent of records having a nonnull value (a value is not missing) for a specific field. This is also called "coverage."

The impact of data completeness on process failure is determined by the nature of the process. For operational processes, missing profile data may exclude likely prospects from a mailing. Trend analysis processes may not be negatively affected, provided there is a normal distribution of completed values. For example, if all health care providers supply a value "medical diagnosis code" on claim forms to an insurance company, demographic trends can be analyzed. However, if health care providers are not consistent in completing this information, the analysis may be skewed. The nature of the pattern of missing values would need to be known in other to correctly interpret the data analysis.

Validity, or Business Rule Conformance

Validity is a measure of the degree of conformance of data values to its domain and business rules. Validity simply means that a data value is from the correct domain of values for a field. The *measure* validity is an assessment of the percent of records having values that conform to the tested business rules for a field.

For example:

- A mailing address street number within the range of street numbers for this street within the city. For example, valid street numbers for Broadway in Nashville, Tennessee, are from 100 to 2099. A street number of 3014 is invalid.

- A medical diagnosis code corresponds to one of the valid diagnosis codes.

- A cargo package weight is within the range of valid weights and unit of measure for the type of shipping operation. Package weight for an express delivery service may be from 8 ounces to 150 pounds (or from 227 grams to 68 kilograms) for normal delivery, but package weights for a transoceanic shipping carrier may be from 1 pound to several tons (or from 0.45 kilograms to several metric tons).

- A birth date of a person is a valid date within the range of possibility for the person type described. A birth date of January 30, 1797, for a currently active employee would not be logically valid. A birth date of January 30, 2004 is not a valid birth date for anybody, until that date in history is reached.

- A latitude or longitude set of values is a valid pair of numbers that constitute a valid latitude and longitude coordinate and is within any constraining parameters of spatial reference.

- The exact amount of cash an ATM customer withdraws will be deducted from the account. Chemical Bank announced in 1994 that ATM customers had twice as much money deducted from their accounts as they had withdrawn. If they withdrew $100 in cash, $200 was deducted from their account. Officials blamed it on "a computer glitch!"

It is important to note that data values that have validity can still be *inaccurate*. Automated data assessments can test validity and reasonability, but they will not be able to assess accuracy of the values. In each of the preceding examples, a given value may be valid, but inaccurate as it describes a specific real object or event.

Automated information quality assessment reports must indicate the limitations of the nature of the assessments so the assessment results can be properly interpreted and understood.

Accuracy to Surrogate Source

A physical assessment to compare data with actual objects or events can be prohibitively expensive or impossible to gain access to the object or a reliable recording of an event. If this is the case, one may have to perform a physical assessment against the most authoritative surrogate source of data within their span of control.

Accuracy to surrogate source is a measure of the degree to which data agrees with data contained in an *original source* of data, such as a form, document, or unaltered electronic record received within the control of the organization. The *measure* accuracy to surrogate source is an assessment of the percent of records whose values for a given field are accurate as compared with the values contained in that "authoritative" source of information.

For example, credit card companies are interested in accurate credit transaction data. This data is created in the sales transactions at merchants around the world, and the credit card companies are not able to observe these events first hand. Their first concern is to assure they accurately capture the data as provided to them by their participating merchants. They may audit the credit transaction data in the databases where that data is created, and where it may be propagated during its credit card transaction processing. A physical assessment may analyze a sample of credit data against its original source document, called a *record-of-charge*, or against the electronic source record received from the merchant.

Conformance to source may be qualified by the point of time represented by the data. For example, the "official" 1996 census population of Brentwood, Tennessee, is 22,255, according to a recent specially conducted census. This population figure is not, nor is it intended to be, the actual population, but a value of 22,255 for the official 1996 Brentwood "census" population would be accurate to source.

This form of information quality assessment is a less-than-perfect measure. People can fill out forms incorrectly. Sales clerks at a credit card company's merchant may incorrectly enter a price. Errors in electronic sources can be introduced in a variety of ways. Credit card companies are (or should be) interested in the accuracy of the credit data entered at the point of sale because they will be the first point of complaint should their customers perceive errors in their transactions.

In data assessments it is important that the reporting of accuracy to reality and "accuracy" to a source document be clearly distinguished. Knowledge workers must know specifically how data is measured if accuracy is implied. Experience indicates source documents have at *best* around 4σ (99 percent) accuracy unless effective quality assurance and controls are in place for the source data acquisition.

Accuracy (to Reality)

Physical data assessments are required to measure the accuracy of data values. There are two types of accuracy assessment. The ultimate goal is for data to be accurate to reality. Auditing to reality requires confirmation of data values to measurement of the actual object or observation of the actual event or its recording.

Accuracy to reality (simply referred to as *accuracy*) is the degree to which data accurately reflects the real-world object or event being described. From an inherent standpoint, this is the highest measure of information quality. The *measure* accuracy is an assessment of the percent of records whose values for a given field are accurate as confirmed with its actual values.

Accuracy may be qualified by the point of time represented by the data. For example, a person's weight will be "accurate" as of the particular date weighed. Furthermore, the accuracy of *any* measured characteristic will be affected by the accuracy of the measurement device. Information quality measurement devices must be calibrated to assure they are measuring properly.

When should an organization measure accuracy to surrogate source, rather than accuracy to reality? The answer lies in the impact of defects in either. For legal documents, and other regulatory issues, one must assure the electronic data reflects the actual source data, even if the source data is not accurate to reality. For example, a person's name may be misspelled on a financial account; the incorrect name spelling actually becomes the account name. Here, the name spelling, though an inaccurate spelling of the person's name, is required to be maintained as listed on the account name. As a matter of observation, the name on the account has the definition and meaning of the *account name*, and not the person's name.

Accuracy to reality is important when the impact of inaccurate data is significant. *Critical* data should have a physical assessment at least once a year for quality assurance. For example, physical inventory is an example of a physical data assessment. The costs of physical data assessments can be minimized with effective random sampling described later.

Precision

Precision is the characteristic of having the right level of granularity in the data values. The *measure* precision is an assessment of the percent of records having values to the right degree of granularity for a specific field.

The precision of data values depends on the processes using the data. For example, dimensions of lumber used in housing construction can tolerate variances of up to 3/32nds of an inch (approximately 2.4 millimeters). However, the dimensions of optical fiber used in fiber optic cable for telecommunications requires a variation in diameter of no more than ± 0.5 micron (0.5 μmeter or 5/10,000 of a millimeter) from its specification.

Precision of population of a municipality has to be exact (to the census count) for allocating state funding. For marketing purposes, however, a precision of population to the nearest 1000 may be adequate.

Where there are multiple requirements in precision, the most stringent requirement must be adopted as the required precision. Precision is like derived and base data. A finer granularity value can always be rounded up. A coarse granularity value cannot be broken down to a more precise value.

Nonduplication

Nonduplication (of occurrences) is the degree to which there is a one-to-one correlation between records and the real-world object or events being represented. The *measure* nonduplication is an assessment of the percent of records that are duplicates of other records within a data collection. By duplicate records we do not mean the records have identical values, but that the records are duplicate representations of a single real-world object or event.

Duplication is a significant problem in many large databases. Duplication is also a significant problem in data maintained redundantly across independently distributed databases that are not controlled. Problems of duplicate data are compounded across these uncontrolled databases and files.

Duplication is most insidious in customer databases. Our office recently had this experience with one of our suppliers. Diane recently called our telephone equipment supplier to request a new catalog. When the customer service representative asked for company name and address detail, Diane told her that we already had an account and she could give her the account number. The rep responded that she could not just key in a company name or account number to pull up our record. So Diane had to give her company name, address, and telephone number (again). The rep came back to her with the reply, "There you are; no, there is a second record; oh, there are four of you!" One record had the company name keyed as "Information Impace" [sic, should be "Impact"]. The representative said she would clean them up and that we should get a catalog in 5 to 10 days.

Several truths jump out of this single episode:

- The company really did not know us as a customer. Having four records about us indicates that customers are treated as "Sales."

- The company cannot calculate customer lifetime value to really know the significance of its customers.

- The data entry processes are labor-intensive and prone to error.

- The company spent 400 percent more time and money than was necessary to capture our name and address information (including the catalog request). Capturing data once electronically is enough. Once captured electronically, it can be accessed millions of times without being destroyed.

- Three hundred percent more disk space was required to maintain information about us in their files. While disk space is becoming cheaper, the costs of handling, backup, and performance degradation all add up in the costs-of-nonquality-information column. It is conceivable that this company has twice as much disk space tied up than necessary due to redundant customer data.

- The company spent time and money to clean up the customer records. By now the previous order history is probably gone, and they will not see a complete picture of our sales history.

- From a customer "service" perspective, Diane was required to give information the company already had, thereby wasting her time.

To be truly customer focused, an organization must eliminate or at least minimize duplication. One publishing company, seeking to be customer service oriented, did not require customers to give their account numbers when ordering. If the customers did not know their number, the order representative would create a temporary account number for them and take their order, in order to get their order out quickly. When the marketing department decided to contact nonordering customers, the "customer serviceness" of this practice was exposed. Politely, the letter read something like this: "We have noticed that your organization has not ordered from us within the past six months. If there is any way we can be of better service to you to meet your needs, please let us know. . . ." The publishing firm received some scathing letters responding, "What do you mean we have not ordered from you in the past six months. We have ordered thousands of dollars' worth of literature monthly from you!!!"

Customer focus means to know as much as we can about our customers, and to know that information accurately and succinctly. The costs of not doing so will hurt the enterprise.

Equivalence of Redundant or Distributed Data

Equivalence of redundant or distributed data is the degree that data in one data collection or database is semantically equivalent to data about the same object or event in another data collection or database. Semantic equivalence means that the values are conceptually equal; in other words, they mean the same thing in both places. For example, a value of "F" for Gender Code for J. J. Jones in database A and a value of "1" for Sex Code for J. J. Jones in database B means the same thing: J. J. Jones is female. The *measure* equivalence is an assessment of the percent of fields in records within one data collection that are semantically equivalent to their corresponding fields within another data collection or database.

Equivalence is especially important in data warehousing and in distributed data environments that may use different technologies to store information about the same things. This measure measures the effectiveness with which redundant data is managed and controlled.

The real significance of equivalence is its business impact. Are knowledge workers working with the *same* information across the business if they are not able to use information from the same database? What is the impact if marketing, sales, accounting, and customer service have different data values about the same customer because they are using data from different databases?

Concurrency of Redundant or Distributed Data

Concurrency of redundant or distributed data is the corollary to equivalence. Concurrency is the information float or lag time between when data is knowable (created or changed) in one database and is also knowable in a redundant or distributed database. The *measure* concurrency is an assessment of the average length of time from when records are created or updated in one database until the time the same records (or their semantic equivalent record) are propagated to another database. An alternative measure is the percent of records propagated to another database by a specific time frame.

There are two types of information float. Manual information float is the length of delay in the time a fact becomes known to when it is first captured electronically in a potentially sharable database. Electronic information float is the length of time from when a fact is captured in its electronic form in a potentially sharable database to when it is "moved" to a database that makes it accessible to an interested knowledge worker. Unless distributed data is controlled with a two-phase commit, there will always be information float between when the distributed data that is available in one database and when the equivalent data is available in a downstream database.

Concurrency is a measure of the *potential* timeliness with which distributed data is made available to downstream knowledge workers. Because there is a time value to information, unacceptable concurrency of distributed data can cause two types of problems. The first is missed opportunities because of failure to have information available on time. The second problem is a discrepancy problem caused by reports coming from two data sources whose data is not in sync; that is, the data from an upstream data source has not yet been propagated to the downstream data source when the reports were created.

Information float is an issue in data propagation schedules for the data warehouse based on the timeliness requirements of the warehouse customers. It is also an issue in reconciliation of reports coming from the data warehouse with reports coming from the source databases.

Pragmatic Information Quality Characteristics and Measures

Pragmatic quality characteristics are the quality characteristics associated with data presentation quality and how well data supports specific business processes and how well it meets both information producers' and knowledge workers' needs. A given information group may have different quality standards for different processes or uses.

The quality measure of "fitness for purpose" is inadequate. Information must be fit for *all* purposes, even future uses not currently envisioned. Data that has *validity* but not *accuracy* may be fit for operational processes but unfit for decision support processes. "Consistently meeting knowledge worker and end-customer expectations" means meeting *all* information customers' needs to meet the enterprise and customer objectives.

Accessibility

Accessibility is the characteristic of being able to access data on demand. The *measure* accessibility is an assessment of the degree of ease-of-access interested knowledge workers have to the data they require. Accessibility has two components. The first is *potential* accessibility. Does the enterprise possess the data or have access to a data source?

Certain data whose source is outside the enterprise may be too expensive or difficult to acquire. Because the data warehouse supports strategic and tactical processes, competitive intelligence data is a key information ingredient. This data may not be easily available on a timely basis. The more data that is potentially accessible in the data warehouse, the more the value of the data warehouse increases.

The second component is *actual* accessibility. Assuming one has the potential to access data, how easy is it to do so? This is a more subjective measure that will be judged by the knowledge workers in comparison to how easy they are able to do other processes.

Timeliness

Timeliness is the relative availability of data to support a given process within the timetable required to perform the process. The *measure* timeliness is an assessment of the percent of process executions able to be performed within the required time frame because the required data was available. This is an assessment of acceptability of information float. Information float is the length of time from when data is known, until it is available for a specific process or use. The *measure* information float is an assessment of the average time required for data to become "knowable"; in other words, available to one or more knowledge workers from the time it is known somewhere in the enterprise.

One insurance company had significant manual and electronic information float in moving policy data from its creation on paper to its policy administration database to its claims database. The requirement for paying claims within 24 hours necessitated payment of a significant percent of claims before the claims processes had access to the applicable policy in the claims database. The lack of timeliness of policy data caused a financial exposure to the company of around $30 million a year. Process failure occurred in the inability to determine if a claim was: (1) a valid claim, (2) for a loss within the covered time frame, and (3) the claim amount was not in excess of coverage limits. Actual losses due to inability to recover overpayments amounted to $3–5 million annually.

Two measures apply to this example. The first is the concurrency or information float of policy data from point of data capture in the policy database to time of availability of the policy data in the nonintegrated claims database. This measures the timeliness of data availability from original data capture to the time needed to support claims payment in general. The second measure of timeliness measures the percent of failed claims payment processes due to not having the data available to support specific claim payments.

Contextual Clarity

Contextual clarity is the relative degree to which data presentation enables the knowledge worker to understand the meaning of the data and avoid misinterpretation. Contextual clarity includes both the intuitiveness of information layout along with labels and other descriptive information to facilitate communication. The *measure* contextual clarity is a subjective measure of the ease with which information as presented is understandable by the knowledge worker. Objective measures include the percent of correct actions taken as a result of presented information.

Derivation Integrity

Derivation integrity is the correctness with which two or more pieces of information are combined to create new information. The *measure* derivation integrity is an assessment of the percent of correctness of the calculations of derived data according to the derivation formula or calculation definition.

Derivation integrity requires precision of definition of the derived data. Its business rules include an accurate formula or instructions for its calculation or derivation. For example, Average Annual Sales Amount per Sales Representative may be calculated by dividing the Total Sales by the number of sales representatives active at the end of the year. But is this a correct calculation? What if 20 sales reps were active from January to October, and 10 new sales reps were hired and worked from November through December? The results may be misleadingly low.

Derived data is a significant part of the data warehouse and especially data marts. Care must be taken to define and document the calculation rules for derived data.

Usability

Usability is the relative ease of use of the *form* of information presentation required to support the information use. The *measure* usability is a subjective measure of the degree to which the information presentation is directly and efficiently usable for its purpose, such as to perform a process or support a decision.

Consider the differences in presentation quality used to track relative performance of some mutual funds in Figures 6.1 and 6.2.

Rightness, or Fact Completeness

Rightness is the characteristic of having the right kind of data with the right quality to support a given process. It is a measure of completeness of the kinds of facts required to support a process or decision. The *measure* rightness is an assessment of the percent of fact types, weighted, available out of the total fact types required to support a specific process. If all the data available has 100 percent accuracy and completeness, is available in the time frame required, is presented in an intuitive way, but the knowledge worker needs three other kinds of facts not available, the process will fail. For example, if a loan officer has accurate values for all fields on a loan application form, but does not have access to the applicant's credit history, a loan approval decision cannot be made.

Applying Statistical Quality Control to Data

The work of Deming, Ishikawa, Shewhart, Juran, and others in quality confirm that quality improvement is based on the technique of *statistical quality control* (SQC). Statistical quality control is the technique for measuring process

Which stocks are the best and worst performing during the 9-month period?

Stock ID	12/31/96	01/31/97	02/28/97	03/28/97	04/30/97	05/30/97	06/30/97	07/31/97	08/29/97
A	$20.750	$25.375	$26.750	$25.875	$23.63	$19.875	$18.625	$12.000	$13.250
B	$26.250	$25.670	$22.990	$21.890	$21.58	$21.770	$21.760	$21.530	$20.940
C	$28.080	$27.790	$30.420	$29.810	$31.36	$32.610	$30.980	$28.400	$30.480
D	$25.740	$26.610	$29.130	$26.530	$29.72	$30.280	$27.790	$26.130	$27.720
E	$21.390	$20.580	$22.020	$23.070	$26.28	$27.950	$25.910	$22.480	$24.100
F	$9.300	$8.850	$9.980	$9.340	$10.50	$11.140	$10.700	$9.630	$10.050
G	$83.750	$83.500	$103.375	$94.125	$108.75	$106.000	$99.625	$43.375	$43.750

Figure 6.1   Poor data presentation quality using base data to analyze mutual fund performance.

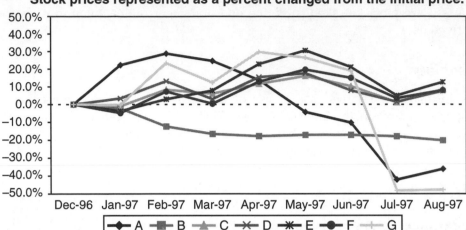

Figure 6.2   Better data presentation quality using graphic presentation of the relative changes in that same base data.

performance, identifying unacceptable variance, and applying corrective actions. Also called *statistical process control* (SPC), the principle underlying SQC is that processes that are "stable" or "in control" perform consistently and produce consistent quality output.

Because data is the product of its business processes that produce or manufacture it, the same principles that apply to controlling manufacturing quality can be applied to information quality. The first component of SQC is measurement. We cannot provide consistent quality if we are not able to monitor the processes to determine the reliability of those processes.

Measurement seeks to quantify the rate at which defects occur. A *defect* is an item that does not conform to its quality standard or specification. However, measurement must be performed from a customer perspective. When Motorola defined its Six Sigma (zero defects) quality program that it applied across its entire business, including IT, it considered a defect to be "anything which caused customer dissatisfaction," whether included in the specifications or not.[2]

For an in-depth discussion of statistical control theory methods, Walter Shewhart,[3] Kaoru Ishikawa,[4] Montgomery,[5] T. P. Ryan,[6] and E. Grant and Levenworth[7] provide excellent discussions. For a treatment of statistical quality control from the perspective of information quality, see Tom Redman's work.[8]

[2]Les Shroyer, "Motorola's Six Steps to Six Sigma," *Total Quality Management in Information Services,* New York: John Wiley & Sons, 1991, p. 33.

[3]Walter Shewhart, edited by W. E. Deming, *Statistical Method from the Viewpoint of Quality Control,* New York: Dover Publications, 1986.

[4]Kaoru Ishikawa, *Guide to Quality Control,* Tokyo: Asian Productivity Organization, 1982.

[5]D. C. Montgomery, *Introduction to Statistical Quality Control,* New York: John Wiley & Sons, 1985.

[6]T. P. Ryan, *Statistical Methods for Quality Improvement,* New York: John Wiley & Sons, 1989.

[7]E. L. Grant and R. S. Levenworth, *Statistical Quality Control, 6th ed.,* New York: McGraw-Hill, 1988.

[8]Thomas Redman, *Information Quality for the Information Age,* Boston: Artech House, 1996.

Assess Information Quality: Process Steps

Information quality assessment seeks to measure the quality of data in a database or file, or data output from a process.

Information quality assessment must assure that quality characteristics of data conform to knowledge workers' expectations of the data in order to perform their business processes or support their decisions successfully. The purpose of information quality assessment is to:

- Assure that processes are performing properly
- Identify processes and data that require improving
- Certify the reliability of data for the knowledge workers who depend on it
- Provide feedback to information producers who create and maintain it
- Develop a baseline to calculate the costs of nonquality information

The effectiveness of an information quality assessment hinges on four factors:

Measuring the *right* data

Against the *right* measures

Using the *right* measurement technique(s)

Providing the *right* interpretation and feedback

Figure 6.3 identifies the steps in the information quality assessment process. For each step I will describe the objective, its inputs and outputs, along with useful tools and techniques that can be used to perform the step. A discussion of the tools and techniques can be found in Chapter 10, "Information Quality Tools and Techniques." Specific uses of tools and techniques will be described in the specific steps.

Step 1: Identify an Information Group for Assessment

The objective is to identify a set of data, where poor quality can cause significant negative impact. Because data assessments are a cost-adding activity, they must be conducted in a way to maximize the benefit and minimize the cost of the assessment.

Inputs

- Information group(s) to be assessed, if identified in the data definition assessment phase
- Known problems in which low information quality is part of the cause

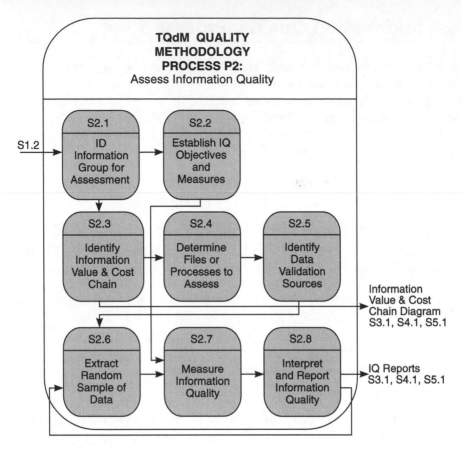

Figure 6.3   Assess information quality process steps.

- Data dictionary, repository, catalog, or inventory of databases

Outputs

- Prioritized information group for quality assessment. Information groups are prioritized based upon relative importance and impact of error and omission.

Techniques and Tools

- Customer satisfaction surveys
- Query tools
- Catalog and data dictionary reporting tools

A general description of these and other techniques and tools is found in Chapter 10 "Information Quality Tools and Techniques" and on the Internet at www.infoimpact.com: select the *Information Quality Resources* button for descriptions of products, techniques, and best practice case studies.

Process Description

Identify a group of data for assessment where low quality can cause significant negative consequences. To identify data for assessment, first identify significant business problems. Examine those problems where information quality is a contributing factor. Examine existing customer complaints, or conduct a customer satisfaction survey. Examine report logs. Examine business processes where process costs are excessively high, or where a high degree of rework exists.

The information group may include one or more entities and includes a few to several attributes. The selected group of data may be the data required for a single process, such as `Customer Billing Address` data, to support Invoicing. Or the group may be a logical information group centered around an important entity type, such as `Product` data, that may support many different processes. The data may be found in several fields in one or more files or databases.

Select data with the knowledge workers who are being impacted by poor quality information. The general selection process is to take a Pareto principle approach. Select data where the costs of nonquality are the greatest and process improvements will be the greatest as the first group of data to assess.

Group the data into different prioritized information groups based upon costs of nonquality. Relate the data to the processes using it. Determine with the process owners the cost of process failure based on error and omission of the various data fields. Group the data into three groups or so based upon relative priority. These groups may be called "A," "B," and "C"; or "Zero-Defect," "High Priority," and "Moderate Priority"; or other names appropriate to the nature of the data and organization.

An information group may consist of any number of fields. A manageable group of data for assessment consists of approximately 5 to 50 fields.

TIP The highest payback comes when you select data for assessment where information quality problems within this information group have reached the visibility of senior management. Negative publicity, catastrophic process failure, or failure to reach management goals as a result of poor information quality become open invitations to information quality improvement.

Select and measure data where the cost of failure is high. High costs of failure include:

- Significant costs of scrap and rework

- **Lost or missed business opportunity**

- **Image or credibility problems**

- **Legal or regulatory risk or liability**

- **Catastrophic or mission failure**

Step 2: Establish Information Quality Objectives and Measures

The objective is to determine the purpose for information quality measurement and what information quality measures to assess.

This step is vital to information quality improvement. The fact of measuring something will influence behavior. It is critical to measure the right things. Measuring the wrong things inadvertently motivates people's behavior to produce the wrong results. In fact, one of the primary causes of poor information quality is process measures that omit measures of quality. Measures of speed of process performance without being coupled with quality measures will virtually guarantee data errors and omissions.

Inputs

- Information group(s) to be assessed
- Information value and nonquality cost assessment, if any

Outputs

- Information quality measurement objectives (see Table 6.1)
- Information quality measures (see the section *Information Quality Characteristics and Measures*, earlier in this chapter)
- Information quality assessment schedule

Techniques and Tools

- Repository, data dictionary
- Customer satisfaction surveys
- Project management

Process Description

For a given information group, identify the processes that require the data and the knowledge workers responsible for those processes. These knowledge workers are the information "customers" who have quality requirements.

Determine the specific assessment objectives or goals. Sample assessment objectives may include one or more of those listed in Table 6.1.

To determine the specific measures of the information, survey the knowledge workers to understand their expectations for the data that they use. Seek to discover the defects that can cause process failure. For example, an incorrect `Mailing Address` will cause the "mail catalog to customer" process to fail. A missing or incorrect value for `Order-Item-Quantity` will cause the "fulfill order" process to fail. A missing value will prevent the order from being fulfilled. An incorrect value will give the appearance of successful order fulfillment, but will fail because the customer will receive an incorrect quantity of the item requested.

The information quality standard (standard of information quality) is determined by the *minimum* information quality required for successful execution of the *most* significant process requiring the data, and by customer satisfaction requirements of those who depend most on the data. These information quality characteristics represent the requirements necessary to "consistently meet knowledge worker and end-customer expectations."

The domain values and business rules discovered or identified in the process, "Assess data definition quality," were described in the previous chapter. They are used to define the specific measures for the data.

TIP Use matrices of process-to-data and person-to-process to identify and document the pertinent quality requirements.

Create a specific repository of the measures to be performed against each file or field. Define with the knowledge workers an assessment schedule. The assessment may simply be a baseline assessment or a regular routine.

Table 6.1 Sample Information Quality Assessment Objectives

OBJECTIVE
Understand state of quality in a database
Assure effectiveness of a process
Identify data requiring cleansing
Identify processes requiring improvement
Assure concurrency of data in multiple places
Assure timeliness of information
Assure effectiveness of data warehouse conditioning processes

Step 3: Identify the Information Value and Cost Chain

The objective is to determine all business processes and applications, and all who create or update a group of data along with the process dependencies. This is to identify all points at which information quality can be impacted and where data concurrency must be assured. It further seeks to differentiate activities that add value to the information customers from activities that add cost.

Inputs

- Information group(s) to be assessed
- Repository, data dictionary, catalog
- System documentation

Outputs

- Information value and cost chain diagram (see Figure 6.4)

Techniques and Tools

- Data flow diagram
- CASE with matrix facility: process-to-data matrix
- CASE with matrix facility: application-program-to-file matrix

Process Description

The information value and cost chain is an extended business value chain or business process. The difference is that it focuses on a logical group of data, such as Customer, Order, or Product, and traces all processes from the knowledge origination to the final database, such as a data warehouse or data mart, into which it may be placed. The actual data origination process may be:

- Automated data creation, as when customers call in to place an order that is captured electronically
- Manual data creation, in which the information is "captured" on paper, such as a customer filling out a paper order form
- Real-time data capture, such as electric meters (for example, process control equipment), or machine-recorded measurements (such as from telephone switches)

The information value and cost chain includes:

- All databases and files, including paper documents, in which the data is stored from its point of origin to its last database of use. This identifies candidate files to assess. It also identifies critical redundant files that are required to contain consistent data.

- All business processes and application programs that create, update, or delete data. This identifies all points at which business and application processes can introduce data error.

- All replicate, extract, and interface programs that copy data from one database and transform it and propagate it to another database. These are cost-adding steps that introduce information float and can introduce data error.

- All information producer and knowledge worker roles in the process. This identifies information customer-supplier relationships. Knowledge workers may invoke standard applications that are part of an application library to access the data, or they may develop ad hoc query programs that are not catalogued in any program library.

- All application programs that retrieve the data, if time permits. Retrieve programs and query programs are the application processes from which information value is derived. The higher the ratio of retrieve programs to programs that create, update, or interface and extract data, the higher the intrinsic value the data has, and the higher quality control one has over the information quality.

INFORMATION VALUE AND COST CHAIN VERSUS INFORMATION VALUE CHAIN

The term *Information Value and Cost Chain* is used instead of what should be called the *Information Value Chain*. Processes in a value chain either add value or cost, or both. However, many information systems architectures have a significant number of interface programs that are only cost-adding. Their only job is to extract data from one database and transform it into a different format "required" by a different system. An important benefit of documenting information value and cost chains is to focus attention on the processes that add value, so they can be maximized, and to focus attention on the processes that only add costs, so they can be eliminated, or at least minimized.

Figure 6.4 illustrates a simple example of an information value and cost chain for Customer information. This specific information flow shows a major problem: three separate application programs can update customer details independently without maintaining consistency of the updated data. Notice that the original "create customer" process application program (OE2101) is the data origination process, and the data is first created in its record-of-origin database

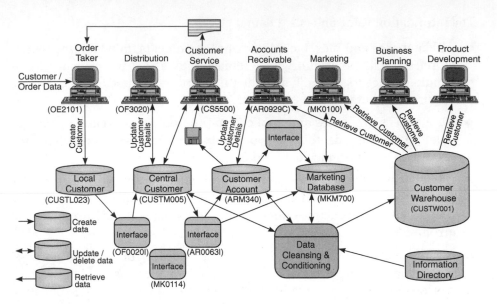

Figure 6.4   Information value and cost chain.

(CUSTL023). However, Customer Service representatives application program (CS5500) may update customer details, such as name and address, in the central Customer database (CUSTM005). There is no guaranteed process to propagate any customer data changes made by the customer service reps to the record-of-origin database. A report of changes sent to the local order-takers may or may not get applied. If applied, they may be applied incorrectly, with incorrect changes sent back to the central database, possibly overlaying the correct values.

Furthermore, the Accounts Receivable software package program (AR0929C) allows updates to Customer account data. Customers may send name and address changes when they send payments. There is no process to assure these updates are applied to customer data in the record-of-origin database or the central distribution database. This guarantees data inconsistencies and inaccurate data in some databases, even after the data had been updated somewhere in the system.

This simple example typifies major design flaws in information value and cost chains created by functional application development processes without effective, enterprise information management across business value chains.

The last database in the value chain should be the data warehouse or data marts extracted from a data warehouse. The information value and cost chain is an important tool with which to identify the appropriate data source files from which to extract and propagate data. This associates the information groups with the maintaining processes where the highest degree of quality is most likely.

TIP   Leverage database and application inventories documented in repositories, data dictionaries, or developed by Year 2000 projects as a starting point.

Measuring Information Float and Timeliness

There are two forms of information float, or timeliness. *Manual float* is a measure of the time from when a fact is known by someone in the enterprise or is available to the enterprise to the point it is captured in an electronic format. At this point, the data is *potentially* knowable to any interested knowledge worker. Data in a paper source or a fact in someone's head is proprietary information, and can be hidden from knowledge workers who need it. It has to be moved, maintained, managed, and protected physically. Once data is in an electronic database, it can be managed electronically, and then becomes a *virtual* resource—anyone with connectivity can access it.

Electronic float is a measure of the time from when a fact is first captured in an electronic format and when it is *actually* knowable by a knowledge worker or group of knowledge workers who need it. The best-case scenario for electronic float is zero time, as is the case for Internet or intranet data and completely shared databases. For example, once a fact is put in a Web page, it is immediately (zero float) available to anyone on the Internet. For data captured in a record-of-origin database, uploaded to a central record-of-reference database over the weekend, and interfaced to multiple downstream databases, electronic float can be from several days to several weeks.

Measure manual information float by taking a random sample of occurrences of facts and timestamping when they become known or are knowable. Extract the electronic records of those occurrences and determine the manual information float. This will consist of average information float in a pertinent duration, such as seconds or fractions, minutes, hours, or days. It may also include minimum and maximum float, and a standard deviation.

Measure electronic information float by comparing the create-date and time of a random sample of records in its record-of-origin database and the create-date and time of the equivalent records in the downstream databases of key knowledge workers. Document the average, minimum, maximum, and standard deviation of electronic information float.

Another way to measure electronic information float is by the percent of data that reaches a specific database by a required time frame. For example, 88 percent of the orders were picked within four hours of receipt. Information float may be measured in absolute time or relative time.

INFORMATION FLOAT AND COMPETITIVE ADVANTAGE

Reuters reported to its shareholders that "when France resumed nuclear weapons tests on 5 September [1995], Reuters customers had news of the explosion a good five minutes before those who relied on our competitors."[9]

---

[9] Reported in the *Reuters Holdings PLC Annual Report 1995*, inside front cover.

Step 4: Determine Files or Processes to Assess

The objective is to identify where data should be assessed to most effectively accomplish the objective for measurement.

Inputs

- Information value and cost chain
- Information quality measurement objectives

Outputs

- Data files and process assessment list and schedule

Techniques and Tools

- Evaluation and selection

Process Description

Select the place where data is to be measured based on the objectives for measurement. Table 6.2 describes the point of information quality assessment based on assessment objectives.

HOW *NOT* TO CONDUCT A DATA ASSESSMENT

To determine process effectiveness, data must be sampled in a way that assures the data is unchanged from the point at which the process created it. If data has been corrected, independently of the process being measured, the assessment results will be skewed.

Here's how *not* to do it: A warehouse crew prepared to take a physical inventory. Two days prior to the inventory, they deleted all quantity-on-hand data in the database. Then they went through the warehouse with their barcode scanners and scanned all inventory. The result of the physical inventory: an amazingly accurate inventory count!

Step 5: Identify Data Validation Sources for Accuracy Assessment

The objective is to identify the authoritative sources from which to validate data *accuracy*.

Table 6.2 Information Quality Assessment Point by Assessment Objective

ASSESSMENT OBJECTIVE	ASSESSMENT POINT
1. Understand state of quality in a database	The entire database or file. This should be a data source that supports major business processes.
2. Assure effectiveness of a specific process	The records output from the process within some time period being assessed but *prior to* any corrective changes.
3. Identify data requiring cleansing	The entire database or file. This should be a data source that supports major business processes.
4. Identify processes requiring improving	The records output from the process within some time period being assessed, but prior to any corrective changes.
5. Assure concurrency of data in multiple places	Sample records from the record of origin, then extract *equivalent* records in the downstream database. If data may be created in the downstream database, you must extract records from both and find the equivalent records in the other.
6. Assure timeliness of information	Sample data at point of origination, then extract equivalent data from database from which timely access is required.
7. Assure effectiveness of data warehouse conditioning processes	Sample data from the record-of-reference, then extract the equivalent record(s) in data warehouse.

Inputs

- Information value and cost chain
- Information group(s) to be assessed

Outputs

- Data validation sources list (see Table 6.3)

Techniques and Tools

- Information flow diagram
- CASE with matrix facility: data-to-data validation source

Process Description

For the data being assessed, identify the most authoritative source of information from which to assess the accuracy of the data being measured. There are two types of authoritative sources:

The actual object itself or observation of an event

A surrogate, or substitute, source document or recording that is expected to authentically reflect the source

There are six basic categories of entity types: person, organization, physical thing, concept, location, and event. Entities within a specific category tend to have similar validation sources. Sample authoritative validation sources for various entity types are listed in Table 6.3.

For purposes of accuracy assessment, it is important to differentiate between confirmation of values against a surrogate or the actual object. The surrogate may contain errors and, in fact, often does. For example, restaurant bills are a surrogate document for a meal. Experience shows the quality of accuracy is, on the average, less than 4-sigma quality, or more than 10,000 errors per million restaurant bills.[10]

For each information group, document official validation sources and surrogate sources, if any. Physical assessment of data accuracy against the actual source tends to be more expensive than comparing data to a surrogate source. For economic purposes, you may conduct assessments to actual sources less frequently than against its surrogate sources or using automated assessments.

The baseline physical assessment (first assessment to benchmark information quality) should include an assessment against *both* the actual source and a surrogate source you consider using. You must verify the accuracy of the surrogate sources to actual source to determine if it is a reliable source. Depending on the accuracy of the data in the surrogate sources, the processes that produce the surrogate data sources may need to be improved. For example, the accuracy of information on an insurance or mortgage application form may be low. The root causes may include faulty form design, lack of definition of the data being requested, or deficiencies in the process instructions.

If the process that produces the surrogate data source is stable, and producing acceptable information quality, then the majority of data assessments may be conducted against the surrogate source. However, periodic actual source assessments should be conducted to assure the processes are performing properly.

TIP Define and maintain an official list of the sources and surrogate sources for each information group. Get confirmation for these sources from the Internal Audit department.

---

[10]Les Shroyer, "Motorola's Six Steps to Six Sigma," *Total Quality Management in Information Services*, New York: John Wiley & Sons, 1991, p. 35.

Table 6.3   Data Validation Sources by Data Type

DATA TYPE	ACTUAL VALIDATION SOURCE	SURROGATE VALIDATION SOURCE
Person (Customer, Employee, Claimant, Organization Contact, etc.) details	Persons themselves	Person-completed forms, such as: employee application form, credit application form, customer application form, official records offices, such as governments and court clerk and record offices; demographic data sources, such as Equifax, etc.
Organization (Customer, Supplier, Broker, Financial Institution, Regulatory Body, etc.	Public relations or legal department	Annual report, letterhead, publicly available legal records, organization's Web site, etc.
Physical objects ([physical] Product, Package, Equipment, Building, etc.)	Samples of actual objects, products from warehouse,	Published official product specifications, blueprints, patent applications, etc.
Concepts (Financial products, such as Loan, Checking, Insurance Product; Process types, such as Manufacturing Process)	Concept conceiver, such as product manager	Official documents, such as product specifications, product marketing literature, process specifications and formulas, etc.
Locations (Country, Address, Plot (of land), Road Way, etc.)	Actual location	Legal documentation and records, official site surveys, etc.
Events (Order, Contract, Sale, Share Trade, Claim, Payment, Accident, Loss Exposure, Treatment, Process Execution, Phone Call, etc.)	Event observation, event recording, such as the telephone switch that captures telephone call data	Authoritative (source) paper documentation, legal records, record-of-charge documents

Step 6: Extract Random Sample(s) of Data

The objective is to select a sufficient number of records to assure the quality analysis of the sample accurately reflects the state of the total data population being assessed, while minimizing the cost of the assessment.

Inputs

- Database files list or process for quality assessment

Outputs

- Random sample of data

Techniques and Tools

- Random number generator
- Information quality analysis software
- Data extract software

Process Description

Sampling of data for information quality assessment is a critical success factor for the "quality" of the information quality assessment process itself. When conducting assessments of data files containing millions of records, the expense of a full data assessment is prohibitive. If the objective of the assessment is to understand the state of quality of the database itself, a small, random sample of records can provide an accurate picture of the information quality when conducted properly.

We will not treat the concepts of statistical sampling exhaustively here. These principles are well known and treated in many statistical books. Some references that provide a layperson's orientation to statistics include works by Wagner,[11] Graham,[12] and Hayslett.[13] Here we will focus on sampling techniques and methods that apply to data and data sampling.

Data Sampling Process Design

The overriding principle in assessment is to design and conduct the assessment in a way as to rule out "bias."[14]

Bias is the tendency or inclination of outlook that tends to cause error in human sensing or interpretation. Sampling of data must be conducted in a way that assures the sample closely approximates the state of the data population; in other words, the entire collection of records or the output of a specific process within some time period. Figure 6.5 represents the impact of sampling

---

[11]Susan F. Wagner, *Introduction to Statistics*, New York: Harper Perennial, 1992.

[12]A. Graham, *Teach Yourself Statistics*, Chicago: NTC Publishing, 1993.

[13]H. T. Hayslett Jr., *Statistics Made Simple*, New York: Doubleday, 1968.

[14]J. M. Juran, *Managerial Breakthrough*, New York: McGraw-Hill, 1964, p. 97.

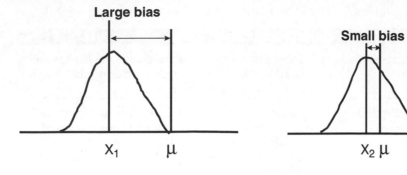

μ = mean of population

X_1 = mean of sample 1 with large bias

X_2 = mean of sample 2 with small bias

Figure 6.5   Sampling and sampling errors.

error, in which sample 1 was taken in such a way as to not reflect the total population accurately. Sample 1 is said to have a large bias. Sample 2, on the other hand, has a small bias, and is much more representative of the population.

The first step in preventing bias is to have identified the right place and time of sampling as defined in the previous step. Principles for effective sampling include:

- *Sampling performed in a way to assure each record in the population has an equal chance of being selected.*

- Sampling performed independently of data production. Information producers should not select samples.

- Sampling performed at a time unknown to the information producers. Knowing when data is to be sampled will influence behavior at those times.

- Sampling performed in a way to assure all variables in the process are within the scope of selection. If measuring specific processes, the time frame of the sampling should include any start- and end-time periods. For example, Monday mornings and Friday afternoons may be times during which there is a higher incidence of errors because of the weekend phenomenon. Anticipation of the weekend might affect attention span, and startup time may include higher volume of work or getting back in the routine variations.

The specific design of a random sample of data will be based on the objectives of the assessment. See Table 6.4 for sample design guidelines for specific assessment objectives.

Table 6.4   Data Sampling Guidelines by Assessment Objective

ASSESSMENT OBJECTIVE	DATA SAMPLE DESIGN GUIDELINES
1. Understand state of quality in a database	Sample data so that every record in the *file* has an equal likelihood of being selected using statistical random number generation.
2. Assure effectiveness of a specific process	Sample data so that every record output from the *process* has an equal likelihood of being selected. The time period of sampling must include all conditions of potential variation, such as startup and shutdown time.
3. Identify data requiring cleansing	Sample all records, or all records with a likelihood of being in error, such as with missing data, or unusual frequency distribution of values.
4. Identify processes requiring improving	Sample data so that every record output from the *process* has an equal likelihood of being selected. The time period of sampling must include all conditions of potential variation, such as startup and shutdown time.
5. Assure concurrency of data in multiple places	Select the sample from the origination file first. Then match the sampled records to their respective counterparts in the downstream file. This sequence is required to assure that no records from the record-of-origin file have been dropped in the propagation process. Sample data from both files if data may be created in both files.
6. Assure timeliness of information	Sample data and point of origin and timestamp it there. Timestamp the arrival of those records in the target file.
7. Assure effectiveness of data warehouse conditioning processes	Sample data in the record-of-reference file that are eligible for propagation to the data warehouse. This may be a full file load, or changed records only. Match the selected records to their respective counterpart records in the warehouse. The records may be consolidated with other records in the conditioning process, and fields may be split out into different records in the warehouse. Data values from before must be compared semantically based on the defined transform rules. For example, Marital-Status-Code values of "1," "2," and "3" in the source file may be transformed to code values of "S," "M," and "D" in the target file.

Data Sampling Techniques

There are several sampling techniques that may be employed in different situations. Sampling techniques include random, systematic, stratified, cluster, and two-stage sampling.

Random sampling. Statistical sampling in which every record within the target population has an equal likelihood of being selected with equal probability. Use a random-number generator in an extract tool or data analysis tool, or query select tool. Determine the required sample size and the number of records in the total population. Program the random-number generator to calculate a number between 1 and the total number of records in the population. Select records where the number generated is less than or equal to the number of records required for the sample plus 1 or 2. For example, a file contains 923,441 records. The required sample is 723 records. Program the random-number generator to calculate a number between 1 and 923,441. Select records where the number generated is less than or equal to 724 or 725. The greater number allows for the statistical chance that a smaller number of records will be selected than is actually required.

Systematic sampling. Sampling in which every nth record is selected. Select a ratio based on the ratio of required sample size to total population of records. Randomly select the first record to be chosen based on the ratio used. Systematic sampling is appropriate when the data population is ordered in a truly random sequence, and there is no bias in its ordering. Use systematic sampling when random sampling of the desired population is not feasible.

Stratified sampling. Sampling a population that has two or more distinct groupings, or strata, in which random samples are taken from each stratum to assure the strata are proportionately represented in the final sample. Use stratified sampling when the file being sampled is a distribution in records such that a small number of records exist for one subtype. For example, a customer database has 100,000 customer records. If there are only 300 "preferred" customers, a sample size of 1000 could have the potential to include no records from this group. Stratified sampling seeks to assure the sample has an equivalent proportion of "preferred" customers selected, based on the stratification by the preferred customer code. The sample should contain approximately three preferred customers in a sample of 1000 records (300:100,000 = 3:1000).

Cluster sampling. Sampling a population by taking samples from a smaller number of subgroups (such as geographic areas) of the population. The subsamples from each cluster are combined to make up the final sample. For example, in sampling sales data for a chain of stores, one may choose to take a subsample of a representative subset of stores (each a cluster) into a cluster sample, rather than randomly selecting sales data from every store. This technique may be used to represent all retail sales data only when the clusters truly represent the same relative kinds of data and the same relative process consistency. For example, if the files contain the same fields, the processes are the same, and the training and performance measure of information producers is consistent.

Two-stage sampling. Sampling from multiple files of the same data type, and then conducting a sample from the combined subset or group of data. This technique is used when collecting data randomly from distributed data files or from different time periods, and then randomly selecting a final sample from the merged samples. This is appropriate when there are many different files to sample and the size of the merged samples is larger than necessary for assessment. The first stage of sampling assures an adequate representation of data from each file or time period. Each sample of the first stage should be proportionate to its subpopulation so no one group inordinately biases the final sample. In other words, randomly select an equivalent percent of data adequate to represent the state of its subpopulation. The second stage of sampling assures adequate representation of the combined samples to represent the complete distribution of data.

Calculating Data Sample Size

A critical success factor in sampling a small set of data is to use an adequate sample size to assure statistical validity of the results. The number of sampled records taken is dependent on the confidence level you have in the sample, or the degree of confidence you desire that the measurement of the data in the sample be within an acceptable variance of the total data population you are measuring. The confidence level is the degree of certainty, expressed as a percentage, that the value for the mean of a population is within a specific range of values around the mean of a sample. For example, a 95 percent confidence level indicates you are 95 percent sure that the estimate of the mean is within a desired precision or range of values called a *confidence interval.* Another way to state this is that a 95 percent confidence level means that if you were to take 100 samples from the same population, the mean of the population is expected to be contained within the confidence limits, or confidence interval, of 95 of the samples.

Statistical methods call for a minimum of 30 records to be examined, in order to draw any meaningful conclusions. However, 30 records randomly selected from a large file that has minimal variation in errors would be unlikely to yield an accurate measure of the quality of that file. If you sample 100 percent of the records of the file to measure accuracy, you can be 100 percent confident that the result of the measurement has zero variation from the accuracy of the file. However, this may be too costly for your measurement objective.

Fortunately, there is an acceptable statistical formula to determine an appropriate sample size to balance your measurement objectives and budget. The formula includes three variables and is represented by the following equation:

$$n = ((z \times s) / B)^2$$

where:

n = **the number of records to extract.**

z = **a constant representing the confidence level you desire.** How confident are you that the measurement of the sample is within some specified variation of the actual state of the data population? The confidence level is the degree of certainty, expressed as a percentage, of being sure about the estimate of the mean. For example, a 95 percent confidence level indicates one is 95 percent sure that the estimate of the mean is within a desired precision or confidence interval. There are statistical charts containing these constants. However, the three most-used confidence levels and their constants include:

90%: $z = 1.645$

95%: $z = 1.960$

99%: $z = 2.575$

s = **an estimate of the standard deviation of the data population being measured.** This is the degree of variation of errors within the data population. The larger the variation, the larger the sample size required to get an accurate picture of the entire population. The smaller the variation, the smaller the sample size required.

B = **the Bound or the precision of the measurement.** This represents the variation from the sample mean within which the mean of the total data population is expected to fall given the sample size, confidence level, and standard deviation. If a sample (see Figure 6.6) has a mean of 0.4400 errors per record, and a Bound of 0.1100, the mean of the total data population is expected to fall within a range of 0.4400 ± 0.1100, or from 0.3300 to 0.5500 errors per record, given the sample size, confidence level, and standard deviation.

Because the information quality measure of accuracy is the most significant quality characteristic, the variation of interest is the variation in the number of errors from record to record.

TIP To calculate an initial standard deviation of a data population, create a random sample of from 30 to 50 records of the information group. Conduct an assessment of its quality to discover its "initial" standard deviation. Then once you conduct the actual assessment, update and maintain the standard deviation for that information group. Use this new standard deviation for the next sample size.

You can also use this new standard deviation to recalculate the confidence level for your assessment.

Figure 6.6 represents a sample of 50 customer records with 13 fields in each record being assessed. While the sample has a total error opportunity of 650 record fields (50 records times 13 fields), we will use the degree (number) of errors per record or information group to calculate standard deviation and sample size.

The sample reveals 22 errors (represented by the dark-shaded cells) in 10 records (represented by the light-shaded rows). Ten of the 50 records (20 percent) have at least one error. Twenty-two of the 650 record fields, or 3.4 percent of the fields, are inaccurate.

Calculating the Standard Deviation of a Data Sample

Standard deviation is a widely used measure of variability that expresses the measure of spread in a set of items. The standard deviation is a value such that approximately 68 percent of the items in a set fall within a range of the mean

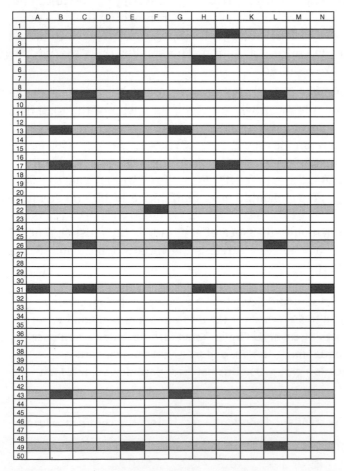

Figure 6.6 Customer data sample with errors.

plus or minus the standard deviation. For data from a large sample of a population of items, the standard deviation, σ (standard deviation of a population), or s (standard deviation of a sample), is expressed as:

$$s = \sqrt{(\Sigma d^2 / (n - 1))}$$

where:

- s = the standard deviation of a sample
- d = the deviation of any item from the mean or average
- n = the number of items in the sample
- Σ = "the sum of"

To calculate the standard deviation of a data sample, perform the steps in Table 6.5.

Table 6.5 Steps to Calculate Standard Deviation of a Data Sample: $s = \sqrt{(\Sigma d^2 / (n - 1))}$

STEP	FORMULA FOR FIGURE 6.6	RESULTS
1. Count the number of records in the data sample.	50	50
2. Count the number of fields containing an error in each record.	22	22
3. Calculate the mean ($\bar{X}$) or average number of errors per record by dividing the number of errors by the number of records.	22 / 50 =	0.4400
4. Calculate the deviation (d) of each record by subtracting the mean number of errors from the actual number of errors in the record.	R1. 0 - .4400 = R2. 1 - .4400 = . . .	-0.4400 0.5600 . . .
5. Calculate the deviation squared (d^2) for each record by multiplying the deviation by itself.	R1. (-.4400)² = R2. (.5600)² = . . .	0.1936 0.3136 . . .
6. Calculate the sum of the deviations squared (Σd^2) by adding all of the deviations squared together.	0.1936 + 0.3136 + . . . =	46.3200
7. Calculate the standard deviation of the data sample (s) by dividing the sum of the deviations squared (Σd^2) by the value of one less than the number of records in the sample ($n-1$) and taking the square root of the result.	46.3200 / 49 = $\sqrt{0.9453}$ =	0.9453 0.9723

Determining a Desired Confidence Level and Confidence Interval

Once you have an estimate of the standard deviation of errors for a data population you can calculate the number of records to sample, depending on the confidence level in and degree of precision (confidence interval) of the results of the sample to be taken. The first decision is the degree of confidence you desire in the sample. The second decision is how wide a variation from the mean of the sample is an acceptable set of limits, called the *confidence limits*.

This data that has an average or mean ($\overline{x}$) of 44 errors per 100 records (0.4400 errors per record), with a standard deviation (s) of 0.9723. To have a 95 percent confidence level that the mean number of errors of the data population is within 10 percent of the mean number of errors of the sample, you would need to select 1876 records. See calculation steps in Table 6.6. For a 90 percent confidence level for the same sample, you would need to select only 1322 records. The smaller the sample size, the less the confidence level.

If you take a sample size and have the standard deviation of the sample, you can calculate the bound at a desired confidence level, and plug these figures

Table 6.6 Steps to Calculate Sample Size: $n = ((z \times s) / B)^2$

STEP	FORMULA FOR FIGURE 6.6	RESULTS
1. Calculate the mean and standard deviation of the sample as described in Table 6.5.	mean ($\overline{x}$) = standard deviation =	0.4400 0.9723
2. Determine the desired confidence level and the z constant. (99% = 2.575; 95% = 1.960; 90% = 1.645)	z = 95% =	1.960
3. Determine the Bound. This can be an actual spread such as ± 0.1100 errors per record, or it could be a fraction of $\overline{x}$ or the mean of the sample, such as ± 10% of the mean.	1) Bound 2) Fraction: 10% x 0.4400 =	1) ± 0.1100 2) ± 0.0440
4. Multiply the z constant times the standard deviation.	1.960 x 0.9723 =	1.9057
5. Divide the result by the bound.	1) 1.9057 / 0.1100 = 2) 1.9057 / 0.0440 =	1) 17.3245 2) 43.3114
6. Square the result.	1) $(17.3245)^2$ = 2) $(43.3114)^2$ =	1) 300.14 2) 1875.88
7. Calculate the actual sample size by rounding the number *up* to the next highest whole number.	1) 300.14 = 2) 1875.88 =	1) 301 2) 1876

into the formula for calculating the sample size and calculate the Bound. If you took a sample of 1600 records in the above sample with a standard deviation of 0.9728 and wish a 95 percent confidence level, the calculation is $1600 = (1.960 \times 0.9728) / B)^2$. Taking the square root of both size of the equation yields $40 = (1.960 \times 0.9728) / B$. Multiply by B to get $40 \times B = 1.960 \times 0.9728 = 1.9067$. Divide both sides by 40 to get the value of the bound, where $B = 1.9067 / 40 = 0.0477$. Now you have a 95 percent confidence level that the mean of the population lies within 0.4400 ± 0.0477.

What is the impact on sample size if the sample has the same error rate of 44 errors per 100 records (0.4400 errors per record), but has a standard deviation of 1.4165? (This standard deviation occurs in a sample of 50 records with 22 errors concentrated in only 5 records, in which those records had 5,3,4,3,7 errors respectively.) A confidence level of 95 percent with a bound of $\pm$ 10 percent of the mean would require a sample size of 3982 records. Because the errors are concentrated in a smaller percent of the records, a larger sample size is required.

Step 7: Measure Information Quality

This step analyzes information quality against its quality criteria. Data assessment is composed of two forms of quality inspection. The first form of assessment is automated information quality assessment that analyzes data for conformance to the defined business rules. The second is a physical information quality assessment to assure the accuracy of data by comparing the data values to the real-world objects or events the data represents.

Its objective is to measure a data sample against one or more quality characteristics in order to determine its level of reliability and to discover the kind and degree of data defects.

Inputs

- Random sample of data
- Defined business rules and measures
- Data validation sources list

Outputs

- Information quality characteristic measurements

Techniques and Tools

- Information quality analysis software

- Query tools
- Spreadsheets
- Customer satisfaction survey questionnaire
- Customer satisfaction telephone survey
- Physical inspection
- Event recording

Data assessment consists of designing and conducting data measurement tests that measure the quality of data. There are two categories of quality assessment techniques which we will break up into two distinct process-description sections:

Automated data assessment for conformance to business rules. Electronic assessments can determine whether data conforms to business rules and whether data values are valid values or are within reasonable limits. Automated tests cannot determine that the data is accurate in many situations, however.

Physical data assessment for accuracy. Physical assessments compare data values to the real-world objects and events that the data represents in order to confirm that the values are accurate.

Automated Information Quality Assessment: Process Description

Automated data assessment is information quality inspection using software tools to analyze data for business rule conformance. Automated data assessments can be performed rather quickly, once business rule tests have been defined and coded into a data analysis product or internally developed measurement programs. Once the initial assessment tests have been developed, routine measurement is easy to schedule.

The fact of measuring data requires you to define the business rules. In fact, this may be the first time an organization formally defines its business rules.

The kinds of assessment tests that may be automated include:

- Completeness of values based on life-cycle state
- Validity or business rule conformance. This includes:
    - Domain values
    - Ranges, reasonability tests
    - Primary key uniqueness
    - Referential integrity

- Dependency rules
- Format consistency
- Accuracy to surrogate source, as measured against an authoritative electronic source
- Nonduplication (automated assessments may be able to identify potential duplicate occurrences of data)
- Equivalence or consistency of redundant or distributed data
- Concurrency of redundant or distributed data
- Timeliness
- Derivation Integrity

There are three general categories of automated data analysis tools:

Rule discovery products with exception-reporting capability

Information quality analysis software

Internally developed information quality analysis programs

Rule Discovery Products with Exception-Reporting Capability

The easiest form of automated analysis is the use of rule discovery products that have exception-reporting capability. These products require no definition of business rules—this also is a limitation. The only potential errors are those against the rules the tool is able to discover. The strength of rule discovery products is the discovery of obscure or informal business rules that may not be uncovered through business rule definition analysis with knowledge workers. A second strength is that these tools may successfully identify patterns of fraud, the most grievous form of information quality problems.

Rule discovery products require the following steps:

1. Identify the files where data relationships may have business rule constraints. Use defined business rules and data whose relationships may reveal fraud patterns to identify the specific data for analysis.

2. Extract and format the data in a form readable by the rule discovery product.

3. Tune the rule discovery analysis by identifying data that may not be associated with meaningful business rules and exclude those fields from being evaluated. Performance of rule discovery products is a function of how many fields are being analyzed as opposed to how many records are being analyzed. There is a geometric increase in performance time due to comparing a field to every other field within its record or information group.

4. If an information group has a very high number of fields, it may be feasible to break the fields into two or more groups of data for analysis. Each grouping should have fields that logically participate in the meaningful business rules. For example, if you are analyzing order data, one information group might include total-order-amount along with all fields that are involved in its calculation, such as item-identifier, item-order-quantity, item-price, discount-percent or discount-amount, tax percent or tax-amount, tax-jurisdiction, and so forth. A second group of Order data might include discount-amount, along with order-date, order-taker-identifier, customer-identifier, order-location, for example. These attributes might analyze whether consistent discounting rules are being applied.

5. For files that have a large volume of records, a random sample of 10,000 or so may be selected for analysis to minimize discovery of meaningless rules.

6. Experience with each information group will lead to knowledge about tuning the specific analysis tests.

See Chapter 10 for a list and description of rule discovery software products.

Information Quality Analysis Products

Information quality measurement products differ from rule-discovery products in that you must define the specific business rule tests to be performed. These products have a business-rule specification language for business-rule definition. These business rules are stored in the product's repository or dictionary. They may then be executed individually or in a collection of tests against a single group of data.

The strengths of this kind of product are that you can define as many or as few business-rule assessment tests as you wish to analyze. Once the business rules are defined, they can be reused until the business rules are changed. Another strength is that the business rule specification language prevents having to code common kinds of business rule tests.

One downside to this type of product is that you may have to redundantly specify business rules that exist in your repository. A second downside is that you may have to specify and maintain domain values or other business rules redundantly, that could be tested with an internally developed measurement program against the original and authoritative domain values. If the product operates on a different execution platform and the data being tested has to be ported into a different file type, assure the data is extracted without corruption of the original data values.

A standard audit principle is to separate the function of audit from process performance. It will be necessary to have a procedure to update the assessment business rules and domain values when the actual process business rules and domain values are changed. Otherwise, when the actual domain values are changed, the audits measure the data against invalid business rules and domain values, and the resulting reports as to business rule conformance will be in error.

Information quality measurement products require the following steps:

1. Develop business rule test naming and definition standards carefully so they are semantically grouped and easily usable.

   a. Name business rule tests by information group (Customer, Product, Order), then by business rule test. For example, Cust-Id-Uniqueness, and Order-Total-Amount-Calculation.

   b. Define the business rule test so that it is easily maintainable. "[Order-Total-Amount-Calculation] tests that the total order amount of an order is derived correctly according to order pricing formula as defined in the 'Corporate Order Pricing Policy.'"

   c. Document the business information steward responsible for the specific data and business rule.

   d. Document the information quality analyst responsible for maintaining the business rule in the information quality product.

2. Identify the files and information groups.

3. Define the specific business rules to measures to be assessed.

4. If the measurement product allows the definition of weights or costs to be associated with types of information quality errors, confirm with the knowledge workers the relative impact or costs of each defect of this business rule.[15] This will be used in reporting of the errors based on impact, and not just number of occurrences of error. Step 8 describes how to report errors by impact.

5. Group the business rule tests into assessment groups, and execute them as a package.

TIP

- You may wish to use the information quality analysis software's dictionary or repository as the record-of-reference source for all business rule definitions that are not easily maintained in another repository or data dictionary.

- Define business rule specification procedures to minimize data capture of business rule definition.

- Create automated replication of business rule definition where possible to minimize unnecessary rekeying of business rules.

See Chapter 10 for a list and description of information quality assessment products.

---

[15] See the discussion of calculating the costs of noninformation quality in Chapter 7, "Measuring Nonquality Information Costs."

Internally Developed Information Quality Analysis Programs

You may develop your own information quality assessment programs to measure business rules conformance. The benefit of this lies in easy-to-develop-and-maintain programming languages or generators, coupled with the ability to use existing authoritative domain value sets and reference data, without having to maintain them redundantly. These assessment programs may be executed on the platforms where data is actually created and used. Internally developed programs may be able to extract business rule definitions from your repository if it has the ability to export business rules.

Internally developed business rule tests provide another benefit: they may be coded in a way that they may also be assembled into reusable routines that can be invoked dynamically from the data-producing applications. This elevates the value of these routines from "inspection" to "defect prevention."

The downside of internally developed analysis programs is the time and cost of developing and maintaining the programs. Business rule definition and program code logic must be maintained separately.

TIP

- Recognize the strengths and limitations of automated assessment.

- Exploit automated information quality analysis assessments to reduce the costs of physical data assessments.

- When reporting the results of automated information quality assessments, be sure to communicate the limitations of the assessments, so the readers do not misinterpret validity for accuracy.

- The sample size for an automated assessment can be substantially greater than that of a physical assessment due to the difference in costs. Use periodic physical assessments using a subsample of the automated assessment sample to develop a correlation of automated validity test to accuracy to reality tests. This can ultimately decrease the frequency (and costs) of physical assessments if a direct correlation exists.

Physical Information Quality Assessment: Process Description

Physical information quality assessment measures the accuracy of data values to the attributes of the real-world object or event. While physical assessments require more time than automated assessments, they are required to confirm the accuracy of many data fields. Conduct physical inspections for the baseline quality assessment, and then only as often as required.

Physical inspection of data is the converse of physical inspection of manufactured products. Quality assessment of manufactured products requires measurement of the products to get *data* about the product to confirm its quality against its *specifications*. Ishikawa graphically represents quality control in manufactured products in Figure 6.7.[16]

Quality assessment of the information product (manufactured data) requires comparing the *information product* with the object the data represents to confirm its quality against the real world *objects or events themselves*. Figure 6.8 depicts quality control of information products.

The objective of physical inspection is to confirm the accuracy of data values against an authoritative validation source as identified in step 5. The form of physical assessment varies based on the data entity type. Table 6.7 describes different forms of physical assessment.

Physical Assessment of Person Data

Telephone or personal surveys with people are the best way to confirm accuracy of current personal details such as name, address, and other current data. For some historical data, surrogate sources, such as legal records, may be a more accurate source of accuracy confirmation, as memory can be faulty over time.

For a telephone survey, develop a script carefully. The survey must put the contact, especially customers, at ease that this is a customer service or customer satisfaction survey and not a marketing call. The integrity of the results and the integrity of future surveys can be jeopardized if the contacts perceive that you have ulterior motives.

The survey script should contain an introduction, a body, and a conclusion. The introduction communicates the purpose of the survey and the benefit to the contact. It should assure the individual that this call is for customer satisfaction, and that the objective is to verify the accuracy of the personal information. It must ensure that the information confirmed, along with any new information discovered, is kept confidential and private and only for internal purposes. By ensuring confidentiality you encourage truthful responses. If your organization does sell or use the information in any other way, you should describe how the information is used. Honestly state the expected length of time the survey should take. If this is too long, seek to schedule an appointment with the individual at a time that is convenient. You may offer some concession or benefit for participating in the survey.

The body is the script for verification of data values. The survey form may be electronic or paper depending on your resources and resource skills. Telephone survey design guidelines include:

- Format this section to be intuitive for both the interviewer and the contact.

- Design questions to be concise and require minimal time on the phone.

[16] Kaoru Ishikawa, *Guide to Quality Control*, Tokyo: Asian Productivity Organization, 1982, p. 109.

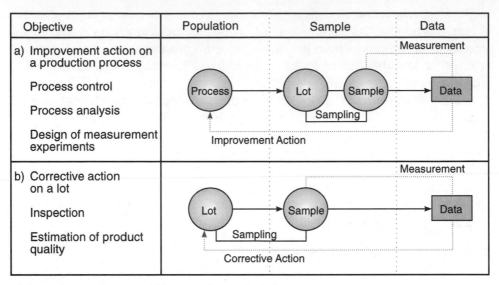

Figure 6.7 Quality control in manufactured products.

Source: Ishikawa, *Guide to Quality Control.*

- If the contact is not the actual person whose details are being validated, note the survey respondent name and their relationship to the subject of data verification.

- Design the questions so that the contact can verify spellings and other details with accuracy.

- Allow space for corrected or new information to be captured.

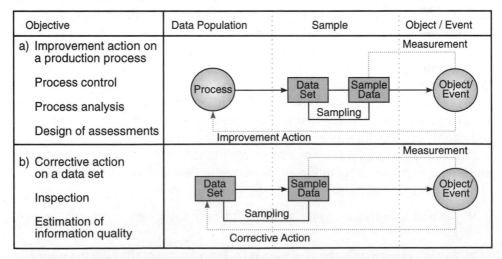

Figure 6.8 Quality control in information products.

Source: L. English, adapted from Ishikawa.

Table 6.7   Physical Data Assessment by Data Type

DATA TYPE	ACTUAL SOURCE ASSESSMENT	SURROGATE SOURCE ASSESSMENT
Person (Customer, Employee, Claimant, Organization Contact, etc.) details	Telephone survey Mail-out form with return	Compare data to data on original forms or source documents
Organization (Customer, Supplier, Broker, Financial Institution, Regulatory Body, etc.)	Confirm data with public relations, liaison, or legal department	Compare data to annual report, letterhead, publicly available legal records, etc.
Physical objects ([physical] Product, Package, Equipment, Building, etc.)	Measure samples of actual objects Confirm with product manager	Compare data to published, official product specifications, blueprints, patent applications, etc.
Concepts (Financial Products, such as Loan, Checking, Insurance Product; Process Types, such as Manufacturing Process)	Confirm with product manager or process owner	Compare data to official documents, such as product specifications, product marketing literature; process specifications and formulae, etc.
Locations (Country, Address, Plot (of land), Road Way, etc.)	Survey actual location Postal authority	Compare to legal documentation and accords, official site surveys, postal authority database, etc.
Events (Order, Contract, Sale, Share Trade, Claim, Payment, Accident, Loss Exposure, Treatment, Process Execution, Phone Call, etc.)	Observe event real time Record event Measure the real-time device that captures data	Compare data to authoritative source documents, legal records, record-of-charge documents

The conclusion serves to thank the respondent for their time. This should include an open-ended question to ask the contact if they have any other comments or suggestions for how your organization can better serve them as customers. Pass this on to the customer care area for attention and follow up with the contact. Reassure the confidentiality of the results and reconfirm any promotional benefit you may have promised for participation.

Another form of physical assessment is a mail-out form that contains the information to be verified. This form is less expensive and can reach more people. This technique is used especially for data cleanup. As a measure of actual information quality, the results will be biased based on response patterns. Another limitation is the personal contact with the ability to probe answers.

Mail-out survey form design includes:

■ Design for return of bad-address mail.

- Minimize respondent's effort to correct wrong information or include new information.

- Include only partial numbers of sensitive data, such as social security or social insurance numbers, bank card numbers, etc. This prevents legal exposure should someone other than the addressed subject open the mail.

- Provide appropriate incentives to increase response.

- Design intuitive questions with definitions of data to avoid miscommunication of the data being verified.

TIP

- With telephone survey, expect 25 to 30 percent of the selected persons to be unreachable in one or two attempts. The sample size must allow for enough occurrences to meet your confidence level due to unreachable contacts.

- "Test" the questionnaire internally to assure communication and intuitiveness.

- Allow for persons not willing to answer the questions. Document, if possible, the reasons for their position. This is useful for future survey design.

Physical Assessment of Organization Data

The nature of physical assessment of organization data is very similar to that of person data. The imperative here is to reach an authoritative person who can speak for the organization. This individual will usually be found in the public relations, communications, or legal departments. Surrogate data sources include publicly available legal records or documents such as annual reports, prospectuses, and other official communications materials including Web sites.

Physical Assessment of Physical Object Data

Physical attributes of tangible objects, such as materials, consumer products, or equipment, can be inspected and measured directly. Dimensions, weights, and components can be measured directly. Chemical composition and other scientific attributes can be analyzed with scientific measurement equipment. Nonphysical attributes of tangible objects can be assessed in the same way as concepts, described next.

Physical Assessment of Concept Data

Concept data, such as loan type or insurance product type, requires validation of data with the product owner or the process owner of the process creating the concept. Surrogate validation sources include product specifications, or publicly available legal documents. Other official documents, such as marketing or descriptive reports, may be required to validate marketing-related data.

PHYSICAL OBJECT ASSESSMENT

A major passenger airline performed an assessment of the reported weight of its freight cargo as supplied by the shipping party—cargo weight determines shipping fees. Freight packages were randomly selected and weighed. A significant number of discrepancies in the reported and actual weights were uncovered. Understated weights were reported twice as many times as overstated weights. This defect translated to annual revenue losses of approximately $15 million per year.

Physical Assessment of Location Data

Location data is of two types: address locations and geo-spatial locations. Validation sources for address locations include the postal authority for mailing locations, internal facilities management for office and warehouse locations.

Physical assessment of geo-spatial data requires engineering surveys. Surrogate sources include official survey maps and plats of land.

Physical Assessment of Event Data

Event data is the most difficult to assess because the data values reflect facts that describe a happening at a specific point in time; yet this data may be the most important for quality assessment. Errors in business and financial transactions directly impact the bottom line.

Fraud is simply information quality "error" intentionally introduced for personal gain. Fraud geometrically accelerates that bottom-line impact.

The validation source of event data is authoritative observation of the event itself. This is usually not practical. However, event data, such as orders, payments, sales, and inventory movements, can be monitored for information quality assessments and for information quality control.

Events that occur over the telephone can be recorded with participants' knowledge and approval. These recordings become the validation source for these events. Stock brokerages record telephone-placed trade transactions to assure stock trades are made correctly and that there are no misunderstandings. Mail-order companies have monitors that randomly listen in on calls to assure customer satisfaction and event quality.

Surrogate validation sources include the "paper trails" of business transactions beginning with original source documents, such as order forms, checks, record-of-charge documents, contracts, movement authorizations, for example. These surrogate data sources may be used to verify data entry has been properly performed. Discrepancies in surrogate data sources and electronic data sources may reveal defects in either the data entry processes or in the form creation processes, or both.

Some surrogate data sources will be electronic in form. Electronic Data Interchange (EDI) data is received into the organization as electronic data. This data should be maintained for validation that the initial data handling processes format the data into the record of origin database properly.

As more business transactions, or electronic commerce (e-commerce), occur over the Internet, these transactions and data sources become the surrogate validation source. Because the actual information producers are outside the "scope of control" and training of the organization, the forms require a high degree of presentation quality. These electronic forms and transactions must be ergonomically designed, intuitive for the information producer, and provide clear meaning of the data being captured.

TIP Each document to be considered as a surrogate validation source should be assessed as to its reliability. To do this, perform an audit on a random sample of source documents against the actual data validation source. This establishes a reliability level of this form of validation that should be disclosed in the assessment reports.

Step 8: Interpret and Report Information Quality

Once data is analyzed it must be communicated in a way that facilitates improvement through teamwork. The findings must be shared in a way that is illuminating, but not punitive. The objective is to communicate the state of information quality in a way that:

- Enables knowledge workers to know the reliability of the data with which they work
- Provides feedback to information producers and process owners on how well their processes are performing, and encourages improvement
- Identifies processes that require improvement based on the impact of data defects and facilitates root-cause analysis for process improvement

Inputs

- Assessed data

Outputs

- Data assessment procedure report
- Information quality assessment reports
- Exception reports
- Information quality control charts

Techniques and Tools

- Information quality analysis software
- Pareto diagrams
- Bar charts
- Statistical control charts

Process Description

Interpreting and reporting information quality findings is the process of analyzing the raw data of the assessment, understanding the meaning of the findings, comparing the findings to knowledge worker expectations, and presenting the findings clearly. The reports must communicate effectively to knowledge workers, information producers, and process owners.

Information quality errors in interpreting and presenting information quality assessment findings are some of the most grievous and even incredulous. Juran cites the following example of interpreting the results of an experiment (*Managerial Breakthrough*, p.99):

> A scientist trained a flea to jump on the command "jump." Then the scientist conducted some experiments on the flea. He removed the flea's front legs. On the command "jump," the flea jumped, but not as far as before. Removal of the middle legs cut the distance further. Finally, the scientist removed the remaining two legs and commanded "jump." The flea did not move. Over and over again came the command "jump," and still no movement.
> Then the scientist solemnly recorded his conclusion: "Removal of a flea's legs impairs his hearing."

The most well-defined information quality assessment can be wasted, or even destructive, if the conclusions are wrong or presented incorrectly. A 99.9 percent accuracy level may be concluded as excellent quality, unless inaccurate data in the 0.1 percent could cause a $1-billion loss.[17] At the same time, information quality accuracy of only 90 percent might be perfectly acceptable, if the knowledge workers know its level of accuracy.

Data Assessment Report

The assessment report is a cover report that states how the assessment was conducted and what kinds of tests were applied. It is similar to the report of independent accountants of a financial statement. Figure 6.9 is a cover report template.

---

[17] Conversation with an information quality manager whose client stated that this is the potential impact of decisions made by inaccurate data.

We have conducted an assessment of the _____
data in the _____ files. This assessment covers
data created for the period _____ to ____. The business
processes measured include: _____.

   This data is the responsibility of the process owners
of the respective processes. The information quality
assessor's responsibility is to express an opinion on the
data's reliability based on our assessment.

   We conducted this assessment in accordance with
generally accepted statistical sampling procedures and
internally developed assessment standards. The
accompanying attachment documents the specific
procedures used for this assessment.

   In our opinion, according to customer surveys of
expectations of this data, [conclusions and
recommendations].

Information Quality Team

Figure 6.9   Information assessment cover report statement.

The assessment procedure report lists what kinds of measures were performed and how data was validated. See Figure 6.10

Information Group Name: _____   Date Assessed: _____
Time Period Covered: _____   IQ Analyst: _____
File(s) sampled: _____   Process(es) sampled: _____
Sample size:_____ Sample percent: _____% Std Dev:_____
Confidence level: ❏90% ❏95% ❏99% ❏ _____% Precision:_____
Assessment type: ❏ Electronic ❏ Third-party corroboration
        ❏ Physical to surrogate source ❏ Survey
        ❏ Physical to real object / event
        ❏ Other: _____

Quality characteristics assessed:
   ❏ Completeness of values
   ❏ Reasonability tests / distribution analysis
   ❏ Validity: conformance to business rules
   ❏ Accuracy: correctness of values to: ❏ Source _____
                        ❏ Surrogate _____
   ❏ Non-duplication of records
   ❏ Timeliness of data availability
   ❏ Equivalence and consistency of redundant data
   ❏ Usefulness and value-adding

Figure 6.10   Assessment procedure report.

Information Quality Summary Reports

Measurement reports generally include graphic representations of the information quality findings. They may be summaries of errors by record, by field, or by information group. They provide a "big picture" of the quality of the data assessed. Figure 6.11 illustrates a summary report using a column chart. This summary reflects both the actual assessed information quality percent of errors compared with the information quality standard. The three measures are completeness of data, accuracy of data, and level of duplicate data.

The completeness and accuracy measures have two summaries: one by record and the other by field. The summary by record represents the percent of records in the sample where at least one field has a missing or inaccurate value. The summary by field represents the same assessed data, but the percent of total fields assessed has a missing or inaccurate value. The accuracy measure represents the findings presented in Figure 6.6 in which 10 of 50 records (20 percent) contained at least one error, while out of 650 fields (50 records times 13 fields) contained 22 errors (3.4 percent).

If certain fields are significant, you may wish to report that the second field (column B in Figure 6.6) has 3 errors out of 50 possible errors, for a 6 percent error rate. Each of these summaries may be important to different knowledge workers.

Information Quality Detail Reports

Measurement reports are generally graphic representations of the information quality findings. They may be aggregations of errors by record, by field, or by

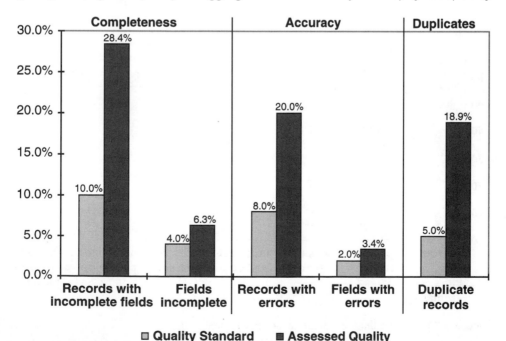

Figure 6.11 Information quality summary report.

information group. They may include Pareto diagrams of specific kinds of errors or defects.

The Pareto principle, commonly known as the "80–20 Rule," is important in quality. For example, it can be used to distinguish between what Juran calls the "vital few" and the "useful many" customers.[18] The vital few customers represent the 20 percent of the customers who account for 80 percent of the sales.

The Pareto principle is also useful in analyzing the 20 percent of the defect types that account for 80 percent of the information quality problems. For a given set of data, Pareto diagrams may be used to represent the types and extent of information quality defects.

Address quality, for example, may be reported by error type. Figure 6.12 is a Pareto diagram of address error counts reported by type based on *frequency* of

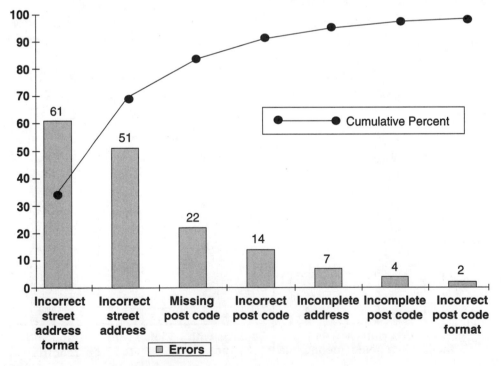

Figure 6.12   Pareto diagram: Address errors by type.

[18]J. M. Juran, *Juran on Planning for Quality*, New York: The Free Press, 1988, p. 27.

errors. The line represents the running total percent of errors by count. This type of reporting calls attention to the most frequent errors first.

While this is useful, it is more useful to report errors based on the impact those errors have. Some errors cause significant impact in costs of nonquality, while others may represent only minor problems. For example, the highest-frequency address error was an incorrect street address format, while an incorrect street address value was the second most-common error. The impact of these two error types is vastly different. The incorrect format will not delay the delivery of the mail, but an incorrect address will most likely cause failure or delay of delivery.

A more effective and informative way to report specific error types is by impact or cost of nonquality. This requires having the knowledge workers quantify the costs of nonquality for each error type based on what processes fail and how frequently they fail based on each error type. Costs of nonquality include costs of irrecoverable materials, rework, workarounds, complaint handling, data correction, and missed or lost opportunity. Identify the pertinent categories of costs as described in the next chapter.

From this, you can calculate the true economic impact of the degree of errors discovered. The weighting can be calculated in a simple spreadsheet, as depicted in Figure 6.13. With this weighting, a new "weighted" Pareto diagram can be generated to illustrate a more informative picture of the costs of the data errors (see Figure 6.14). Note that the most *frequent* error is a relatively insignificant error (fourth out of seven) in terms of costs. Some quality analysis software products include this capability.

Equivalence and Consistency Reports

Other reports compare the equivalence or consistency and accuracy of data where records about the same object or event exist in multiple databases. These establish whether data maintained in multiple files are being kept in sync. Figure 6.15 illustrates some inconsistencies and accuracy problems of

A	B	C	D	E	F
Error Count	Error Weight Cost/yr	Weighted Result	Error Type	Total Error Cost/yr	Sample Percent of Population
61	$0.20	$12.20	Incorrect street address format	$1,220	1%
51	$5.00	$255.00	Incorrect street address	$25,500	1%
22	$2.00	$44.00	Missing post code	$4,400	1%
14	$7.50	$105.00	Incorrect post code	$10,500	1%
7	$1.00	$7.00	Incomplete address	$700	1%
4	$1.00	$4.00	Incomplete post code	$400	1%
2	$1.00	$2.00	Incorrect post code format	$200	1%
161				$42,920	Total
		(A x B)		(C ÷ F)	

Figure 6.13 Weighting data errors by cost of error.

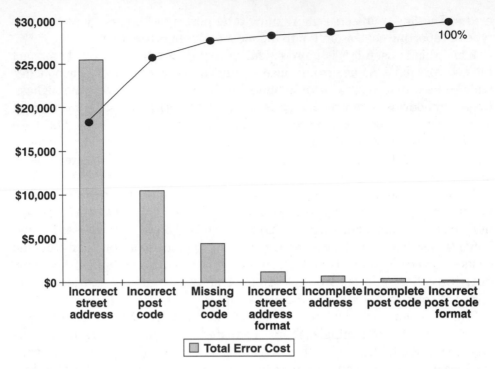

Figure 6.14 Weighted Pareto diagram: Address error impact expressed as a cost of errors per year.

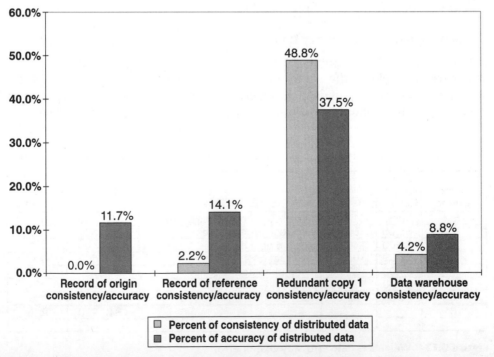

Figure 6.15 Distributed data consistency and accuracy comparison report.

customer data captured from a record-of-reference database, an independently maintained redundant copy, and within the data warehouse.

Exception Reports

Exception reports simply show the data discovered to be in error along with the correct values, if known. Pass them to the process owners for data correction.

Information Quality Control Charts

Quality control charts are used to provide a picture of information quality over time. They are used as the means of assuring that processes are maintained in control, or, in other words, are achieving their quality standards. Figure 6.16 illustrates a quality control chart over a 12-month period illustrating assessed information quality against its quality standard.

Report the actual information quality assessment against the data's information quality standard. Set quality standards that can be attained within a reasonable time frame. When the level has been met and sustained for a reasonable time, redefine the quality level to a higher standard. Continue this until the optimum quality level is met and sustained.

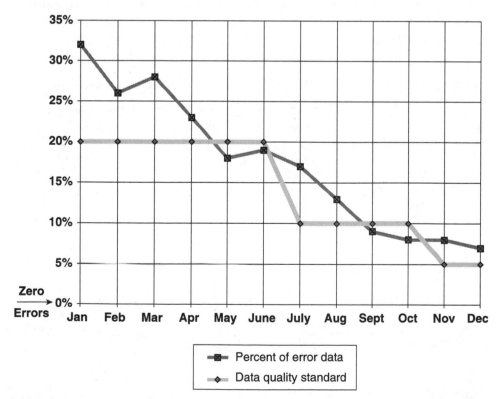

Figure 6.16   Information quality control chart example.

> **TIP** *After* conducting a baseline assessment of an information group, set a target quality standard that is realistic and obtainable during an agreed timetable. As you accomplish this, raise the standard until the "real" quality goals are consistently met.

Conclusion: Data Certification

By assessing information quality against knowledge workers' (the information customers) quality criteria, and following generally accepted audit procedures, you can now certify whether data meets its quality standards (customer expectations). This can be reported in a number of ways. A statement of certification, a seal, a citation, or other form of communication is in order (see Figure 6.17).

Data certification is a warranty of information quality. Most companies provide some guarantee or warranty of quality of their products. In the Information Age, in which information is the differentiating resource, shouldn't the information producer organizations warrant their information product's quality to their downstream information customers?

Now that you know the level of information quality, you must quantify its costs. Management is not interested that a file contains 1.1 percent errors in one database and 22 percent duplication in another. It is interested that the 1.1 per-

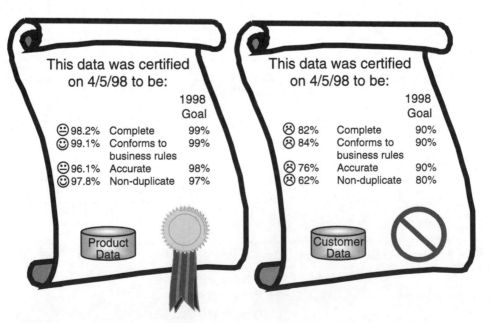

Figure 6.17 Certified information quality.

DATASTREAM'S INFORMATION QUALITY GUARANTEE

DataStream is a company whose product is information. It collects and sells financial information, mostly about U.K. organizations and their share prices. DataStream guarantees its information quality. If a customer discovers an error in its data, DataStream will pay them £40, approximately $68, for each data point in error.

cent of errors just cost the company $1.5 million, and that the 22 percent duplication resulted in $400,000 in a single mail-out, but lost $8 million in missed customer lifetime value. Assessing information quality is a precursor to quantifying the costs of nonquality information, and is described in the next chapter.

CHAPTER 7

Measuring Nonquality Information Costs

"All organizations are at least 50 percent waste—waste people, waste effort, waste space, and waste time."

—ROBERT TOWNSEND

The real costs of poor-quality information are most tangible, directly affecting the bottom line in two ways. The first is in the form of direct costs as a result of "information scrap and rework." The second is in the form of missed and lost opportunity. Missed and lost opportunity due to poor information quality, while intangible, can be estimated fairly accurately given customer attrition patterns and complaint data.

There are three reasons for measuring the costs of poor-quality information:

- To determine the real business impact of information quality problems
- To establish the business case for information quality improvement initiatives
- To provide a baseline for measuring the effectiveness of information quality improvement projects

In this chapter we describe the cost and value basis for information. They consist of the five processes of the resource life cycle, required to effectively manage and exploit the value of any resource. Four of the five processes constitute the cost basis of a resource, and the fifth process makes up the value basis. We describe how the same principles and cost and value basis apply to information and its information resource life cycle.

Next we describe the costs of information quality, including the three distinct categories of the cost of quality. We focus especially on the costs of nonquality information and how it negatively affects business operations and "steals" profits from the bottom line. Finally, we describe how to measure and quantify the real costs of poor-quality information in business measures.

Measuring the costs of nonquality information is perceived as being difficult or intangible; however, it is actually quite straightforward.

Value and Costs of Information

To determine the value of a resource you must understand its costs, and the benefits derived from its use. The basic formula for value, or profitability, is:

Value = Benefit − Cost

As a product, information has the same cost components as a manufactured product. Costs are divided into *fixed* and *variable* costs. Fixed costs are the costs to create the *capacity* to produce something, including the infrastructure costs, machinery, and other costs required to be able to produce a product. Fixed costs represent the costs to create the infrastructure required before a single item can be produced or before a single record can be created electronically. Fixed costs do not vary with the number of items produced up to the production capacity. Variable costs are those costs required to produce a single item or record, such as materials consumed and personnel time. Variable costs increase incrementally based on how many items are produced or records created.

Information production has both fixed and variable costs. Fixed costs are those required to begin producing information. They are the costs of developing applications and databases. Variable costs are those incurred in operating the applications in which information is created, updated, and used.

However, the costs of information must be broken out into two areas: the *cost basis* and the *value basis*. The cost basis of information is the cost of developing and maintaining the infrastructure. This includes the cost to define information requirements; develop information, application, and technology architectures; and to design and build applications and databases. The value basis of information is the costs of applying information—for example, the costs of applications that access or retrieve data—and to use it to perform work or to solve a business problem. The cost and value basis of information can best be seen in analyzing the resource life cycle.

The Universal Resource Life Cycle

The resource life cycle consists of the set of five processes required to manage any resource. All major resources of an enterprise (people, money, facilities and equipment, materials and products, and information) require these resource life-cycle processes for effective management. Figure 7.1 represents the processes of the resource life cycle.

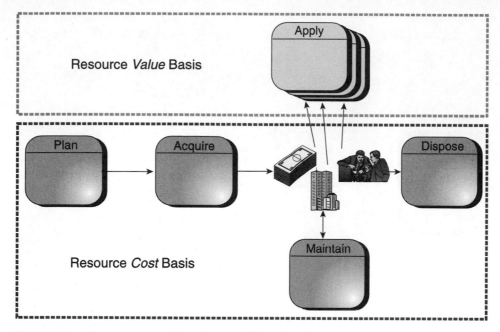

Figure 7.1   Five processes of the resource life cycle.

The five processes of the resource life cycle are:

Plan resource. Resources require planning. They have costs and can be used to create value. Planning is required to optimize the resource; in other words, get the maximum return at the lowest cost.

Acquire resource. Before you can use a resource you must have it.

Maintain resource. Resources require maintenance to keep them at their optimum effectiveness.

Dispose resource. When a resource is no longer needed it is disposed of; else, unnecessary costs are being incurred without corresponding value being produced. Idle resources produce negative value.

Apply resource. Here you use the resource in ways that add value.

The first four processes—*planning, acquisition, maintenance,* and *disposition*—represent the cost basis of the resource. Each of these processes costs money, without producing value. Consider the resource life cycle for people as illustrated in Figure 7.2.

- You *plan* for the people resource to capitalize its value. It begins with the mission and strategies of the enterprise. Having defined them, what skills are required, and at what skill level? How many people are required to accomplish your mission? Tactical planning consists of recruitment planning. Where will you get your people resources?

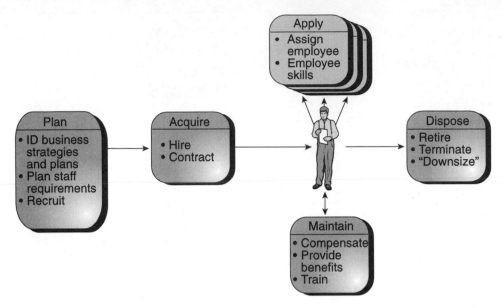

Figure 7.2 Resource life cycle for human resources.

- You *acquire* people resources by hiring permanent employees or contracting labor on a just-in-time basis.

- You *maintain* people resources to keep their value high. They must be paid a fair wage or they soon become ex-employees and contractors. They must be developed and trained to learn the specifics of the work they perform.

- You *dispose* of through retirement, layoffs, or downsizing. While the term *dispose of* is an inappropriate term for this aspect of the most important enterprise resource, you can see the analogy in the resource life cycle.

Each of these four processes incurs *costs*. Human resource planning and recruiting are costs. Hiring has costs. Personnel agencies may take a third of a placed employee's first-year's salary. Signing bonuses are not unheard of. Costs of training, benefits, and salary make up the maintenance costs. Disposition costs include retirement benefits and costs of layoffs or downsizing. When IBM conducted its first-ever layoff of 20,000 employees, it took a charge of $6 billion.

The *value* of human resources lies in the application of people to use their skills to perform their jobs. The value of any resource is in its *use*.

There is an economic formula for enterprise profitability and survival. The economic formula is simple: *Economic Value occurs when the benefit derived from a resource's application is greater than the costs incurred from its planning, acquisition, maintenance, and disposition.*

Financial resources fall into the same life cycle. You must plan for financial resources. What are your strategies? What resources are needed? How much money will be needed (for acquisition, maintenance, and disposition)? Where will you get it? Money acquisition may be in the form of getting a loan or issuing shares of stock. Maintenance is in the form of paying the interest on the loan or paying dividends or increasing stock value. Disposition comes in the repayment of the principal or buying back the stock shares. The value of money is found in its application. Money has value only when it is invested wisely or used to purchase things that add value.

The aggregation of benefit derived from the application of all of the enterprise's resources minus their costs incurred will equal its profit or loss.

The *Information* Resource Life Cycle

If information is a resource, it will follow the same life cycle for effective management. Figure 7.3 illustrates the information resource life cycle in an information-managed resource life cycle. The same five processes hold for information as a resource.

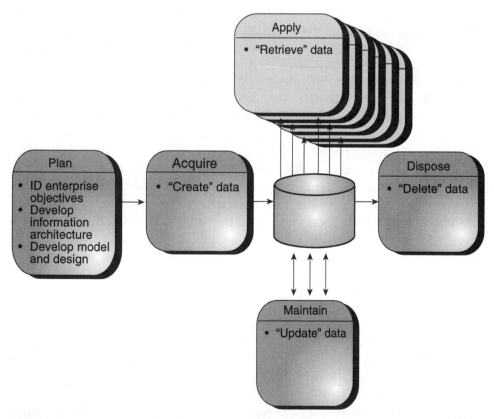

Figure 7.3 Resource life cycle for information resources.

Cost Basis of Information

The cost basis of information is in the same four processes, as described next.

Plan Enterprise Information Requirements

Planning for information begins with understanding the mission, objectives, and strategies of the enterprise. The question, "What do you need to know to accomplish your mission and objectives?", determines the information requirements in the same way human resource planning determines people and skills requirements.

Planning includes modeling and developing information models and physical databases of the required information, modeling and developing the application systems across business value chains that will "acquire" (create), "maintain" (update), "dispose of" (delete), and "apply" (retrieve) the information resource.

Planning represents the *fixed* costs of information. These costs, like manufacturing costs, are incurred before the first fact of information can be acquired and stored electronically for shared use.

Acquire Information

Processes that acquire information are comprised of the business processes and computer applications that "create" data. The application programs that create information are like manufacturing machinery that produces manufactured products.

The business process and application create process may be bound together, as when an order clerk takes a customer's order and enters it into a system electronically. Or the business process and application process may be separate, as when a salesperson takes an order on paper, and an order entry clerk enters that order from the paper form. The real information production occurs when the knowledge is created. In the first example, the order clerk is the actual information producer as far as the enterprise is concerned. This is where the knowledge becomes known in the enterprise. In the second example, the salesperson is the information producer, while the order entry clerk becomes a data intermediary, transcribing the information from paper into a database. Here an additional step adds cost and the potential for introducing error.

Maintain Information

Processes that maintain information are comprised of the business processes and computer applications that "update" data. They are like the processes that keep equipment or facilities maintained. Equipment that is not maintained breaks down and fails. Information that is not maintained when it changes becomes unquality and causes the processes that use it to fail. This phenomenon is called *information quality decay.*

The cost of maintaining information is a cost item. It does not add value directly, but it is required to keep subsequent value-adding processes from failing.

INFORMATION QUALITY DECAY

Information quality decay occurs in information when it is not updated as the facts about the real-world object change. For example, if a company changes prices of products, but fails to update the prices in the database, information quality decay occurs. The quality of the data has decreased. The processes' pricing orders or sales will now fail, causing lost revenue when the price change is an increase, or customer dissatisfaction when the price change is a decrease.

Individual address data has an information quality decay rate of 17 percent per year in the United States, according to the U.S. Postal Service. This means that a customer database without any maintenance processes would see its address data accuracy decrease by about 17 percent per year.

Dispose of Obsolete Information

When information is no longer needed it is disposed of or deleted. Processes and applications that perform these processes make up the resource disposition processes. There may be some value derived by freeing up computer storage and computing resources or physical storage for physical information records. This may be offset, however, by the requirement to archive information required to be maintained due to legal requirements or transforming data to other archived formats, such as CD-ROM, or the cost of shredding or deleting electronic residual traces of sensitive data, as in erasing computer disks.

Performing the create, update, and delete processes and executing the corresponding applications represent the *variable* costs of "information production."

There are two components of the information cost basis: infrastructure development and redundancy costs.

> **Infrastructure development and maintenance costs.** Infrastructure costs are those associated with the development of sharable, reusable information architecture, and the single create, update, and delete programs that capture and maintain information in authoritative record-of-reference databases. Included in infrastructure development are the costs of modeling and building *sharable* databases, and authoritative *sharable* create and maintenance applications.

> Sharable infrastructure costs increase the value of information. By building authoritative record-of-reference databases, you eliminate the need for redundant proprietary data sources.

> **Redundancy development and maintenance costs.** Redundancy costs are those associated with development of the redundant databases that house the same or same kind of data that is maintained in existing record of reference databases. Also included are the costs of redundant applications that create data redundantly and interface programs that transform data from one database to another.

Redundancy costs are the duplicate costs of capturing the same or same kind of information a second or third time, and are described in the section *The Unmanaged Information Life Cycle*, and illustrated in Figure 7.4.

Value Basis of Information

The value basis of any resource is when it is *applied*. Until it is used, any resource only has *potential* value.

Apply Information

Data residing in a database, even if 100 percent complete and 100 percent accurate has no tangible value; it only has *potential* value. Information value comes from its use, not its existence.

Data residing in a single sharable database has more than 43 times the value of the same data residing in 43 redundant databases. The redundancy actually diminishes its value because of costs to capture of interface it 43 times coupled with the costs of inconsistent data that *will* occur in such unmanaged information environments.

The value of any resource is realized when it is used to accomplish something that adds value. The business processes that use information and the computer applications that retrieve information to perform a meaningful process make up the value basis of information. The retrieval of information is the *basis* for value. The realized value comes when it is used to enable automated processes to perform correctly, and when knowledge workers exploit the presented information to perform work and make decisions correctly.

The value of information is increased when the organization *minimizes* the costs of planning, acquisition, maintenance, and disposition of data, and *maximizes* the exploitation of information by using it. One caveat: beware of reducing costs of *planning*. If you fail to *invest* in a well-defined information architecture, you will cripple the knowledge infrastructure that is the foundation for the intelligent learning organization. To maximize information value requires:

- Well-defined information architecture that is designed to meet *all* knowledge worker needs, not just immediate departments or organization units
- Information create processes and applications that acquire *all* data needed about the business events or objects processed, to prevent downstream knowledge workers from having to rediscover and acquire data that was knowable during an earlier process
- Information maintenance processes that update data on the most feasible and timely basis

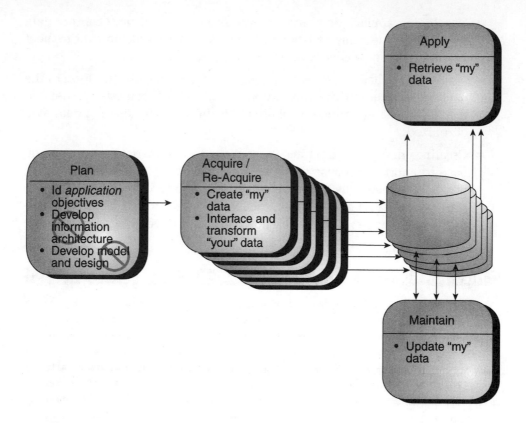

Figure 7.4 Information resource life cycle in the *unmanaged* information environment with high redundancy of databases and interface programs.

The Unmanaged Information Life Cycle

Many organizations, unfortunately, have designed and built legacy applications and databases from a "systems approach" life cycle rather than a resource life cycle. Figure 7.4 illustrates what happens when information is not managed.

The result is significantly increased costs of information by:

- Creating application-specific databases with little or no attention to an enterprise information architecture or downstream knowledge worker's needs. Such databases are generally not widely sharable and data definition tends to be usage specific, rather than inherent. For example, Vendor files designed for Accounts Payable departments will generally only contain data required to pay bills. They may not have the Supplier data required by Purchasing to develop contracts, or data required by Manufacturing, such as ISO 9000 certification information. Even the name "Vendor" denotes a single, functional view of organizations from which supplied materials are essential to the enterprise.

- Developing application-specific create programs that only capture data required for the immediate beneficiaries or departments and not to meet downstream knowledge worker needs.

- Acquiring application software packages without paying attention to the data architecture of the application, resulting in inconsistently defined data from the enterprise databases and difficulty in keeping data synchronized.

- Creating unnecessary interface programs to transform data from one database to another, because the original databases are not sharable or are designed to meet only the departmental needs. Interface applications that retrieve data from one database, transform it, and store it in another database are resource *reacquisition* processes. Interface programs represent

---

THE HIGH COSTS OF NOT MANAGING INFORMATION AS A RESOURCE

Large organizations often have data redundantly stored 10 times or more.

To be sure, there are times when data must exist in multiple databases because of business logistics. This data should be replicated if required to be stored redundantly. If software packages require electronic transformation of data, those interface programs need to be tightly controlled. There is no business case for unnecessary duplication of the only enterprise resource that is nonconsumable. The retrieval or use of information does not consume or destroy it. Every other resource is consumable. Once you spend a sum of money, it is gone. When you assign employees to perform a job, they cannot be assigned to another task. When you use materials to make a product, those materials are consumed. When you hold a meeting in a conference room, no other event can take place in that facility at the same time.

Fundamental management principles applied to all other resources include planning for it to minimize the costs of the resources. If an organization has data stored redundantly 10 times for 10 different applications, it is paying the costs of acquisition, maintenance, and disposition 10 times. If the same principles where applied to other resources, the following would happen:

- **Accounts Payable would pay an invoice 10 times.**
- **Human Resources would hire 10 employees to perform the same job redundantly 10 times.**
- **Purchasing would buy 10 times the raw materials necessary to manufacture a product.**
- **Facilities management would build 10 buildings when only one was needed.**

Think about it. If organizations have 10 times redundancy of information, what costs are being totally wasted? If those same organizations had spent *twice* as much to develop enterprise information, process and application architectures, they would have *80 percent less cost* to develop the same functionality as they have today. Or, with the same development budgets, they could deliver *500 percent more* value.

the redundant reacquisition of a resource the enterprise has already acquired and paid for.

Not only does the unmanaged information environment cost an organization far more than is necessary, it creates complexity and increases the number of points at which information quality problems can occur. Every time an interface program is developed, maintenance or change to the data must be applied *three* times: once to the origination database, once to the interface program, and finally to the target database and application.

Costs of Information Quality

Now that we have described the costs of planning for information, or the costs to develop the capacity to have information, we turn our attention to the costs of information production quality. There are three categories of information quality costs:

Nonquality information costs. These costs of process failure and information scrap and rework are harmful to the enterprise—and they are avoidable.

Information quality assessment or inspection costs. These costs are to assure processes are performing properly. Minimize these costs.

Information quality process improvement and defect prevention costs. The real business payoff is in improving processes that eliminate the costs of poor quality information.

Each of these is described next.

Nonquality Information Costs

These are the costs incurred as a result of missing, inaccurate, untimely, imprecise, not well presented, or misleading or misunderstood information. These costs include:

- Process failure costs
- Information scrap and rework costs
- Lost and missed opportunity costs

Process Failure Costs

Process failure costs result when poor-quality information causes a process to not perform properly. Inaccurate mailing addresses cause correspondence to be misdelivered. Incorrect prices cause customers to be charged the wrong amount, resulting in the cost to issue a credit, or in lost revenue. Process failure cost examples include:

Irrecoverable costs. These are expenditures made in vain, such as the costs of mailing a second catalog to the same person due to duplicate records for the same customer.

Liability and exposure costs. These include actual costs and potential risk. An insurance company had to pay claims sometimes before the policy information created in the policy administration system made its way through the interfaces to the claims database. The volume of claims paid in the absence of policy information were over $30 million a year. This represents their risk. The actual losses incurred as a result of overpayment or payment of ineligible claims was from $3 to 5 million a year. Inaccurate environmental data may put an organization at risk for liability. Inaccurate information about individuals or improper use of information governed by privacy laws can put an organization at risk. Exposure is the potential liability an organization has due to nonquality.

Recovery costs of unhappy customers. If a customer or supplier becomes dissatisfied as a result of information quality problems, an organization may have to provide compensation, spend time to correct a problem or to restore the strained relationship.

Information Scrap and Rework

Like manufacturing scrap and rework, when information is defective, it requires cleansing (rework), or rejecting, or marking as in error (scrap). Information scrap and rework examples include:

Redundant data handling and support costs. If data is not usable from one database, the knowledge workers who have to spend time and money to collect and maintain the data in another database is a scrap-and-rework cost. The original database is "scrapped" and a redundant, and many times private, database is reworked up to the knowledge workers' requirements.

Costs of hunting or chasing missing information. When knowledge workers have to stop their work to go find missing information, they are performing rework of earlier processes that failed to capture the data they need accurately and completely. This is like halting an assembly line to fix a faulty component.

Business rework costs. These are the costs of reperforming processes that failed, such as reissuing a new bank card because of errors on the card itself or reprinting checks because of an incorrect account number. Multiple runs in accounting of "trial balances" until the debits and credits balance is an example. If the data were correct at the source, no trial balances or reruns would be required.

Workaround costs and decreased productivity. Time and money spent in performing alternative work, when nonquality information prevents you from performing the normal case. For example, missing or inaccurate diagnostic information may require a doctor to have to order additional tests on a patient.

Data verification costs. When knowledge workers cannot trust the data, they have to perform their own "quality inspection." Because they are further removed from the source, it takes them longer, sometimes 5 to 10 times longer to get back to the information source to verify its accuracy.

Software rewrite costs. The costs to fix application programs when they fail, recover from the problems caused, and rerun the programs.

Data cleansing and correction costs. While there is value in information *product* improvement, just like the value of manufacturing rework, the costs are unnecessary if the information was correctly created and maintained.

Data cleansing software costs. The costs of software to cleanse data from a source database fall into this category. The costs of software that can be invoked by data create and update applications falls in the category of defect prevention costs, described later.

Lost and Missed Opportunity Costs

Lost and missed opportunity is the revenue and profit not realized because of poor information quality. These costs must be analyzed not just in light of immediate sales lost. It must be examined from the standpoint of customer lifetime value. Customer lifetime value is the average profitability of a customer over his or her life of relationship with an organization. Customer lifetime value is valuable measure of the costs of nonquality information and is described later in this chapter in steps 4 and 5 in the section, *Measure Nonquality Information Costs: Process Steps*.

Opportunity costs include:

Lost opportunity costs. Lost opportunity occurs when you alienate and lose a customer. If you misspell customers' names or incorrectly bill them, and they go to the competition, you have lost their future revenue.

Missed opportunity costs. In addition to losing an unhappy customer's lifetime value, you may have also missed some prospects they influence. But missed opportunity also includes many other areas. For example, lack of accurate profile information may cause prospects to be omitted from a mailing campaign in which they may be highly interested. Lack of accurate trend information may lead product developers to miss a new product idea until it is too late to enter the market. Or, inaccurate economic data may be the basis for a failed campaign made in a new market that, with accurate information, would not have been attempted.

Lost shareholder value. Accounting data errors and other information quality problems that create unexpected surprises in the stock markets have caused share prices to decrease—in some cases over 50 percent of value—in a short period of time. But the real loss in shareholder value comes from the result of the drain of profits resulting from information scrap and rework and lost opportunity caused by nonquality information.

Assessment or Inspection Costs

The costs to assess information quality are inspection costs. The purpose of assessment is to assure processes are performing properly. Assessment in and of itself does not add value; it is a cost item. It must lead to process improvement to have value.

The solution to any kind of quality problem is not to add a step that checks quality for defects to correct. This adds time and inspection costs to the value chain. The solution is to improve the processes to prevent defects. The objective for assessment is to minimize the costs of the actual assessment. Using statistical sampling of data and effective sampling and measurement techniques, you can maximize the value of information quality assessment.

Assessment costs include:

Information quality analysis software costs. The costs of software to analyze and measure information quality fall here.

People time in the assessment processes. This includes time in conducting both automated and physical information quality assessments.

While assessment is a cost item, what you do with the results can add value. By providing timely feedback to information producers, assessment information can be a stimulus for process improvement and error reduction. By providing interpreted assessment information to the knowledge workers using databases or data warehouses, they know the reliability of the information and can factor that into their usage and decision-making.

Process Improvement and Defect Prevention Costs

Investments made in process improvement to prevent defects yield the highest benefits to the enterprise. An interesting phenomenon is that requests to establish an information quality program are met with requests for cost justification of the new initiative—and rightfully so. However, the real cost justification must be made for the first category of costs: the costs that result from not creating and maintaining quality information in the first place.

THE BUSINESS CASE FOR INFORMATION QUALITY

The fundamental business case for an information quality improvement initiative is not, "What is the business case for information quality improvement?" but rather, "What is the business case for the costs of resulting from information scrap and rework in the status quo?"

The cost justification for information quality initiatives is made from analyzing and quantifying the costs of nonquality information. You must know the costs of the status quo. These costs of process failure, business rework, decreased productivity, redundancy upon redundancy, have been accepted by businesses as a "normal cost of doing business." When management recognizes that the costs of information scrap and rework, process failure, and lost and missed opportunity are crippling the bottom line, changes will be made.

Measure Nonquality Information Costs: Process Steps

The steps for measuring nonquality information costs are illustrated in Figure 7.5. They are described individually next.

Step 1: Identify Business Performance Measures

Information has value to the extent it enables the enterprise to accomplish its mission and objectives. To measure information costs and value, you must begin the business performance measures of the enterprise. The bottom line of any for-profit organization is to make a profit while accomplishing its mission and objectives. The business case for information quality improvement is established by documenting how poor information quality decreases profits and how improving information quality increases profits.

The objective is to identify the basis for valuing and costing information.

Inputs

- Business vision and mission
- Business plans and strategies
- Strategic business objectives

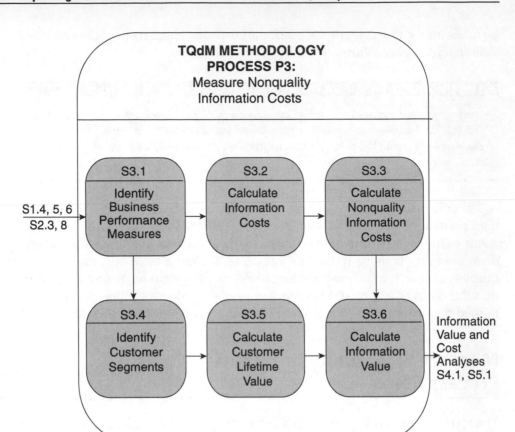

Figure 7.5 Process steps to measure information costs and nonquality information costs.

Outputs

- Business performance measures

Techniques and Tools

- Repository, data dictionary, or modeling software

A general description of these and other techniques and tools is found in Chapter 10, "Information Quality Tools and Techniques," and on the Internet at www.infoimpact.com: select the *Information Quality Resources* button for descriptions of products, techniques, and best practice case studies.

Process Definition

The only reason for spending money on information is because it is a resource required to accomplish the mission and objectives of the enterprise.

1. Identify the *enterprise* business performance objectives. While some tactical objectives are useful, the key to sustainable information quality initiatives is when they create value at the enterprise level. A short list of objectives might include some of the following:

   a. Accomplish mission

   b. Increase profits

   c. Reduce costs

   d. Reduce cycle time

   e. Increase quality

   f. Increase customer satisfaction

   g. Increase employee satisfaction

   h. Increase productivity

   i. Increase market share

   j. Increase shareholder value

2. Select those measures that are most significantly hindered as a result of poor quality information.

3. Define how these performance objectives are measured. You must use the same measurements for calculating the impact of nonquality information on hindering the accomplishment of business objectives.

This becomes the basis for steps 2 and 3.

Step 2: Calculate Information Costs

This step analyzes the costs of the information resource itself. It includes both the fixed and variable costs of information.

The objective is to identify what percent of information systems and data development and maintenance is value-adding and what percent is cost-adding only in order to improve information systems productivity and effectiveness. This step determines the relative amount of costs of application and data development in the three categories of information development expense: infrastructure, value basis, and cost-adding basis.

Inputs

- Business performance measures
- Application portfolio
- Database inventory

Outputs

- Information development cost analysis (see Figure 7.6)

Techniques and Tools

- Repository, data dictionary, and modeling software
- Catalogs and information directories
- Cost analysis
- Spreadsheets

Process Definition

This process analyzes the costs of developing information systems in three categories:

Infrastructure basis or investment. These are the costs of developing reusable databases and applications that create and maintain the information resources.

Value basis. These are the costs associated with the access and retrieval of information for use to add value. Such uses include accessing information to perform a process, create a report, analyze the business, or support a decision.

Cost-adding. These are the costs of redundancy of both application and data development and maintenance, including redundant databases, redundant create and update applications and interfaces.

1. Count or estimate of the number of application programs in the production portfolio. This includes application software packages as well as internally developed applications and applications developed and operated by outsourcing organizations. This includes interface and extract applications. This provides a quick inventory of how many applications exist.

TIP Reuse the inventory of application programs and databases compiled from the Year 2000 projects. This should be an exhaustive inventory.

2. Determine the relative percent of application programs that are create only, retrieve only, or a combination of retrieve some data in order to create other data. This provides a way to differentiate between the data acquisition costs, or the costs basis of information from the retrieval costs, or the value basis of information.

3. For programs that retrieve some data in order to create other data, calculate the relative percent of data retrieved only (the value basis) and the percent of data created or updated.

TIP To calculate the relative percent of a program that both creates or updates, and retrieves data, take a statistically valid random sample of 30 to 50 programs that both retrieve some data and create other data. For example, an Order Entry program will retrieve `Customer` and `Product` data and then create an `Order`. Count the number of fields that are either created or updated in a program. Count the number of fields that are retrieved only.

4. Count or estimate of the number of database tables or other files in the production environment. This provides a quick inventory of how many database tables or other files exist.

5. Determine the total Information Systems annual budget for development and maintenance of applications and databases, including acquisition of software and hardware over the typical life of applications, such as 10 years. This excludes production operations and operations support. The figures represent the Resource planning costs, not the cost of operating the applications and databases.

TIP Use net present value when calculating past years' budgets. If actual budget data is not available, use reliable estimates.

6. Determine the relative percent of application programs in three categories: infrastructure, value, and cost-adding basis.

 - Infrastructure basis or investment. These include:
   - Reusable, record-of-reference database files including *replicated* databases. Independently maintained redundant databases are excluded. For example, if there are 15 independently maintained Customer files containing some overlapping Customer data such as customer-name, only one of those files is the record-of-reference file. The others are redundant, even if they contain different attributes about Customer and even if they are not accessible by all applications or knowledge workers. The other 14 files are counted in the cost-adding basis.
   - Authoritative, source applications (one for each entity type, such as `Customer`) that create and maintain the information resources.
   - The first strategic extract or interface program for a given data type. This is an extract of operational data to propagate data to a *data warehouse* to support strategic and decision processes. If there are 15 Customer files merged into the data warehouse, the first extract and transformation program falls into this category. The other 14 are classified in the cost-adding basis. The reason? If there were only one sharable or standardly defined database, only one extract would be required.

- Value basis. These include:
  - Application programs that access and retrieve information to perform a process. For programs that both retrieve data and create/update it, take the relative average percent of retrieved data calculated in activity 3 and multiply that times the number of applications in this category.
  - Report programs.
  - Query programs.
  - Data analysis programs to determine business patterns or trends.
  - Decision support application programs.
- Cost-adding basis. These include:
  - Redundant databases. The second and subsequent databases about a single entity type represent redundant files. Because electronically recorded data stored is completely reusable and nonconsumable, all redundant copies create additional costs. This does not include replicated databases.

TIP Note that some redundancy may be cost justified. Data stored in pre-relational database technology may not be generally accessible to all operational processes. Extracting this data to an open, accessible database makes this data generally available to knowledge workers and is sharable. However, the requirement for storing the data in two places does, in fact, represent additional costs of storage, backup, processing, and data integrity management that are not incurred if the data were maintained and shared out of a single database.

- Redundant applications that create and update data. For example, if there are 10 application programs that create and update data about a single entity type, such as Product, then 9 of them are redundant, even if there may be some different Product fields in the different files.
- Interface and extract programs. This includes all interface programs that extract data from one operational database file, possibly transforming it, and storing it in another operational database. This also includes the second and subsequent redundant strategic interface programs that extract data from operational databases, and storing it into data warehouses or data marts.

7. Aggregate these cost estimates into an Information Development Cost Report, illustrated in Figure 7.6. This report analyzes a development environment of 3800 application programs and database files with development and maintenance costs of $50 million over a 10-year period.

Category	Portfolio Total Number	Relative Weight Factor*	Average Unit Dev/Maint Costs	Total Development/Maintenance Expenses**	Total Infrastructure/Value-Adding/Cost-Adding Expenses	% of Budget Expenses
Infrastructure Basis:						
Enterprise architected DBs	200	0.75	$15,000	$3,000,000		
Enterprise reusable create/update pgms +	300	1.5	$30,000	$9,000,000		
Total Infrastructure expenses					$12,000,000	24%
Value Basis:						
Total retrieve equivalent pgms+	300	1.00	$20,000	$6,000,000		
Total value-adding expenses					$6,000,000	12%
Cost-Adding Basis:						
Redundant create/update pgms	500	1.50	$30,000	$15,000,000		
Interface/extract programs	400	1.00	$20,000	$8,000,000		
Redundant database files	600	0.75	$15,000	$9,000,000		
Total cost-adding expenses	1,500				$32,000,000	64%
Lifetime Total**	**3,800**				**$50,000,000**	**100%**

* Determine relative effort to develop average unit of each category using effort to develop a retrieve program as "1.00"

\+ For programs that retrieve some data and create / update other data, determine the percent of retrieve only attributes and percent of create / update attributes (e.g., to retrieve customer data to create an order)

** Based on 3,800 application programs and database files in portfolio and $50 million in development

Figure 7.6 Information development cost analysis.

TIP The relative weight factor used here is based on experience that create and update programs require 50 percent more effort than retrieval programs, and that database files require 25 percent less effort than developing a retrieval program. Your experience may vary. You should determine your own ratios based on time studies or facilitated brainstorming.

8. Create a column chart to illustrate the relative costs of development divided into infrastructure, value basis, and cost-adding categories. Figure 7.7 illustrates an example of the report listed in Figure 7.6.

9. Relate the costs of information to the business performance measures. Is the money spent in information technology, data, and applications being spent as an investment in reusable architectures that can support long-term business strategy, or in short-term quick wins that create redundancy and high maintenance?

This represents the *quality* of application development in the form of building reusable components. Reuse is a measure of quality of databases and applications.

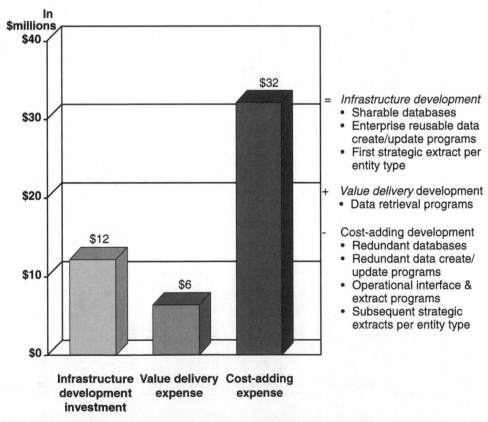

Figure 7.7   Information development costs by value-centric category.

Step 3: Calculate Nonquality Information Costs

This step identifies the costs of poor-quality information in the form of bottom-line drain and in the form of how it hinders the accomplishment of the business objectives.

The objective is to quantify, in bottom-line currency figures, the cost of non-quality information to assess the business impact of information quality problems, raise awareness of the importance of information management, and establish a benchmark for measuring information quality initiatives.

Inputs

- Business performance measures
- Information group
- Process-to-data matrix
- Information value and cost chain
- Business case studies and anecdotes

Outputs

- Nonquality information cost analysis

Techniques and Tools

- Cost analysis
- Time and motion analysis
- Spreadsheet

Process Definition

This process identifies the categories of costs of poor-quality information and calculates the costs of information scrap and rework.

1. For the data to be analyzed, review the information value and cost chain and the process-to-data matrix. See step 3 in Chapter 6, "Information Quality Assessment." If this does not exist, develop a matrix of processes to the information groups whose costs are to be analyzed (see Figure 7.8).

2. With the subject matter experts of each process, identify the impact of missing or inaccurate data in relative terms. These may be high, medium,

Information Groups \ Processes	Customer Name Group	Customer Address Group	Customer Profile Group	Product Description Group	Product Price Group	Product Inventory Group	Order Group
Marketing Campaign	H	H	H	M	M	M	NA
Sales	L	M	M	M	H	H	NA
Order Fulfillment	M	H	NA	NA	NA	H	H
Invoicing							
Payment Application							
Product Performance							
Customer Analysis							
. . .							

Legend: H = High; M = Medium; L = Low; NA = Not Applicable

Figure 7.8   Information to process impact analysis.

low, or not applicable, in which the process does not use the data and is not affected by poor quality problems (see Figure 7.8).

3. Select the high- and medium-impacted processes for cost analysis.

4. Interview the information producers and knowledge workers in the information value chain to identify what happens when there are data defects, and what they must do. See the kinds of costs-of-process failure and information scrap and rework described earlier in the section, *Nonquality Information Costs*.

5. Explore what resources are consumed using the following checklist. For each instance of data error, determine how much time and other resources are consumed. This can be done informally by interviewing information producers and knowledge workers. However, it can be more accurately calculated through time and motion analysis, in which you observe the scrap and rework time or process recovery by observing and timing the actual processes.

❏ Time resources:
  ❏ Business personnel
  ❏ Information systems personnel

❏ Money resources:
  ❏ Direct payments and credits
  ❏ Fines
  ❏ Future revenue lost or missed

❏ Materials resources:
  ❏ Raw materials consumed
  ❏ Products scrapped

❏ Supply or support materials consumed

❏ Facilities and equipment resources:

   ❏ Space requirements

   ❏ Equipment

❏ Computing resources:

   ❏ CPU resource time

   ❏ Network and communication

   ❏ Data storage

6. Determine the cost rate for the various categories of resource.

TIP **Many of these resources will have rates established by their respective management offices. The Human Resources department will generally have loaded rates for personnel time. Facilities Management will have the rates for facilities by the square foot or meter. Information Systems will generally have the average CPU, communication, and data storage cost of a transaction and record.**

Keep your measures simple. Good estimates will suffice. For example, every job may have a loaded rate. Rather than use this precisely, use two or three general rates; for example, clerical time, professional and first-line management, and senior professional and senior management time. Simply document the source and assumptions of your cost figures. If the figures are challenged, you can defend or adjust them. Involve subject matter experts to set cost rates.

7. Determine the number of instances of error per some time period. This may be done through the information interview process, or it may have been established in an information quality assessment as described in the previous chapter.

8. For each process, calculate the costs for each component of cost and annualize them. Figure 7.9 represents a case study of address errors in 36.0 percent of a database of 1 million address records. Figure 7.10 represents the analysis of costs of this quality of data on the process of conducting a marketing campaign.

Total Address Records	Duplicate Customers	Duplicate Customer Percent	Missing Data Count	Missing Data Percent	Data Error Count	Data Error Percent	Total Nonquality Count	Total Nonquality Percent
1,092,431	167,142	15.3%	44,790	4.1%	181,341	16.6%	393,273	36.0%

Figure 7.9 Nonquality information costs case study.

Marketing Campaign	Per Instance	Number Instances	Total Number Per Year	Total Cost Per Year
* Time: ($60/hour loaded rate)				
– Creating redundant occurrences	2.4 min	167,141	1	$401,138
– Researching correct address	10 min	5,000/mo	12	$600,000
– Correcting address errors	0.3 min	6,000/mo	12	$21,600
– Handling complaints from customers	5.5 min	974/yr	1	$5,357
– Mail preparation	0.1 min	393,273	4	$157,309
* Money				
– Credits to customers	—	—	—	—
– Fines	—	—	—	—
* Materials				
– Marketing brochure	$1.96	393,273	4	$3,083,260
– Postage	$0.52	393,273	4	$818,008
* Facilities and Equipment				
– Warehouse storage	$0.01	393,273	4	$15,731
– Shipping equipment and maintenance	$5,000/yr	36.0%	1	$1,800
* Computing resource				
– CPU transactions	$0.02/trans	393,273	4	$31,462
– Network	—			
– Data storage	$0.001/mo	393,273	12	$4,719
– Data backup	$0.005/mo	393,273	12	$23,596
Total Annual Costs				**$5,163,980**

Figure 7.10 Analysis of direct costs of nonquality information in the marketing campaign process.

9. Aggregate all costs for a given information group across its major processes. Document the degree of completeness of the study. For example, you may analyze 40 percent of the processes that make up 80 percent of the costs on nonquality information. The other 60 percent of the processes will comprise only 20 percent of the total costs of nonquality for this information group (see Figure 7.11). Extrapolate the costs estimated from the unstudied processes, and document your assumptions. This gives an intelligent estimate of the total costs of nonquality for this information group.

10. Continue this process for other information groups to be analyzed.

11. Determine the percent of data and processes analyzed for costs of nonquality data. Extrapolate the relative nonquality information costs of information other than what you studied, based on your findings. Involve the stakeholder business subject matter experts in this calculation. You can draw some meaningful estimates.

Data Groups \ Processes	Customer Name Group	Customer Address Group	Customer Profile Group	Product Description Group	Product Price Group	Product Inventory Group	Order Group	Total
Marketing Campaign	. . .	$5,163,980						
Sales	. . .	$4,675,000						
Order Fulfillment		$2,422,600						
Invoicing		$1,821,100						
Payment Application		$0						
Product Performance		$0						
Customer Analysis		$250,200						
. . .								
Total		$14,332,880						$14,332,880

Figure 7.11   Nonquality information cost report.

12. Develop an analysis of your findings along with the assumptions that make up the study. This background provides the support of the figures reported and estimated.

   This represents the direct costs of nonquality information. Next we analyze the indirect costs of lost and missed opportunity.

Step 4: Identify Customer Segments

This step identifies groups of customers that tend to have common tendencies and common customer lifetime value. The objective is to identify meaningful groups of customers to be valued. This provides a customer segment to establish customer lifetime value. It also provides the basis for measuring the costs of nonquality information in terms of lost and missed customer lifetime value.

Inputs

- Customer segment lists and definitions, if any

Outputs

- Customer segment profile

Techniques and Tools

- Facilitated brainstorming

Process Definition

This process identifies meaningful segments of customers for customer lifetime value analysis.

1. Identify any existing customer segment lists. The marketing and sales departments may already have this segmentation. Most organizations have ways of identifying their "most profitable" customers or distinct groups. For example, airlines have their frequent flyer groups and have them differentiated into different "elite" categories based upon mileage which, of course, translates into different customer lifetime values for each customer segment. Retailers have their "frequent shopper groups." Institutional customers may be segmented into a top-10 or major account customers. Utilities have commercial and residential consumer segments.

TIP Keep this task short and simple. Focus on the highest value segment first.

If no customer segmentation exists, and customers tend to be relatively homogenous, use the entire customer population for customer lifetime value.

2. Document the characteristics or profile of the customer segments. This allows you to extract samples of each segment.

TIP Multidivisional organizations may have customer segments by division. Seek to identify relationships of customers and segments across divisions where pertinent. Enterprisewide customer segmentation can open significant areas of cross-divisional marketing and customer relationship opportunities.

Step 5: Calculate Customer Lifetime Value

This step analyzes the average revenue and profit of a typical customer in a customer segment over the life of relationship with the organization. The objective is to establish a meaningful hard currency metric by which to value customers and determine information value. This establishes a baseline for measuring the impact of nonquality data.

Inputs

- Segmented customer profile
- Sales history database(s)

Outputs

■ Segmented customer lifetime value table

Techniques and Tools

■ Random sampling
■ Data extract tools
■ Spreadsheet

Process Definition

This process extracts customer sales data from a sample of customers to calculate average revenue and profit for a customer segment.

1. Define customer lifetime value and the derivation formula for your organization. Customer lifetime *profit* is the important measure. Some organizations, however, use it to refer to total sales. Some organizations identify this value as the total value of a customer independent of their sales. For example, Sewell Cadillac, in Dallas, Texas, knows that a typical customer of luxury cars, will purchase 13 automobiles over their "lifetime" of driving. Their definition includes total possible revenue to be derived from this customer segment. Two books, both entitled *Strategic Database Marketing*, one by Arthur Hughes, the other by Rob Jackson and Paul Wang, are excellent references for examining the makeup of customer lifetime value. They are referenced in the bibliography to this book. Figure 7.12 illustrates a template of customer lifetime value.

   The template is divided into three sections: revenue, expenses, and profits, with a running total customer lifetime value over five periods of time. These may be yearly periods or other meaningful time periods. Both revenue and expenses are accumulated over the lifetime using a discount rate to calculate net present value revenue and expenses. Customer lifetime value is the net profit over a five-year lifetime.

   TIP For the discount rate for calculating net present value, use the figures used in your Accounting department. This may be a constant percent, or each previous year may have an actual percent based on inflation for that year.

   Figure 7.13 is an example of calculating customer lifetime value. This is the result of the following step activities.

2. Determine your organization's cost-of-goods-sold (sometimes abbreviated COGS) percents or calculation to calculate expenses. If possible,

	Period 1	Period 2	Period 3	Period 4	Period 5
Revenue					
New Customers					
Repeat Customers					
Retention Rate					
Average Period Sales					
Total Revenue					
Discount Rate					
NPV Revenue					
Cumulative Revenue					
Customer Lifetime Revenue					
Expenses					
Non-Customer Acquisition Cost %					
Non-Customer Acquisition Costs					
Customer Acquisition Cost %					
Customer Acquisition Costs					
Customer Relationship Cost %					
Customer Relationship Costs					
Total Costs					
Discount Rate					
NPV Costs					
Profits					
NPV Profit					
Cumulative NPV Profit					
Customer Lifetime Value					

Figure 7.12   Customer lifetime value template.

separate out the first-time customer acquisition costs from customer retention costs and from overhead and manufacturing cost-of-sales. This is valuable information for analyzing the importance of customer relationships and customer satisfaction focus.

The example in Figure 7.13 has noted that first-time customer acquisition costs account for 26 percent of the cost-of-sales. Customer retention costs for the second and subsequent periods are only 6 percent of sales. This means there is an extra profit of 20 percent from sales to already acquired customers. Noncustomer cost-of-sales is a constant 40 percent of sales. It represents the costs of manufacturing and overhead as a percent of sales.

TIP For customer acquisition and retention costs, see your marketing and sales department. Accounting or manufacturing may have the cost-of-goods sold with a breakdown of the cost categories. Use your enterprise cost breakdown figures.

	Period 1	Period 2	Period 3	Period 4	Period 5
Revenue	1991	1992	1993	1994	1995
New Customers	1000				
Repeat Customers		400	180	90	50
Retention Rate		40%	45%	50%	55%
Average Period Sales	$1,500	$1,500	$1,500	$1,500	$1,500
Total Revenue	$1,500,000	$600,000	$270,000	$135,000	$75,000
Discount Rate	0.66	0.73	0.81	0.90	1.00
NPV Revenue	$2,272,727	$821,918	$333,333	$150,000	$75,000
Cumulative Revenue	$2,272,727	$3,094,645	$3,427,978	$3,577,978	$3,652,978
Customer Lifetime Revenue	$2,273	$3,095	$3,428	$3,578	$3,653
Expenses					
Non-Customer Acquisition Cost %	40%	40%	40%	40%	40%
Non-Customer Acquisition Costs	$600,000	$240,000	$108,000	$54,000	$30,000
Customer Acquisition Cost %	26%				
Customer Acquisition Costs	$390,000				
Customer Relationship Cost %		6%	6%	6%	6%
Customer Relationship Costs		$36,000	$16,200	$8,100	$4,500
Total Costs	$990,000	$276,000	$124,200	$62,100	$34,500
Discount Rate	0.66	0.73	0.81	0.90	1.00
NPV Costs	$1,500,000	$378,082	$153,333	$69,000	$34,500
Profits					
NPV Profit	$772,727	$443,836	$180,000	$81,000	$40,500
Cumulative NPV Profit	$772,727	$1,216,563	$1,396,563	$1,477,563	$1,518,063
Customer Lifetime Value	$773	$1,217	$1,397	$1,478	$1,518

Figure 7.13 Customer lifetime value example.

3. Select the customer segment to be analyzed.

4. Identify the customer sales databases from which data will be extracted. See process step 1 in Chapter 8, "Information *Product* Improvement: Data Reengineering and Cleansing" to identify the source files. In multidivisional organizations, there may be separate sales databases. Customers may exist in multiple databases.

5. Determine the typical lifetime period of that customer segment. For retail customers, this may be relatively short, from 3 to 5 years. When Kimberly-Clark introduced its Huggies diapers, they knew their customer lifetime value. A parent spent on average some $1,300 for diapers for each baby over a 2- to 3-year "lifetime." For organizational customers, the lifetime may be 10 years or longer.

6. Extract a random sample of from 1000 to 3000 customers within the custom segment from the earliest sales period of all sales. Calculate their total

and average sales. Calculate their acquisition costs and nonacquisition costs from percentages. If possible, select customers who are first-time buyers that year.

In the example in Figure 7.13, 1000 customer records were extracted from sales five years earlier. The total sales of $1.5 million were discounted by an annual 10 percent discount rate compounded over five years. The net present value of the total sales resulted in a net present value of $2,273 per customer. Using the defined percents of acquisition costs and nonacquisition costs, the calculated net-present-value expenses subtracted from the revenue results in a profit of $773 per customer.

TIP Duplicate customer records will skew customer lifetime value results. Make every effort to identify and consolidate customer sales data to eliminate this. See Chapter 8, process steps 2–5, for how to consolidate data.

A shortcut is to take the customers in the random sample and attempt to match any duplicates within the sales files and across multiple sales files from different divisions or product lines if sales are handled differently. Estimate the percent of duplication and adjust the customer lifetime value accordingly. If there is 10 percent duplication, 1000 records represents only 900 customers. After calculating the customer lifetime value for the 1000 records (without de-duping them) divide the final lifetime value calculation by 90 percent to reflect the actual value.

7. Take the randomly selected customers and extract only their sales data from each of the next four periods. From this you calculate the number of repeat customers and the retention percent. Derive their total and average revenue and total expenses, discounted by the compounded discount rate and their accumulated profit. The final year or period results in the customer lifetime value.

   Note that the profits are calculated against the original 1000 customers in this example. This represents the average customer lifetime value within the segment.

The customer lifetime value figure will be used to calculate lost and missed opportunity due to poor information quality. It is also most useful in understanding the importance of customer satisfaction and its role in profit. In the example, the profit rate on first-year sales is only 34 percent of sales due to the high customer acquisition costs of 26 percent. Subsequent sales result in a 54-percent profit margin due to the lower customer retention costs of 6 percent. Increasing efforts in customer relationship management 2 percent (from 6 percent to 8 percent) may decrease the profit margin to 52 percent, but increase customer retention by an additional 10 percent (from 40 to 50 percent in the second year). The result would be a *20.4 percent increase* in *profits* in the second year alone and an overall increase in customer lifetime value (profit) of 18.4 percent, to $1,798.

Step 6: Calculate Information Value

There are many ways to calculate information value. One is replacement value. How much would it cost to replace a set of information if it were destroyed and could not be restored electronically? Another is market value. How much would information be worth if it were sold to a third party, such as a competitor or other stakeholder?

Information value may be *actual* or *potential*. Actual value reflects the benefits derived from the current use of information. Potential value represents the increased value of a set of information were it to be used in new or different ways from its current use.

Here we address information value in its role in lost and missed customer lifetime value and the exposure or risk an organization faces due to inaccurate information. This calculation is not just the value of customer information, but all information that influences customers. For example, omission of product information in a catalog misses the opportunity of any sales. Incorrect billing or pricing data may alienate customers and cause them to move to a competitor. Lack of access to customer-complaint data may cause an overzealous sales rep to further offend complaining customers and drive them away.

The objective is to establish the relative importance of information to the business and to establish an economic justification for information quality improvement.

Inputs

- Information group
- Customer lifetime value
- Nonquality information cost report
- Customer complaint data

Outputs

- Information value, and lost and missed opportunity cost analysis

Techniques and Tools

- Facilitated sessions
- Spreadsheet

Process Definition

Calculate the lost and missed sales and profit opportunity and organizational exposure or risk as a result of poor-quality information.

1. Select the processes analyzed in step 3 to calculate missed customer lifetime value due to poor-quality information. These include customer-intensive processes such as marketing, sales, and invoicing. Other missed opportunities include casual customer contacts in which employees fail to capture updated knowledge or corrected facts about customers.

2. Establish the number of instances or percent of customer opportunities missed.

   The example cited earlier in Figure 7.9 represents missed opportunity. The duplicate address rate of 15.3 percent means 167,141 catalogs were not sent to potential customers. The 20.7 percent address error rate means that 226,131 catalogs did not reach the intended prospect. The result is new customer lifetime value from these misdirected catalogs can be calculated using the response rate and customer lifetime value figures.

3. Calculate the missed customer lifetime value by multiplying the number of *new* customers not acquired as a result.

   Figure 7.14 shows the calculation of missed opportunity in the form of missed customer lifetime value. Based on a response rate of 1.5 percent from the target audience, and a 0.4 percent response rate from the misdirected catalogs, there were 2487 missed first-time customers (1.5–0.4, or 1.1 percent missed response rate times 226,131 misdirected catalogs). 2487 missed customers times a customer lifetime value of $1,518 results in missed customer lifetime *profits* of $3,775,266.

Information Value	
Catalogs mailed	1,092,431
– Duplicate addresses (15.3%)	167,142
– Wrong/missing address (20.7%)	226,131
– Total catalogs "scrapped"	393,273
– Costs per catalog	$2.61
Non-recoverable costs	**$1,026,443**
Response rate of target customers	1.5%
Response rate of "missed" prospects	0.4%
Missed customer opportunity rate	1.1%
Misdirected catalogs	226,131
Missed first-time customers	2,487
Customer lifetime value	$1,518
Missed customer lifetime value	**$3,775,266**

Figure 7.14   Missed opportunity costs due to nonquality information.

4. Identify sources of customer complaint data to document lost customer lifetime value. There is a direct relationship between customer complaints and customer attrition, and with it, lost profits. Customer service organizations, help desks, and other points of contact with customers should have complaint data in databases.

5. Classify customer complaints that have information quality as a component. Examples include billing errors, name misspelling, wrong addresses or multiple addresses not updated when a customer has informed you of a change, unclear customer procedures or instructions, incorrect prices or product information.

6. Count the number of complaints that have an information quality component.

7. Determine the attrition rate of customers who have complained. This may already be known in the customer service or marketing organization.

Every industry tends to have distinct patterns of customer attrition. The variables include the economic magnitude of the complaint and how the organization handles the complaining customers. Figure 7.15 represents the retail industry average as established in a TARP study. Minor complaints consist of a value less than $5, and major complaints have a value to the customer of more than $100. The first three columns describe attrition percentages based on how an organization handles the customer's complaint. While you still may lose customers, the faster you deal with it and resolve it, the lower the attrition. The fourth column represents the attrition of those who have a complaint but do not tell you. They have the highest attrition, 9 out of 10 if it is a major complaint, and 6 out of 10 if it is a trivial complaint. More significantly, a full 96 percent of retail customers fall into this category. While they are not telling you of their complaints, they tell an average of 8 to 10 others about it, influencing your existing and prospective customers.

8. Calculate the number of lost customers due to information quality-related complaints by multiplying the complaining-customer attrition rate times the number of complaints. Figure 7.16 illustrates an example. Of all the complaints listed in the example, the percent of complaints with an information component is 49.5 percent. Experience shows a 40 percent attrition rate for complaining customers.

9. Calculate the number of lost customers by multiplying the noncomplaining customer attrition rate times the estimated number of noncomplaining customers. The estimated attrition rate is 75 percent. Notice how a relatively small number of complaints a year (972, of which 482 are information related) results in lost customer lifetime value of over $14 million annually.

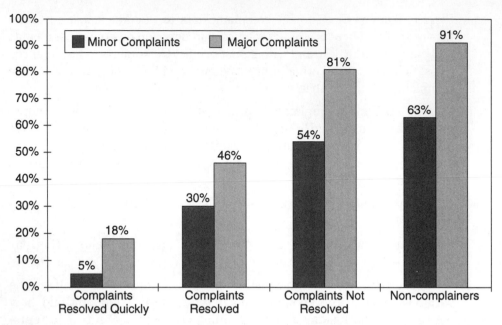

Figure 7.15 How many of your customers with a complaint will *not* buy from you again.
Source: TARP.

TIP Document your assumptions and calculations for estimating your organization's experience. Involve the business in these estimations. Use as much real data as you can.

Be conservative.

10. Report the information to the sponsors of change.

TIP Use this data to establish the information quality standards for each information group.

		Per Year
Total Customer Complaints		974
Customer complaints involving IQ problems	49.5%	482
Ratio of complaints to "non-complaints"	1:26 (Retail Industry avg.)	
Non-complainers with complaints	482 x 26	12,532
Total customers with complaints		13,014
Complainer attrition	40% (x482)	193
Non-complainer attrition	75% (x12,532)	9,399
Total lost customers		9,592
Customer Lifetime Value		$1,518
Opportunity Costs of IQ problems		$14,560,656

Figure 7.16 Lost opportunity costs due to nonquality information.

Conclusion

Measuring the costs and value of information serves to translate the extent of information quality problems and translate them to their impact on the bottom line. Pareto charts and statistical control charts of the incidents of information quality problems are meaningful to information quality improvement teams, but they are irrelevant in the executive office and to the board of directors. Pareto charts of the costs and missed opportunity caused by poor information quality will speak volumes. Statistical control charts of increased revenue and profits generated as a result of improved information quality will sustain information quality improvement initiatives as a business management tool.

Early experience indicates that the direct costs alone of poor information quality may well consume from 15 to 25 percent of revenue or operating budget expenditures. This is based on a number of cost analyses conducted by the author, and is corroborated by the experiences of Deming, Juran, Imai, Crosby, and others in manufacturing and service quality.

Until you quantify these costs as costs of nonquality information, management may continue to perceive them as normal costs of doing business—until leading-edge companies raise the bar by eliminating these costs and exploiting the opportunities through high-quality information.

Information *Product* Improvement: Data Reengineering and Cleansing

"After the first four years, the dirt doesn't get any worse."
–QUENTIN CRISP, *THE NAKED CIVIL SERVANT*

Data reengineering and cleansing is the process of information *product* improvement. It serves to take existing data that is defective and correct the deficiencies to bring it to an acceptable level of quality. This process of information "scrap and rework" is similar to the process of manufacturing scrap and rework. Like a defective manufactured product that requires rework to correct the defects, missing or incorrect data requires rework to be cleansed. Data that cannot be cleansed (completed or corrected) is "scrapped"; in other words, thrown out or identified as not correctable in the same way an unfixable manufactured product is scrapped.

In this chapter we define what is meant by information *product* improvement. Information *product* improvement, basically the correction of defective data, is sometimes called *data reengineering, data cleansing, data scrubbing,* or *data transformation.* We define the three areas of information product improvement: cleansing data at the source database, for data conversion, and for data warehousing.

We next describe the kinds of data problems encountered in a data cleanup project. Information quality problems exist in the data definition and data architecture itself, as well as in the data within databases and files.

We then describe the steps of the data reengineering and cleansing process, covering all three categories of data cleansing. The term *data reengineering* implies the transformation of unarchitected data into architected and well-defined data structures. The terms *cleansing, cleaning, cleanup,* and *correcting* data are used synonymously to mean correcting missing and inaccurate data values.

Finally, we show you how to leverage the costs and knowledge gained in data cleansing in data warehousing to create additional value. By developing an enterprise data architecture, the operational data store can become a transition record-of-reference database. It can be used to migrate disparate legacy databases into a shared data environment.

Information *Product* Improvement

The objective of data reengineering and cleansing is to take defective data and rework it, correct it, reformat it, consolidate it, discover hidden "data within data," and standardize it so that the information product meets the quality requirements of its information customers. While this process is most notably used in data warehousing, it may be required to cleanse data within an existing database to improve the performance of operational processes and use, or in converting data to a new data architecture or application software package database.

Data cleansing is a cost-adding process. The ultimate goal of information quality improvement is to eliminate the need to perform error correction. This process is most effective when coupled with the last process in the TQdM methodology, "Information *Process* Improvement." Based on the lessons learned from the data being cleansed, one can attack the root cause of the defective data. While information *product* improvement attacks the symptoms of defective data, information *process* improvement attacks the root causes.

There are three categories of information product improvement or data cleansing:

- Data cleansing of source data in place
- Data cleansing for data conversion
- Data cleansing and reengineering for data warehousing

These three data cleansing areas are incremental. The tasks required to cleanse source data are also required for cleansing for data conversion. Likewise, the cleansing and transformation activities for conversion are required for data cleansing and reengineering for data warehouses, data marts, or operational data stores. Each cleansing category is introduced next and the process steps are described later.

Source Data Cleansing

The objective of source data cleansing is to improve quality of existing data in its existing files in order to maximize its value and use, and to minimize the costs of process failure due to poor information quality. Many supposedly authoritative enterprise databases go unused by many potential customers because they lack confidence in the databases' reliability for their needs. This happens far more frequently than the typical organization believes, even though the processes supported by the database are apparently operating correctly.

Knowledge workers who cannot access these record-of-reference databases or who have found integrity problems are forced to look for other sources of data or resort to creating their own "private" database files in a spreadsheet or a PC DBMS.

The process of cleansing is to improve the quality of data within the existing data structures. This means standardizing nonstandard data values and domains, filling in missing data, correcting wrong data, and consolidating duplicate occurrences. The results of data cleansing enable all knowledge workers to trust the information and use it with confidence and to prevent process failure.

Cleansing for Data Conversion

The objective for data conversion is *not* just to transform legacy data to a target data architecture. The objective must include improving the existing information quality, filling in missing values and new fields, not simply *converting* it to the target architecture. The task includes discovering the meaning of the data in the source database and mapping the legacy data to a target data architecture. The tasks include:

- Extracting complex data from legacy files and identifying its use, standardizing it, and mapping it to the corresponding fields in the target data architecture

- Identifying any data fields required in the target architecture that are missing from the legacy data structures and acquiring correct values for those fields

- Identifying important data in the data sources not contained in the target architecture that is required in the new environment and making a place for it

- Auditing and controlling the data transformation and cleansing processes

Filling in missing data and correcting inaccurate data should be performed. The data should be cleansed within the source databases only if the data will still be used from those sources or is required for parallel operations.

Cleansing and Reengineering for Data Warehousing

The success of a data warehouse is dependent on collecting, managing, and disseminating quality information products that support the strategic and tactical business processes of the enterprise. Without quality information, the data warehouse *will* fail. With quality information, the data warehouse can be used for competitive advantage in ways not currently envisioned.

The aspects of information quality in the data warehouse context can be seen in Figure 8.1. The components of the data warehouse include:

Information directory. The information directory houses the data definition, data architecture, and data transformation rules that control the data acquisition and cleansing processes. The information directory demands data definition and data architecture quality because it is the basis for specifying the meaning of the data in the warehouse. Data definition is to data what a product specification is to a manufactured product. See Chapter 5, "Assessing Data Definition and Information Architecture Quality," for a discussion of the characteristics of data definition and metadata quality.

Data warehouse database. Quality of the data content applies here. Data must have completeness, nonduplication, accuracy, precision to the right degree, derivation consistency, and timeliness for the knowledge workers. See Chapter 6, "Information Quality Assessment," for a description of information quality characteristics.

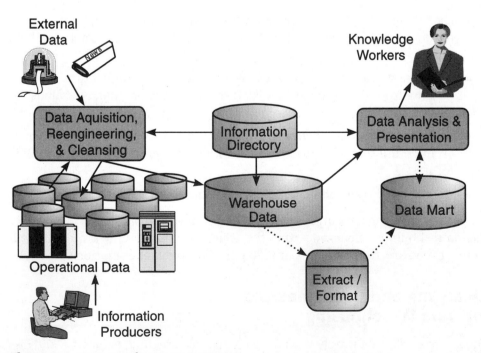

Figure 8.1   Data warehouse components.

Data analysis and presentation processes. These processes require quality of presentation to correctly represent information so that it can be understood and assimilated easily. Presentation quality is the characteristic of the presented information to easily communicate the meaning and *significance* of the information to knowledge workers.

Data acquisition, reengineering, and cleansing processes. These processes extract data from its source files, apply the transformations required to propagate data to the data warehouse architecture, and cleanse the data to improve its quality to meet data warehouse customer needs.

Data cleansing and reengineering for data warehousing is the most complex of the cleansing tasks. While the objective of creating a data warehouse is to load clean data to the warehouse, data should be cleansed and corrected within the source databases as well. Any data corrected for the data warehouse should be updated in the source if it is still being used from the source databases. This increases its reliability in the source database for subsequent processes. Furthermore, queries run against the source database and data warehouse that should give the same answer will not. This can cause confusion and undermine the credibility of both operational data and the data warehouse. If you are not able to update the data at its source, document that the corrected data is available from the warehouse and seek to have the data warehouse become the record-of-reference for that data.

In addition to the tasks required for cleansing data in place or for conversion, data warehouse data reengineering and cleansing involves:

- Identifying data not maintained in existing data sources required to support strategic and tactical processes from the data warehouse or data marts.

- Defining new summary and derived data required to support tactical and strategic processes.

- Consolidating data from multiple legacy data sources into a single integrated data architecture.

- Enhancing the data with external data that adds value to existing operational data. For example, external economic data, such as inflation, weather conditions, geopolitical changes such as the breakup of the former Yugoslavia into the new countries of Slovenia, Croatia, Bosnia, etc. are appended to operational data for trend analysis.

- Propagating changed data from the data sources to an operational data store, data warehouse, or data mart.

- Auditing and controlling the ongoing data extract, transformation and cleansing processes.

These activities are described in detail in the section, *Reengineer and Cleanse Data: Process Steps*, later in the chapter.

Data Defects

Data defects are like manufactured product defects. There are two categories: defects in product or data specification (i.e., its definition and architecture), and defects in the actual produced information products.

Data Definition and Architecture Defects

Organizations attempting to build data warehouses in an environment lacking a strong information management function are challenged by many problems in data content and in data definition and data architecture. These kinds of defects abound in both older legacy databases and files as well as in recently designed databases and application software packages. Data definition and architecture defect types include:

A high degree of redundant files containing information of the same type. These include legacy databases, files, and application software package files. This complicates what should be a simple process of identifying the authoritative record-of-reference for a given entity type.

Inconsistent definitions of attributes and domain value sets across different redundant database files. A publishing company found huge problems in maintaining consistency of `customer-name` data between its internal record-of-reference `Customer` database and its accounts receivable `Customer` file. The `customer-name` field in the internal C master had each atomic component of the name defined. The `customer-name` field in the accounts receivable `Customer` file was a single free-form text field. Because of this and other data anomalies, the company ended up replacing the accounts receivable package, using its internal `Customer` data model to evaluate the software package data architectures.

Data of the same type maintained redundantly in different database management systems (DBMS) and file systems. This creates problems in converting data across different data management technologies. Data types may not be handled consistently in the different technologies. Null, or the absence of data, may be treated differently by the different DBMSs. These differences must be resolved in the data transformation processes.

Nonstandardized data fields. Data of the same type stored in multiple files tends to be defined to meet one set of functional needs.

Legacy data may not have formal definition or specification of business rules. The business rules may only exist in the application code. Informal rules may exist as anomalies within the files themselves.

Legacy data may *have* formal definition and specification of business rules, but over time the meanings of the data and business rules have changed, but the documentation has not been kept current. Once again, the real rules may exist only in the code or data.

Historical data may have a different definition over time, as a database design has been changed to meet new information requirements. The historical archived data sets may or may not have the corresponding historical data definition and business rules maintained.

Data defined and designed to meet high-performance transaction processing may be highly cryptic, with much embedded meaning. This type of data may be understandable only to the programmed processes and understandable only to a small set of subject matter experts.

Legacy data architectures are generally inadequate to support all knowledge workers' information requirements. This forces information producers and knowledge workers to use data fields to store data in ways different from the formal, intended definition of the field. Or worse, it forces them to create their own private PC or departmental database for such required data.

TIP Some of the organization's most accurate data will be found in private databases. Knowledge workers who do not trust the enterprise databases or who do not have appropriate access, may create their own databases in spreadsheets, PC database files, or in word-processing documents. Because they depend on this data personally, they will keep it maintained.

Document PC and private databases and explore them as a source of data for conversion or data warehousing.

Use this data to cleanse data at its originating source or record-of-reference database. Then implement processes to keep the source data correctly maintained and accessible. In this way, the knowledge workers develop trust in the information quality and return to using that data source.

Follow this up with education and incentives to maintain the information quality at the source.

The data definition and architecture problems must be overcome in the information architecture for the data warehouse. If common enterprise data definition is not achieved, the problems of the legacy environment will only be compounded, increasing the cost of information systems, further reducing the effectiveness of the information systems organization and jeopardizing the business.

Data Content Defects

Several patterns of data defects plague legacy databases. These defect patterns have common patterns of corrective actions. Defect patterns include:

Domain value redundancy. Nonstandardized data values, or synonym values in which two or more values or codes mean the same thing.

Missing data values. Data that should have a value is missing. This includes both required fields and fields not required to be entered at data capture, but are needed in downstream processes.

Incorrect data values. These may be caused by transposition of keystrokes, entering data in the wrong place, misunderstanding of the meaning of the data captured, or values forced due to fields requiring a value not known to the information producer or data intermediary.

Nonatomic data values. Data fields may be misdefined as nonatomic or multiple facts may be entered in a single field.

Domain chaos. Fields may be used for different purposes depending on a specific requirement or purpose.

Embedded meaning in data values. Primary keys and other fields may have positional digits or characters where specific values hold meaning. For example, the VIN, or vehicle identification number, has embedded meaning, such as the manufacturing plant, identified within the single number.

Duplicate occurrences. Multiple records that represent one single real-world entity. This may be caused by poor edit rules, business procedures that do not effectively determine duplication, data that has changed since its original data capture causing a failure to match, or incentives of productivity in the information producers.

Inconsistent data values. Unmanaged data stored in redundant databases often gets updated inconsistently; that is, data may be updated in one database, but not the others. Or, it may even be updated inconsistently in the different databases.

Information quality contamination. The result of deriving inaccurate data by combining accurate data with inaccurate data.

A specific pattern type tends to have common causes of the defect as well as a common approach to cleansing or correction. In this chapter we describe data cleansing and correction actions. In the next chapter we discuss root cause analysis and process improvement actions.

Reengineer and Cleanse Data: Process Steps

Figure 8.2 illustrates the steps in the general reengineering and cleansing process of source data, and Figure 8.3 illustrates the steps in the reengineering and cleansing process for operational data store, data warehouse, and data mart data. While these steps are listed individually, many may be performed as a single process. For example, steps 5 *Match and Consolidate Data* and 7 *Transform and Enhance Data into Target* may be performed together. Step 9 *Audit and Control Data Extract, Transformation, and Loading* will occur within each step. For example, you audit *source* data during step 2, *Extract and Analyze Source Data.* You audit data transformation during step 4, *Correct and Complete Data,* step 5, *Match and Consolidate Data,* step 7, *Transform and Enhance*

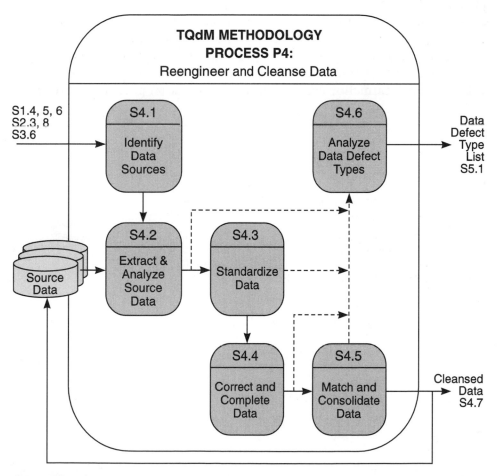

Figure 8.2   Reengineer and Cleanse data process steps.

Data into Target, and step 8 *Calculate Derivations and Summary Data.* You audit the Load process during step 9.

If you are starting a data warehousing initiative and do not have a formal information quality function, you may wish to follow the steps in Figure 8.4 as a guide.

Organizations seeking to develop a data warehouse should conduct a baseline data assessment of the data early, including assessing the quality of the existing data definition to know the extent of data cleansing required. Use rule discovery assessment to discover how the data is currently being used, as well as hidden patterns in the data.

A most important step for the data warehouse is to develop an information architecture that supports both the base data and derived data required to support the strategic and decision processes of the enterprise. The rules and data relationships, as well as hidden attributes discovered in the legacy data required for the data warehouse or target database, must be included in the target information architecture.

The baseline assessment and resulting cleansing activities become the basis for an analysis of the costs of poor information quality. This cost assessment provides a basis for establishing an information quality environment as described in Part Three, "Establishing the Information Quality Environment," with ongoing information assessment and information process improvement activities.

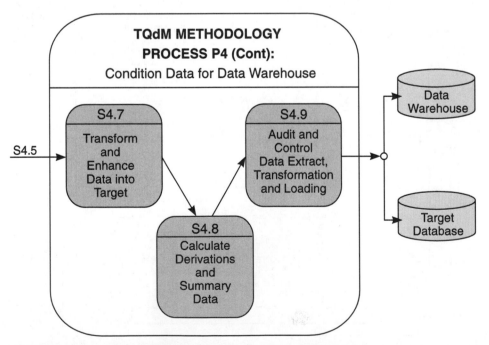

Figure 8.3   Condition data for data warehouse process steps.

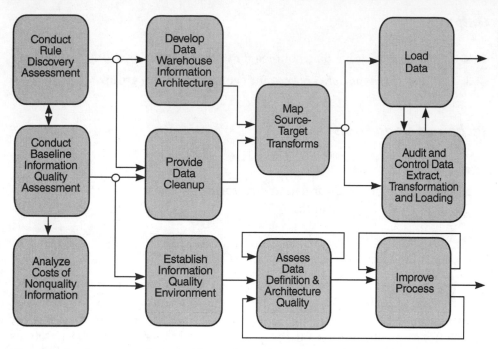

Figure 8.4   An approach to implementing information quality in the data warehouse environment.[1]

Now we discuss the steps of Data reengineering and cleansing.

Step 1: Identify Data Sources

Step 1 documents all pertinent files from all files that may hold data about a given entity, and determines which is most authoritative, if any, and where to cleanse or extract data for conversion or propagation to a target database or data warehouse.

The objective is to determine the record-of-reference databases or files where the improvement of information quality will enhance business performance.

Inputs

- Information groups for cleansing
- Database and file inventory
- Information value chain

---

[1]Larry P. English. This was first published in "Help for Data-Quality Problems," *InformationWeek*, October 7, 1996, p 54.

Outputs

- List of authoritative data sources for each information group
- List of redundant data sources for each information group

Techniques and Tools

- Repository or data dictionary
- Data catalogs and information directories
- CASE with matrix facility
- Reliability assessment
- Information quality assessment (see Chapter 6)

A description of these and other techniques and tools is found in Chapter 10, "Information Quality Tools and Techniques," and on the Internet at www.infoimpact.com: select the *Information Quality Resources* button for descriptions of information quality products, techniques, and best practices case studies.

Process Description

This step seeks to identify the most reliable data of a given type, such as `Customer` or `Order`, for propagation to the warehouse. It is not as simple as selecting a single file for loading to a data warehouse or data mart. The reality is that most large organizations have multiple redundant databases or files with much duplicated data.

Here you identify which groups of *fields* from the different redundant or overlapping files are most likely to be the most reliable. You also identify the rules for when to select data for a given occurrence from one file versus another. For example, if Joe Bloggs is a customer, and has records in the Order Fulfillment Customer file, the Accounts Receivable file, the Marketing Customer/Prospect file, and others, from which file do you select the data such as customer-name, date-of-first-service, and mailing address?

1. Identify all operational databases and files containing the information to be cleansed. Use the information value chain as documented in step 3, *Identify the Information Value and Cost Chain*, described in Chapter 6. Otherwise, use all data dictionaries, repositories, and catalogs to identify the files.

TIP Reuse the inventory of application programs and databases compiled from the Year 2000 projects. This should be an exhaustive inventory.

2. Identify private PC or departmental databases and files containing the information. Communicate with the major stakeholders of the information to discover personal files they may have. Use e-mail to survey knowledge workers.

3. Document the processes and uses made of the data against the individual files.

4. Document in an authoritative repository or directory all files discovered, along with the processes using the data from the specific files.

5. Determine the authoritative record-of-reference files. If there is no single record-of-reference file for an information group, identify the candidate authoritative files and use steps 2 and 3 to determine best sources.

Guidelines for reliability assessment to select the most authoritative data:

■ The process that has the largest stake in the correctness of a value is usually most reliable. If the cost of failure to a process is high, the data create and update processes are likely to be the most effective. For example, the Accounts Receivable department has the largest stake in `billing-address`. If this is incorrect and customers do not get the invoices, payments cannot be made. This causes cash flow problems and expensive debt collection rework.

■ Data recently updated is *generally* more accurate than older data. However this rule must be examined against the next rule.

■ Data updated by a stakeholder in the data (both information producer and knowledge worker who depends on the data) is favored over data updated by an information producer who does not use or depend on that data. Information producers who do not have an incentive for capturing data they do not need will neglect that data if there are time pressures.

■ Data created and updated by information producers who have performance measures for information quality is generally more accurate than data created and updated by information producers who have performance measures of speed or "productivity" only.

■ Historical data, such as date-of-first-service, should be extracted from the *oldest* record for a given occurrence.

The most effective way to determine the most authoritative source for an information group is to conduct an information quality assessment on the various files to discover which files have the highest-quality information for each group of data fields. The steps for information quality assessment are described in Chapter 6.

TIP   If a full information quality assessment may be too time consuming, you can conduct an abbreviated assessment with a quick *random* 50 occurrences of the various files containing the redundant or overlapping data. This will give you a basis for which source is the most reliable, especially if there is much discrepancy between the files.

After determining the authoritative data sources, document and communicate that these are the enterprise record-of-reference files for that information group; for example, Customer Name and Address, Customer Profile, Order, and so forth. Use these record-of-reference files for distributing data to redundant data files. Focus on making process improvements to maintain the highest possible quality within these record-of-reference files.

Step 2: Extract and Analyze Source Data

Step 2 extracts representative data from the source files and analyzes it to confirm that the actual data is consistent with its definition and to discover any anomalies in how the data is used and what it means. This uncovers new entity types, attributes, and relationships that may need to be included in the target data architecture.

The objective is to discover the "hidden" data and its meaning stored in fields contrary to the definition of that field. The purpose is to identify attributes required to be defined and where new fields need to be implemented, either in the source file or in a new target data architecture.

Inputs

- List of authoritative data sources for each information group
- List of redundant data sources for each information group

Outputs

- Discovered new attributes requiring new fields for storage
- Discovered, defined business rules
- Data anomalies to be corrected; such as domain chaos, in which one field is used for several different purposes with different meanings

Techniques and Tools

- Data extraction software
- Business rule discovery software
- Data mining software
- CASE and data modeling tools
- Data analysis

Process Description

Extract data from the selected source files to analyze the data for "hidden" data in fields whose meaning is different from the official definition of the field. For example, the Claims department of an insurance company had no field to identify problem claimants. So, in a creative move, the department used the medical-diagnosis-code field for that purpose. They used the value for the diagnosis of "hemorrhoid" to identify those problem claimants who were a "pain in the a__!" Other examples include using free-form text fields for storing many facts for which there are no defined fields for that data. The "account-name" field in financial institutions may have hidden data denoting relationships such as "trustee," "custodian," and "joint tenants."

Other examples include overloading of one field to capture different fact types. A `customer-classification-code` may be used in some cases to mean "preferred customer" or "delinquent customer," and in other cases to represent the standard industry classification of the customer. One major manufacturing firm discovered one field used *19* different ways, an excessive case of domain chaos.

1. Extract a representative sample of data from a file or set of related files. This sample should be large enough to discover most if not all anomalies. Data analysis using rule discovery software enables larger samples of data to be analyzed. For data analysis performed with the subject matter experts, assure an effective and representative random sample of data is selected.

TIP Random samples of 10,000 to 20,000 records of related data is sufficient for rule discovery, even in multimillion-record files.

2. Parse the data into atomic level facts. This involves breaking out multiple components of facts into individual attributes. For example, break out person-name into the different components of name, such as first-name, middle-name, and last-name. Take domain chaotic fields such as `customer-classification-code` described earlier and break it into separate attributes.

3. Analyze the meaning of the data with the subject matter experts for the source data. Even if rule discovery tools are used, confirm the findings with subject matter experts. Define the meaning of new attributes and entity types discovered.

4. Document the definition, domain value sets, and business rules for each atomic level attribute as used in its source file. Use CASE, data modeling, or repository tools to capture the documentation of the source data.

5. Map and document the relationship of the atomic level attributes to the source files and fields. This will be used in the transformation processes.

This data must be discovered, broken out into atomic level attributes, and defined for three reasons. The first is to assure that you have identified all required attributes that need to be included in the data warehouse. The second is to identify the proper meaning of existing data and how it is used so that the data is transformed and migrated to the correct fields in the data warehouse. Failure to do so minimizes the capability of data mining tools to properly determine correct relationships and trends. The third reason is to identify the domains and business rules of the source data. This is input to developing the transformation rules in step 6.

Step 3: Standardize Data

This process standardizes data into a sharable, enterprisewide set of entity types and attributes. The definition and domain value sets for each standardized attribute become the authoritative enterprise definition.

The objective is to standardize data into atomic values, and to standardize the formats and data values to increase business communication and to facilitate the data cleansing process. This step enables a consistent format so that data from multiple sources can be consolidated, and duplicate records identified.

Inputs

- Atomic attributes discovered with existing source domain value sets
- Discovered business rules
- Data anomalies

Outputs

- Standardized and defined data, including entity types, attributes, domain value sets, and business rules
- Source data to standardized data map

Techniques and Tools

- CASE with matrix facility
- Business rule discovery software
- Data reengineering, transformation, and cleansing software
- Facilitated data definition workshop

Process Description

This step formats nonstandardized data into standardized fields with standardized domain value sets.

Nonstandardized data values include data in which two different values mean the same thing, or are in inconsistent formats that create problems in data usage. Examples include:

Domain value redundancy. Product may have a Unit-of-Measure attribute. Different Products may have different values that all mean a Product is sold in units of 12 to a package. This problem, illustrated in Table 8.1, causes the inability to analyze data consistently by Unit-of-Measure.

   Correction action. A team consisting of the business information steward for Unit-of-Measure working with the information resource manager and representatives of all Unit-of-Measure stakeholders should determine an enterprisewide standard set of Unit-of-Measure domain values. Define the data transform rule to transform the nonstandard values into the standard value. Notify information producers.

Format inconsistencies. Data whose presentation requires formatting, such as Telephone-Number or Tax-Identification-Number, may be stored as unformatted or formatted data inconsistently (see Table 8.2). This prevents simple query programs from matching duplicate occurrences.

   Correction action. A team consisting of the business information steward working with the information resource manager and representatives

Table 8.1   Example of Nonstandard Unit-of-Measure Values

PRODUCT-IDENTIFIER	...	UNIT-OF-MEASURE
123	...	Dozen
456	...	Doz
789	...	Dz
987	...	12

Table 8.2   Example of Nonstandard Data Formatting

PARTY-IDENTIFIER	TELEPHONE-NUMBER	TAX-IDENTIFICATION-NUMBER
123	1-800-555-2121	123456789
456	18005552121	123-45-6789
789	800 555 2121	12-345678-9
987	555-2121	

of all stakeholders should determine an enterprisewide standard format. In the example of `Telephone-Number`, there should be fields to store all required attributes, such as `area-code` or `city-code`, and `country-code` if international telephone numbers are included in the occurrences. Define a process and transform rule for standardizing the formatting of the data. Assure information producers have effective procedures and training.

Nonatomic data values. The principle of atomic data values means that data attributes and fields should be defined in a way in which a field contains the lowest level, or most atomic level, fact required to be known. For example, consider the `party-name` field in Table 8.3.

Correction action. Break out the individual atomic level components of a field into separate attributes for analyzing its meaning. The `party-name` field in Table 8.3 is nonatomic. It contains no fewer than six separate attributes. Table 8.4 standardizes this into the lowest-level (atomic) attributes.

Atomic level data is more easily used in simple query programs. For data cleansing purposes, it enables matching for duplicates more easily and supports consolidation more effectively. For information management, atomic level data enables better definition and control. Business rules can be applied more effectively.

Embedded meaning in data values. A common problem in legacy data is embedding meaning in data to conserve space or to create identifiers for data in which facts are contained in a record's primary key. A publishing company had a `product-identifier` with `product-line` and `product-sub-line` embedded into the single field (see Table 8.5).

Table 8.3   Example of Nonatomic Data Field

PARTY-ID	PARTY-NAME
123	Dr. John A. Smith, Jr. MD

Table 8.4 Example of Standardized Atomic Data Fields

PARTY-IDENTIFIER	PARTY-NAME-PREFIX	PARTY-FIRST-NAME	PARTY-MIDDLE-NAME	PARTY-LAST-NAME	PARTY-NAME-SUFFIX	PARTY-PROF-SUFFIX
123	Dr.	John	A.	Smith	Jr.	MD

The embedded meaning in the `product-identifier` is:

Digits 1 and 2 identify the `product-line`

Digits 3 and 4 identify the `product-sub-line`

Digits 5 and 6 identify the unique `product` within the `product-sub-line`

> **Correction action.** Break out the embedded meaning components into separate attributes. This facilitates queries and data mining analysis. It further enables the ability to relate historical data in which the meaning embedded in the identifier has changed, causing the primary key value to change for the same product. Table 8.6 illustrates the standardized `Product`. Now, if the `product-line` or `product-sub-line` changes over time, the `product-identifier` remains the same.

The following are the activities to standardize data:

1. Identify the common attributes across all the pertinent source files.

2. Identify the information stakeholders who use this data from those source files.

3. Select representative subject matter experts of the data.

4. Select a business information steward to be the official enterprise representative and champion for this data.

5. Convene a data definition workshop to achieve consensus in the data definition, business rules, and standardized data values. If this is not feasible, the information manager with some subject matter experts may develop a suggested definition and set of standardized domain values. Distribute this to the information stakeholders for their review, comments, and suggestions. Revise as necessary and redistribute for consensus.

Table 8.5 Example of Embedded-Meaning Data Field

PRODUCT-ID	PRODUCT-NAME
114533	History of Teaching [book]
223456	Teacher Quarterly [journal]

Table 8.6 Example of Normalized Atomic Data Field

PRODUCT-ID	PRODUCT-NAME	PRODUCT-LINE	PRODUCT-SUB-LINE
114533	History of Teaching	11 [book]	45
223456	Teacher Quarterly	22 [journal]	34

6. Document the consensus data definition, including the business information steward for the data, whose role it is to validate and approve future changes along with the information manager.

7. Validate the quality of the data definition and information architecture against the criteria defined in Chapter 5 under the section entitled, *Information Product Specification Quality*.

8. Document the data map of the source files and fields to the standardized data. The metadata model for this data is represented in Figure 8.5. The source files and fields are documented as instances on the left side of the data map. The standardized enterprise information architecture is documented on the right side. The middle column represents the mapping of the current files and fields to the standardized entity types and attributes.

9. Document the merge and transformation rules of data from the source files to the standardized entity types and attributes. This is documented in the middle column of the data map shown in Figure 8.5. Merge rules describe the relationship of the source and target files. Transformation rules are documented in the relationship of the source and target fields.

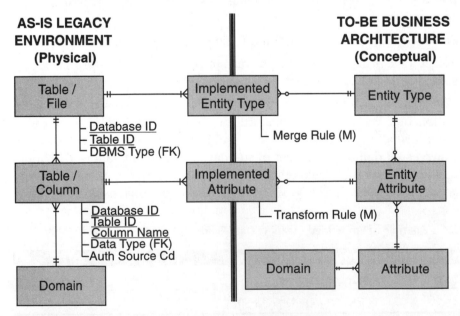

Figure 8.5 Data map of source data to standardized data.

Step 3 influences and augments the data architecture or data warehouse design process. The attributes discovered and standardized become input to the data architecture design.

Step 4: Correct and Complete Data

This step improves the quality of the existing data by correcting inaccurate or nonstandardized data values, and finding and capturing missing data values.

The objective is to improve the quality of the data to the highest level *feasibly* possible to meet the minimum needs of the knowledge workers.

Inputs

- Files requiring cleansing
- Data definition and business rule documentation
- Data map of source files and fields to standardized entity types and attributes
- Discovered, defined business rules
- Data anomalies

Outputs

- Completed, cleansed, and corrected data
- Rejected, uncorrectable data

Techniques and Tools

- Data reengineering, transformation, and cleansing software
- Physical information quality assessment and update

Process Description

In this step you take data with missing values, known errors, and suspect data, and seek to identify the correct values and correct the data. Use electronic correction processes where possible and human investigation and correction processes where required. Involve the information stakeholders in the correction process.

To correct data errors, you must know that they exist; you cannot cleanse data if you do not know what needs cleansing. To understand what requires cleansing, assess data using the information quality assessment process described in Chapter 6—the steps will not be repeated here. All data being transformed to a new database architecture or propagated to a data warehouse should have *automated* assessments to assess *completeness* and *validity* (conformance to business rules). The most important data, data in which errors can cause the most catastrophic or most expensive problems, should have *physical* assessments to assess *accuracy*. Physical data assessment is described in Chapter 6, step 7, *Measure Information Quality*.

There are three general categories of data that dictate specific cleansing techniques:

Name and address data. Postal service data, such as valid street addresses or ranges and national change-of-address (NCOA) data may be used to validate your address data. Name data tables can be used to match names such as nicknames for formal names for individuals (Bob for Robert, or Jennie for Jennifer), and common names can be matched against legal institution names (HP for Hewlett-Packard Company, and DuPont for E. I. DuPont de Nemours).

Permanent object entity types, such as `Product`, `Material`, `Location`, `Facility`, and shared data or reference data, such as `country-code`, `[General-Ledger]` `account-code`, etc. This data tends to be relatively static, with some changes over time. It may require historical occurrences in a data warehouse to capture the changed values over time. For example, a `Product` may have a changed `product-description` or `product-price` that must be known along with the effective dates. A `Warehouse-Facility` may have a changed `warehouse-inventory-area-square-footage` that can change over time, and historical occurrences are required for analysis of distribution patterns. The change in `square-footage` will have an impact on understanding those distribution patterns.

Event entity types, such as `Order`, `Sale`, `Claim`, `Inquiry`, `Deposit`, `Chemical Process Execution`. Event entity types are transactions that happen at a point in time or over some duration of time. The only historical data that may be required are changes to the state of the event, such as an `Order` that is `placed`, `validated`, `picked`, `shipped`, `invoiced`, and `paid`. Once the life cycle for an occurrence has taken place, no changes are allowed to any values.

Some data, unfortunately, will never be able to be corrected because the data values may not have been recorded anywhere and are no longer recoverable. Important data found to contain an unacceptable level of uncorrectable errors and omissions is a candidate for reviewing and improving the create processes.

Some data will be correctable electronically. Data such as name and address data, matched against postal service files, including change of address data, and other public database sources, such as demographic data, can be "cleansed" electronically. Existing reference data, such as enterprise defined codes, may be used to fill in or correct data in legacy files.

Some data can only be corrected through human research. This is the most expensive form of correction, but required for some of the most important data where information quality problems could cause catastrophic results in data warehouse queries. Human error correction may consist of calling people who are experts in the subject being analyzed to verify details. Physical data, such as product dimensions, may require product sampling and measurement. Event data, such as orders, credit transactions, claims, airline on-time arrival data, for example, requires observation or reviewing the original source documents.

The activities to complete and correct data include:

1. Identify missing data. Missing data may not be simply blank or "null" in which no value exists where it should exist. Default values may be used in some fields to indicate missing data.

2. Identify obvious incorrect data and suspect data. Suspect data "jumps out" at knowledgeable persons because it "doesn't look right." Examples include:

    Data out of normal distribution or domain value sets.

    Data with high values or low values when numeric data is expected to be within a certain range.

    Duplicate data values when unique values are expected, such as with `social-security` or `social-insurance-numbers`. One company found a high frequency of `Customers` who had a `social-security-number` of 111-11-1111. Another found many `Claimants` who had the same `social-security-number`. When one information producer came upon a `Claim` form without a `social-security-number`, she entered her own.

3. Identify the approach for data cleansing:

    Electronic data correction. Transformation routines in either transformation software or internally developed programs can correct or fill in some kinds of data. This data may be filled in or corrected using business rules to identify correct values. For example, `Customers` may have a `preferential-customer-code` to identify important customer segments, such as airlines have with frequent flyers. The correct `preferential-customer-code` may be derived from a `Customer`'s `Order` data.

    Human data correction from the *authoritative* source. Some data may be discovered only through human investigation. Calls to a person to verify personal details about the person. For permanent objects, such as `Person`, `Product`, or `Material`, physical measurement or investigation must be conducted.

Human data correction from a *surrogate* source of information. Some data, such as event data, will not be able to be physically inspected. Event data that happens at a point in time may not be discoverable directly after the event has occurred. Events such as `Sale`, `Order`, `Credit Charge`, `Deposit`, `Flight Arrival`, `Loss Event`, may not be directly observable. However, there may be a surrogate source of information about that event that may serve as a source to audit and correct or complete missing data. Examine any paper documents or other information sources used to enter data into a computer system.

Hybrid data correction using electronic transformation of obvious errors and human investigation and correction of data not able to be cleansed electronically.

4. Prioritize data to be cleansed based on value of correct data compared to correction costs. This is driven by the uses to be made of the data, including impact of wrong decisions in light of inaccurate or missing data.

5. Select the data for cleansing. Some data may be selected for cleansing of the most obvious errors and omissions. The Pareto Principle, or 80-20 rule, applies here. Cleanse the most obvious of data requiring a minimum of correction costs. If, however, the costs of cleansing all of the data is less than the costs and consequences caused by any remaining errors, you should invest in cleansing all of the data.

6. Document the type of data cleansing approach taken for each data type in the repository or information directory.

7. Determine how to handle uncorrectable or suspect data. The knowledge workers, as the information customers, must be involved in the decision. Alternatives include:

Reject the data and exclude it from the source file or information group to be propagated to a data warehouse. This is viable if the data is not used in summaries, and will not cause queries to have incorrect results.

Accept the data without change or documentation.

Accept the data without change, but document that it is suspect. This enables the information customers to know that there are problems.

Accept the data and estimate the correct or approximate values. To avoid discarding occurrences that have missing values and creating a new information quality problem, some will estimate the data. For example, numerical data, birth dates, and so forth, may be estimated from other known data. Approximate birth dates may be estimated based upon school completion data or employment history. Approximate order amounts may be estimated using all orders for a customer. Approximate income may be estimated based upon neighborhood or specific house price, census figures, and so forth. There are some problems in using this approach. First, the estimate will be just that. The estimates may even be significantly overstated or understated, creating a worse result than using a suspect value. On the other hand, using estimates or averages enables you to keep all occurrences so that counts of data are correct. If the data is used in aggregate and summary queries, this may not create a significant problem. The upsides may outweigh the downsides. In any case, if you decide to use some form of estimation technique to supply missing values, you must document that you are doing it, which records have been estimated, and the algorithms or assumptions used to calculate the derived data.

8. Document records or important fields that are not able to be corrected, or where values have been estimated. Also document the records that were corrected, and how they were corrected (surrogate versus actual source). This alerts knowledge workers using the data that it has missing or questionable data values, or that the data has been estimated. If some processes and knowledge workers require the original (incorrect) values, capture these in a before-image field.

Create an attribute to codify the cleansing results (at either record or field level). Codes might include:

X   Error, not correctable

E   Error in original records, corrected value has been estimated

C   Corrected and verified against authoritative source

S   Corrected and verified against surrogate source

9. Capture and document the time and other costs in the cleansing process. Cleansing costs are part of the costs of information scrap and rework, and become part of the business case for process improvement to eliminate defective data during information production along with the costs of data cleansing. Costs of data cleansing include:

Time to develop transformation routines

Costs of data cleansing software

Time in investigating and updating missing or inaccurate values

Costs of computer time

Costs of materials required to validate data

Step 5: Match and Consolidate Data

This step examines data to find duplicate records for a single real-world entity such as Customer or Product, both within a single database or file and across different files, and then consolidates the data into single occurrences of records. Consolidation also includes re-relating associated data with the consolidated occurrences. For example, when two `Customer` records are consolidated into a single record, the related `Order`, `Policy`, or `Account` records must be re-related to the new occurrence-of-reference.

The objective is to create a single authoritative electronic *occurrence* of reference to represent a single real-world object or event.

Inputs

- All database files for an entity type

Outputs

- Matched, consolidated, and re-related data
- Duplicate data match list
- Duplicate data suspect list

Techniques and Tools

- Data matching techniques, such as phonetic, match code, cross-reference, partial text match, pattern matching, fuzzy logic
- Data cleansing software with matching and merging capabilities

Process Description

The standardized and corrected data can now be matched within a file and across multiple files, even if the same entities have different identifiers in different files, and can now be consolidated into a single record. It is not uncommon for data warehouses to have to consolidate data from more than a dozen redundant files. Some data warehouses have consolidated data from over 50 files into single records in one warehouse file.

Data reengineering and cleansing tools can be very helpful in this process. While many tools are able to provide matching of address data based on postal service data, some tools that utilize rule discovery techniques are able to match possible duplicates based on similarities of occurrences.

1. Establish match criteria for the data. Select the attributes to become the basis for possible duplicate occurrences. Names, addresses, identifying attributes both from internal and external sources can be helpful in matching possible duplicates.

2. Determine the relative strength of any matched data to represent a duplicate occurrence. An exact match on `person-name` is stronger than an exact match on `street-name`. An exact match on `social-security-number` with similarity of `person-name` is stronger than an exact match on `person-name` and similarity of `social-security-number`.

3. Determine the impact of incorrectly consolidating records. If the negative impact of consolidating two different occurrences such as different `Customers` into a single `Customer` record, assure that you create high controls to prevent such consolidation. Here it is better to have duplicate occurrences than to consolidate two `Customers` into the same record. Human intervention should be required to assure consolidation of data that cannot be guaranteed to be duplicate.

TIP   Identify and capture data about occurrences that minimize duplicates from being created. For example, identify attributes that are not likely to change about a real-world entity. For people, `mother's-maiden-name` will never change. While `social-security-number` or other national identification numbers have restrictions on use, using the last four digits can be useful, even if not a guaranteed match criteria, since people may apply for and be assigned more than one or reuse someone else's number illegally.

4. Determine the relative weights of each match attribute. This may be governed by the specific cleansing software used. If you develop your own software routines, use an aggregate total weight of 100 and allocate that among the attributes used in matching.

5. Determine the matching techniques to be used:

    Exact character match of values in two corresponding fields, such as:

    Wild card match.

    Phrases contained in.

    Key words.

    Intelligent key words or aliases; e.g., "customer" and "client" or "education" and "training" are considered a match. In name matching, this includes matching formal names with typical nicknames, such as "Bob" for "Robert" or "Beth" and "Liz" for "Elizabeth."

    Phonetic match to identify words whose variations in spelling may be due to pronunciation similarity. Names such as "Smith" and "Smythe" or "blue" and "blew."

    Close match, such as one or two characters different or transposed.

    Match codes created from parts of attributes.

6. Compare match criteria for a specific record with all other records within a given file to look for intrafile duplicate records.

7. Compare match criteria for a specific record with all records in another file to look for interfile duplicate records.

8. Evaluate potential matched occurrences to assure they are in fact duplicate.

9. Consolidate data into single occurrences with most authoritative data values.

10. Document the matching and merge rules in the data map of source to target. Document this in the relationship of entity type to source table or file. This model is represented in Figure 8.5 and described in step 3.

11. Establish a control mechanism to cross-reference duplicate occurrences in multiple files in which primary keys cannot be kept identical. For example, use a cross-reference table of primary keys to related the same real-world entity of one file to the equivalent record in the other files. Use the occurrence of reference identifier as the primary key. Use the identifier key and file name or identifier to relate that to records in other files (see Table 8.7).

12. Examine and re-relate data related to the old records being consolidated to the new occurrence-of-reference record. Be sure to validate that no related data is overlooked.

13. Maintain an archive of the original source data for an appropriate length of time for error recovery purposes. In the event of a consolidation error, you must be able to recover. A building society in the U.K. consolidated some customer records in error. After one year, one customer's accounts had yet to be straightened out.

Table 8.7 Cross-Reference File Example

PRODUCT-IDENTIFIER	RELATED-PRODUCT-NUMBER	RELATED-PRODUCT-FILE-NAME
123	123	Item Master (record of reference file, and occurrence of record)
123	789	Item Master (duplicate record, not able to be consolidated—avoid this if possible)
123	AB121	Item Planning Master
123	4644	Inventory File
123	11-321	Product Catalog Master
123	6321	Material Master

> **TIP**   Select the most complete data versus more cryptic. For example, if consolidating occurrences of a person with the names "Robert R. Brown" and "R. R. Brown, MD," the consolidated name should be "Robert R. Brown, MD." You can derive the initials if you have the full name, but not vice versa.

Step 6: Analyze Data Defect Types

This step analyzes the patterns of data errors for input to process improvement.

The objective is to leverage the knowledge of the data cleansing work to discover patterns of data errors, improve business processes, and eliminate the most significant problems caused by data errors.

Inputs

- Data anomalies
- Rejected, uncorrectable data

Outputs

- Data defect type list

Techniques and Tools

- Data reengineering and cleansing software
- Business rule discovery software
- Data analysis

Process Description

Analyze the results and outcomes of the other steps to understand the kinds of errors, their frequencies, and the costs and impacts of the errors on the business.

There are several patterns of data defects that plague legacy databases. A specific pattern type tends to have common causes of the defect as well as a common approach to cleansing or correction. Defect patterns are described earlier.

1. List and analyze examples of the various kinds of data anomalies discovered in the earlier steps.
2. List two or three representative examples of each defect type.
3. Categorize the information quality problems and patterns.

4. Estimate the frequency of each information quality problem.

5. Estimate the relative costs or impacts, if possible.

6. Summarize the impact by data defect type.

This information provides patterns of errors useful in information process improvement.

Step 7: Transform and Enhance Data into Target

This step prepares the base data for loading into the warehouse or target database. This includes converting or formatting the cleansed, consolidated data into the new data architecture, and possibly enhancing internal operational data with external data purchased or acquired from various information service providers.

This step also consolidates external data, such as geographic or demographic data, from external sources by appending it to records or to new files.

The objective is to successfully map the corrected and consolidated data into the data warehouse data architecture. This requires transforming any data from the data types, domain values, and formats into the respective data types, domain values, and formats of the data warehouse or target database.

Inputs

- Cleansed, consolidated data
- External data from information providers
- Data warehouse or target data architecture
- Data map of source data to standardized data

Outputs

- Transformed, enhanced data
- Updated data map of source data to standardized data
- Data map of source data to target data architecture

Techniques and Tools

- Data transformation software
- External, online or public databases
- Information providers

Process Description

This step has two parts. The first part transforms the standardized data into the target data warehouse or operational data store data architecture. The second part optionally combines external data from one or more information providers with internal data. This step requires:

- Cleansed and standardized data
- Data from external information sources for integration with internal data
- Business rules governing the source data
- Business rules governing the target data warehouse data
- Transformation rules governing the transformation process

At this point, data from external sources may be combined with the internal operational data to "enhance" it or to increase its value. For example, you may enhance customer address data by appending to it geographic data (latitude and longitude), demographic data such as neighborhood average house value or average income, or census data such as population or density.

There are many types of data that may be purchased or acquired from information suppliers. Much external data may be acquired by the data cleansing product suppliers. Types of data that may be used to enhance existing data:

- Personal data such as `birth-date` and `gender-code, marital-status`, household data, etc. Use caution in using names to "assign" a gender code for people. While gender may be generally derivable from a person's name, even obvious gender-specific names can have exceptions. I know women named Lee, George, and Sam.

- Geographic data, such as `latitude, longitude`, and `altitude`. Other attributes include time zone and maps or directions to a specific address.

- Postal data, such as address standardization and address-change data. Other postal data includes carrier routes, and delivery point data for an address.

- Census data, such as household income and makeup, home ownership and ethnic data.

- Demographic data, such as area population, density, average or mean income, home value.

- Economic data, such as stock exchange data, interest rate changes inflation data. This data can be used to better understand spending and other financial transaction patterns.

- Political and world event data, such as political leader changes, coups, embargoes, and other significant events that can have a direct or indirect impact on the enterprise business. This data has an impact on business decisions and strategies. It also serves to help interpret historical operational data patterns and business trends correctly.

- Meteorological data, such as dates and locations of catastrophic events like hurricanes, tornadoes, and volcanic eruptions. This data helps explain weather-related anomalies in retail sales or insurance claims, for example.

- Behavioral data, such as marital status, religion, magazine subscription patterns, credit card purchase patterns, contributor patterns.

When acquiring data from external sources to enhance existing data, you should know:

- The definition of the data, including the meaning of any codes used.

- The date the data was collected.

- The source from which the data was acquired.

- Its reliability level or information quality level. What is the level of completeness and accuracy of the data including its confidence level?

- Whether or not data estimation techniques were used to fill in missing data. If so, what and how much data was estimated, and what kind of estimating algorithms and rules were used?

If you buy or acquire external data, you should expect the information supplier to provide you with a reliability level (completeness and accuracy) and confidence level (confidence in the reliability level reported is sometimes reported as "margin of error"). If you do not have this you should audit a sample of the data to discover its reliability. You may do this by corroborating it against other sources. Investigate any discrepancies with the data providers.

1. Using the data map of source data to standardized data and the data warehouse architecture, extend the data map of the standardized data to the data warehouse data architecture. This extended data map is represented in Figure 8.6. The target data architecture may have some compromises of the standardized data. Any compromises must be for performance of the data and not compromise the *meaning* or *domains* established for the standardized data. For example, an attribute may be implemented in more than one data warehouse file to facilitate query performance. Keep the meaning and domain values consistent across both files.

2. Define the data transformation rules and develop the transformation routines for the transformation software or internally developed programs. This should extend the transformation rules defined in step 3 to map them to the physical files and fields if any changes from the standardized model are required, as for software package databases.

3. Define the data propagation schedule. This includes conversion of data to new operational databases or software packages and for initial data warehouse loading when a single load process is used. For data warehousing,

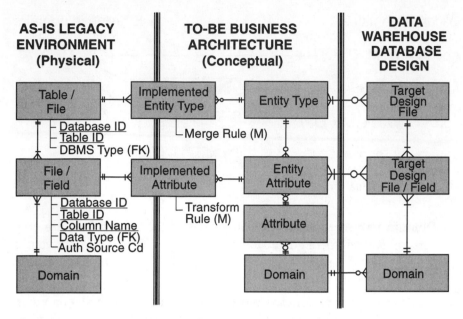

Figure 8.6 Data map of source data to target data.

ongoing propagation of changed data will be required. Define the data propagation schedule based on:

Timeliness requirements for the warehouse data.

Volume of changed data.

The time windows for the extraction, transformation, and load processes.

Complexity of the data consolidation processes. For example, the more files that must be consolidated, the more complex the data synchronization.

4. Develop the transforms for the data to be converted to the target data architecture. There are several transformation categories. They include:

Simple data extraction. Data is extracted as is, selecting only the fields to be mapped to the target (see Figure 8.7).

Cust ID	Cust First Name	Cust Last Name	Mail Stop	Tel Number

Cust ID	Cust First Name	Cust Last Name	Tel Number

Figure 8.7 Simple data extraction.

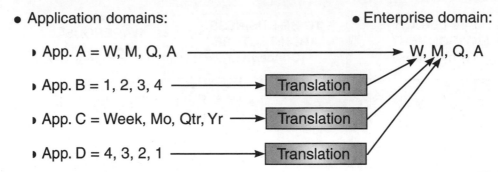

Figure 8.8   Domain value conversion.

Domain value conversion. Data values in the source field are converted to standardized data values in the target field. Different values for `publication-frequency` are converted to a standardized domain value set as illustrated in Figure 8.8.

Codify or classify textual data. Analyze data in textual, comment, or free-form fields, and create discrete classification codes. This facilitates data mining tools to identify meaningful patterns. See Figure 8.9. This is useful for taking complaint data, for example, and identifying categories of complaints. For information quality assessment, customer complaints may be categorized by whether there is an information quality problem that forms the basis for the complaint. This facilitates data mining discovery of trends.

Vertical filter. When you discover one field is used for many different purposes, you must identify all of those different uses, and define them and the respective domain value sets. Map them to atomic level attributes and fields. Define their transformation rules. Figure 8.10 illustrates the filtering of three different uses of `customer-source-code` into three appropriately defined attributes. In this example, source code was used in some cases to identify the `Acquisition Source`, such as from a purchased mailing list. In other cases, a specific `Promotional Campaign` was documented in this field. For other `Customers`, this field was used to identify the organizations `standard-industry-code`.

Complaint

Complaint ID	Complaint Description	...

Complaint (Data Warehouse)

Complaint ID	Complaint Type Code	Complaint Description	...
	10		
	33		
	4		

Figure 8.9   Codify or classify textual data.

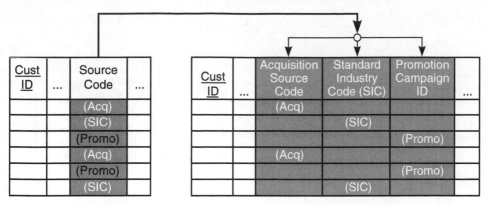

Figure 8.10 Vertical filter.

Horizontal filter. Horizontal filtering is used to extract atomic level components of data from a nonatomic or complex data field, such as name, address, etc. Figure 8.11 represents this type of transformation.

Matching and consolidation. This transformation is used to consolidate or "de-dupe" multiple records of data both within a single file and across different files in which common occurrences might exist. Consolidating duplicate `Customer` or `Product` data are examples (see Figure 8.12). Other data, such as `Order` data, may be matched and consolidated across `Order Fulfillment`, `Accounts Receivable`, and `Order Analysis` databases.

Data evaluation and selection. Data stored redundantly, either in interfaced databases or with software packaged data files, requires determination of the most reliable data for propagation to the target database. This transformation routine implements business rules to differentiate among redundant data the most authoritative or highest-quality information for selection. In Figure 8.13, `birth-date` is determined to be more authoritative and credible from the Marketing `Customer` database rather than the Accounts Receivable (A/R) `Customer` database. Marketing is more dependent on correctness of this data than is Accounts Receivable. In another organizations, however, A/R uses birth date to verify `credit-rating`. The

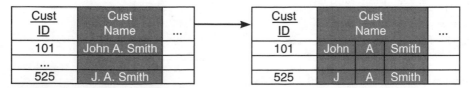

Figure 8.11 Horizontal filter.

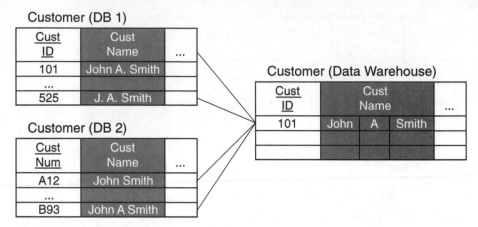

Figure 8.12 Matching and consolidation.

cost of failure is higher in this case, and therefore the A/R database would be more authoritative.

Guidelines for reliability assessment to select the most authoritative data:

> The process that has the largest stake in the correctness of a value is usually most reliable. If the cost of failure to a process is high, the data create and update processes are likely to be the most effective. For example, the Accounts Receivable department has the largest stake in `billing-address`. If this is incorrect and customers do not get the invoices, payments cannot be made. This causes cash flow problems and expensive debt collection rework.

> Data most recently updated is *generally* more accurate than older data.

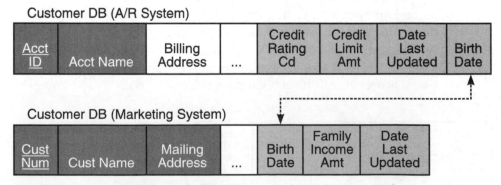

Figure 8.13 Data evaluation and selection.

Historical data, such as date-of-first-service, should be extracted from the *oldest* record for a given occurrence.

Data updated by a stakeholder in the data (a knowledge worker who depends on the data) is favored over data updated by an information producer who does not use or depend on that data. An information producer who does not have an incentive for capturing data they do not need will neglect that data if there are time pressures.

Data created and updated by information producers who have performance measures for information quality is generally more accurate than data created and updated by information producers who have performance measures of speed or "productivity" only.

The most effective way to determine the most authoritative source for an information group is to conduct an information quality assessment on the various files to discover which files have the highest-quality information for each group of data fields. The steps for information quality assessment are described in Chapter 6.

Integration. Data integration represents the aggregation of all the transformation processes. See Figure 8.14.

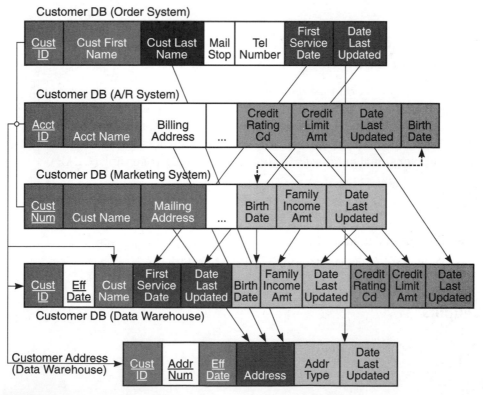

Figure 8.14   Integration.

5. Develop or define to the transformation software the criteria specifying any data to be appended.

6. Develop the job streams to execute the data transformation on the appropriate schedule.

7. Test the data transformations to assure the processes perform according to specification.

The following is a checklist for formatting and enhancing data into a target data architecture:

❏ Assure consensus enterprise definition of data in the target data architecture

❏ Assure definition and business rules of source data

❏ Assure definition of data transformation rules

❏ Assure transformation consistency of data types if data is transformed across different database management systems

❏ Assure the definition and meaning of any external data used to enhance existing data

❏ Assure any external data used to enhance operational data is matched to the right data

Step 8: Calculate Derivations and Summary Data

The objective is to optimize data warehouse performance by determining and storing derived data for the most frequently asked queries requiring complex calculations. The goal is to balance the cost of data storage against the cost of the online calculation of the derived data. This step is required for storing data in multidimensional databases for online analytical processing (OLAP).

Inputs

- Formatted, enhanced data
- Data map of source data to target data architecture

Outputs

- Derived and summarized data

Techniques and Tools

- Data transformation software
- Internally developed software

Process Description

Determine the various dimensions or views of the data, based on frequent or most important queries. Confirm the formulas and business rules for calculating the derived data with the business subject matter experts. Document the definitions and calculations of the derived and summarized data in your repository.

The importance of quality of the base facts is evident in this step. Derived data can be contaminated if correct data values are derived or calculated using inaccurate data. This phenomenon causes the "50% = 75%" error problem, illustrated in Table 8.8.

The step activities for calculating derived data include:

1. Model and define the derived and summarized attributes and fields required in the data warehouse or data mart.

2. Define the calculation rules and algorithms.

3. Verify the data definition and calculation rules with the subject matter experts and business information steward.

4. Develop the software parameters or routines for the data derivation or summarization.

5. Test and certify that the routines perform according to specification.

Step 9: Audit and Control Data Extract, Transformation and Loading

This step controls the data extraction, transformation, and loading processes of data converted to a target data architecture.

Table 8.8   Information Quality Contamination in Derived Data

FACT ONE	FACT TWO	DERIVED RESULT
Correct fact	Correct fact	Correct result
Correct fact	*Incorrect fact*	*Error result*
Incorrect fact	Correct fact	*Error result*
Incorrect fact	*Incorrect fact*	*Error result*

The objective is to assure that the *right* data is extracted from the *right* files, *properly* transformed according to the defined transformation specification, and loaded *properly* into the *right* fields in the target database or data warehouse.

Inputs

- Extracted, consolidated, transformed, source data and loaded target data (at each stage)
- Source data definition and business rules
- Target data definition and business rules
- Data transformation, enhancement and summarization rules

Outputs

- Audit and control reports

Techniques and Tools

- Quality assurance

Process Description

Nonquality data is a symptom of a defective or broken process—processes that are in control produce quality information. Quality information in the source files is irrelevant if the data extract, transform, and load processes fail or transform quality information into nonquality information.

Once you have accomplished the steps just listed, the data audit and control processes are a matter of implementing procedures, both electronic and human, that assure the processes perform as specified.

TIP Internal Audit can be an excellent ally in setting up audit and control procedures.

To control the data, define audit and control processes to monitor and verify:

- All data that *should* be extracted *is* extracted.
- Data is consolidated, merged, or enhanced correctly into the right records.
- Transforms are performing according to specification.

- Data is loaded according to the mapping specification.

- Errors and exceptions are identified. Processes for handling errors and exceptions include notification of problems to proper individuals and addressing those problems prior to any usage of the suspect data.

The following is a checklist for audit and control in data warehousing:

❏ Assure all extract, consolidate, transform, and load jobs ran. Post the last load date and time in a way that knowledge workers know the currency of the data.

❏ Investigate any job reruns immediately. Assure that data has not been loaded or added to summary data twice before knowledge workers use the newly loaded data.

❏ Assure all extract jobs extracted the appropriate data; in other words, the right set of data by date, changed data only, or complete extract.

❏ Assure all valid inputs to data transformations have corresponding outputs.

❏ Assure data consolidation of duplicate or merged data was properly handled. Maintain source data in audit files for only as long as required to assure proper consolidation. If the consolidation or merge process fails, you must be able to back out the results

❏ Assure currency totals and numeric counts of inputs and outputs balance according to transform business rules. Define appropriate counts and cross totals for balancing.

❏ Capture and verify counts of records extracted, records accepted, records and fields corrected, records consolidated, records rejected (along with reject reason), and records loaded. These should all balance across the extract to load processes.

❏ Check a sample of domain transformations to assure they are properly changed.

❏ Check a sample of derived and summarized data transformations, using a separate audit process to recalculate the data.

❏ Maintain audit and control data in the information directory or other repository for the data warehouse customers. This alerts them to the currency and state of the information products they are accessing.

❏ Maintain information quality assessment data, if any, as to the percent of data accuracy and completeness in the information directory or other repository for the data warehouse customers.

Activities for audit and control of data extraction, transformation and loading include:

1. Assure the source data has clear data definition, domain value specification, and business rules specification.

2. Assure the target data architecture has clear data definition, domain value specification, and business rules specification.

3. Assure all transformation rules, summarization rules, and matching and consolidation rules have clear specification.

4. Define the data audit and control requirements. Because all data is not equally important, concentrate on the highest-priority data first. Validate these requirements with the subject matter experts and target data customers.

5. Define the appropriate processes in which to implement the audit and control procedures. For example, audit source data in step 2 (*Extract and Analyze Source Data*). Audit data transformation during steps 4 (*Correct and Complete Data*), 5 (*Match and Consolidate Data*), 7 (*Transform and Enhance Data into Target*), and 8 (*Calculate Derivations and Summary Data*). Audit the data loading during step 9.

6. Develop procedures for monitoring and controlling data extraction, transformation, and loading. This defines how to handle exceptions and program failures. Knowledge worker involvement will be required when physical inspection or correction of data errors is required.

How to Leverage Data Reengineering and Cleansing

The complexity of data integration for a data warehouse is geometrically proportional to the number of redundant files and fields to be transformed. The phenomenon of data warehousing is required in most organizations because of the lack of enterprise information architecture. Even answering simple queries may be difficult, time consuming, and costly, because data must be extracted and analyzed from many different, disparately defined databases, files, and application software-package data structures.

The data warehousing opportunity is an opportunity to correct the albatross of the legacy data environment. Here's how. The operational data store (ODS) can become a transition database for an enterprise data architecture for operational data. As a staging area for data in transit to a data warehouse only, an ODS is a cost-adding component. But you can leverage the operational data store to create value in two ways:

It can house base data for a period of time to allow summarized and derived data in the data warehouse to be audited for correctness.

The costs of storing huge volumes of base data may be cost-prohibitive, or the base data may not have significant value over time. The ODS serves as a temporary data store for that data until the summary data is audited and certified.

The operational data store can become the basis for a new architected information environment. By defining the base data with enterprise consensus definition, the ODS can become a transition database that evolves to become the record-of-reference database for operational data.

Figure 8.15 illustrates the typical data warehouse environment with multiple source database files for a single entity type, such as `Customer`, `Product`, or `Order`. This is an *interface-based* information environment that is a legacy of the industrial-age organization. Extract and transformation processes must be defined for each file about a single entity type. Match and consolidate software or routines are required to attempt to identify duplicate data across the multiple files. In a managed information environment with high data sharing, there is no requirement for matching customers across different files because any data distribution is replicated or tightly controlled. A single occurrence of a given type will have the same primary key in all controlled and managed databases.

The operational data store can become the basis for reengineering existing applications to an architected enterprise database. Figure 8.16 illustrates how to use an ODS to reengineer applications in a controlled fashion to produce a truly shared operational data environment. As a transition database, applications and legacy databases can be reengineered when feasible. The reengineering projects can be managed in increments, thereby reducing the risk.

A byproduct benefit of this approach is that for every disparate source database eliminated, the extract, cleansing, standardizing, correcting, matching and consolidating, and transforming processes are eliminated. This reduces the costs and complexities of the data warehouse over time. This reverses the current trends in which new unarchitected databases and applications serve to increase costs and complexities of information systems and processing over time.

The end-state of this transition is an environment of information management and information sharing. Figure 8.17 illustrates data warehousing in the *information-based* value chain. Here, all unnecessary transforming interfaces are eliminated. The operational data store has evolved completely to become the enterprise record-of-reference database. If data must be distributed because of performance and location requirements, this record-of-reference database becomes the hub for distributing the data, via replication or other controlled data distribution techniques.

Significant benefits of this new managed information environment accrue. Business effectiveness is increased because all information created by information producers is immediately knowable to all knowledge workers. The value of the information is increased because more people use it for a single

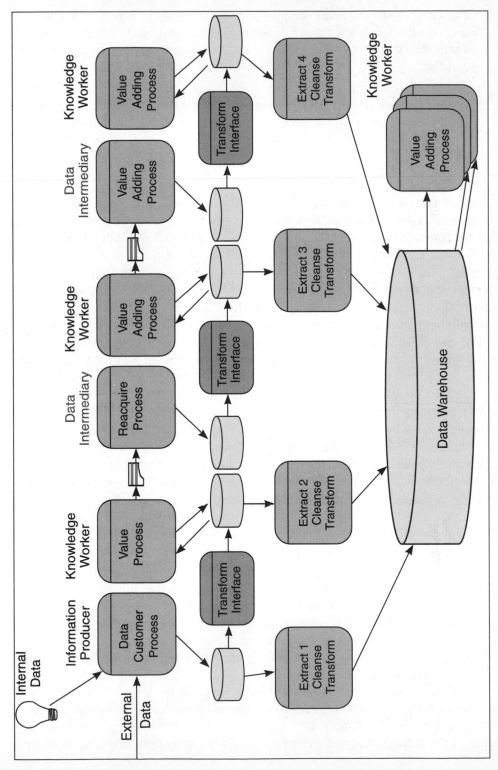

Figure 8.15 Data warehousing in a redundant data environment requires multiple transformation processes for the same data type.

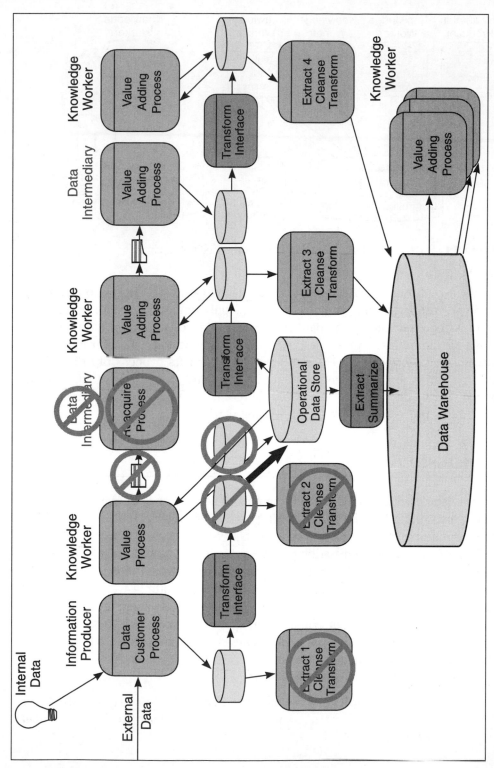

Figure 8.16 Operational data store as a transitional data environment to reengineer applications to a shared data environment.

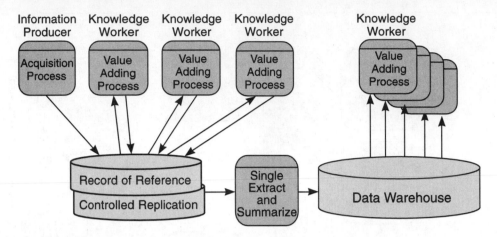

Figure 8.17   Data warehousing in an information-based value chain.

database or from managed replicated databases. Costs of information handling go down within the data warehouse because only one data transformation program is required for a given data type. Costs of information handling also go down for operational processes because all unnecessary transforming interfaces are eliminated. Data is captured only once at its process of origin. Data intermediaries are no longer needed to redundantly enter data that is maintained with quality in a single sharable source. Those valuable human resources can be redeployed to perform value-adding work.

Conclusion

If knowledge workers cannot trust the data in source or data warehouse databases, data reengineering and cleansing are required. These are the processes of information *product* improvement.

Data cleansing is a cost-adding process. It, like manufacturing scrap and rework, reduces the profits of the enterprise. The ultimate objective of a data cleansing initiative is to eliminate the need for it. If data is well-defined, and correct and complete at the source, no costs are wasted in correcting or completing it, standardizing it, or transforming it to a new data architecture to make it usable for the data warehouse. The only costs are to extract it, summarize it, enhance it, and load it into the warehouse.

There are two values to data cleansing:

To improve information *product* quality up to a level of quality acceptable for the knowledge workers to use it effectively to solve strategic and tactical business problems.

To motivate the enterprise to improve information *process* quality to eliminate not only the need for data cleansing, but also to eliminate the costs
and problems caused by poor-quality information within the operational
processes.

By focusing on the quality of the product of the data warehouse to meet the
needs of its information customers, you can enable the intelligent learning organization. The result is not technical success—it is *business* success.

Improving Information *Process* Quality: Data Defect Prevention

*"People forget how fast you did a job—
but they remember how well you did it."*

–HOWARD NEWTON

This is where the payoff is. The first four processes of an information quality improvement methodology represent the costs of inspection or the costs of information scrap and rework. The efforts expended in information process improvement eliminate defective data, and with it the costs of process failure caused by unquality information. By focusing on information *process* improvement, the enterprise will see its costs (of information scrap and rework) go down, and its profits (of exploited business opportunity) go up. The motivation for this is simply to reduce costs, increase profits, increase value, and increase customer satisfaction.

In this chapter we first describe the business case for data defect prevention through process improvement by analyzing the costs of correction and the costs of quality data production at the source. The fact that nonquality data exists is a symptom that the information processes are broken.

We describe how to improve business processes to eliminate the cause of unquality data. The same process applied to improving manufacturing processes works effectively for improving information production processes.

We conclude with a section of *Best Practices and Guidelines for Information Quality* to help you jump-start your own process improvement program.

Why Make Information Process Quality Improvements?

Because it is more expensive to do things over, around, or instead of as a result of poor-quality data. And, because improved processes increase the effectiveness of the enterprise, which in turn increases customer satisfaction, which in turn increases profits.

The Low Costs of Information Process Quality Improvement

There are two fundamental approaches to dealing with reoccurring problems:

Be *reactive* to problems and fix the symptoms or *consequences*.

Be *proactive* by analyzing the cause of problems and eliminating the *cause*.

Western society today tends to be reactive. We tend to treat illnesses when they occur, rather than take preventive measures to prevent the illness. We tend to ignore the maintenance schedules in our automobiles and have them serviced only when something breaks.

In business we tend to ignore problem signs until they become crises. And then we put out the fires, rather than seek and eliminate the cause. Why is so much business effort focused on short-term problem-solving? The economics of quality are clear. "It is much less expensive to prevent errors than to rework, scrap, or service them."[1] "Reliable service reduces costs."[2] Shortcuts taken to produce information fast without attention to quality are paid for multiple times over in the costs to find and correct the data and to recover from the process failure. The results of several quality initiatives reveal the costs of finding missing data or verifying and correcting information problems after the knowledge-originating business event has passed are 5 to 10 times the costs of capturing and verifying all information at the source of original information capture. Figure 9.1 illustrates the costs of downstream data error discovery and correction.

The vertical axis represents the costs of data capture or correction. The horizontal axis represents the degree of quality and completeness. Many processes in typical businesses only capture data at the point of origin required for departmental needs and ignore the needs of downstream knowledge workers. These processes typically only capture 70 to 80 percent of the information needed by downstream knowledge workers. When the downstream knowledge workers receive the data, and find it incomplete or inaccurate, they must perform processes to find the missing data or verify and correct the inaccurate data.

[1]Philip B. Crosby, *Quality Is Free*, New York: Penguin Group, 1979, p.149.
[2]Mary Walton, *The Deming Management Method*, New York: Putnam Publishing Group, 1986, p.58.

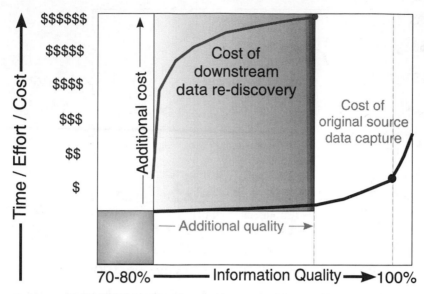

Figure 9.1 Cost curve for capturing and correcting data *after* the originating processes.

Many of the costs of this rediscovery process are incurred in simply getting back to the source of data to recapture or verify it. This adds no value, only cost. Further complications in this after-the-fact data acquisition include the problem that some data, especially event data, may not be able to be rediscovered or verified. Details about accidents or oral contracts made or business transactions that were not recorded may never be reconstructed.

Figure 9.2 illustrates the preventive costs of capturing and verifying all data at its source. There is minimal additional time and costs to discover additional data required by downstream knowledge workers. More data can be captured and verified at this point than when the opportunity passes.

Effective people are proactive. This is the first of the seven habits of highly effective people, according to Stephen Covey.[3] The highly effective enterprise will be proactive. Effective organizations seek to improve their business processes to eliminate unnecessary waste and cost. Effective *learning* organizations seek to improve the business processes that create and manage their information resources not just to eliminate unnecessary waste and cost, but more importantly to maximize its value through the sharing of knowledge.

Kaizen, or continuous process improvement, forms the basis for this process of information process improvement. Kaizen is cited by James Martin as the *first* of 23 enterprise learning techniques.[4] This is the mind set that any and every process in the enterprise is a candidate for improvement. Information process improvement must become a habit of every person in the enterprise.

---

[3] Stephen Covey, *The Seven Habits of Highly Effective People*, New York: Simon & Schuster, 1989.

[4] James Martin, *Cybercorp*, New York: American Management Association, 1996, p.261.

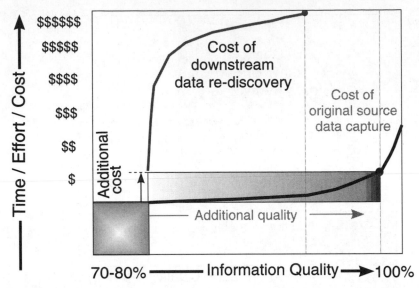

Figure 9.2 Cost curve for capturing and correcting data *during* the originating processes.

Reactive management will seek to justify the costs of process improvements. *Proactive* management will see the waste caused by unquality information and ask for justification of the costs of the waste. Reactive management will accept the costs of information scrap and rework as "normal" costs of doing business. Proactive management will reject processes that add unnecessary cost and waste, and invest in processes that add value.

Defective Data Is a Symptom of Defective Processes

Information quality problems are symptoms of broken processes. The long-term solution to information quality problems is not to "fix" the *data*, but to fix the *process* that produces defective data. This requires identifying the root cause and eliminating it.

This principle is true in other areas. When people are sick, they demonstrate *symptoms* of the actual illnesses. Doctors analyze the symptoms to diagnose the illness; in other words, the cause. The solution is to treat the patient to eliminate the illness, not the symptoms. However, treatment of illness occurs after the problem has happened. Some illnesses are preventable. The costs of preventing illness can be much less expensive than treating the illness itself.

Data cleansing fixes the symptoms of information quality problems after the problems have occurred. Information process quality improvement analyzes and eliminates the cause. It is the most cost-effective means of dealing with information quality problems.

Walter Shewhart developed the technique for process improvement that has become the normative technique for improvement. The Shewhart Cycle is

---

INFORMATION QUALITY THROUGH PREVENTIVE MAINTENANCE

Aircraft maintenance provides a model that is useful for information quality improvement. There is a strict procedure for routine maintenance of aircraft parts based on a zero-defect policy. Because of the importance of air safety, rigorous guidelines control the inspection and replacement of all parts before they fail. A faulty or malfunctioning part can cause catastrophic failure in the process of flying the aircraft safely.

Some information, if faulty, can cause catastrophic or severe failure to key business processes. This information should be subject to rigorous information preventive maintenance processes. This information preventive maintenance applies to volatile information such as name and address data, product price information, and other data that creates expensive problems when it is defective. Preventive maintenance establishes processes to control the creation and *maintenance* of that data and may include assessment of that data *before* critical processes use it.

---

known as Plan-Do-Check-Act, or PDCA for short. Deming used it, and in Japan it became known as the Deming Cycle. The four steps are simple:

1. **Plan.** Having identified some unacceptable problem, analyze the cause and plan an improvement to the process.

2. **Do.** Implement the improvement in a controlled environment.

3. **Check.** Assess the results of the improvement to see if it achieved the desired results.

4. **Act.** If so, act to implement and "standardize" the improvement.

The Shewhart Cycle is the basis to improve information process quality.

Improve Information
Process Quality: Process Steps

There are three categories of costs of quality: cost of information scrap and rework; cost of information quality assessment; cost of information process quality improvement. The objective of this process, the third cost category, is to eliminate or minimize the first category of costs and increase business effectiveness. The process steps for improving information process quality incorporate the PDCA cycle and are illustrated in Figure 9.3.

Step 1: Select Process for
Information Quality Improvement

This step identifies a problem caused by defective data and selects the process associated with the defective data. The objective is to identify a process where improvements can prevent business problems that cause nonquality information.

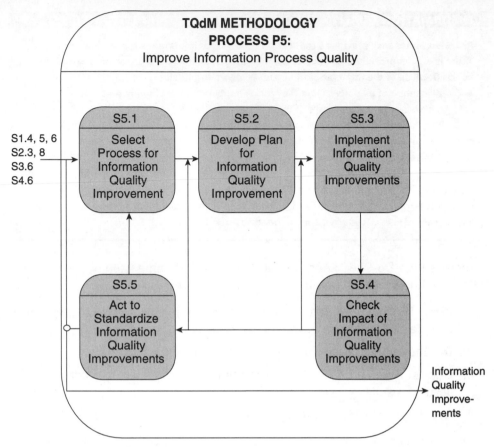

Figure 9.3 Improve information process quality process steps.

Inputs

- Technical data definition quality assessment
- Information architecture and database assessment
- Data definition customer satisfaction survey
- Information quality assessment
- Information costs and value analysis
- Information value and cost chain

Outputs

- Candidate processes for improvement
- Information quality improvement project

Techniques and Tools

■ Pareto diagram

■ Information quality analysis software

A description of these and other techniques and tools is found in Chapter 10, "Information Quality Tools and Techniques" and on the Internet at www .infoimpact.com: select the *Information Quality Resources* button for descriptions of information quality products, techniques, and best practices case studies.

Process Definition

From a known problem resulting from nonquality information, identify the processes that are likely producing the information. It is possible that the ultimate root cause is earlier in the information value chain.

If you are faced with multiple potential projects, prioritize them. Analyze the business costs relative to the specific project. One data area with only a small percent of error may be more vital than another having a significant percent of error.

TIP Focus first on the most significant payoff based on the consequences of data errors. Not all data is created equal; therefore, not all data requires the same degree of quality control. Dr. Genichi Taguchi won Japan's Deming Prize for the concept known as the *Taguchi Loss Function*. The principle is that the economic loss of nonquality increases with deviation from the ideal. The greater the deviation, the poorer the quality, and the greater the economic loss. While the costs are incremental with some defects, other defects may produce significant economic loss with only small variation.[5] The same is true for information. The costs of some data quality problems result in minimal costs, such as an incorrect address format or misspelling of words in a product description. Other data quality problems, such as inaccurate location of oil well pipes or aircraft location on an air controller's radar screen, can have catastrophic consequences.

Improvement projects can be initiated anywhere, at any time. Specific process failures could generate an improvement project. Conducting internal or external customer satisfaction surveys can identify serious information quality problems. Business objectives may trigger improvement activities.

1. Appoint an information quality problem "owner" with accountability for problem resolution. The owner for the process in which the defective data is produced should play this role.

[5]Rafael Aguayo, *Dr. Deming: The American Who Taught the Japanese about Quality*, New York: Simon & Schuster, 1990, p. 162.

2. Identify a project sponsor, if needed. This may be someone other than the problem "owner" or process owner. The sponsor will generally be a downstream information stakeholder who may not be responsible for the process that creates or maintains the information.

TIP Sometimes a neutral facilitator is required. This helps overcome personal and territorial issues, especially when dealing with cross-organization boundaries.

3. Identify the information quality improvement team members. They should include representatives of all activities within the process or value chain, including the process owner, information producers and data intermediaries, as well as downstream knowledge workers who suffer from the results of information quality problems.

There are four levels of information quality improvement teams based on the nature of the problems to be solved:

Individual. Anyone can, and should, be empowered to improve their own work procedures.

Intradepartmental. Departmental improvement teams. This team creates improvements for problems whose scope is within the department activities. Department manager is the sponsor.

Cross-functional. Business value chain improvement teams. This team creates improvements for problems whose scope is within a cross-functional business value chain. Higher-level management or business value chain owner is the sponsor. The impact of these problems is greater, as is the benefit derived when they are solved.

Systemic. Enterprise improvement teams. This team creates improvements for problems whose scope is enterprise-wide factors such as performance measures, information policy, and culture change. Executive management is the sponsor.

TIP Include the hands-on information producers and data intermediaries on the improvement team for two reasons: Being the closest to the processes that create and maintain the information, they know the problems in the process; and because any improvements may affect them, they should have a voice in any process change. This reduces resistance to implementing the changed process.

4. Establish an information quality improvement project. While the size of some projects will cause them to fall within your project planning and control procedures, keep this as informal as possible. The goal is to have a quick, decisive, results-oriented, and value-adding project.

Step 2: Develop Plan for Information Quality Improvement

This step analyzes an information quality problem to identify its root cause, and then plans improvements to eliminate the problem cause. The objective is to identify the root causes of an information quality problem and identify corrective actions to eliminate/minimize the causes.

Inputs

- Candidate process for improvement
- Technical data definition quality assessment
- Information architecture and database assessment
- Data definition customer satisfaction report
- Information quality assessment
- Information costs and value analysis
- Information value/cost chain
- Information quality improvement lessons learned (from previous improvement initiatives)

Outputs

- Recommended process improvements

Techniques and Tools

- Pareto diagram
- Cause-and-effect diagram
- Delphi approach
- "Why?" analysis
- Benchmarking
- Training
- Information quality defect prevention software
- Quality circles

Process Definition

Define the business problem to be solved, analyze root cause, and analyze and recommend process improvements. In cause-and-effect analysis, the problem statement is the unacceptable "effect" or information quality problem.

1. Develop a project plan for the information quality improvement project. This varies from very informal plans for small scope improvements, to varying degrees of formal plans based on the scope and nature of the problem.

2. Define the measures against which to measure the improvement project success. These should be related to the business performance measures. See Chapter 7, "Measuring Nonquality Information Costs," step 1, *Identify Business Performance Measures*.

3. Analyze the existing state of information quality. This will be the effectiveness of the current information processes, not necessarily the state of information quality within a database. If the problems are within the application and data development processes, see Chapter 5, "Assessing Data Definition and Information Architecture Quality." If the processes to be improved are business processes, see Chapter 6, "Information Quality Assessment."

4. Analyze and quantify the costs of the problem, if this has not been previously done. This provides the benchmark against which to measure the success of the improvement initiative. See Chapter 7.

5. Develop a cause-and-effect diagram for root cause analysis. Also called the *fishbone diagram* or *Ishikawa chart*, the cause-and-effect diagram identifies four major categories of cause called the four "Ms": huMan (Manpower), Materials, Machines, and Methods. Figure 9.4 represents a template cause-and-effect diagram for data definition and information architecture quality problems. Figure 9.5 represents a template cause-and-effect diagram for business information quality problems.

6. Brainstorm the possible causes with representatives across the information value chain. Group causes around the four main categories. There are several principles for cause-and-effect analysis:

   Create a solution-focused and blame-free environment. The objective of this is not to find fault or punish the guilty. The goal is to identify *what* has caused the process to be broken.

   Describe the effect clearly. This keeps everyone focused on the problem to be solved.

   Everyone must participate. The groups must congeal and identify as a team.

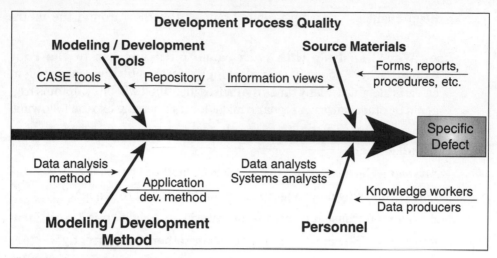

Figure 9.4 Application and data development cause-and-effect diagram template for data development process improvement.

Do not criticize ideas. While brainstorming ideas, refrain from commentary. This may stifle the brainstorming process. It may also keep shy persons from contributing.

Keep the diagram visible for all to see. Use printing whiteboards and overhead projectors, so diagrams are visible as you develop them.

Group causes together around the four categories. Group causes related to the people producing the information together around the human "spine" of the of the fishbone diagram in Figure 9.5, for example.

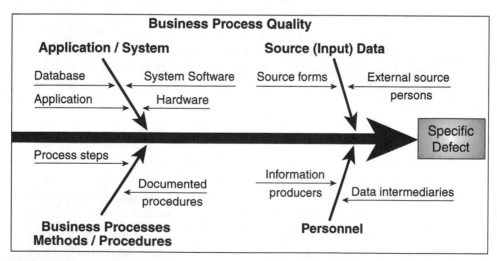

Figure 9.5 Business process quality cause-and-effect diagram template for business process improvement.

Keep business procedure-related causes together around the methods spine.

Use "Why?" analysis with each cause until you get to the root cause. "Why?" analysis keeps asking "why?" until the real problem cause is identified. Many times the causes identified will be symptoms triggered by other causes. A scenario might look something like the following:

Question: "Why do 80 percent of the claims have a diagnosis code of broken leg?"

Answer: "Because we let the systems default to broken leg."

Question: "Why do you let the system default to broken leg?"

Answer: "Because it is faster than entering the right code."

Question: "Why must you enter it faster rather than correctly?"

Answer: "Because I have a quota and don't have time."

Question: "Why don't you have time?"

Answer: "Because I get paid for how many claims I process each day."

The next question is for management:

Question: "Why do you set quotas for how *many* claims processors enter a day rather than on the accuracy of the claims?"

Answer: The only explainable answer to this—although not a legitimate business one—is that management of the claims processing area does not suffer from the fact that claims data is incorrect. Another part of the business may suffer, but "that's not my problem." One of the major real causes of information quality problems is that management sets the wrong measures for information producers because they do not have objectives that are enterprise-goal-centric. Objectives in one department often contravene the objectives of others. The improvement of information quality will happen when management of information producers shares in the goals of all parts of the enterprise requiring the information produced.

If the diagram becomes too busy, create multiple diagrams according to cause category, or redefine the problem into small component parts, each with its own diagram. One scenario is that the problem itself is too big. Break it into smaller "sub" problems. The second is that there may be so many potential causes, you may need to tackle each group separately. Create one diagram for application and process problems and another for people-oriented problems.

After all ideas have been exhausted, circle the most likely causes. Use the Delphi approach or another technique to isolate the two to four most likely causes.

7. Examine the circled causes to identify the major causes. If it is not clear, you may need to observe the process to determine by fact the major causes. Figure 9.6 illustrates a cause-and-effect diagram in which the problem "effect" analyzed is "duplicate customers are being created."

Monitoring order takers over a period of time with results presented in a Pareto diagram revealed that a lack of knowledge of the customer lookup procedures was the major cause.

TIP Not every problem will require observation. Use this when the costs of improvement may be high and there are several potential problem causes with different improvement techniques required.

8. Having identified the major cause or causes, brainstorm and plan an appropriate improvement with the team. It is critical to involve representatives of the process activities in the improvement. In the example cited in Figure 9.6, the team (notably, the order takers) identified the need for refresher training in the procedures for customer lookup. A checklist of best practices and quality improvements is listed in the last section of this chapter, *Best Practices and Guidelines for Information Quality*.

TIP Analyze lessons learned from previous information quality improvement initiatives to assure you emulate the successes and reduce the risk of failure.

Now you are ready to implement the planned improvements.

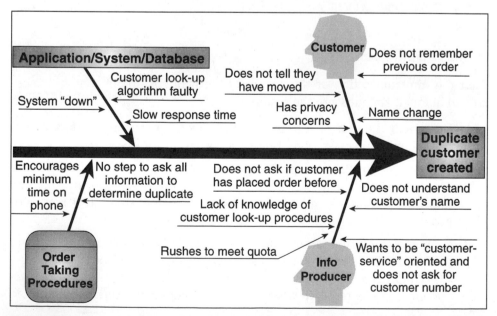

Figure 9.6 Cause-and-effect diagram for "duplicate customer created" effect.

Step 3: Implement Information Quality Improvements

This step implements the process improvement. The objective is to implement improvement actions in a controlled manner to improve information quality to verify that the recommended improvements do solve the real problem.

Inputs

- Recommended improvements

Outputs

- Controlled implementation of improvements and measured results

Techniques and Tools

- Information quality analysis software
- Pareto diagram
- Statistical control charts
- Training
- Procedure development
- Project management

Process Definition

Plan the implementation of the process improvement, implement in a controlled manner, and measure the results.

1. Document the new procedures, training, software changes, data model and database changes, and other changes required.

2. Identify a controllable scope for test implementation of the improvement. This pilot implementation is to assure the improvements do, in fact, improve the process and do not introduce negative side effects or other problems.

3. If people and business procedures are involved, provide orientation and draft procedures to be tested. If software changes are to be made, implement them in a test mode. For example, in the "Duplicate customer" problem cited in Figure 9.6, in which refresher training was the recommended

improvement, a dozen order takers were selected at random. The refresher-training module was developed and given to the pilot team. After about a month, their work was monitored to identify process improvement success.

TIP If several changes are planned, consider implementing them in phases. Too much complexity can cause the project to fail. Furthermore, some of the changes may not be effective. You must be able to identify those effective from those that are not, so they will not be implemented permanently.

Sample the newly implemented process after the learning curve has been completed, and at a time the subjects, if new procedures or training is involved, are not aware of the sampling. This keeps the results from being biased.

Step 4: Check Impact of Information Quality Improvements

Test the effectiveness of the improvements by comparing the before and after results, and against your success criteria. The objective is to verify the effectiveness of the improvement actions implemented.

Inputs

- Implemented improvements and measured results
- Original information quality assessments

Outputs

- Verified improvement results
- Recommendations for further improvements, if necessary
- Information quality lessons learned

Techniques and Tools

- Information quality analysis software
- Pareto diagram
- Statistical control chart

Process Definition

Compare the information quality from the improved process against the information quality before the improvement. The goal is to achieve the desired improvement without creating new problems.

1. Measure and quantify the benefits gained against the appropriate business performance measures.

2. Quantify the economic gains resulting from the improvement. It is important to have quantified the costs before the improvement so that the *value* of the improvement can be quantified.

3. Record the lessons learned. Record the state of quality and costs before the improvement. Record the state of quality and benefits derived from the improvement. Were there difficulties in implementation? If so, why? If implementation went smoothly, what were the critical success factors? These are important inputs to subsequent improvement initiatives.

TIP   Document information quality lessons learned in an intranet-accessible document for both communicating the benefits and for guidance to other information quality improvement teams.

4. If there was acceptable improvement and no negative side effects, proceed to step 5, *Act to Standardize Information Quality Improvements*.

5. If there was not acceptable improvement, or negative side effects were created, you must analyze why:

    If there was acceptable improvement *but* there were *negative side effects* created, return to step 2, *Develop Plan for Information Quality Improvement*. For example, a change to a procedure to capture new customer profile attributes inadvertently leaves out the verification existing customer preference codes, resulting in an increase of missing preference codes. You must plan changes to eliminate the negative side effects.

    If there was *unacceptable* improvement because the implementation was faulty, return to step 3, *Implement Information Quality Improvements*. You must reimplement the changes effectively.

    If there was *unacceptable* improvement, but the implementation was *not* faulty, return to step 2, *and* replan changes to solve the right problem.

Step 5: Act to Standardize Information Quality Improvements

This step rolls the improvements out to the rest of the enterprise and standardizes them, so the old defective processes become permanently replaced. The objective is to make the effective information quality improvements a baseline habit.

Inputs

- Verified improvement results

Outputs

- Documented and standardized information quality improvements
- Updated business process definition and procedures
- Modified application programs and databases
- Trained or oriented information producers and other stakeholders
- Changed performance measures and systemic factors

Techniques and Tools

- Documentation and procedures
- Statistical quality controls
- Communication
- Training
- Policy

Process Definition

1. Roll the improvements out formally.
2. Formalize the improved business procedures and documentation.
3. Implement software and database changes into production, or across the enterprise.
4. Identify and implement quality controls and assessment schedules as necessary.
5. Provide communication and training to all affected information stakeholders.

TIP Get feedback quickly as the procedures are being implemented. As the procedures are implemented in different parts of the business, new problems may occur.

6. Take the knowledge learned from this improvement initiative and add it to your "Information Quality Lessons Learned and Best Practices Handbook."

7. Maintain a history of all information quality improvement initiatives. Keep the following information:

> Project name and description
>
> Initiating and triggering cause; for example, information quality assessment, customer-satisfaction surveys, management request, or process failure
>
> Project team
>
> Process improved
>
> Process improvements implemented
>
> Before improvement, information scrap and rework costs
>
> After improvement, cost reduction and benefits gained
>
> Lessons learned

This establishes the value of the projects, or in cases of failure provides lessons for subsequent projects. It further creates a valuable source of knowledge for others embarking on information quality improvement initiatives. This can become the basis for developing your own Best Practices handbook.

Best Practices and Guidelines for Information Quality

Additional best practices case studies can be found on the Internet at www.infoimpact.com: select the *Information Quality Resources* button.

The following compendium of best practices and guidelines is the result of projects with many clients and others who are creating value for their organizations. Use this as a basis for your own Information Quality Handbook. The best practices are classified under four categories:

> Data Definition and Information Architecture Checklist
>
> Business Process and Application Design Checklist
>
> Business Procedures and Data Capture Checklist
>
> Management and Environment Checklist

I describe important best practices in each category.

Data Definition and Information Architecture Best Practices

Best practices for data definition and information architecture assure higher-quality databases. High-quality databases are *stable*, *flexible*, and *reusable*.

The measures of quality in information architecture are a high degree of reuse and minimal transformation in the actual structure, only adding new files or new fields within existing files.

Data definition and information architecture checklist:

❑ Assure data standards quality through feedback from information stakeholders.

❑ Assure agreement of data definitions among representatives of all knowledge workers and information producers.

❑ Assure understanding of data definitions through customer satisfaction surveys.

❑ Assure information architecture stability and flexibility by walking representative information views through the conceptual model with information stakeholders before physical design.

❑ Model entity types and subtypes to assure business understanding of the similarities and differences in data.

❑ Implement critical types and subtypes in single generic files where it makes sense. For example, `Customer`, `Supplier`, `Distributor`, `Competitor`, and `Stakeholder` may have many common attributes, and there may be a high degree of role overlap. That is, a `Customer` may also be a `Supplier` and a `Competitor` at the same time. Capture them once in a shared generic `Party` file, and identify their roles by relating them to each `Party Role` they may play.

❑ Define generic entity types for volatile data types or descriptive data. This can be used to code the data names or labels as data values. For example, most people now have multiple phone numbers. If these are implemented in a related file along with their type and use, new types of phone numbers can be added *without changing the data structure*. In a file implemented this way, when cell phones came along, no change to the database file would be needed. Only the creation of a new code value to identify `cell-phone` type. Then all that would be needed would be to add a record for the `Person` with a `telephone-type` of "cell-phone" and the number.

❑ Define all code values to insure clarity of meaning and nonduplication of codes.

❑ Assure data design supports all information views.

❑ Appoint business information stewards for critical data.

❑ Name and label data clearly and consistently across the information value chain.

❑ Name and label data clearly and consistently across all presentation, including business term, repository and data dictionary names, field names, screen names, and report names.

❏ Develop policy and guidelines for evaluating application software packages that include evaluating their data structures and data definitions against your enterprise data model for that subject of information.

❏ Create a policy to document local data applications in which new derived data is being created. This inventory may identify data that should be part of the record-of-reference data. The applications may also be of interest to others in the enterprise. Set policies and guidelines to coordinate and leverage these "local" applications and data resources.

TIP The proliferation of these local applications may be a symptom of inadequate database design or of inaccessible data. If there are information architecture quality problems or information quality problems, identify the cause and improve the processes. Local data solutions may benefit one knowledge worker, but at the expense and time of the worker having to develop and maintain them. Shared data solutions benefits all knowledge workers who need the information.

❏ Define check digits for important primary keys, such as customer or account identifiers. This can prevent most common transposition errors in keying.

❏ Define cross checks for numeric and financial data to prevent update errors from going undiagnosed.

❏ Allow a value of "unknown" for attributes that may not be known to the information producer at create time. Many data errors are created by having "required" fields for which information may legitimately not be known. The irony is that the edit test that is supposed to guarantee quality actually causes nonquality data.

REAL APPLICATION PRODUCTIVITY THROUGH INFORMATION ARCHITECTURE QUALITY AT FREMONT INDEMNITY

Fremont Indemnity eliminated application backlogs, and I/S had to go out to the business looking for new applications in order to keep their application developers busy. They accomplished this through absolute control over the design of the databases as an information "infrastructure" with minimal redundancy.

"Eighty percent of the information is infrastructure" representing fundamental business entity types, such as Building and Facility, with only 20 percent transactions. "It is the infrastructure that lets you develop fast." For example, one developer developed 42 programs in two weeks. The data "infrastructure" was already there, fully sharable and reusable. All that was needed was to develop the calculations to extract the data and present it to the knowledge workers in the ways they needed to see it.

The chief information officer and data manager left as a team and accomplished the same result at another insurance company.

❑ Define reasonability tests for data ranges.

❑ Control replication of data and publish replication schedules.

❑ Include audit and verification fields in order to trace problems back to application programs and processes.

Business Process and Application Design Best Practices

Best practices for process and application design assure higher-quality information. High-quality data cannot be consistently produced by processes that are not defined well or controlled.

Business process and application design checklist:

❑ Identify a business process owner for each important process and hold that process owner accountable for the outcomes, including both tangible and information products.

❑ Define each process completely, including its objective, process, and product specification with quality measures. Identify and document the downstream stakeholders for the information products of each process.

❑ Identify the business value chain across functional lines, so that the interdependence of all process activities is known. For example, the "pick order" process activity is dependent on the "validate order" process, but is required for the "ship order" process. Identify and document the downstream stakeholders for the information products of each process.

❑ Identify the authoritative information create and update processes and applications.

❑ Develop a single, nonredundant data create and update program for each data type, such as `Party` or `Item`, to capture common attributes. Develop single, nonredundant application modules for each subtype, such as `Person` or `Organization`; and `Customer`, `Supplier`, and `Employee` subtypes; and `Supply Item` or `Big Ticket Item`. These capture the different attributes required about each subtype. This maximizes the reuse of applications and business rules.

❑ Use value selection from a list versus free-form entry when time allows.

❑ Minimize data entry keystrokes.

❑ Implement reasonability tests, but allow an override.

❑ Eliminate unnecessary interfaces and intermediary steps.

❑ Maximize data reuse and sharing.

❑ Eliminate redundant data entry. Identify record-of-reference files and encourage reuse. Create automated extracts of data to eliminate the need for knowledge workers to have to enter data from reports into spreadsheets for their personal analysis if this cannot be done from the record-of-reference files.

❑ Automate data capture where feasible.

❑ Place data capture at actual point of origin.

❑ Make forms and screens simple and intuitive; provide definitions and explanations. Involve information producers in the design process.

❑ Provide automated help with data definitions.

AUTOMATING INFORMATION QUALITY CONTROL AT IMS AMERICA

IMS is a marketing research company with large databases. Its old parameter-driven control system for data entry and processing errors proved to be ineffective and labor intensive. IMS designed a new data-editing process in which transactions were classified as "good" or "bad" using neural network technology. Training cases for the network were taken from previous data corrections made by their staff.

   Benefits. Now error correction is automated, providing greater accuracy and speed than data quality analysts could perform. Automated error correction increased from only 1 percent in the old system to 38 percent in the new. Edit time to produce the same results was reduced 67 percent from 6 days to 2.

   Tips. Keep the project scope of data manageable and focus on critical data. Take into account the needs of the knowledge workers at all stages. Conduct a pilot to assure the methodology is effective.

Business Procedures and Data Capture Best Practices

Business procedures represent the instructions for people performing processes. Best practices ensure ease of understanding and performing the process. Best practices minimize the chance for error introduction.

Business procedures and data capture checklist:

❑ Create guidelines for procedures for information create processes. Quality characteristics include:

   ❑ "Novice-friendly" and "power-worker friendly." New information producers should be able to learn them easily. Use simple words, short sentences, with direct actions. Avoid making the reader have to hunt to find the actions to be taken. Allow shortcuts for the experts.

   ❑ Intuitive. Procedures should be natural to the order in which information is gathered.

   ❑ "Foolproof." Design procedure to eliminate or minimize inadvertent error. Prototype procedures with a variety of information producers.

❑ Fault-tolerant. Exception conditions and errors should be able to be handled easily.

❑ Graphic and visual. Graphics can reinforce the learning and performance.

❑ Automated. Define procedures electronically, so that they are updated in only one place and immediately accessible by all who require them.

❑ Maintained. Keep them current. Get feedback. If errors occur, examine root cause and improve that part of the process. Listen especially to new information producers to identify where procedures are unclear.

❑ Use every point of contact with customers and other volatile data sources to verify information and update decayed data.

❑ Maintain frequent contact with customers and data sources to assure currency of volatile information. Create processes that create points of contact, such as sending out customer profile information periodically for verification.

TIP Be careful not to alienate customers who are frequent customers and who may have verified their details recently.

❑ Use "clean" templates; don't use old correspondence or completed forms for new letters or forms.

❑ Verify third-party information; if not all, at least a sample.

❑ Develop a data update process that empowers any employee to get data updated in the record-of-reference (origin) database.

❑ Don't force knowledge workers to create private databases, reports, or unintegrated files. Instead, provide access to the authoritative record-of-reference or controlled replication.

❑ Don't accept bad data. Send it back to the originator.

❑ Provide immediate feedback, both positive and negative.

❑ Repeat vital information given verbally. Repeat the data back in a way that forces the source to listen and think about it. For example, if numbers are given such as "1, 2, 3, 3, 2," repeat it back as "1, 23, 32."

❑ Don't assume you know correct spelling. Confirm it.

❑ Train information producers and intermediaries adequately.

❑ Make sure information producers know their downstream information "customers" and what processes use their data. In this way, they can feel the importance and identify with the finished results.

❑ Use standard guidelines for procedure development for consistency. This is especially true for the same kind of information captured in different parts of the business.

❏ Observe training of new information producers to identify ways to improve the process.

HOW DOFASCO IMPROVED INFORMATION QUALITY AT THE SOURCE

Measuring piece quality of steel is often subjective and difficult to validate through edit checks at the source. In 1993 Dofasco implemented processes in which the people who produced the steel also entered the data at its origination into the operational systems. This data is used to measure costs of poor quality of steel as a corporate metric. Soon after the implementation, the metrics appeared to show a significant change in steel quality had taken place. An assessment of the data against other data revealed a data quality problem in the source data.

Dofasco implemented a "Quality Data Integrity" project and corrected the data quality problems. The improvement included:

- Clear, concise, business definition of data definition and business rules for critical data elements
- Data stewards responsible for data definition and business rules
- Implementing a process for continuous data monitoring and correction with automatic report generation, for which stewards are responsible
- Control charts to monitor the correction performance

Benefits achieved: Increased quality of decision making that contributed to reducing product "downgrades" in steel quality by 50 percent. The data continues to be used to ensure Dofasco focuses on severe problems and tracks the "real" results of changes made.

Tips for others: Consensus data definition and business rules are keys to success. Keep processes for monitoring and correcting data simple, easy to do, and easy to monitor. Provide data stewards the tools, training, and measures to perform their roles.

Management and Environment Best Practices

Sustainable information quality will only occur when management values information and the environment encourages quality information.

Management and environment checklist:

❏ Create value statements and information policies for information as a business resource, and stewardship of and accountability for information based upon its role in accomplishing the business objectives.

❏ Senior management has information quality as a performance measure because of its impact on business costs, customer satisfaction, corporate profits, and shareholder value.

❏ Funding of applications separates funding for information development into three areas:

❑ Infrastructure. The development of enterprise-architected databases and single create application programs should be funded as a capital expenditure and allocated equitably over the enterprise.

❑ Value delivery. The programs that retrieve and apply information to solve business problems can be charged back to project sponsors that benefit.

❑ Unnecessary redundant cost-adding. Redundant applications and databases, including interface programs that avoid using enterprise record-of-reference databases, are discouraged by charging penalties to the business areas that insist on not using the enterprise databases. In addition, the "offending" business area "requiring" these proprietary applications is held responsible for the costs of maintaining the redundant data in sync, and the costs of process failure when there are information quality problems resulting from the redundancy.

❑ Hold process owners accountable for information quality.

❑ Provide adequate training for information producers, including identifying the customers of their information products, what processes use the data for what purposes, and the costs and consequences when the data is missing or inaccurate.

❑ Create performance measures and incentives for information producers for quality, not just quantity or speed.

❑ Create information quality awards for those who make process improvements that result in the elimination of data errors.

❑ Encourage and recognize all employees who identify problems in information quality and recommend improvements.

❑ Involve information producers and data intermediaries in information quality improvement teams. They know the barriers and problems in the way of quality information. They will also be more amenable to change if they have a hand in the process design.

❑ Provide new employee orientation on information management principles and stewardship.

ACCOUNTABILITY FOR INFORMATION QUALITY AT COMINCO, LTD.

Because quality of information about mine shafts is important to the safety of all miners at Cominco, a mining company, the miners are accountable for accuracy of information they report at the end of their shifts. This information accountability is written into management's job descriptions, the miners' job descriptions, as well as in the collective agreement with their contract miners.

Conclusion

We began this chapter with the question, "Why make information process quality improvements?" The answer is simply that the costs of unquality information are too expensive in the global competitive economy. But more than that, improving processes to prevent defects means everyone has more time to do things that add value. They become happier employees who can focus their attention on increasing customer satisfaction in both their internal information customers and their external customers—and profits go up.

CHAPTER 10

Information Quality Tools and Techniques

"If the only tool you have is a hammer, you tend to see every problem as a nail."

–ABRAHAM MASLOW

Information quality tools are tools that can be used effectively—or abused. Tools are not "solutions," nor are they "silver bullets." With a strong culture that values customer satisfaction in information products and a set of robust information quality processes, information quality tools can be effectively used to increase the efficiency of information quality assessment, control and cleansing, and improvement. Without an information quality culture, those same tools may not be maximized, or worse, they may be used as a means to absolve one's personal accountability for information quality.

In this chapter we identify the *categories* of information quality products, the problems each product category addresses, and a list of representative tools in each category. We describe some of the major functions the tools provide and highlight criteria for evaluating information quality products.

Finally, we classify categories of information quality improvement techniques and list the techniques cited in all of the information quality process steps. Due to space limitations they are not described here. Some are described in the process step but descriptions of the others may be found on the Internet at www.infoimpact.com under *Information Quality Resources*.

Tools for Information Quality Management

Information quality tools provide automation and management support for solving information quality problems. Effective use of information quality tools requires:

- Understanding the *problem* you are solving
- Understanding the *kinds* of technologies available and their general functionality
- Understanding the *capabilities* of the tools
- Understanding any *limitations* of the tools
- Selecting the *right* tools based on *your* requirements
- *Using* the tools properly

There are five categories of information product functionality useful for supporting information quality. These categories fit in the information value chain illustrated in Figure 10.1. A current, comprehensive, and annotated listing of information quality products is maintained on www.infoimpact.com under *Information Quality Resources*.

Information Quality Tool Categories

The classifications of products supporting information quality improvement are:

Information quality analysis tools. Analysis tools that extract data from a database or process, measure its quality, such as validity or conformance to business rules, and report its analysis.

Business rule discovery tools. Rule discovery tools that analyze data to discover patterns and relationships in the data itself. The purpose is to identify business rules as actually *practiced* by analyzing patterns in the data.

Data reengineering, cleansing, and transformation tools. Data "correction" tools that extract, standardize, transform, correct (where possible), and enhance data, either in place of or in preparation for migrating the data into a data warehouse.

Information quality defect prevention tools. Defect prevention tools that prevent data errors or violations of business rules from getting into a database in the first place. Application programs that create and update data call defect-prevention product modules or routines. These products apply business rule and quality tests during the create and update processes.

Metadata management and quality tools. Management and control tools that provide quality management of metadata, such as definition and control of business rules, data transformation rules, or provide for quality

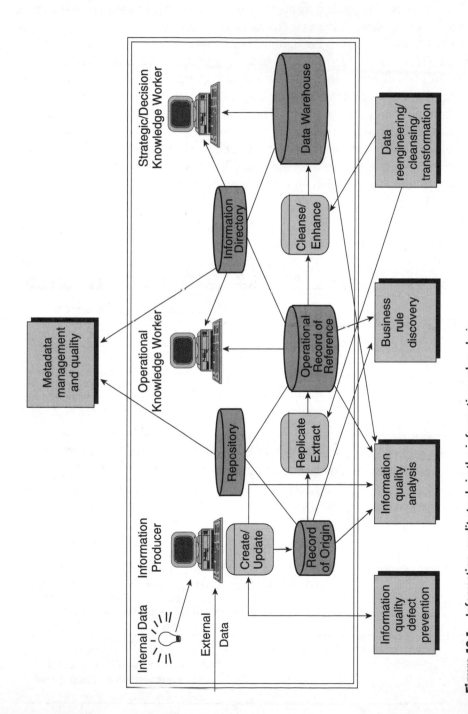

Figure 10.1 Information quality tools in the information value chain.

Source: Larry P. English. This was first published in "Help for Data-Quality Problems," *InformationWeek*, October 7, 1996, p. 56.

assessment or control of metadata itself, such as conformance to data naming standards.

Many information quality products perform functions in more than one category. For example, a product may discover business rules, and then report exceptions to the rules. Several data cleansing tools that cleanse and transform data from existing databases also have modules or routines that may be invoked and executed directly from the data create and update programs themselves.

Table 10.1 lists the various classifications of information quality tools for information quality management. This IQ classification code will be used in the tables listing information quality products. They identify the five major classifications listed previously. The legend also identifies whether a data reengineering and cleansing tool is a general tool (CG) that can be used to transform or correct any data type, or is name and address specific (CN). Some of the product suppliers provide third-party services in addition to selling the products (S), or they may only provide services (SO).

Table 10.1   IQ Classification Legend

IQ CLASSIFICATION CODE	CLASSIFICATION NAME	CLASSIFICATION DESCRIPTION
A	Analysis	Automated data assessment.
C	Cleansing	Data extract, reengineering, transformation, and/or cleansing.
CG	Cleansing: general data types	Reengineers, cleanses, and transforms data of any data type.
CN	Cleansing: name and address data	Cleanses and enhances name and address data.
M	Metadata quality	Provides quality assessment or management of metadata.
P	Data defect Prevention	Prevents data errors in source applications that create and update data.
R	Rule discovery	Analyzes and discovers business rules in data.
S	Service provider	The supplier provides the quality services or has third-party suppliers who use the products for quality services.
SO	Service provider only	The supplier only provides information quality services and does not sell information quality products.

Next we describe the basic functions of each tool category, along with general limitations. A representative set of products that fall into each category is listed. An annotated list of the products is found on the Internet at www.infoimpact.com. Products may fit into more than one category.

Information Quality Analysis Tools

Quality analysis tools automate parts of the information quality assessment and audit process. They automate quality measurement of data. These tools are used during automated information quality assessment, described in Chapter 6, "Information Quality Assessment."

Tool Capabilities

Assessment functions test whether or not data conforms to its definition and business rules. Quality analysis software provides automated assessment. Analysis software generally requires you to define business rules within its repository. It translates those business rules to code for testing the defined business rules against a data sample. Some tools discover the business rules from the data itself and identify records that deviate from the discovered rules.

Analysis products can measure such information quality characteristics as:

- Completeness of values
- Validity (conformation to business rules), such as:
  - Valid domain values
  - Data within defined ranges
  - Referential integrity
  - Primary key uniqueness
  - Derived data calculations
- Precision of data values
- Equivalence of data across multiple redundant databases

Information quality analysis tool functions:

- Data extraction, including random sampling
- Business rule definition and quality measurement test specification
- Automated assessment of data against defined business rules
- Reporting of data assessment findings in a variety of ways:
  - Exception reports
  - Pareto charts or bar or column graphs of relative error counts or percents

- Weighted Pareto charts or graphs, illustrating weighted impact or costs of errors analyzed
- Control charts showing history of assessments over time

The strengths and capabilities of information quality software tools are that they can perform automated functions accurately and quickly. The integration of reporting capabilities is a plus, saving time in analysis presentation. The repository may become a source for documenting business rules, if it is generally sharable.

There are some limitations with any software product, however, of which the information quality manager must be aware.

Tool Limitations

Quality analysis products only measure *validity* and *completeness*—they cannot measure most types of data *accuracy*. For example, an address may be a valid address, but the person may have moved. Product prices may be within a reasonable range of prices, but the actual product price is wrong and not updated in the database. Various code values may be a valid domain value, but incorrect for a given entity. These are examples of data validity without data accuracy.

In the example cited earlier in which 80 percent of `medical-diagnosis-codes` in `Insurance Claims` contained a value of "broken leg," the code was a valid code. Quality analysis software can identify that this is a highly suspicious distribution of values, but it cannot tell you which "broken leg" values are in fact correct and which are not.

When reporting the results of automated information quality analysis results, you must differentiate between accuracy and validity. Knowledge workers must not assume that if the data has passed validity tests its data is accurate.

Representative Products

Table 10.2 provides a representative set of products that perform information quality analysis functions. For a legend of the information quality product classifications, see Table 10.1.

Business Rule Discovery Tools

Business rule discovery tools are used to understand how data is used. These are specialized data mining products that focus on understanding the business rules that are actually practiced. These rules support the preparation of data for cleansing, described in Chapter 8, "Information *Product* Improvement."

Tool Capabilities

Business rule discovery tools analyze data in fields, files, or across multiple files to discover useful patterns, relationships, and rules in the data. They use

Table 10.2   Representative Information Quality *Analysis* Products

SUPPLIER	PRODUCT NAME	IQ CLASSIFICATION
DataFlux Corp.	Data Quality Workbench: SmartScrub; Datalogue; Extend; MatchMaker; IntelliMerge; Inspector	CG; A; R; CN
DBE Software,	DB-Examiner	AM, PM
Decisionism Inc.	Aclue Decision Supportware	A
DupeKiller, Inc.	DupeKiller	A,CN, S
Gamma Research	OCRProof	A, P
Gladstone Computer Services	DQ Administrator, Warehouse Quality Administrator	CG, A
Innovative Systems	Analyzer; Verify; Dictionary; Edit; Match; Scrub; Household; CorpMatch; Find	CN, CG, A, M, R, P, S
MatchWare Technologies (a subsidiary of Vality)	AutoStan; AutoMatch; MatchWare/CL; MatchWare/ PACE	A, R, C
Mobius Inc.	INFOPAC-ABS	A, R
OTS Group	Global Third Party Name/Address Cleansing & Enhancement Service	A; CG, CN, SO
Pine Cone Systems	Content Tracker, Refreshment Tracker	A, M
Prism Solutions (acquired by Ardent Software, Spring 99)	Prism Quality Manager	C, G, A
Rockwell Automation DataMyte	Quantum SPC/DC; Quantum SPC/QA	A
Search Software America	NAME 3, EXTENSIONS, Data Clustering Engine	A, R, CN, P
Unitech Systems	ACR / Plus (Detail, Summary, Data)	A
WizSoft	WizRule, WizWhy	R, A

Note: The author has made every attempt to provide accurate information about the listed products. Information quality decay will cause some of this data to be out of date by the time you read it. Some suppliers have not replied to requests for verification, and if there are errors, we apologize for the inconvenience. We will maintain correct information on our Web site for all updates supplied to us. For a current list of information quality products, including a brief annotation and operating platforms, visit www.infoimpact.com and select *Information Quality Resources*.

data mining or artificial intelligence-like algorithms to analyze data to discover business rules useful for information quality management.

Business rule discovery tools analyze several kinds of patterns and rules:

- Domain value counts
- Frequency distribution of data values
- Patterns of data values in nonatomic data, such as unformatted names and addresses or textual data
- Formulas or calculation algorithms, such as the formula to calculate an `order-item-price`
- Relationships, such as duplicate data within or across files
- Similarities of items, such as spelling
- Correlation of data values in different fields, such as `address` and `postal-code`, or `customer` and `order-discount-percent`
- Patterns of behavior that may indicate possible fraud, intentional or unintentional

Tool Limitations

Business rule discovery tools may not be able to discover all pertinent business rules. Business rules may actually have more variables than the rule discovery algorithm examines. Some discovered "rules" may not be pertinent. Tuning of the rule discovery parameters can minimize this.

There may be performance problems with large files or with many fields. This may be minimized through random sampling and making separate analysis runs against different sets of fields, grouped in ways that meaningful business rules are likely to emerge.

Be sure that all variables that may be subject to business rules are available to the discovery analysis products. Exclude from analysis, fields that may be irrelevant to the kinds of rules you seek to discover.

Representative Products

Table 10.3 provides a representative set of products that perform business rule discovery functions. For a legend of the information quality product classifications, see Table 10.1.

Data Reengineering and Cleansing Tools

Data reengineering and cleansing tools are used to improve the quality of the data itself. They provide automation of data "correction," as described in Chapter 8.

Table 10.3 Representative *Business Rule Discovery* Products

SUPPLIER	PRODUCT NAME	IQ CLASSIFICATION
DataFlux Corp.	Data Quality Workbench: SmartScrub; Datalogue; Extend; MatchMaker; IntelliMerge; Inspector	CG; A; R; CN
Evoke Software (formerly DB Star)	Migration Architect	R
Information Discovery	The Data Mining Suite	R
Innovative Systems	Analyzer; Verify; Dictionary; Edit; Match; Scrub; Household; CorpMatch; Find	CN, CG, A, M, R, P, S
Integral Solutions Ltd. Basingstoke, Hampshire, UK	Clementine	R, CG
MatchWare Technologies (a subsidiary of Vality) Brutonsville, MD	AutoStan; AutoMatch; MatchWare/CL; MatchWare/ PACE	A, R, C
Mobius Inc.	INFOPAC-ABS	A, R
Re-Genisys	rulefind:R; analyze:R	R
Search Software America	NAME 3, EXTENSIONS, Data Clustering Engine	A, R, CN, P
Trillium Software (a division of Harte-Hanks)	Trillium Software System	CN, CG, R, S, P
Vality Technology	Integrity Data Re-engineering System	CG, R
WizSoft	WizRule, WizWhy	R, A

Note: The author has made every attempt to provide accurate information about the listed products. Information quality decay will cause some of this data to be out of date by the time you read it. Some suppliers have not replied to requests for verification, and if there are errors, we apologize for the inconvenience. We will maintain correct information on our Web site for all updates supplied to us. For a current list of information quality products, including a brief annotation and operating platforms, visit www.infoimpact.com and select *Information Quality Resources*.

Tool Capabilities

Data reengineering and cleansing tools perform one or more of the following functions:

- Extracting data
- Standardizing data

- Matching and consolidating duplicate data

- Reengineering data into architected data structures

- Filling in missing data, based upon algorithms or data matching

- Applying updated data, such as address corrections from change of address notifications

- Transforming data values from one domain set to another

- Transforming data from one data type to another

- Calculating derived and summary data

- Enhancing data, by matching and integrating data from external sources, such as census, demographic, geographic, or behavioral (purchase pattern) data

- Loading data into a target data architecture

Tool Limitations

Data reengineering and cleansing tools are not able to correct all missing or inaccurate data. The same limitations that apply to analysis tools apply here. Data cleansed by automated tools can only be as clean as the automated business rules allow. Much error correction will have to be conducted by people.

Knowledge workers must be aware that "automated cleansing" does not automatically mean accuracy. Physical data assessments can confirm the accuracy level of the cleansed and transformed data.

Representative Products

Table 10.4 provides a representative set of products that perform data reengineering, transformation, and cleansing functions. For a legend of the product classifications, see Table 10.1.

Information Quality Defect Prevention Tools

Defect prevention tools are used to automate information process quality improvement by minimizing error introduction at the source. They provide automation of business rule tests in the applications that create and update data, as described in Chapter 9, "Improving Information *Process* Quality."

These tools provide callable program modules, subroutines, or libraries of functions and data tables to implement data edit and validation rules.

Table 10.4 Representative *Data Reengineering, Cleansing, and Transformation* Products

SUPPLIER	PRODUCT NAME	IQ CLASSIFICATION
Ardent Software	DataStage	CG
Carleton Corp.	Enterprise Integrator, Passport	CG
Century Analysis	CAI Integration Toolset: TDM Interface Engine	C
Constellar Corp.	WarehouseBuilder	CG
D2K	Tapestry	CG
DataFlux Corp.	Data Quality Workbench: SmartScrub; Datalogue; Extend; MatchMaker; IntelliMerge; Inspector	CG; A; R; CN
DupeKiller, Inc.	DupeKiller	A,CN, S
Evolutionary Technologies	EXTRACT	CG
GB Information Management	Accelerator; Originator; Enhancer; Address Manager; Postcode Manager	CN, P
Gladstone Computer Services	DQ Admin-istrator, Warehouse Quality Admin-istrator	CG, A
Global-Z Int'l	Third party name/address cleansing	CN, SO
Group 1 Software Inc.	NADIS: ScrubMaster, SearchMaster; OnLooker; Model 1 Cross-Seller	CN, P, R
Harland	Harland Warehouse Data Prep System	CN
Hopweiser	Probe, RAINS	CN
HotData, Inc.	HotData, HotData Developer's Kit	CN, S
i.d.Centric, a Firstlogic technology	i.d.Centric Data Quality Suite	CN, P, S
Information Builders	EDA-SQL; SmartMart; SNAPpack Data Warehouse	C
Innovative Systems	Analyzer; Verify; Dictionary; Edit; Match; Scrub; Household; CorpMatch; Find	CN, CG, A, M, R, P, S
Integral Solutions Ltd.	Clementine	R, CG
International Software Products	Third-party cleansing	C, SO

Continues

Table 10.4   Representative *Data Reengineering, Cleansing, and Transformation* Products (Continued)

SUPPLIER	PRODUCT NAME	IQ CLASSIFICATION
Leonard's Logic. Ltd.	Designer; Scheduler; Engine; Data Links	CG
MasterSoft	Nadis: ScrubMaster, SearchMaster, Onlooker, ModelMAX, dbPROFILE	CN, P, R
MatchWare Technologies (a subsidiary of Vality)	AutoStan; AutoMatch; MatchWare/CL; MatchWare/ PACE	A, R, C
OTS Group	Global Third Party Name/Address Cleansing & Enhancement Service	A; CG, CN, SO
Pinnacle Software	Parse-O-Matic	CG
Pitney Bowes Software Systems	ReUnion	CN, P, S
Platinum Technology	InfoRefiner; InfoPump; InfoTransport; InfoHub; DecisionBase	CG
Prism Solutions (acquired by Ardent Software, Spring 99)	Prism Warehouse Executive; Prism Quality Manager (formerly QDB Analyze)	C, G, A
QAS Systems	Quick Address: Rapid, Pro, Batch, Names, DataPlus, Address-Point, Updater	C, P
Qualitative Marketing Software	Centrus Suite	CN, P
SAS Institute Inc.	SAS Warehouse Administrator: Transformation Engine	CG
Search Software America	NAME 3, EXTENSIONS, Data Clustering Engine	A, R, CN, P
SmartDB Corp.	SMART DB Workbench	C
Trillium Software (division of Harte-Hanks)	Trillium Software System	CN, CG, R, S, P
Vality Technology	Integrity Data Re-engineering System	CG, R

Note: The author has made every attempt to provide accurate information about the listed products. Information quality decay will cause some of this data to be out of date by the time you read it. Some suppliers have not replied to requests for verification, and if there are errors, we apologize for the inconvenience. We will maintain correct information on our Web site for all updates supplied to us. For a current list of information quality products, including a brief annotation and operating platforms, visit www.infoimpact.com and select *Information Quality Resources*.

Tool Capabilities

Defect prevention tools provide the same kind of functions as data cleansing tools. However, they provide "cleansing" during the online data creation process, rather than in batch mode.

Tool Limitations

Defect prevention tools can only implement edits and automate validity tests. They can provide reasonability tests and assure valid values, such as valid codes or valid addresses, or confirm postal services change of address, but cannot necessarily assure the correct values. Quality of information input requires trained and incented information producers.

Representative Products

Table 10.5 provides a representative set of products that perform information quality defect prevention functions. For a legend of the information quality product classifications, see Table 10.1.

Metadata Management and Quality Tools

Metadata management and quality tools provide automated management and quality control of data definition and information architecture development. These tools are used to support data definition assessment, described in Chapter 5, "Assessing Data Definition and Information Architecture Quality."

Tool Capabilities

Metadata management and quality tools perform one or more of the following functions:

- Assure conformance to data naming standards
- Validate data name abbreviations
- Assure all required components of data definition are provided
- Maintain metadata for control of data reengineering and cleansing processes
- Evaluate data models for normalization
- Evaluate database design for integrity, such as primary key to foreign key integrity, and performance optimization

Table 10.5 Representative *Information Quality Defect Prevention* Products

SUPPLIER	PRODUCT NAME	IQ CLASSIFICATION
DBE Software,	DB-Examiner	AM, P, M
Gamma Research	OCRProof™	A, P
GB Information Management	Accelerator; Originator; Enhancer; Address Manager; Postcode Manager	CN, P
Group 1 Software Inc.	NADIS: ScrubMaster, SearchMaster; OnLooker; Model 1 Cross-Seller	CN, P
i.d.Centric, a Firstlogic technology	i.d. Centric Data Quality Suite	CN, P, S
Innovative Systems	Analyzer; Verify; Dictionary; Edit; Match; Scrub; Household; CorpMatch; Find	CN, CG, A, M, R, P, S
Kismet Analytic Corp.	KisMeta Validator, Analyst	P, M
MasterSoft	Nadis: ScrubMaster, SearchMaster, Onlooker, ModelMAX, dbPROFILE	CN, P
Pitney Bowes Software Systems	ReUnion	CN, P, S
QAS Systems	Quick Address: Rapid, Pro, Batch, Names, DataPlus, Address-Point, Updater	C, P
Qualitative Marketing Software	Centrus Suite	CN, P
Search Software America	NAME 3, EXTENSIONS, Data Clustering Engine	A, R, CN, P
Trillium Software (a division of Harte-Hanks)	Trillium Software System	CNG, R, S, P

Note: The author has made every attempt to provide accurate information about the listed products. Information quality decay will cause some of this data to be out of date by the time you read it. Some suppliers have not replied to requests for verification, and if there are errors, we apologize for the inconvenience. We will maintain correct information on our Web site for all updates supplied to us. For a current list of information quality products, including a brief annotation and operating platforms, visit www.infoimpact.com and select *Information Quality Resources*.

Tool Limitations

Metadata management and quality tools support the documentation of the specification of the information product. The basic components include data name, definition, and business rules, along with the relationship of data such as is represented in a data model or database design. These tools cannot determine whether data required by knowledge workers is missing, or that included data is defined correctly, or whether that data is required data in the first place.

Metadata quality tools may audit or assure that data names and abbreviations conform to standards, but they cannot assess whether the data standards are "good" standards that produce data names that are understandable to knowledge workers.

Representative Products

Table 10.6 provides a representative set of products that perform information quality analysis functions. For a legend of the information quality product classification, see Table 10.1.

FOR A CURRENT, ANNOTATED LIST OF INFORMATION QUALITY PRODUCTS

Because information quality product offerings are developing rapidly, product information will be out of date by the time this book reaches you. A current, regularly updated list of information quality products is maintained on the Internet at www.infoimpact.com under *Information Quality Resources*.

This list includes supplier name, product name, Information Quality (IQ) classification, operating platforms, and brief product description.

Table 10.6 Representative *Metadata Management and Quality* Products

SUPPLIER	PRODUCT NAME	IQ CLASSIFICATION
Compedia	SA Name Cop, EnComp	A, M
DBE Software,	DB-Examiner	A, M, P
Innovative Systems	Analyzer; Verify; Dictionary; Edit; Match; Scrub; Household; CorpMatch; Find	CN, CG, A, M, R, P, S
Intellidex (a subsidiary of Sybase)	Warehouse Control Center: User Module; Administrator Module; Meta Data Manager	M
Kismet Analytic Corp.	KisMeta Validator, Analyst	P,M
Pine Cone Systems	Content Tracker, Refreshment Tracker	A, M

Evaluating Information Quality Tools

You should evaluate any software tool from the standpoint of how well it solves the business problems and supports accomplishing the enterprise business objectives. The objective is not what is the "best" tool, but rather, what are the tools you can use "best" to accomplish your information quality goals.

First, define all the business problems you are solving. Because information quality is an enterprise issue, the evaluation and selection of information quality software should be an enterprise initiative.

Once you understand the business problems you are solving, determine what category or categories of information quality function automation are required. For example, the fact that you are developing a data warehouse does not automatically mean that your problem is cleansing data for the warehouse. The real problem may be data defects at the source, and the business problem to be solved is that the information producers do not know who uses the information they create. Therefore, data defect prevention software and training are required to solve the real business problem.

Having defined the business problem, work with the information stakeholders, those who are in the value chains of the business problem, to define the requirements for both automation support and for business procedure and management support.

Translate those requirements into evaluation criteria, such as:

Cost relative to business value. Some information quality products are very expensive, but the cost-savings derived may be multiple times the ownership costs of the product. Lowest price does not necessarily mean "best value." And highest price does not necessarily mean "best of breed." Quality from a customer perspective means the product solves your information quality problems easily, minimizing your cost to use the product while maximizing the quality functions performed.

Cost of ownership. The cost picture to evaluate is not "How much does it cost?" This only represents the cost of acquisition, and this might be only a fraction of the overall cost of the product. Rather, the right cost figure is "How much does it cost to acquire, maintain, and use?" This is the cost of ownership. A less expensive product to buy that is difficult to learn and use, and requires extraordinary training or supplier-required consulting may be more expensive in the long run than an easy-to-use product with a higher purchase price tag. On the other hand, an inexpensive product may be easier to learn and use, and while it may have less functionality than other products, it may be the best overall value.

Platform type support. How does the product work in your information environment? Does it run on your hardware and operating system, or will new technology be required?

Data access support. Does the product access the data in your information environment directly and easily? The more data has to be converted to a non-native data type, the more cost is involved, and the more the potential for error is introduced. Or does it rely on third-party extract products? The more that different tools must be "integrated," the more complex the environment.

Database/file type support. Does the product access data directly from your databases and files, or will conversion of data be required? This adds time and cost, as well as potential for error to be introduced.

Data type support (generic versus specific). Does the product support the type of data your enterprise requires? Geographic data analysis or cleansing functions in a tool are irrelevant if you do not have geographic data types. Likewise, a sophisticated name and address cleansing product is not needed if your organization's customer base consists of 50 commercial customers.

Comprehensive duplicate record identification criteria. How well does the tool utilize several different matching criteria to be able to match duplicate records? Can the criteria be used to match data of any type, or name and address only?

Comprehensive duplicate record consolidation criteria. How well does the cleansing software support complex business rules to define and determine data consolidation requirements, such as:

- Files precedence, or occurrence of reference.

- Sets of fields within files. For example, select fields 1–3 from file A, but select fields 4–7 from file B. The record-of-reference may be by groups of fields in different files, and not necessarily all fields from one file.

- Exception selection criteria. Can you specify rules for when to select the same attributes from several files, such as most recently updated or least recently updated? Can you specify multiple selection rules?

- How do you specify and maintain those rules?

Comprehensive transform logic. What kinds of templates of data transformations are provided? Do they support *all* enterprises' data types, both from the source data to the target data?

Ease of defining transform rules. How easy is it to define transform rules that may not be "predefined"? Are there easy-to-use rule definition features, or does the tool require coding the business rules into callable routines? How flexible and easy are they to write?

Ability to update both source and target data. Does the cleansing product have the capability to cleanse data in the source files, or does it only provide for cleansing and transformation of extracted data? While it is a business decision to update data within the source database, the basic rule of thumb is that if the data is still being used at the source, correct it there. If data is inconsistent between the source and target, queries run against both sets of data will yield inconsistent answers.

Multiple source file to single target file synchronization. Does the cleansing product enable data from multiple source files to be matched and consolidated into a single target file?

Single source file to multiple target file synchronization. Does the cleansing product enable data from a single source file to be transformed and propagated into multiple target files? For example, poorly designed legacy database files may contain hundreds of fields about many different entity types that must be propagated to several different files.

Multiple field business rule transformations. Is the product able to perform transforms combining multiple fields? Is there a limit on the number of fields the tool can use to compute derived data? Can it perform multiple Boolean logic tests in order to make transformations of data?

Extraction of single field to multiple target fields. Can the tool provide for extracting different types of facts from a single field (domain chaos), and propagate them to the appropriate target fields? For example, if one field, such as `Customer-Source-Code`, may contain two facts, one being the `sales-rep-id` and the other being a `marketing-campaign-code`, can a data transformation extract and propagate the right facts to `sales-rep-id` and `marketing-campaign-code` fields?

Free-form text and business rule analysis. How well does the tool analyze business rules and other characteristics about the data? Are you able to discover anomalies in the data with the tool, or must you physically discover them yourself?

"Integration" with enterprise repositories. Must you recode business rules to the information quality product, or can you extract business rules and other metadata from your own repositories and dictionaries? Can this product's repository become a central "enterprise" repository for business rules? This would require multiple people to be able to extract information from the tool. Are there extract tools from which you can extract the business rules in a form that can be integrated into an enterprise repository?

Flexibility of changing transform business rules. How easy is it to update business rules? Can they be maintained centrally, but updated from different locations? Can updated transform rules be applied easily to data that was transformed already from the previous business rule? For example, if you have a domain value set, such that a value of "10" is now split into two values, those of "12" and "14" on the basis of known data, can the tool automatically update data that has a value of "10" into its proper "12" or "14" value?

Comprehensiveness of external profile data. Does the product provide externally provided data such as postal service, census, geographic, demographic, or other profile data that can be appended to Address or Customer data? If so, does it provide the kind of data *your* organization needs to better understand its markets and customers.

Definition of external data. How well is external data defined? (See Chapter 5 "Assessing Data Definition and Information Architecture Quality.") Is the meaning of the data clear from the way it will be presented to knowledge workers? How easy is it for the end knowledge workers to access its definition? What is the original source of the information supplied?

Accuracy and completeness of external data. Does the supplier provide accuracy and completeness measures of the data it provides? Has the provider conducted an information quality assessment to document its reliability? Does it warrant its quality in any way?

Currency of external profile data. If this product provides external data, what is the currency, or "age," of that data? As a hypothetical example, suppose postal service change of addresses are provided to the IQ tool supplier every other month. Suppose the postal services requires two weeks to log changes of address, one week to prepare the data to be sent to the supplier, and one week to deliver it. The data is four weeks old, or has a currency of the data four weeks prior to receipt by the IQ tool supplier. If the IQ supplier takes one week to update its files and one week to deliver the address updates to you, the data is now six weeks old. If you require two weeks to install the updates, the data is eight weeks old. Given an annual decay rate of 17 percent—17 percent of people in the United States change addresses every year, or 1.4 percent every month—the information quality of change-of-address data that is two months old contains approximately 2.8 percent incorrect addresses. If census data is provided, what is the date of the census?

Ease of use. Because data cleansing and information quality assessment are cost activities, you must minimize the effort required to perform them. You must weigh the tradeoff of using a labor-intensive but comprehensive tool versus an easy-to-use but less comprehensive tool. Compare the relative quality goals achievable to the effort and expense to achieve them. Can you learn to use the tool easily, or must you hire the supplier's consultants for long periods of time?

Knowledge transfer. If training is required to learn how to use the tool, what resources are available? What are the training length and costs for you to become proficient?

Methodology support. Does the supplier have a methodology for the use of the tool? If so, is the methodology a full information quality improvement methodology, or does it only address the capabilities of the tool? If the latter is true, does the supplier market the methodology as a "complete" methodology? It is okay if a supplier has an *incomplete* methodology that addresses the effective use of its tool, as long as they truthfully advertise and communicate its scope and limitations. Organizations will be either tool providers or methodology providers. It is very difficult to be both at the same time.

Multiuser support. How widely accessible is the tool? Does it require a central "administrator," or can multiple people cooperatively use the product?

Automated scheduling features. How easy is it to schedule and manage the jobs to run the quality assessments or transformations?

Data defect prevention capabilities. Does the product (assessment and cleansing) have the ability to be executed real time from applications that create and update data? Are the same business rules that have been defined for assessment or for cleansing reusable by your own data create programs? This significantly increases the value of the product. You define the quality test or transform rules once. However, you can use them both for assessing information quality or for cleansing the data, and then can also use the same defined quality rules to prevent data defects using the same defined rules.

Benchmark sample data. Are you able to run a benchmark against a sample of your own data? This applies to both information quality assessment and data cleansing products. Is the benchmark actually run against your data, or is the benchmark a simulation of the results you would get? Benchmarks run directly against your data tend to indicate better ease of use.

Quality of results. Is the output of the tool quality results? How well does a cleansing tool correct data *correctly* or *enhance* it with accurate data? How well does the analysis tool's results measure accuracy of data? Conduct a physical assessment as described in Chapter 6 "Information Quality Assessment," step 7, *Measure Information Quality*, to compare the results of the tool to the accuracy of data cleansed or measured.

Techniques for Information Quality

There are many techniques useful in information quality management and cited as techniques used in various information quality assessment and improvement steps in Part Two of this book, "Processes for Improving Information Quality."

Information Quality Technique Categories

There are five major categories of techniques useful for information quality management. The categories of techniques are described here, with a list of the techniques referred to in Part Two. Due to space limitations in this book, a description of the information quality techniques is maintained on the Internet at www.infoimpact.com under the button *Information Quality Resources*. They include:

Information gathering and analysis techniques. These techniques help us understand the nature or extent of information quality problems.

Documentation techniques. These techniques are useful for managing information and communicating information that should be shared.

Presentation techniques. These are techniques that help communicate information such as information quality assessment results in ways that facilitate improvement.

Problem-solving and improvement techniques. Once you have discovered information quality problems, these techniques help you improve the process or data.

Information quality control techniques. Once you have improved a process, these techniques help you keep it improved.

Information Quality Techniques

The techniques are listed in alphabetic order for ease of reference. Descriptions of information quality techniques are maintained on the Internet at www.infoimpact.com under the button *Information Quality Resources*.

Bar and column charts

Benchmarking

Catalogs

Cause-and-effect diagram

Checklists

Communication

Cost analysis

Customer satisfaction survey questionnaire

Customer satisfaction telephone survey

Data analysis

Data dictionary

Data flow diagram

Data matching techniques

Data modeling software

Delphi approach

Edit and validation software routines

Error correction procedure

Evaluation and selection

External, online, or public databases

Facilitated brainstorming

Facilitated data definition workshop

Facilitated sessions

Information directories

Information flow diagram

Internally developed software

Modeling software with matrix facility

Pareto diagram

Performance measures

Physical information quality assessment

Policy statements

Prioritization

Process procedure documentation

Project management

Quality assurance review

Quality circles

Quality function deployment

Random number generator

Random sampling

Repository

Root cause analysis

Sharable spreadsheet or database

Statistical control chart

Structured information view walkthroughs

Time and motion analysis

Training

"Why?" analysis

Conclusion

Information quality products can be powerful tools in the war against information quality problems. Successful use of the products requires understanding the business problems you are solving, understanding the functions and limitations of the products, understanding how to apply the products effectively within effective information quality processes, and accountability for information.

Information quality techniques are proven, reusable activities to assist you in analyzing, measuring, documenting, cleansing, preventing, and controlling information quality. These should always be seen and used as a means to an end, and not an end in themselves. Measure information quality not to create reports, but to increase customer satisfaction and business effectiveness by eliminating problems caused by poor-quality information.

Now that you have defined processes to measure and improve information quality, and have tools and techniques to support those processes, you must make sure your organization makes the cultural changes to "make" quality happen and to sustain information quality as a business management tool. Part Three shows you how to establish the information quality environment.

Establishing the Information Quality Environment

*"The only place where success comes before
work is in the dictionary."*

–VIDAL SASSOON

Information quality improvement is not simply "scrubbing" data to put it into the data warehouse. Information quality is not simply auditing data to measure it. Information quality improvement is:

- Fundamental changes in how the information systems organization defines, develops, and delivers its products and services
- Fundamental changes in how the enterprise operates

These changes are systemic and permeate the entire organization. Sustainable information quality improvement will be accompanied by a change in the way people think and act about their information products. The information quality mind-set is a change from a selfish and competitive spirit, "I create the information I need to do my job," to a helping and cooperative spirit, "I create the information *we* need to do *our* jobs."

This culture shift is counterintuitive in the hierarchical, downsized organization where employees are strapped for time. However, the evidence reveals that when information producers create complete, reliable information, downstream knowledge workers can use it with trust. As a result they save the costs of having to verify the data, find missing information, and correct inaccurate data. Not only has the organization saved money, it has increased productivity of employees and employee morale, which translates to increased customer satisfaction and ends in increased profits.

How does one achieve this culture transformation and implement an effective process for information quality improvement? This can be implemented only through an organized movement of planning and implementing information quality improvement principles and processes.

Chapter 11 describes Deming's 14 Points of Quality and their direct ramifications for information quality improvement. There is no better place to begin than with the same principles the Japanese incorporated into the very fabric of their organizations' culture to achieve a continuous quality improvement mind-set.

Chapter 12 describes information stewardship, the business accountabilities for information products. Without individual accountability for the information everyone in the enterprise creates, updates, uses, or defines, models, and builds databases for, there cannot be lasting information quality improvement.

Chapter 13 describes the steps to implement an information quality environment. It begins with how to conduct an information quality management maturity gap analysis to help you identify where to begin.

Chapter 14 concludes with a summary and celebration of the tremendous benefits that your information quality journey will bring as you move your organization into the Realized Information Age.

The 14 Points of Information Quality

"You don't have to do this—survival is not compulsory."

–W. EDWARDS DEMING

The reader is forewarned that the following pages are X-rated. No, this is not the pornographic section; however, the following pages contain material objectionable to managers who have hidden agendas and employees who purposely hoard knowledge to advance themselves and their careers. W. Edwards Deming's ideas have been contrary to many concepts of traditional management education. As a result, Deming's principles did not achieve permanent acceptance in postwar America until the economic crisis of the 1980s when the Japanese quality revolution transformed the economics of doing business.

Deming identifies 14 points of quality for real and permanent quality improvement. These points of quality, which Deming applied to manufacturing quality, apply directly to data as the product of business processes.[1]

Deming's 14 Points for Management Transformation

Dr. W. Edwards Deming has provided the basis for transforming management not for quality's sake, but for business survival. "Adoption and action on the 14 Points are a signal that management intends to stay in business and aim to protect

---

[1]The following 14 Points of Information Quality have appeared in the *DM Review* in my monthly column, "Plain English On Data Quality," which began June 1997.

investors and jobs."[2] These points provide the principles to any business endeavor, large or small, manufacturing or service sector, enterprise or business unit, or organization within an enterprise.

DEMING'S 14 POINTS OF QUALITY[3]

1. Create constancy of purpose toward improvement of product and service, with the aim to become competitive and to stay in business, and to provide jobs.
2. Adopt the new philosophy. We are in a new economic age. Western management must awaken to the challenge, must learn their responsibilities, and take on leadership for change.
3. Cease dependence on inspection to achieve quality. Eliminate the need for inspection on a mass basis by building quality into the product in the first place.
4. End the practice of awarding business on the basis of price tag. Instead, minimize total cost. Move toward a single supplier for any one item, on a long-term relationship of loyalty and trust.
5. Improve constantly and forever the system of production and service, to improve quality and productivity, and thus constantly decrease costs.
6. Institute training on the job.
7. Institute leadership. The aim of supervision should be to help people and machines and gadgets to do a better job. Supervision of management is in need of overhaul, as well as supervision of production workers.
8. Drive out fear, so that everyone may work effectively for the company.
9. Break down barriers between departments. People in research, design, sales, and production must work as a team, to foresee problems of production and in use that may be encountered with the product or service.
10. Eliminate slogans, exhortations, and targets for the work force asking for zero defects and new levels of productivity. Such exhortations only create adversarial relationships, as the bulk of the causes of low quality and low productivity belong to the system and thus lie beyond the power of the work force.
11a. Eliminate work standards (quotas) on the factory floor. Substitute leadership.
11b. Eliminate management by objective. Eliminate management by numbers, numerical goals. Substitute leadership.
12a. Remove barriers that rob the hourly worker of his right to pride of workmanship. The responsibility of supervisors must be changed from sheer numbers to quality.
12b. Remove barriers that rob people in management and in engineering of their right to pride of workmanship. This means, *inter alia*, abolishment of the annual or merit rating and of management by objective.
13. Institute a vigorous program of education and self-improvement.
14. Put everybody in the company to work to accomplish the transformation. The transformation is everybody's job.

[2]W. Edwards Deming, *Out of the Crisis*, Cambridge, MA: MIT Center for Advanced Engineering Study, 1986, p. 23.

[3]Ibid., pp. 23–24.

Point 1: Create Constancy of Purpose for Information Quality Improvement

Deming's first Point of Quality describes the beginning point of a quality environment: "Create constancy of purpose for the improvement of product and service."[4] Constancy of purpose means dedication to quality as a way of doing business. The purpose of this constancy is to become competitive, stay in business, and provide jobs.

Business and IS (Information Systems) management must balance two sets of problems: those of today and those of tomorrow. Businesses fail when management focuses too much attention on today's immediate needs, such as quarterly profits, at the expense of adequately solving tomorrow's problem, such as discovering and satisfying customers' emerging requirements. The pressure of solving today's problems—meeting project target dates, converting applications and databases to support the Year 2000, "fixing" application bugs to get operations back up, cleaning data from legacy databases for the data warehouse—must be balanced with creating tomorrow's solutions. What good is it that applications are "Year 2000 enabled" if the enterprise goes out of business because it was not able to develop applications that drive critical new processes? What good is clean data in the data warehouse if it is the *wrong* data? What good is measuring information quality if it only leads to finger pointing, blame, and deeper entrenchment into political fiefdoms of proprietary databases? Deming says no company without a plan for the future will survive. No IS organization without a plan that positions the enterprise to meet tomorrow's knowledge requirements and to rapidly adapt to new ways of performing business processes can—or should be allowed to—survive.

Constancy of Purpose

One aspect of constancy of purpose is innovation. Innovation, however, is not innovation for innovation's sake. New IS products and services must not simply be new applications or new technology platforms. Creating a Web site because it is the technology du jour is not innovation.

What is its purpose? How does it move one to accomplish the mission? IS must improve how its business partners achieve *strategic* business objectives, and at the same time improve its end-customers' lives. The ramification is that information producers may be asked to capture attributes about business events that are needed by downstream knowledge workers. These attributes may not be needed within the information producers' department, but are required to effectively serve the end customer.

[4]Deming, *Out of the Crisis*, p. 24.

Constancy of purpose for information quality means that Data Resource Management (DRM) must continually ask, "How are its information products going to capture and deliver knowledge resources that enable the business to achieve its mission, and how will it improve end-customer satisfaction?" It also means application development must continually ask, "How is this application going to support reengineered processes that enable the business to achieve its mission, and how will it improve end-customer satisfaction?" Quality information systems products will be reusable and require low maintenance. Quality databases will be minimally redundant (except where planned *and* managed) and reusable by subsequent applications and business areas by simply adding any newly required data and not requiring structural database changes. Quality applications will be nonredundant (except where replacing planned obsolete applications) and will add value.

To achieve quality innovation, Deming says, top management must have a "declared unshakable commitment to quality and productivity." Permanent information quality improvement occurs only when senior IS and business management recognize two facts: one, the amount of time and money spent fixing today's problems as the result of nonquality information is unacceptable. And two, this wasted time results from creating short-term nonintegrated applications and not spending enough time building a stable and flexible information infrastructure that solves tomorrow's problems.

Information systems productivity is not, "How fast can we develop and implement an application?" It is, "How fast we can develop the next application by reusing quality data and application components produced in the first application?" Information systems quality is delivering *stable* (not requiring a lot of enhancement requests) applications as a result of reusable quality components such as shared data. This requires planning and development of reusable information infrastructure components that enable the enterprise to accomplish its mission and continually satisfy its end customers.

A critical aspect of constancy of purpose of information quality is that the "obligation to the customer never ceases." IS products and services must always be planned, designed, built, and implemented with the *downstream* knowledge worker and *end* customer in mind. The only success measure is how well do they satisfy the end customer and meet their needs and expectations. This does *not* mean how well it satisfies the immediate beneficiaries of that application. It *does* mean how well the product of this application (data) satisfies all downstream knowledge workers' needs to satisfy the end customer.

The ramifications of Deming's Point 1 for information quality are twofold:

Does the enterprise vision and mission include the concepts of information as a strategic business resource that adds value to its products and services for customer satisfaction?

Does IS have a vision and mission that includes developing products and services with success criteria being measured not just by the immediate beneficiaries of the services, but by downstream knowledge workers and end customers? Does it subscribe to its responsibility that "the obligation to the knowledge worker never ceases"?

How to Create Constancy of Purpose for Information Quality Improvement

The following are steps to take to create constancy of purpose for information quality:

1. Create a vision and a mission statement if your IS or DRM organization does not have one.

2. Assure that the mission statement is directly driven by (not just linked to) the enterprise vision and mission.

3. Assure that the IS and DRM objectives have measures that illustrate how they contribute to the long-term enterprise objectives.

4. Assure that the mission statement focuses on your customers (the downstream business beneficiaries and not just the immediate beneficiaries of IS products and services).

5. Assure that the mission statement focuses on the enterprise customers (the ultimate beneficiaries of IS products and services).

6. Develop plans that are both strategic and long range, and that can be delivered quickly and incrementally and are reusable.

7. Measure the reuse of IS and DRM components as a measure of quality against the development of redundant and nonvalue-adding interface programs.

8. Assure that everyone in IS and DRM subscribes first to the business and then to the IS and DRM vision statements.

9. Once you have done this, make constancy real by reading and contemplating your vision and mission statements daily for the first five minutes of the day, until your mission becomes the subconscious driver of your daily activities.

10. Keep asking yourself, "Is what I am doing or about to do moving me closer to achieving our vision and mission?" Try this daily for a month, and see if it does not help you achieve a constancy of purpose for information quality.

Doing this creates a new drive and purpose for information quality.

Point 2: Adopt the New Philosophy of Quality Shared Information

Quality Point 2 extends Point 1: "Adopt the new philosophy of quality information." Deming admonishes that quality must become the new religion. This is not religion of quality for quality's sake, but a passion for continually delighting the customer. This quality "religion" demands behavior changes. The new economic era has redefined the rules for successfully competing in the global marketplace. Quality is no longer optional. Consumers have new expectations based on the availability of reliable products and services. The new economics demand new standards—not new data naming conventions, but new standards of information quality.

"Reliable service reduces costs," Deming says. Mistakes, rework, and delays are what raise costs. Philip Crosby in *Quality Is Free* reconfirms this. What increases costs are the "unquality things," such as doing things over, around, or instead of because of poor quality.

Quality Point 2 really means a transformation of management, according to Deming. Management must dismantle the organizational structures that have created barriers to quality, and caused inefficiency in performing business processes.

Information Quality Point 2 likewise means information quality is no longer optional. Every data warehouse project reconfirms this. The requirement for information quality is driven by the fact that business can no longer afford the costs and problems caused by poor-quality information. Every hour the business spends hunting for missing data, correcting inaccurate data, working around data problems, scrambling to assemble information across disintegrated databases, resolving data-related customer complaints, and so on, is an hour of *cost only*, and either reduces profits or is passed on in higher prices to the customer. That hour is never again available to add value.

Two information product and service facts are also clear: Reliable information management reduces information systems costs, and reliable information reduces business costs.

Reliable Information Management Reduces Information Systems Costs

Unfortunately, conventional wisdom does not understand this. Information management is often perceived as *adding costs* to an application. To be sure, an information management function that only adds costs to information systems *should* be eliminated and *replaced* with an effective, value-adding information management program. Information management is not simply developing application-specific data models and defining application data. Quality information management defines and models data that is *reusable* throughout the enterprise. Quality information management is measured by how much of its defined data and databases are reused and shared. By eliminating the need for redundant applications creating data redundantly, redundant databases, and unnecessary transforming interfaces, quality information management actually *reduces* costs of applications development and maintenance, and *eliminates* the costs to fix problems caused by inconsistent redundant data.

Reliable Information Reduces Business Costs

Quality information likewise reduces business costs by eliminating the costs of scrap and rework caused by inaccurate or missing data. But more significantly, quality information *minimizes* missed and lost business opportunity due to poor customer service caused by nonquality information. When customers receive poor service because of problems, they may not complain to you. They simply go elsewhere, and take with them their customer lifetime value. If all companies provide the same level of (non)quality, they may simply trade unhappy customers. Even this has costs. It costs four to five times as much to gain a new customer as to retain a happy one. But when someone raises the quality bar, the rules change for everyone.

Ramifications of Point 2 for information systems management:

The purpose of applications is not to automate processes. Applications must capture, maintain, and deliver the knowledge of the enterprise.

Data, as a product of information systems, demands new standards of excellence to reduce the costs of nonquality.

Point 2 means a transformation of information systems management. In 1980, James Martin asserted that one should not view a database as a grandiose project, but rather as a change in the management of data processing. Some 20 years later, many IS organizations still do not understand this. The IS mission is not to deliver automation "solutions" to business areas; IS must deliver solutions that solve *boundary* problems between business areas. This is where nonquality information kills the effectiveness and the efficiency of the enterprise. When IS solves these problems it enables information as a strategic enterprise resource. Without this, IS cannot transform the enterprise into a realized Information Age organization.

How to Adopt the New Philosophy of Information Quality

1. Revisit your information management mission. Does it focus on the customer of information? Does it include guarantees of quality of information

systems and databases? Does it include a philosophy of partnership with the business community to guarantee information quality for downstream knowledge workers?

2. Make information quality a habit.

3. Eliminate a fire-fighting reaction when problems occur. Instead, look for ways to eliminate the problem cause.

4. Document the number of transforming interface programs (omit *managed* replication programs and extract programs that retain the same data definition and domain values) and redundant applications and databases that capture data about the same or similar data types. The truth horrifies most management: 43 redundant applications and files maintaining a "key data element"; 92 different part files, many with different primary keys with no ability to integrate them; and 175 customer files—requiring 6 people 4 months to answer the question, "Who is our best customer?" Do not gloss over this. Ignoring it can cripple the enterprise.

5. Estimate the costs of developing *and* maintaining a transforming interface program, create program, and database file over their respective lives. Multiply this times the number of redundant occurrences to get the cost of redundancy.

6. Estimate the amount of time IS spends in resolving problems due to inconsistent data to get the cost of redundancy "scrap and rework" (nonquality of the redundancy).

7. Add these two figures together. This represents only a portion of the costs of nonquality information in the enterprise.

8. If you are unhappy with the results, develop a plan to make fundamental changes in your IS organization, including:

   - A strategic information management program that provides leadership and education for quality shared information.

   - Data model development by teams of business subject matter experts, not simply the primary beneficiaries of an immediate application. It can, and *must*, be developed rapidly by involving the right people with the right charter.

   - Data models developed in three levels of abstraction: 1) Enterprisewide business information model that senior business management can understand; 2) Detailed conceptual data models by business resource (subject) that support cross-functional business value chains; and 3) Physical databases that are stable, flexible, and reusable.

   - Application development around value chains that reuse data and are nonredundant.

- Information policy that articulates the enterprise values for information as a strategic business resource, business accountability for information quality, and acceptable behaviors for stewardship of information. Top management issues this policy.

- An inventory of critical information redundancy and a plan to eliminate unnecessary redundancy and maximize quality shared information.

- An information quality improvement process whose objective is to increase business effectiveness and decrease nonquality information costs by measuring information quality, identifying defective processes, facilitating root-cause analysis, and providing education in information quality principles.

Adopting the new philosophy of information quality does not mean *saying* one believes in it and creating slogans. It means acting on those beliefs and *changing behavior* to make it happen.

Point 3: Cease Dependence on Information Product Quality Assessments Alone

Ironically, the practice of "quality assurance" inspections and walkthroughs to provide quality of products and services is actually a deterrent to quality. Quality assurance, as in inspection of products to assure conformance to specifications, actually increases costs and provides a false sense that one is providing quality. The goal of inspections (such as data model review, program testing, or data audits) is to discover defective products and fix the defects, or throw out defective products that are too costly to fix. The end result of inspection as a means of quality assurance is expensive, ineffective because it cannot assure 100 percent discovery of defects, and does not achieve real process improvement.

True quality comes from the improvement of the process to eliminate defects, rather than from inspection, according to Deming's third Point of Quality. Quality is achieved by designing *good* quality in, rather than by inspecting *bad* quality out. When quality is built in, it reduces costs and increases productivity. The costs of nonquality result from the scrap and rework of defective products and services, and in lost customer lifetime value when nonquality causes one to miss a new opportunity, or to lose customers.

To be sure, some inspections and quality assurance reviews will always be required. For one thing, inspection is required to tell you how well you are doing. Periodic data assessments are required to assure the reliability of the quality of data being produced. In some cases, where the impact of nonquality is significant, as in safety or in totally unacceptable costs, quality review is required, possibly in 100 percent of product cases. Several fatal airline crashes have had information quality problems as part of the cause. An information quality problem of an incorrect wing flap setting was the immediate cause of one fatal airline crash. The root cause was that the crew had failed to go through the standard quality assurance "checklist," during which time they would have assured that they had set the wing flaps properly.

When one designs quality into the process, the net result is that the quality assurance process simply confirms that quality is taking place and discovers few, if any, defects.

From Data Model Inspections to Quality Information Model Development

Here I discuss the ramifications of Deming's Quality Point 3—"Cease dependence on mass inspections"—for building in quality in the data definition process. In the next section I discuss the ramifications for building in quality in the business processes that create and update data.

How does one achieve data definition and data model quality? Not by post-model development walkthroughs, but by performing a data definition process that achieves quality during data model development.

How to Be Sure Your Data Development Process Produces Quality Information Architecture

To assure quality data definition and information architecture, the data development process must have the following characteristics:

❑ It is defined. It describes the why, what, how, when, where, and who of the process.

❑ It is repeatable. Different modeling teams can produce consistent data model results using the process.

❑ It has a process owner ultimately accountable for the integrity of the process and its outcome.

❑ Individual process participants are trained, empowered, and held accountable for their role as a team in the outcome.

❑ It incorporates reuse of already defined components. How many times should an organization need to define person name or address?

❑ It has multiple levels of abstraction that separate business model from detailed conceptual model from the physical model.

❑ It incorporates controlled evolution. Experience has demonstrated that data models at a detail level cannot be "created" in one sitting, but require managed evolution to develop.

❑ It begins with a high-level, business information model that has identified fundamental business resources or subjects and fundamental entity types and major attributes with business-agreed definitions, examples, and fundamental business rules. Senior management must be able to "read" this model and say, "This is what we must know to accomplish our mission." If no high-level business information model exists, this must be developed first.

❑ Detailed abstractions of models are driven by the business information model.

❑ It is inclusive, supporting all objectives, processes, and knowledge workers having an interest in the data being modeled.

❑ It includes representations of data or information views that *business* subject matter experts can "read" and can confirm that the enterprise information requirements are met.

❑ It associates groups of data with respective business information stewards who are "accountable" for the integrity of data names, abbreviations, definitions, domain values, and business rules.

❑ It involves developing a data model to support the major information views across the enterprise:

   ❑ All primary processes requiring the data across its natural—and cross-functional—value chain.

   ❑ Major downstream processes not part of its value chain, but requiring the data.

   ❑ Key business indicators, queries, reports, and decisions requiring the data.

❑ It results in reusable and reused data models and definitions.

❑ It results in reusable and reused physical databases.

❑ It results in improved *information systems* communication and productivity.

❑ It results in improved *business* communication and productivity.

❑ The resulting databases *can* house the data that satisfies the knowledge workers requiring it and increases their communication and productivity.

From Data Audit to Quality Information Production

The previous section asserted that the practice of "quality assurance" inspections, whose intention is to provide quality of products and services, actually becomes a *deterrent* to quality. Audit or "cleansing" of data only attacks the symptoms and not the root cause. The result is a perpetuation of a process to fix data errors, rather than improving the process to eliminate errors that require fixing.

Consider the case of a large insurance company that implemented an information stewardship program. Business personnel interviewed about their expectations for the stewardship program identified one major and common expectation: the need for quality information "at the source." Some of the knowledge workers shared their frustration of having to spend as much as 70 percent of their time verifying and correcting data received from upstream processes before they could perform their "real" jobs. Or consider the case of the large mail-order company that had implemented an "information quality" function in the marketing department to assure the correctness of addresses and profile data for marketing purposes, because the order-taking process caused unacceptable errors. The result: high costs of information "scrap and rework" to correct inaccurate data and to find missing data.

True information quality comes from improving business processes to eliminate the cause of data defects, not from inspecting and cleaning it. Real information quality is achieved when one designs *good* quality in rather than inspecting *data errors* out. When quality is built in, it reduces costs and increases productivity and effectiveness. The costs of nonquality result from product scrap and rework, and in lost customer lifetime value due to missed opportunities or lost customers.

Some quality assurance reviews will always be required, to tell you how well the key processes are working. Periodic information assessments are required for the most critical information to assure its reliability. In data warehousing processes, for example, critical information should be assessed from its source to measure its completeness, accuracy, and nonduplication. Data audits and controls should be performed in data warehouses to assure the extract, cleansing, transformation, and load processes are performing properly and are not dropping or redundantly loading data.

As much as 80 to 90 percent of the effort of data warehousing is in extracting, cleansing, and transforming data to improve its quality to a usable level or to eliminate unusable data. Surveys at major data warehousing conferences consistently reveal that information quality is the most significant issue facing data warehousing.

Is anyone asking the question, "If the data was correct at the source in the first place, and in an enterprise-defined format, would we need to spend so much on data cleanup?" Very few people seem to be. Extraction and summarization would still occur, but quality information at the source eliminates or minimizes the need to clean up, de-dup, and throw away. The time saved could be spent in activities that add value.

The message of Deming's Quality Point 3 applied to information quality is clear: The cheapest and most effective way to assure information quality is at the source, where the actual information producers have the knowledge.

Achieving Quality Information Production

How does the enterprise achieve information quality consistently at the source? How does the enterprise create information in a way that minimizes the costly scrap and rework activities required for downstream processes to be able to use the data? The answer is simple, and the benefits are significant; yet the implementation challenges the status quo.

Information quality must be designed into the process. But who determines information quality? The immediate beneficiaries of the information may determine that the information quality meets their needs. This is insufficient in itself, however. It is the downstream knowledge workers in other business areas who depend on that same information—as the ultimate consumers of the information—who define its quality requirements. If information does not meet their needs, those downstream knowledge workers, such as data warehouse customers and other process owners, must implement additional processes to discover missing data, capture additional facts not required by the original information producers, and correct data to their required quality level. Studies indicate the cost to reconstruct data after the fact is 5 to 10 times the amount required to capture it properly at its source. In fact, it may be impossible, or prohibitively expensive, to rediscover or capture data about some business events after the event has taken place.

To design information quality into the process, one must identify the downstream processes and activities that require the process's outputs, including information. The process must be defined to capture and maintain all data knowable within the process, to the quality level required by the downstream processes and knowledge workers.

How to Assure Business Processes Produce Quality Information

To assure quality information, assure that the following characteristics exist for each critical business process:

❑ It is defined. It describes the why, what, how, when, where, and who of the process.

❑ It is defined "horizontally" across business value chains. This means the information products are designed in a way that is integrated (not interfaced) with the downstream processes that depend on its products and outcomes. Data is defined consistently for all processes using it. The process will capture data required for downstream processes even though it is not required by the immediate beneficiaries of the process.

❑ It is repeatable. Different information producers produce consistent quality information.

❑ It minimizes or eliminates unnecessary data intermediary steps.

❑ It has a process owner ultimately accountable for the integrity of the process and its information product quality.

❑ It has information producers who are trained and aware of the downstream "customers" and uses of their information products.

❑ It has information producers who are held accountable for the information quality they produce. See Chapter 12, "Information Stewardship," for a discussion of data accountability.

❑ It captures information as close to the point of origin of the data as is feasible.

❑ It does not capture data redundantly. For example, the process does not reenter data from a report produced from another database. Nor does it capture, independently, data that is naturally captured by a process closer to its source of data origin.

❑ It results in reusable and reused data.

❑ The information products produced consistently satisfy the knowledge workers who require them, and result in increased business communication, productivity, and effectiveness.

Point 4: End the Practice of Awarding Information Business on the Basis of Cost Alone

"Price has no meaning without a measure of the quality being purchased,"[5] Deming asserts. The lowest price for a competing product may turn out to be the most expensive in the long run. What has one gained by saving money in buying something if the cost of maintenance is high? Without knowing the quality of a product purchased, price alone cannot be used as an accurate measure. What appears to be a bargain price may turn out to be the most expensive alternative.

Deming's Quality Point 4, "End the practice of awarding business on the basis of price tag alone," strikes harshly at three commonly accepted IS practices that virtually guarantee nonquality information. Those three practices are:

■ Reward project development for on-time/within-budget alone, without real measure of the quality of the product delivered.

[5]Deming, *Out of the Crisis*, p. 32. Deming cites Walter A. Shewhart, *Economic Control of Quality of Manufactured Product*, Van Nostrand, 1931; repr. ed., American Society for Quality Control, 1980; reprinted by Ceepress, The George Washington University, 1986.

- Model and build databases based upon the application requirements alone, without involvement of stakeholders outside of the project scope.

- Capture data close to where it is convenient for a given business area or application, without considering if this is the best source of data capture for the enterprise.

Bad Practice 1: Reward Project Development for On-Time and Within-Budget Alone

The practice of lowest price has had the impact of actually increasing costs while increasing defects. "Value for money," is how the British describe quality. Yet it is so common for the almighty deadline and budget estimates to control how application project success is determined. To be sure, both of these measures are important. But quality of the resulting product must be factored into the equation in order for an application to be considered successful. To use only two of these three measures of success is like trying to stand on a two-legged stool. It cannot stand the test of time. When a deadline is a critical requirement, one must consider carefully the tradeoffs between budget and quality. The "right" investment up front may prevent future headaches and save money.

The history of this is no doubt that target dates and money are easy enough to measure, while quality is not. However, quality *can be measured quantitatively*, in financial terms as well as in customer satisfaction measures. These measures apply to inhouse developed applications, outsourced applications, and application software packages alike.

The first measure of quality compares cost of the development (or acquisition) and implementation to the estimated costs of "enhancements" and "fixes" requested in the first six months of operation against the *requirements in the original scope* of the project. Enhancement requests represent the "expectations" of the customer. The ratio of the estimated (and modified by the actual hours as the modifications are implemented) modification hours to actual development hours demonstrates the quality of development to meet customer expectations. Information quality is "consistently meeting knowledge worker expectations."[6] If the modification requests are 0 to 10 percent of the original development costs, development quality is high. If the modification costs are 30 percent or higher, development quality is low. One organization implemented two projects of comparable complexity about the same time. One project had a 10 percent modification-to-development ratio, while the second had a 200 percent modification-to-development ratio. Both projects were implemented "on-time and within-budget." Which one was quality?

[6]Larry English, "Information Quality: Meeting Customer Needs," *DM Review*, November 1996, p. 46.

The second measure assesses the downstream knowledge workers' satisfaction with the data created by the application. These knowledge workers, generally in another department or organization unit, have a stake in the information product. A simple customer satisfaction survey, much like the ones completed by seminar and conference attendees, can measure knowledge satisfaction with the information received from upstream applications.

The measures are simple. Does the application capture values for all data elements (about the business events within the scope of the application) you require? Or do you have to go find missing data not captured in the original upstream event capture. Does the application capture all data elements (about the business events within the scope of the application) you require? Or do you have to go research to find additional facts not captured about the original event. Is the quality (accuracy) of the data sufficient for you to perform your required work effectively and efficiently? Or must you clean the data or perform workarounds to use it. Do you get the data on a timely basis? Or must you delay essential processes or find data from alternate sources to accomplish them.

In addition to the customer satisfaction ratings, one can quantify the costs of additional data capture and data correction and business rework. This is the data equivalent of manufacturing "scrap and rework," a measure of nonquality.

This second measure assesses cross-functional quality of application development. The quality of data from upstream applications and business processes directly impacts the costs and quality of downstream applications and business processes. As cross-functional information quality goes up, the costs of application development and maintenance go down.

Bad Practice 2: Model and Build Databases Based upon the Application Requirements Alone

The classic application development and delivery methodology uses a divide-and-conquer approach: Narrow the scope of an application so it can be developed quickly and cheaply. This development approach does not involve stakeholders outside of the project scope. After all, to involve personnel outside the scope of the project increases project development time and costs. Or does it?

This practice is what I call the "systems approach" to application development. The systems approach is a divide-and-conquer approach that calls for carving up a problem into small and manageable chunks. The rationale is to reduce the scope and complexity of projects into manageable application areas.

The unwitting side effect of this, however, is that it focuses on the project requirements independently of how the application "integrates" within its larger context. The traditional method of application "integration" is through building interface programs to move data from one application's databases or files to another application's databases or files.

It must be noted that this "systems approach" is *not* the same as "systems thinking," Senge's fifth discipline of the learning organization. The essence of systems thinking is *holism* and interconnectedness.[7] Holism is a theory that the universe, or enterprise, is correctly seen in terms of interacting wholes that are more than the mere sum of elementary components. What this means for information quality is that the business enterprise is a whole, and that business functions and processes have an interconnectedness that must be understood when developing applications and databases.

The concept of an "interface" is a useful concept, but often misapplied in application development. *Webster's Dictionary* defines an interface as "the place at which *independent* [emphasis mine] systems meet and act on or communicate with each other (the man-machine ~)." Interfaces, when properly used, increase productivity and quality by providing a mechanism for collaboration among truly independent systems. For example, the electrical cord plug and electrical outlet are interfaces of independent (that is, different kinds of) systems. The one is an interface to a device that requires electricity, the other an interface to a source of electricity. These interfaces allow an electricity-requiring device, such as my computer, to gain access to an electricity source, such as provided by Nashville Electric Service.

The problem with application system interfaces is that application systems are *not* independent systems. Otherwise, why would they need to share data? Application systems are *interdependent* or interconnected systems if they require the same data. Information quality problems become magnified if the interconnectedness of the components of the enterprise is not carefully considered in requirements definition and design.

The typical practice of building interface programs that transform data as a means of "data flow" among business processes has several inherent information quality problems:

- It focuses on only the requirements of the project at hand without consideration of the requirements of downstream processes or information customers. This virtually guarantees that the data will be minimally reusable directly and will require transforming interfaces or separate data create applications.

- Any interface program increases information float, the time delay from when data is electronically captured and when downstream knowledge workers can derive value from it.

- An interface is a source of potential data error introduction. This is not intentional. It is a fact that any point of interchange is a point of loss, noise, or other problem.

[7]Peter Senge, *The Fifth Discipline*, New York: Doubleday, 1990, p. 375.

- Interfaces increase both development and operations costs over and above commonly defined and implemented data that can be either directly shared or propagated through managed replication.

Deming disagrees with this "systems approach" with its interface mind set when he says that purchasing should be a team effort, consisting of "product engineer and representatives of manufacturing, purchasing, sales, or whatever other departments will be involved with the product."[8] Why? The quality of raw materials has an impact on the entire enterprise, not just engineering or manufacturing. Everyone affected by purchasing decisions should have appropriate involvement in the "requirements specifications" and supplier selection.

Application development is to the information product what purchasing is to raw materials. Application development designs and builds or purchases applications that are used to acquire (create and maintain) data. Ineffective purchasing can increase manufacturing problems by acquiring lower-quality materials, while achieving "cost savings." In the same way, ineffective application development can increase information quality problems by creating application-specific data that lacks quality to meet the information needs of other business areas.

The alternative to interface development is an enterprise data infrastructure that has shared data defined in a way that meets both the immediate beneficiaries of an application as well as the downstream beneficiaries. These downstream knowledge workers are customers of that data, are they not?

The argument generally posed against enterprise data models is that it will lengthen the project and increase the costs of "the project." In fact, it *will* increase the costs of the project, although these costs should not be charged back to the sponsor. However, enterprise data model development does not have to lengthen project delivery time. Using rapid data modeling sessions with a skilled facilitator can actually reduce the time required for data modeling. Involving stakeholders from other processes that require the data within the project scope assures that the data defined and implemented meets the knowledge needs of the enterprise, not just the isolated project beneficiaries.

The counterintuitive results are that enterprise data modeling, when conducted and implemented into production databases properly:

Reduces the costs of application development and maintenance. Once data is defined and implemented in a way that meets all stakeholders of that data, it does not need to be redefined and implemented again. It can be either shared or replicated as necessary, reducing the costs of building, maintaining, and operating interface programs.

Increases information quality. By defining data consistently among all stakeholders, the data needs to be captured only once at the best source location.

---

[8]Mary Walton, *The Deming Management Method*, New York: Putnam Publishing Group, 1986, p. 64.

It can then be used directly by all knowledge workers or replicated as required without having to be transformed into a different coding structure.

Data is a shared resource. Some information-intensive organization units generate only a small percent of the data they require. Therefore, data modeling and definition must be a team effort, just as purchasing must be a team effort, according to Deming.

There is something worse than "spaghetti" code, and it is exponentially worse: "spaghetti *systems*." Interface programs as a solution for "integrating" applications and business processes creates information quality problems, application maintenance problems, and actually increases costs. The message of Quality Point 4 is that an application development or acquisition decision based on "cost of acquisition" may be the most expensive alternative in the long run. "Cost of ownership" decisions factor quality into the decision by considering the long-term ramifications and the interconnectedness of the component parts.

Bad Practice 3: Capture Data Where It Is Convenient for a Given Business Area or Application

This practice is a double whammy that stems from the combined paradigms of the Industrial Age functional organization and the isolating "systems approach" of application development. These two paradigms have resulted in the notion that every business area and every application should have its own source (supplier) for the information it needs to operate. The presupposition is that we (in our department) cannot trust your data (data that you create in your department). So we create our own information needed to do our job (or, function). Because we cannot "control" the information you create in your department, or it is in the wrong format or incomplete to meet our needs, we develop our own data sources and databases.

The result of this practice is incredible data redundancy. Worse yet is the fact that the data is created by one of two means, both of which create potentially significant information quality problems. The first option is to develop separate and uncoordinated applications that capture the same type of information, such as `Customer` or `Product`. The second option is to use interface programs to extract—and transform—data from "your" database into "my" database in the way I want to see it. For example, the interface of Orders from the sales department may be transformed to go into the Fulfillment System, because it does not "need" all information captured by the Order System. Both of these options significantly increase the cost of capturing and maintaining data and the complexity and cost of maintaining applications.

Deming's fourth Point of Quality is the fundamental truth that purchasing or acquisition decisions based on price alone result in decreased quality and higher costs in the long run. If there is no measure of quality, business tends to select the lowest bidder with "low quality and high cost being the inevitable result."[9] The quality solution is for the organization to develop a long-term relationship with a single source of supplied goods. This "partnership" provides the basis for consistency of materials resulting in higher-quality goods and reduced costs.

Single-Source Information Suppliers

The same principles of quality hold with data acquisition. In business there should be a single source of data of a given type (`Customer`, `Product`, `Order`, etc.). The natural data suppliers—information producers—are those who are responsible for the process at the point of data origination; in other words, information producers, who are closest to the point at which data becomes known within the enterprise, should create it. Those closest to business events that create and update knowledge are the ones best able to capture data with quality for the entire enterprise. The enterprise should leverage those information producers as the preferred supplier of choice.

Data should be captured in a single, authoritative record-of-reference database in a way that it can meet the needs of all interested knowledge workers. If the enterprise is geographically dispersed and this is not economically feasible, the data may be created in local record-of-origin databases and *replicated* to an enterprise record-of-reference database to support nonlocal knowledge workers.

The enterprise is best served when it establishes a partnership between the knowledge workers and the single source of data. This requires a relationship of trust between knowledge worker and information producer. A trust relationship eliminates the need for every department or business unit to have to create and maintain their own sources of that data.

Unfortunately, most applications are built vertically. Many will create secondary sources of data with interfaces that transform data to fit their specific functional requirements. Others will "hire" their own data suppliers to take information from computer-generated reports and reenter it into another database. In fact, as much as 70 percent of computer input comes from other computer output, according to Kathryn Alesandrini.[10]

However, there is no valid business reason for an organization to need internal personnel to have to reenter data that is available electronically. The argument may be that they cannot trust the data, which is precisely the point! Develop information quality in the originating information producers. Then downstream knowledge workers do not need to look for an alternative data supplier or source.

[9]Deming, *Out of the Crisis*, p.32.

[10]Kathryn Alesandrini, *Survive Information Overload*, Homewood: Business One Irwin, 1992, p. 67.

How to Develop Single-Source Information Suppliers

It is important to note that the concept of single-source information suppliers does not mean centralizing the capture of information. It means providing the resources and training to those information producers that are the natural point of knowledge discovery, and creating information at those knowledge discovery points with quality so that all information customers can trust it. This eliminates the need for every organization to have their own information suppliers to *re-create* the information for their own needs.

1. For a particular type of data, identify the originating process and information producers.

2. Identify the redundant processes, databases, and information producers that are re-creating it.

3. Analyze the reasons for the redundant create and maintenance (inaccessibility, low information quality, incompleteness of attributes, inconsistent definition or domain values).

Knowledge worker management should contract with the information production process owner for the level of quality to satisfy their needs. This eliminates the need—and cost—to find a new "supplier" of the data. Based on the root cause, seek to eliminate the problem by:

- Controlling replication (inaccessibility)

- Negotiating quality standards and possibly reallocating resources to the originating processes (low information quality)

- Redefining data models and databases (incomplete attributes)

- Redefining data definition of attributes (inconsistent data definition)

- Planning migration to authoritative, single sources of data (with improved quality)

Benefits of Single-Source Information Suppliers

The benefits of single-source information suppliers are many:

- Decreased costs of data capture and maintenance (eliminate redundancy and complexity)

- Increased value of the data resource (create once with quality; use many times)

- More timely information (once captured, all knowledge workers have access)

- Increased confidence in the data resource (capture with quality)

- Increased ability to exploit new opportunities (by minimizing resources to maintain data and applications redundantly, they can be deployed on new opportunity applications and data)

What is the message of Quality Point 4? "Best" price may be the most expensive alternative in the long run. Organizations with a quality mind-set are developing and buying applications on the basis of "cost of ownership" rather than "cost of acquisition." What have you gained if the project comes in on time and within budget, but you must spend twice as much to bring it up to the expectations of the knowledge workers as defined in the original specifications?

Point 5: Continually Improve the Process of Data Development and Information Production

Deming's fifth Point of Quality has strong implications for every IS organization that builds applications and databases, buys software packages, or develops data warehouses. The key question is, "Are all—including downstream—beneficiaries of the delivered application and information products generally happy with the results?"

Deming's Point 5, "Improve constantly and forever the system of production and service," holds two messages. The first is the recurring theme that quality *must* be built in at the design stage. Quality begins with intent (Point 1). Management establishes intent by creating constancy of purpose for quality. Management must translate this intent into plans, specifications, and tests that deliver quality to the customer.[11]

The second message of Point 5 is that improvement is not just a one-time project; it is a continual, unending process, involving everyone in the enterprise. We each should ask ourselves every day, "What have I done this day to advance my learning and skill on this job, and what have I done to advance my education for greater satisfaction in life?"[12] An important byproduct of Quality Point 5 is that when we improve the processes for information quality, we also improve our satisfaction in work and in life!

Information Quality Improvement versus Data Cleanup

Deming cites Joseph M. Juran for the following illustration. A hotel catches on fire. Someone yells, "Fire!", grabs a fire extinguisher, and pulls the fire alarm.

---

[11]Deming, *Out of the Crisis*, p. 49.
[12]Ibid., p. 50.

The fire is extinguished. But does putting out the fire improve the hotel? No. It is not quality improvement, it is simply putting out fires. And putting out fires is not the same as process improvement.[13]

Information quality improvement is not the same as data cleanup. Data cleanup is fire fighting. Fixing bad or missing data is not information quality improvement; it is putting out fires. Data cleansing and transformation of data into a usable state for the data warehouse knowledge workers is fire fighting. It is the manufacturing equivalent of "scrap and rework." What then, is information quality improvement?

Information Quality Improvement Equals Information Production Process Improvement

Improvement that leads to genuine enterprise benefit is the improvement of processes that create, maintain, and deliver information. Information production process improvement requires teamwork between the process owners and information producers, and the downstream knowledge workers and process owners.

Information Quality Means Teamwork

Information quality improvement means getting the information producers and customers together to rethink and redesign the processes in which data defects are caused. Both management and professionals in the information value chain are required to improve processes. Professionals who perform the processes know them best. Management must enable staff to make process improvements, and to communicate that it is imperative to always look for better ways of performing the process.

Process owners alone cannot define quality for the data created by their process if other processes depend on that data. Only the downstream information customers can define its quality and therefore the data specification and requirements. To improve information quality the process owner must look to the downstream processes that require it for information quality requirements. Then the process owner must involve the information producers to determine how to improve the process to meet downstream knowledge workers' expectations.

Information Quality Improvement Processes

Information quality improvement is not just one process. There are several ways of improving information.

---

[13]Deming, *Out of the Crisis*, p. 51.

Innovation in information products and information services. Develop information that you do not currently have. Much work may be performed because of a lack of knowledge. The first change question is, "What is it that you do not know today, but if you did know, would fundamentally change *what* you could do?"

Innovation in the process that creates data. Handheld computers eliminated the need for utility meter readers to physically read the dials on meters. Embedded chips in the meters eliminate the need for utility meter readers, who are freed to perform value-adding work. This is process innovation.

Improvement of existing data (data cleanup). Correcting inaccurate or missing data makes that data usable for the downstream knowledge workers and data warehouse customers.

Improvement of the existing process. By analyzing defects and their cause, you can identify improvements that prevent future defects. Defect prevention eliminates the costs caused by the defective data as well as the costs of correcting it to make it usable. The costs of correcting data can be 5 to 10 times as much as the cost of defect prevention.

All of these processes are a part of an information quality program; however, none is sufficient *by itself*. For example, improvement to inventory management processes to reduce the cost of inventory becomes moot when the competition innovates with Just-In-Time inventory management.

Data cleanup becomes an unnecessary expense if processes can be improved to eliminate data defects. However, if data required to support decisions and strategic processes cannot be used because of unacceptable error, then it must be cleaned, reengineered, and transformed for the data warehouse data to become usable.

How to Improve Information Quality

The techniques for information quality improvement are addressed in Deming's Quality Point 14 and described in detail in Chapter 9, "Improving Information *Process* Quality." The steps are listed next.

1. Define the information value/cost chain for a collection of data, such as `Customer`, `Order`, and `Loan`. This identifies all processes that can create or update the data, as well as those that use the data.

2. Identify the information producer and process owner roles.

3. Identify the knowledge workers, and downstream process owners.

4. Conduct an information quality assessment to discover the degree and nature of data errors.

5. Identify categories of data defects and prioritize them based on their economic impact.

6. Analyze the history to see what variables and patterns are involved in the data defects.

7. Bring representatives from the pertinent processes to analyze root cause.

8. Identify potential causes and agree on the most likely cause(s).

9. Plan process improvements and implement them in a controlled pilot environment.

10. Study the implemented improvements to see if they achieved the intended quality.

11. If so, roll out the improvements and make them "permanent."

12. Look for the next critical data defect to eliminate.

Information quality improvement is not a onetime activity. Information quality improvement is a cultural mind-set that realizes the status quo is not sufficient. It is the actions and behavior that implement the philosophy of providing quality to all our customers, whoever they may be.

Quality Improvement versus Problem Fixes

Deming attended an awards ceremony in which the highest award was presented to a man who saved his company $250,000 by discovering that labels were missing from bottles of vaccine that were about to be shipped. The second award went to someone who discovered contamination in a shipment before it went out, resulting in the condemnation of the shipment. "Those awards were not for improvement of quality, nor of the system, but only for putting out fires," Deming commented.[14]

Fixing program bugs is not quality improvement. Fixing the Year 2000 problem is not quality improvement. It is putting out the largest information quality "fire" the planet has seen to date. "Fixing" the software and databases to support the Year 2000 calendar change does not improve *any* business process; it only allows the business processes to be performed in exactly the same way on Monday, January 3, 2000, as they were Friday, December 31, 1999. The fix does not improve the software development process; it only puts out a fire that was entirely preventable.

Will there be award ceremonies for those who have "fixed" their organization's Year 2000 problems? Probably. Will there be award ceremonies for those who designed their organization's databases with four-digit date fields, preventing the need for a Year 2000 project? These "Year 2000-problem preventers" are the ones who should be honored.

---

[14]Walton, *The Deming Management Method.* p. 66.

Application and Data Development Process Improvement

Many of the business information quality problems can be traced back to poor, unintegrated applications and database design that are based on functional and departmental requirements alone. On the other hand, quality, integrated application and database design based on business value chains can be a major contributor to information quality improvement. The information technology itself is *not* a "solution"; it is only a tool. As with any tool, it can be used effectively or poorly.

Information technology, however, can play an important role in business process innovation and improvement to assist in preventing many types of "human error." Some human error can be attributed to not paying attention, fatigue, lack of training, or other human reasons. But much human error is actually induced by poor application design and unintuitive information presentation that is cumbersome, forces unnecessary keystrokes, or has other ergonomic shortcomings.

Application and database design becomes a very important part of process improvement when information quality is designed into the process. The application represents the capability to transform business processes. And the database or data warehouse represents the capability to "informate" all knowledge workers.

Data Definition Quality Improvement Is Teamwork

If data is defined from a narrow vertical perspective it is highly likely to be insufficient for knowledge workers outside the scope of those who define the data. The only way data can be defined to satisfy all information customers is to define it across business value chains. In other words, data must have a consensus definition for both information producers and *all* knowledge workers who use it.

How to Achieve Data Definition and Application Quality Improvement

The business value chains for data definition are the application and data development methodologies. These value chains contain the processes that identify information requirements, model and define data, and translate data models to databases that store data and applications that create, update, delete, and retrieve data.

1. Analyze the application and data development and delivery methodology:
   - Is it defined *and* followed? Or is it "defined" and ignored? Or is it nonexistent?

■ Does it have a philosophy of teamwork between the business and information systems, and between application development and information resource management groups?

■ Does it focus on only the application for development? Or does it identify the business value chain of which the application is a part and the interrelationships of the value chain?

■ Does it address only benefits to the sponsoring business area? Or does it specify how the business objectives of the application directly support the enterprise mission as a beginning point and provide the potential for benefits to other business areas?

■ Does it define information as a *product*, or does it focus on functional automation as the *product*? In other words, does the methodology differentiate in the concept of performing work—the function—from the work product that has customers?

■ Does it define data requirements only for the scope of the application, even though other knowledge workers in the enterprise have a stake in the data? Or does it identify the knowledge workers and downstream process owners to seek to discover their requirements from the information products being delivered?

■ Does it seek to define all application and data from scratch? Or does it focus on reuse of existing data and application infrastructure, along with developing application and database components that are reusable and sharable to eliminate all unnecessary redundancy?

■ Does it include getting postimplementation feedback from both immediate beneficiary and downstream (outside the scope of the application) beneficiaries?

2. Conduct a customer satisfaction survey among business personnel as to their satisfaction with applications and databases delivered within the past three years.

3. *Listen* to and analyze the feedback. The only way we can make effective improvements in application and data development is to listen to the "customers" who must live with the applications and databases long after the developers have moved on to "greener projects."

4. Analyze the history of business feedback, program and system problems.

5. Bring representatives from the business areas, applications development, and information resource management to analyze root causes of poor application and database design. See Chapter 9 for how to perform root-cause analysis and process improvement for information quality.

6. Identify potential causes and agree on the most likely cause(s).

7. Plan process improvements and implement them in a pilot development project in a controlled environment.

8. Study the implemented improvements to see if they achieved the intended improvement among all knowledge worker beneficiaries.

9. If so, roll out the application and data development process improvements and make them "permanent."

10. Look for the next critical application or data development defect to eliminate.

Information quality improvement is not a one-time activity. Information quality improvement is a cultural mind-set that recognizes that the status quo is not sufficient. It is the actions and behavior that implement the philosophy of providing quality to our customers, whoever they may be.

When I was the manager of application development at a large publishing firm, we implemented a procedure for addressing application problem causes. The person "fixing" the problem completed a "Trouble Report," describing what was done to "fix" the problem. The most important section on this report was a "Recommendation for Problem Prevention" section in which the problem solver had to recommend improvements that could prevent the problem from happening again. This section was the most difficult to complete, but the most valuable. It is this kind of mind-set that Deming's Quality Point 5 is all about.

Point 6: Institute Training on Information Quality

Training is so important that it constitutes not just one, but two of Deming's 14 Points of Quality. Point 6 represents a universal truth: For someone to know how to do something well, they must be properly trained. Point 6 addresses the foundations of training for both management and staff. Point 13 reinforces the requirement for continuous training and augments it to include self-improvement for quality improvement through innovation.

People, not information, are the organization's most important asset. Information today becomes the differentiating resource. With capable, trained, and empowered people armed with quality, just-in-time information, an enterprise will thrive. All other factors equal, the organization with the highest-quality information will emerge victorious in a competitive world. Yet, the "greatest waste in America is failure to use the abilities of people."[15] A manager expressed his anger about the fact that training was wasted money. He confided to a consultant that all he did was train people, and then they left to go elsewhere.

[15]Deming, *Out of the Crisis*, p. 53.

The consultant observed, "Consider the alternative; suppose you don't train your people—and they *stay*."

Early in my career in information management, I worked for an organization that was developing a pilot application to build its first shared database. The project had such an ambitious schedule that the application development manager scheduled the project team's training in the database technology *after* the scheduled implementation date! My objections went unheeded. And my written predictions came true—the project was implemented late. The message of Quality Point 6 is simple. For people to do a good job, they must know how to do that job properly. They must have education as to *why* the quality required is expected and *how* to produce it.

Deming is very clear that training is required, not just for worker employees, but also for management. Management requires training to understand the entire value chain of the enterprise, and to know about all of the processes of the business. Japanese management training and career path development illustrates an important message for companies seeking to transform themselves from functional to business value chain management. Japanese managers start their careers with long internships that vary from 4 to 12 years. During this time, the manager-trainees work in all parts of the enterprise, from the factory floor to procurement, accounting, distribution, and sales. As a result of this on-the-job training, managers have firsthand experience in production problems, as well as those of acquisition, logistics, and sales. This prepares them for understanding how all parts of the business integrate.

Once employees have learned how to do a job improperly, it is very difficult to erase and change their behaviors. I began my career in information systems at Sears, Roebuck and Co. in the early 1970s. Only 2 or 3 of the 25 classmates in my programmer-training class had degrees in computer science. Sears's philosophy was to hire the right people, and then to train them. It was much easier to train someone with a degree in philosophy, music, theology, history (some of the backgrounds in our class) in their approach to application development, than to retrain someone experienced and trained in another approach.

Ramifications for Information Quality

How can information producers provide quality information if they are not properly trained? How can knowledge workers use information correctly if they do not know its meaning?

How can data analysts and systems analysts develop quality information models, data definitions, and quality applications if they are not properly trained? How can database designers and application developers deliver reusable applications and databases if they do not know how?

Every job in the enterprise requires training about information and information management principles. Table 11.1 lists information quality training requirements by broad job or role classification. This list does not include job-specific or tool-specific training. It includes information management and information quality training requirements.

Table 11.1 Education and Training for Information Quality

AUDIENCE	TRAINING TOPICS	DURATION
All new employees	■ General orientation on information policies, management principles, responsibilities	2 hours
Information producers	■ Information quality standards, guidelines ■ Data definition, values, business rules ■ Information value chain and processes requiring the information produced ■ Knowledge worker expectations of information quality	2 hours As required
Knowledge workers	■ Information policy regarding use; responsibilities for update ■ Information value chain and processes producing information ■ Data definition, values, business rules	2 hours As required
Business management and process owners	■ Information policies, principles, responsibilities ■ Downstream knowledge worker expectations ■ Information value chain	1 day + refresher
Senior management	■ Information management principles, information policies, information as strategic enterprise resource ■ Information quality principles and roles ■ Information stewardship roles and accountabilities ■ Creating the Information Age organization (the strategic view of information management)	2 hours + updates Series of 2-hour modules
Business information stewards	■ Information stewardship: roles/responsibilities, data definition guidelines, information quality principles ■ Information management principles ■ Information value chain and information stakeholders	1 day + 2 hours
Data resource management staff	■ Information stewardship ■ Information quality improvement	1 day 3 days
Application development staff	■ Information stewardship principles, roles, responsibilities ■ Data modeling and value-centric development principles	1/2 day 2–3 days

Table 11.1 *(Continued)*

AUDIENCE	TRAINING TOPICS	DURATION
Data warehouse staff	▪ Information management principles ▪ Information quality improvement principles ▪ Data sourcing, transformation, cleanup principles	1 day 1 day 2 days
Information quality staff	▪ Information management principles ▪ Information stewardship ▪ Information quality improvement	1 day 1 day 3 days
Information systems management	▪ Creating the Information Age organization ▪ Value-centric application development principles ▪ Information quality improvement principles	1 day + 1 day 1 day

How to Create Training for Information Quality

For quality information, you must train all employees with respect to their role in information quality.

1. Identify each role that has an accountability for information quality in some way.

2. Identify the impact of each role on information quality.

3. Define training requirements for each role.

4. Define the learning objectives for training to achieve the required skill level.

5. Develop the training curriculum.

6. Deliver the training to a pilot group.

7. Analyze the effectiveness of the training by observing the newly trained personnel.

8. Refine the training as necessary.

9. Conduct the training and continue its refinement.

With effective training you now have the capacity for producing quality information.

Point 7: Institute Leadership for Information Quality

Deming's seventh Point of Quality stresses management's accountability in quality improvement. Information quality will not be achieved solely by professionals measuring and reporting information quality, or by data warehouse staff "cleansing" data extracted from source databases before propagation to the warehouse. Information quality will be achieved when IS and business management lead the way to make process improvement happen, and with it remove information quality defect causes.

The job of management is leadership, not supervision, according to Deming.[16] Management must not just supervise, but must continually work to improve both product and service. Management's goal is to lead process improvement, not supervise workers to achieve quotas. "Focus on outcome (management by numbers, MBO [Management by Objectives], work standards, meet specifications, zero defects, appraisal of performance) must be abolished, leadership put in place."[17] This statement is a bold contradiction to traditional management theory. Deming correctly identifies that focusing on quota and productivity numbers alone is in fact a major cause of quality problems that actually results in decreased productivity and increased costs. Time and time again we see that emphasis on speed and productivity virtually guarantees information quality problems. A major mail-order company found that its goal to reduce time on the telephone caused a high incidence of duplicate customer records and unverified (and incorrect) addresses. A major stock trading firm found unacceptable errors in trade data. The culprit: Trader's bonuses were based on volume of trades, not quality of trade data.

What Is Leadership?

Leaders are the primary *enablers* of improvement. Management must establish the environment for information quality improvement.

Leadership means:

Knowing the work one manages. A manager who does not know the work will be less able to coach workers correctly. Most measurement systems that managers put in place when they do not know the job encourage just the opposite, because the measurement systems reward the wrong things. For example, what is the relationship of function points and application quality? What is the relationship of "on time" and "within budget" to customer satisfaction?

Knowing common causes and special causes of quality problems.[18] "Removal of common causes of trouble and of variation, of errors, of mistakes, of low production, of low sales, of most accidents is the responsibility of management."[19] Leaders must be able to identify problem causes

---

[16]Deming, *Out of the Crisis*, p. 54.
[17]Ibid.
[18]Rafael Aguayo, *Dr. Deming: The American Who Taught the Japanese About Quality*, New York: Simon & Schuster, 1990, p. 176.
[19]Deming, *Out of the Crisis*, p. 321.

within the system or process (common cause). Common causes of information quality problems are those that can be corrected by process improvement. An example of common cause is the creation of a duplicate customer record because (1) the procedure does not have a step to determine if the customer is on file, (2) the operator fails to look for an existing record, or (3) the automated algorithm is deficient and fails to find the customer's existing record. Special causes are those that are outside the system or process, and are "special." An example of special cause is the creation of a duplicate customer record because the computer or network system was down, and the order was taken manually with contingency procedures. Special causes make a process be out of statistical control. Removal of special causes enables a process to be stable, repeatable, and predictable. Processes must first be put into control. Then they can be improved through the removal of common cause of problems. Note, however, that the contingency order procedure should have a step to discover and correct duplication.

Removing the barriers that prevent staff from taking pride in their work, and doing a quality job. Real leaders listen to their staff's suggestions for improvements. When workers understand who their customers are and what their customers need, they know how to improve the processes. If claims processors know that actuaries are their customers and they use Medical Diagnosis Code to analyze risk, they know how to improve the Create Claim process to meet customer quality expectations.

Establishing the right performance measures. Management often sets metrics that measure quality from an internal point of view; in other words, what *management* sees, rather than from an external or *customer* point of view. Such measures as quotas, cost of production, or speed of production without a measure of customer satisfaction are destructive. Even a measure of zero defects is wrong if it is not based on customer expectations.

Knowing how their group's processes fit into the goals of the enterprise. Management by objectives or departmental goal measures can cause organizational groups to set conflicting and counterproductive objectives, even though they are supposedly decomposed from the same enterprise objectives. For example, a large publishing firm found that their order sales department and accounts receivable departments were constantly at odds with each other. The reason? Their objectives were in conflict. The order sales department had an objective "to increase sales" while accounts receivable sought "to reduce bad debt." Order sales took all orders to meet their objective, even though some customers had risky credit. In turn, accounts receivable rejected some truly acceptable orders from marginal customers to assure they met their objectives.

Knowing how their group's processes fit with the upstream and downstream processes. This is what Peter Senge describes as "systems thinking"—seeing a part in the context of its interrelationships with the whole.[20] Quality comes when all activities within the value chain work together to increase customer value. A leader "works in cooperation with preceding stages and with following stages toward optimization of the efforts of all stages."[21]

Knowing that one half of any staff will perform "below the average" of the group. Trying to bring the below-average individuals up to standard is counterproductive and harmful. Leaders provide resources to enable staff to rise to their level of performance and not judge them based on the "norm." "Above average" performers will slow down and fail to achieve their full potential. A person who does not perform quality work is "almost always in the wrong job, or has very poor management."[22]

Building trust and providing help without judging. Leaders encourage everyone as a team to improve the processes.

Leveraging the skills of all. Leaders will encourage teamwork that allows experts to leverage their expertise by training and coaching others. The resulting team productivity is greater than the sum of individual productivity.

Information Quality Leadership

Leadership is required in both information systems and business processes. Information quality will not just happen. There must be a visionary to lead the way.

Information Systems Leadership

Information systems (IS) managers must provide leadership for information technology, application, and database quality. IS leaders will see the interrelationship of technology, application and data components in an information-managed environment. They will further see that IS does not just supply services to departmental customers. Information systems must support optimization of the work across all stages of the larger business processes, or value chains.

A more appropriate metaphor for IS-to-business relationship is that of a partnership, not just a customer/supplier relationship. If IS sees its relationship as customer-supplier, it will have a tendency to deliver applications that meet the needs of one business area, while suboptimizing the needs of other business areas.

[20]Peter Senge, *The Fifth Discipline*, New York: Doubleday, 1990, pp. 6–7.
[21]Aguayo, *Dr. Deming*, p. 177.
[22]Walton, *The Deming Management Method*, p. 71.

IS leaders will:

- Understand how their group's processes fit into the enterprise goals.

- Understand the interrelationships of the three IS components of information technology, application, and data.

- Plan, model, and build or deliver applications and databases across the business value chains. A business value chain is an end-to-end set of activities that begins with a request from a customer and ends in a benefit to a customer.

- Work to improve the information planning and development processes. The key business information systems value chains are:

  - Information infrastructure development. This strategic process provides for the planning and development of the enterprisewide information technology (network), business value chain, and information (database) architectures. Infrastructure is *not* just technology.

  - Information systems component development. This operational process provides for the design, development of information technology, databases, and applications as components of the architectures and their respective business and implementation value chains.

- Manage their employees not by numbers or standards, but by customer-satisfaction and team-effectiveness criteria.

Business Leadership

The organization and management styles are radically different in the Information Age from those in the Industrial Age. The Information Age organization is horizontal, dynamic, entrepreneurial, team-based and rewarded, and customer-focused. Business leaders will:

- Understand how their group's processes fit into the goals of the enterprise.

- Understand how their group's processes fit into the business value chain of which they are a part. This means knowing the downstream customers of their work and information products. It also means knowing the information quality requirements of those downstream customers.

- Understand that information is a strategic business resource and how quality information can be used to improve processes, decrease costs, and increase new business opportunities.

- Work to improve the business processes.

- Manage their employees not by numbers or standards, but by customer-satisfaction and team-effectiveness criteria.

How to Facilitate Leadership

Leadership does not just happen. Change agents make it happen. To facilitate leadership:

1. Be proactive.
2. Identify areas in need of improvement and in which you have influence; lead the team to make improvements.
3. Identify your customers and solicit their feedback as to how you can better meet their needs; then act on that feedback and get their new feedback.
4. Encourage and coach others to do the same.
5. Identify those who are visionaries and those who have information quality problems.
6. Listen to their problems and objectives.
7. Establish the business case for information quality from a perspective of how it enables them to solve their problems and meet their objectives.
8. Provide awareness education to management to sensitize them to the problems in operational efficiency and effectiveness caused by information quality problems.

Management by numbers simply maintains the status quo, and focuses on arbitrary measures of performance and actually has the impact of decreasing productivity and increasing costs as a result of nonquality information produced. Leadership provides vision, focuses on customers' expectations, and implements continual process improvement to continually delight the customer.

Point 8: Drive Out Fear of Data Uncertainty

Deming's eighth Point of Quality describes why information producers cannot perform their best unless they feel secure. Information quality will not be achieved unless information producers are free from fears of making mistakes or feel free to point out problems and suggest improvements to the processes. Quality Point 8 states, "Drive out fear, so that everyone may work effectively for the company."[23]

Fear Sabotages Information Quality

"The economic loss from fear is appalling," Deming says.[24] When people are afraid for their jobs, afraid of management, afraid of being punished for making

---

[23]Deming, *Out of the Crisis*, p. 23.
[24]Walton, *The Deming Management Method*, p. 72.

mistakes, productivity suffers—and it suffers considerably. Fear in the workplace, no matter how subtle, does not improve productivity. In fact, fear drives people to *counterproductive* behavior. People who are afraid invest energy and take action necessary to remove the source of fear.

A common information quality problem in banks is the daily cash shortages and overages bank tellers have compared with their accounting balances. While the discrepancies are generally quite small, sometimes the differences can be substantial. Dr. Joyce Orsini cites an example of how one bank executive "solved" the problem.

HOW FEAR AFFECTS INFORMATION PRODUCERS

A chief executive of a New York bank noticed the [teller shortage/overage] problem and decided he would eliminate it the old-fashioned way. He just wouldn't tolerate it. He issued an edict that any teller with more than two differences a month would be placed on probation. Any teller on probation for three months would be terminated.

Most of the differences disappeared. The chief executive was elated. He reported the results to his board along with an explanation of his form of management. All that was necessary, according to him, was for him to put his foot down and not accept errors. The board of directors was also elated. This was obviously sound management. But why tolerate two differences a month? No one could think of a good reason, so the rule was changed. Just one difference placed a teller on probation. All the differences disappeared.

How could differences disappear so quickly and so completely? In fact, a simple but sophisticated system had been developed by the tellers to deal with the problem that management denied existed. The tellers began operating their own pools of money when the new policy was initiated. When overages occurred, instead of being reported, they were saved. When a teller came up short on a given day, he would withdraw from the funds saved on the days he was over. Those who needed funds borrowed from those with excess funds. A sophisticated system of borrowing and lending had evolved.

This was, of course, contrary to bank policy, but it was the only way of surviving in the bank. Everyone in the bank knew of the existence of these pools of funds except management.[25]

Whenever fear exists in the workplace, people will develop defense mechanisms for survival. This further decreases productivity, because people work first for survival based on how they are judged. Then they give their next efforts to accomplishing their work objectives.

Many knowledge workers and information producers resist information technology and systems, fearing job elimination. The Information Age is a double-edged sword. One edge cuts away unnecessary work that is no longer required due to new ways of doing work, or reduces the number of people required to perform it. The other edge of the sword causes work to be transformed and performed in new ways with new skills. It creates new jobs that

[25]Aguayo, *Dr. Deming*, p. 78.

could never be performed without the technology or the information that the technology enables to be acquired, maintained, manipulated, and shared.

The reality of the Information Age is that work is, and will continue to be, transformed. All workers must embrace that reality of change and see it as opportunity. No workers can live in the dream world that work will stay the same—or the way they want it to—forever. Deming's Point 13 addresses the fact that we cannot rest on our laurels of today's successes; rather, we must proactively engage in opportunities for self-improvement. Point 8 requires management to decrease sources of fear by providing open communication and resources to enable information producers to develop to their potential.

Information systems personnel can also decrease the fear factor among business personnel by recognizing people's fear of the impact of information technology on their job security. Information systems personnel must adopt a partnership relationship with the business in applications development. Planning and analysis for application systems and databases must focus on what processes add value to the end customer and define data that can enable knowledge workers to add new value. Information systems management must be accountable for building applications and databases that add value and not simply automating redundant or nonvalue adding processes. This kind of application development simply creates obsolete jobs that will have to be eliminated later through process improvement or radical business reengineering.

Everyone must see information technology as a means of improving work. If so, they can participate in application development with eyes open to completely new ways of adding value in what they do rather than fearing loss of their job; in other words, "this is the only way I can work." Meter readers praised the handheld computers that read the utility dials, making their work easier and minimizing information quality problems. New chip technology embedded in utility meters to electronically transmit the meter readings will completely eliminate the "job" of the meter reader. Management must help meter readers to see this technology as an opportunity to define a new place for themselves to add value to their end customers.

People are also paralyzed by the fear that if they point out problems, they will be blamed for them or penalized for "insubordination." Unfortunately, "so seldom is anything done to correct problems that there is no incentive to expose them."[26] Management can reduce this kind of fear by encouraging and rewarding problem identification that leads to information quality improvement. Management must *reward* whistle blowers who reveal wrongdoing and waste within the organization—not punish them. Those who call attention to things that cause higher cost through waste and lower quality to the customers are valuable employees.

In the past, the way to keep your job and move up the corporate ladder was "Hunker down, keep your nose clean, and don't make waves." This recipe,

---

[26]Walton, *The Deming Management Method*, p. 72.

however, causes enterprise failure in the Information Age. Management must remove the barriers of fear of suggesting new ideas, being punished for missteps when learning new skills, and for making mistakes because of inadequate training. Perhaps Tom Peters captures the new Information Age credo best when he encourages workers to "Hunker up, keep your nose dirty, and splash like hell."[27] Management must create this environment of "unfear" or the new job security, so all employees can contribute to continual improvement of the enterprise.

How to Remove Fear as a Barrier to Information Quality

To remove fear:

1. Develop relationships of trust and partnership between information producers and knowledge workers. If information producers and knowledge workers recognize they are on the same team, it becomes easier to work for common goals rather than self-preserving hidden agendas.

2. Develop accountability in process owners—i.e., management—for information quality as the first requisite. Management must be held responsible for the integrity of the processes for which they are charged. Management must empower staff and provide resources so they can perform work with the right level of quality.

3. Develop relationships of trust and partnership between the business and information systems. If the business and information systems personnel operate as a team, working toward the common objective of improving processes and providing information for end-customer satisfaction, resistance and fear of sharing will be removed.

4. Provide training for information producers as to how to produce quality information products (Quality Point 6). Knowing how to do something well reduces stress.

5. Provide self-improvement training for information producers in new skills so they are equipped to produce tomorrow's information products (Quality Point 13).

6. Develop mechanisms for providing feedback as to information quality expectations from downstream knowledge workers.

7. Provide incentives for information producers to find ways of improving the processes. Remove any punitive measures for calling attention to information quality problems or process deficiencies.

8. Develop an effective process for information quality process improvement that involves the information producers. When information quality

[27]Charles Butler, "Tom Terrific," *Successful Meetings*, December 1997, p. 33.

problems occur, it is the process that is broken. Information producers who perform the processes know how to improve them.

9. Provide help resources for information producers to go to when they have questions. This may be the name of the business information steward who is the subject matter expert in the data in question. It may be the information resource personnel who are accountable for the data architectures. It may be access to the repository, data dictionary, or information directory where data is defined and business rules are maintained.

10. After the preceding components are in place, develop information quality metrics based upon mutually agreeable information quality characteristics required by downstream knowledge workers and the end customers.

11. Measure information quality and provide the results openly to information producers along with the opportunity for the producers to recommend what needs to be done to achieve the information quality goals.

Point 9: Break Down Barriers between Information Systems and Business Areas

How is it that a company could fail when everyone was doing a good job, and no one in the organization was having problems? Simple. A new company president found that each business area, while working well, was "suboptimizing its own work, but not working as a team for the company."[28] "People can work superbly in their respective departments . . . but if their goals are in conflict, they can ruin the company."[29]

Deming's Quality Point 9 states "Break down barriers between departments. People in research, design, sales, and production must work as a team, to foresee problems of production and in use that may be encountered with the product or service."[30] A fundamental principle of organizational effectiveness is that all parts of the organization work together as a team toward organizational goals for customer satisfaction and not for departmental goals that may be counterproductive. The conflicting objectives between the order sales and accounts receivable departments cited in Point 7 illustrate the tragedy of suboptimization. Who was looking after the interests and concerns of the customers?

Teamwork is intradepartmental as well as interdepartmental. Teamwork requires those who have strengths to help compensate for those who may not be as gifted. It is in teaching and coaching that people sharpen their own skills. Unfortunately, most traditional performance measures incent competition

[28]Deming, *Out of the Crisis*, p. 63.
[29]Walton, *The Deming Management Method*, p. 75.
[30]Deming, *Out of the Crisis*, p. 24.

TEAMWORK PRODUCTIVITY VERSUS COMPETITIVE PRODUCTIVITY

Peter Blau studied two groups of interviewers in an employment agency. One group had a cooperative mind-set. The second group had a competitive environment in which to fill job openings. The workers in the competitive environment tended to "hoard" job notifications instead of posting them as the procedure called for. The first group shared information. By working cooperatively, they filled significantly more jobs than the competitive group.[31] It is this group performance, not individual performance, that is the "clear index of performance."[32] Unfortunately, in a system that puts employees in the position of having to choose between enterprise objectives and performance-based objectives, unless employees are independently wealthy, they will choose to satisfy the objectives on which their merit and pay is based.

---

among employees, not teamwork. The result is "information fraud," the hoarding of information to advance one's own career.

Teamwork for Information Systems and Database Quality

Building quality applications and databases requires teamwork between application development and data resource management, along with teamwork with and between business areas. Yet the majority of today's application development projects are plagued by lack of cooperation, lack of involvement due to time pressure, conflicting objectives, or competing organizational units. And it is not just one type of teamwork that is missing. But most application development and delivery or package selection methodologies today virtually guarantee low-quality applications and databases because they do not define requirements *across* business areas.

Application Development Teamwork

Teamwork in application development must happen at three levels:

- Within the information systems organization
- Between information systems organization and the business organization that is the primary beneficiary of the application
- Among business organizations who are ultimate stakeholders in the information produced by the application

Let's examine each of these.

---

[31]Aguayo, *Dr. Deming*, p. 196.
[32]Alfie Kohn, *No Contest*, Boston: Houghton Mifflin , 1986, p. 52.

1. Within the Information Systems Organization

Teamwork means the data resource management group and the application development group must operate as a single team. Historically, there is often much conflict between these groups. The goals of application development tend to be to deliver applications that solve business problems quickly with minimal costs. The goals of data resource management tend to be to develop reusable information architecture, data models, and databases that can be shared across the enterprise. The goals of speed for narrow application development projects conflict with the goals of defining information with consensus for reuse and shareability.

Whose goals are right? The answer is, both—yet neither is right. Why? It is possible to build an application quickly and within budget and with quality in the eyes of the business unit for whom it is built. That same application may fail to:

- Add value to the end customer
- Increase customer satisfaction
- Help accomplish the real enterprise business drivers
- Have high reuse and low cost of subsequent maintenance

It is also possible to build sharable data models with quality in the eyes of the knowledge workers who use it. That same data model may fail to contain the kind information that:

- Adds value to the end customer
- Increases customer satisfaction
- Helps accomplish the real enterprise business drivers
- Has high shareability and low cost of subsequent maintenance

Both application development and data resource management groups must begin any development project with two ingredients in mind:

- The enterprise mission
- The ultimate customers (internal and external) and stakeholders

The enterprise mission gives the team the context. Knowing the customers keeps the team focused on who they are serving. The list of customers must always include the external customer who is the ultimate beneficiary of the organization's products and services. If not, the application and database will invariably fall short of improving product or service from the end customers' perspective.

2. Between the Information Systems Organization and the Primary Beneficiary Business Organization

Conflict between information systems and the business creates a "blame" environment and assures poor application and data quality. The business often views systems personnel as "technoids" who have no comprehension of the business or ability to translate business requirements to usable applications with any kind of timeliness. Information systems are simply a necessary evil they have to deal with, but avoid when possible. The evidence of this is all the private applications and databases knowledge workers have developed for themselves because they cannot get the information "support" they need to do their jobs.

On the other side, information systems personnel often believe the business people are incompetent and do not know what they want in systems. Some believe that they know the business rules far better than the business; after all, they coded them. All too often, systems personnel do not understand why the "users" do not "like" the applications they develop, and complain about what they feel are trivial requests for changes in their application.

The attitudes described here are real, but they are merely symptoms of the real problem. The problem exposed here is that there is a lack of partnership or team relationship. No common stake in the outcome of the application and data development process exists. What exists is an uneasy relationship of "support." A partnership is something that is either win-win or lose-lose. With a "support"-only relationship, I can divorce myself from the consequences of the resulting failure and point blame at the other party. Win-lose or lose-win scenarios often result.

The relationship between information systems and the business must *not* be a distant customer-supplier relationship. Information systems does not simply provide "support" to business areas. Information systems must be a partner with business in the common goals of transforming work and *improving* processes.

A partnership or team relationship is the only viable relationship between the business and information systems. Partnering in application development means that both information systems personnel and business personnel join ranks for the good of their mutual customers in the development of applications and databases. They both assume responsibility for the outcome of the effort. If it is a success they each can say, "*We* succeeded." If it is a failure, they each can say, "*We* failed." Neither group can say the other *caused* the failure.

The application development and delivery process cannot be delegated. Business units cannot specify requirements and expect information systems to bring back a "quality" system. Application and data development can only effectively be achieved when business and information systems work together throughout the development to satisfy their mutual customers. Outsourcing of data architecture and key business application development reflects a view of information systems as a "support" function that places the enterprise at risk.

3. Among Business Organizations

Organizations may develop the first two team relationships well, yet produce low-quality application systems and databases. A business area must see itself as a team with other business areas that "supply" information to it, and with business areas that are "customers" of the information it produces. The failure of this business teamwork has led to the myriad of standalone, unintegrated applications and databases that consume an inordinate amount of support resources and threaten to cause business failure.

This legacy of unintegrated applications and databases directly results from organizations failing to apply Deming's Quality Point 9. Organizations that ignore Point 9 are characterized by the "my application" or "my data" syndrome. Everything may appear to be working satisfactorily, but the business areas may be achieving their business area goals while suboptimizing the enterprise goals.

This myriad of redundant databases increases the costs of data warehouse initiatives that must aggregate data from disparate data sources to support strategic and cross-functional analytical processes.

"Is it management's job to help staff areas work together? To promote teamwork? Sounds great, but it can't be done under the present system [of management by objectives and individual performance measures]. In spite of the system, you will find teamwork. But when it comes to a showdown under the present system and someone has to make a decision—his own rating or the company's—he will decide for himself. Can you blame him? People work in the system. Management creates the system."[33]

Management must change the system of performance measures to incent teamwork. It must break down the barriers between organizational units to increase the desire to share information rather than to hoard it.

Quality Application Development Methodologies Break Down Barriers

Application and data development methodologies are business processes like business planning and product development or engineering. As such, they are subject to improvement as is any other process. In fact, the application and data development methodologies are vital processes because they create the information "system" that *enables* or *hinders* the work of the organization. While application and database "products" may be built in 3 months' to 2-years' time, the resulting applications and databases will constrain or enable business processes for 5 to 25 years. Many organizations have core "legacy" applications and databases that are now more than 35 years old.

Quality application and data development methodologies must have a customer focus. This customer focus does *not* mean focusing on the customer who is paying for the application. Rather, a customer-focused methodology asks *who* are *all* the customers of the information products delivered by the application, and *who* are the suppliers of information products required by the application. The best place to electronically capture information required by the application may not be within the scope of the sponsoring business area.

Quality development methodologies will focus on the horizontal business value chain rather than vertical functions being automated. Only by focusing

[33]Walton, *The Deming Management Method*, p. 75.

horizontally, will a development methodology ever produce applications and databases that are *seamlessly* integrated *and* that satisfy downstream information-product customers as well as the immediate beneficiaries of the developed applications and databases.

How to Create Quality Application Development and Delivery

To assure a quality application and data development methodology, assure the following characteristics:

❏ The methodology is defined adequately and consistently, so different project teams, adequately trained, can produce quality applications and databases consistently.

❏ Has a role of *business* project manager as well as a *systems* project manager.

❏ Has a role of data architect, data administrator, whose purpose is to assure common definition of data among all information stakeholders.

❏ Focuses on applications as an interdependent component of a larger business value chain, and not simply a standalone application. It defines its scope as a integrated part of the value chain.

❏ Views applications and databases *not* as *end products* in and of themselves, but as *tools* that enable business products to be produced. Applications and databases are to business processes what manufacturing equipment is to manufacturing processes.

❏ Defines application objectives in context with the *enterprise* goals and business drivers, along with how the application supports or enables enterprise goal attainment.

❏ Uses business value chain, information, and technology architectures as input to the development process and identifies how the application fits into them.

❏ Identifies information customers and suppliers outside of the scope of the "project" and considers their information requirements that are within the scope of the application developed.

❏ Has a step to assess whether business activities add value or add cost from the end-customer perspective.

❏ Has a step to reuse existing architected data models and databases.

❏ Has a step to define and model information to meet all information customer (internal and external) needs, not just those of the application project. The only way to develop such a business information model is to have representative participation by all areas that have a stake in a common information subject. Information modeling is best done by modeling and defining information requirements about the various business resources or subjects. Business resources (subjects) include people and organizations (customer, supplier, and human), products and materials, facilities and other assets, financial, and other business resources sometimes called "subject areas." They must be modeled and defined to support all business processes and knowledge workers who require or produce the information about the various resources. These kinds of models cannot be developed with "interview and assimilate" techniques. They can only be developed with interactive modeling sessions involving business subject-matter experts from the different parts of the organization so they can see how their views and processes fit within the context of the other enterprise views and processes. Those who argue this cannot be done must believe teamwork is not possible or desirable within their organizations. Those who argue it's too expensive must justify the costs of redundancy that result from doing it fast without regard for how well it integrates within the enterprise information environment or how much it costs to support.

❏ Separate the funding of application development into three categories:

  ■ Infrastructure costs (shared databases, authoritative data capture applications at the point of data origination, and shared information technology). Infrastructure costs must be allocated equitably across the enterprise.

  ■ Value delivery (the application programs that retrieve and use information to add value to the business processes). Value-delivery programs should be charged back to the beneficiary business area.

  ■ Redundant, cost-adding development (redundant data create applications, interbusiness area interface programs, redundant databases). Redundancy and cost-adding development, whose result is proprietary, inconsistently defined databases must be disincented. Business areas that insist on unintegrated applications and nonshared databases with inconsistently defined data must directly bear the costs of the development and the costs of maintaining consistency of their data with the enterprise shared data. In addition, they must bear the cost of fixing the information quality problems caused by the redundantly or inconsistently defined data.

❏ If evaluating application software packages, evaluate the packages against the enterprise data architecture, not just functional requirements.

❏ If evaluating application software packages, evaluate the packages against the enterprise technology architecture.

❏ If evaluating application software packages, evaluate the ramifications and costs of interfacing (it is a misnomer to call this *integrating*) the package data and technology architectures into the existing environment.

❏ Seek to place the data create programs with the business processes that are the first and natural point of data acquisition.

❏ Maximize the reuse of data, application, and technology objects already defined and implemented.

❏ Develop a step to gather postimplementation feedback of both immediate and downstream beneficiaries (knowledge workers) who are the customers of the application's information products.

❏ Institute a step to analyze the postimplementation feedback for the purpose of improving the application and data development processes.

Teamwork for Business Information Quality

Peter Drucker describes the new management models in the Information Age with the metaphor of the symphony conductor as opposed to the military chain-of-command hierarchy.[34] Working with a single composition, the conductor (Chief Executive Officer [CEO]) must interpret the music (establish the vision, mission, and objectives) and bring out from the musicians (workers) their skills in performing the music for the enjoyment of the concertgoers (the customers). There are a number of important parallels in this metaphor to Deming's Quality Point 9:

The musicians are all specialists. The violinists cannot play the trumpet parts nor can the flautists play the cello parts. In the same way, the business "functions" represent specialist roles in the business processes.

The conductor, as the CEO and leader of the orchestra, is accountable for the musical performance, and for bringing out the best in the performers. In the same way, management is the leader of the enterprise, and must bring out the best in employees. Management must provide its interpretation of what the enterprise must accomplish. It must make clear what is expected of the each section of the orchestra.

The orchestra plays from a single musical composition. In the same way, the business must operate from a common vision, to achieve a common end.

A successful performance can only occur when the orchestra plays *ensemble*. *Ensemble* is from the Latin word that means "working together." It is this ensemble, or "teamwork," that transforms a simple performance into an *enjoyable* performance for the concertgoers. Successful business that brings customer satisfaction occurs when all parts of the business value chain work together in ensemble.

---

[34] Peter Drucker, *The New Realities*, New York: Harper & Row, 1989, pp. 212–213.

The concertgoers are the customers. It is the customers who judge the quality of performance of the orchestra. A *quality* performance may be recognized by a standing ovation. In the end, no matter what "objectives" the enterprise has met, the customers have the final say as to the quality of products and services. They demonstrate their satisfaction by coming back again—or by going to the competition.

There are no conflicting objectives or competing incentives among the orchestra players. The trombonist does not compete with the clarinetist by trying to "drown out" the clarinet passages. Nor does the bass viol player compete with the violist to "finish first." The performance measures are simple. Do the players make music together? Business must examine its performance measures from this metaphor. Performance measures must be team-oriented. They must incent teamwork and encourage working together for common goals without being penalized. Consider performance measures for the musicians such as "how many notes can you play per minute" or "who can finish their part first." This would be ludicrous. If business management creates individual incentive mechanisms, it must expect suboptimal behavior by talented people, and frustration and morale problems along with decreased productivity by those who do not "measure up," and decreased customer satisfaction.

Organizations can achieve significant benefits when they begin operating out of a horizontal, teamwork mind set rather than a vertical, functional (individual) mind-set. This can be exploited exponentially in the Information Age, with our ability now to capture and share knowledge in ways not possible before.

For example, service technicians and customer service reps have significant and valuable knowledge about their company's products and their quality problems. The credit department may be the first place in the company to learn of quality problems when customers refuse to pay. Quality can be improved by incorporating this knowledge in product and service design and delivery. When Hewlett-Packard first used information from customer comments in the design of a new product, the resulting product reached the point of profitability faster than any previous product in its product line. It also went on to become one of the unit's most profitable products.

When all departments and business units are working *ensemble* as a team to accomplish common goals, new ways of productivity can be achieved. This productivity results from eliminating redundant information work or data cleanup that each area has to perform for itself, because it cannot trust the data created by the information supplier departments. Departments must view themselves not as isolated business functions, but as a component in a larger business value chain. While the work may be sequential, unlike the work of a symphony orchestra, there must be cooperation among all parts of the value chain to assure a product that is perceived as *ensemble* to the end customer.

To accomplish this, however, requires changes to the incentives and budgeting for information creation and maintenance. Performance measures must incent business areas that have upstream activities (information suppliers) to capture information needed by downstream knowledge workers, even though they do not need the data within their business area. They must not be forced to pay for that data capture out of their budget alone. The additional data capture must be funded in a way that is equitable for the information producer area and the ultimate downstream beneficiary areas. "If the reward system is competitive, the people in the system will view this as a competitive situation and act accordingly, despite the inherently cooperative nature of the situation."[35] In other words, if you ask an upstream department to capture your data for you, but do not provide funding to cover the additional costs of capturing data from which they do not directly benefit, do you really expect them to do it?

When you find that business areas do not want to cooperate, challenge and change the reward mechanisms. Management creates the performance measures and creates the "systems" in which the business cooperates—or competes—with each other. Management must change the reward mechanisms and performance "systems" that disincent teamwork and cooperation.

Point 10: Eliminate Slogans and Exhortations

The hallways of a major insurance company's information systems area are filled with posters like Figure 11.1 that read, "The Bug Stops Here." With the obvious desire to affect systems quality, you would expect them to develop and deliver quality applications. Did those posters improve systems and information quality? No. In fact, a major pilot project undertaken to bring in a new era of state-of-the-art application development ended as a complete failure. What was to have been the key business system for policy administration with 90 percent reusable components resulted in only 10 percent reusable objects.

Deming's Quality Point 10 condemns the superficial quality improvement technique of quality by edict, that is, "I say it; you do it." Slogans, posters, and exhortations do not result in improved quality. Rather, they "generate frustration and resentment."[36] Point 10 reads, "Eliminate slogans, exhortations, and targets for the workforce asking for zero defects and new levels of productivity. Such exhortations only create adversarial relationships, as the bulk of the causes of low quality and low productivity belong to the system and thus lie beyond the power of the workforce."[37]

[35]Aguayo, *Dr. Deming*, p. 195.
[36]Deming, *Out of the Crisis*, p. 67.
[37]Ibid., p. 24.

The bug stops here

Figure 11.1   The bug stops here.

The problem with posters and slogans is that they are addressed to the wrong people. Most of the causes of problems come not from the workers, but from the "system" in which the workers must perform their jobs. "It is totally impossible for anybody or for any group to perform outside a stable system, below or above it. If a system is unstable, anything can happen. Management's job . . . is to try to stabilize systems. An unstable system is a bad mark against management."[38]

It is a sham for management to put forth exhortations to improve quality without providing the means for accomplishing quality improvement. Superficial exhortations and short-term quality improvement initiatives may bring about some short-term gains, as people see management's focus on quality as an issue. But if management does not provide the resources, quality improvement processes to make process improvement possible, and changes to the system to incent information quality at the source, quality improvement will cease and information quality may even go down.

DEMING CITES THE FRUITS OF QUALITY IMPROVEMENT EXHORTATIONS[39]

1. **Failure to accomplish the goal**
2. **Increase in variability**
3. **Increase in proportion defective**
4. **Increase in costs**
5. **Demoralization of the workforce**
6. **Disrespect for the management**

[38]Walton, *The Deming Management Method*, p. 77.
[39]Deming, *Out of the Crisis*, p. 68.

Ramifications for Information Quality

Information quality will not occur by edict, exhortation, or threat. Information systems management and business management must change the systems in which applications and databases are developed and in which information producers work.

Setting targets for information quality will have only temporary impact unless:

- Processes to improve the processes to eliminate data-defect causes are put in place.

- Incentives are changed to incent quality production rather than "productivity" (regardless of the quality produced).

- Management and process owners have accountability for the quality of the information products produced by the processes in their charge.

Deming describes the process for taking action to accomplish the transformation in his Point 14. I describe the process for information quality improvement in Chapter 9. I discuss how to implement accountability for information in the next chapter.

Point 11: Eliminate Quotas of Productivity with Metrics of Quality

"Quotas or other work standards . . . impede quality perhaps more than any other single working condition."[40] The solution is simple: If management believes quality is important to business success, they will implement Quality Point 11: Eliminate numerical quotas for the work force and numerical goals for people in management.[41] In their place, management will put measures that measure the right things, such as customer satisfaction reduction of information scrap and rework.

The impact of quotas is counterproductive. Peer pressure causes those who perform "above average," whatever that means, to slow down. In essence, they produce less than they are capable of. Those who perform below the average cannot make the rate. The result is loss due to working faster than optimal, frustration, and high turnover. The actual effect is to "double the cost of the operation and to stifle pride of workmanship."[42]

Furthermore, Point 11 strikes against the practice of management by numbers. Internal goals, such as "decrease costs by 10 percent next year," or

---

[40]Walton, *The Deming Management Method*, p. 78.
[41]Deming, *Out of the Crisis*, pp. 70, 75.
[42]Ibid., p. 71.

HOW QUOTAS OVERRIDE GOOD INFORMATION QUALITY PROCEDURES

A senior vice president of a healthcare company hired a telemarketing firm to conduct a customer satisfaction survey of its top 50 customers. The customer list came from the customer service system, and contained customer name, address, phone number, and contact name of its most important customers. The telemarketing company called back to say they were going to have to charge more money than originally planned. "Your data is so bad that we are spending much more time on the phone conducting this survey than we planned," was the reply. "We are having to call directory assistance and then find the correct party within the account because your contacts and phone numbers are out of date."

The senior VP—who had not been particularly supportive of the company's information quality effort—sought to get to the root of this information quality problem. Asking the customer service center questions like, "Why don't you verify address, phone, and contact information when a customer calls in?" he found the reality of Deming's Point 11. He discovered that the customer service procedure in fact does say to verify the customer's address and phone number with every contact. But the reps were not following the procedure *because they were measured by the number of calls they took per day*. If this was the level of information quality for these "best" customers, what information quality could they expect of the rest?

"increase sales by 10 percent," "are a burlesque," Deming says.[43] Meeting a goal may be due to a natural fluctuation rather than to a process improvement. Quotas are even more cruel if they are arbitrary and not accompanied with a plan for attainment. The only numbers that Deming believes are permissible are those that set forth actual facts of enterprise survival, such as, "unless our sales improve 10 percent next year, we shall be out of business."[44]

Ramifications for Information Quality

The information quality problem described in Chapter 1, "The High Costs of Low-Quality Data" (80 percent of insurance claims had a medical diagnosis code of "broken leg"), confirms the application of Point 11 for information quality. The claims processors were measured by how many claims they processed in a day. How can you expect them to take time to enter the correct medical diagnosis code when they could use the system default of "broken leg"? It should come as no surprise that 80 percent of the claims "just happened" to have a medical diagnosis code of "broken leg." While this "quality" satisfied the operational process to pay the claim, it was nonquality information for all other information customers, such as the actuaries who needed to analyze risk from the data warehouse.

When quotas and speed cause information quality problems, it *significantly* increases the costs of the affected information products. The data is not usable

---

[43]Deming, *Out of the Crisis*, p. 71.
[44]Ibid., p. 76.

by other business areas, so they have to look for alternative sources. Or they have to spend a significant amount of time and money to verify, find, and correct the data before they can use it. Or they may even have to create and maintain their own private databases and systems in order to trust the data they require. All of these costly workarounds can be traced to the root cause that the information producers allowed nonquality information because they were being measured by how fast they did work, not whether it was reusable by others who needed it.

The only viable correction to these problems is to change the performance measures for information producers. Rather than measures of "how fast" or "how many," use measures of customer satisfaction by the downstream information customers. Data captured with quality at the source will meet all knowledge workers' needs. This results in decreased costs and increased productivity of those who use the data. The data warehouse team would not have to embark on a major cleanup effort to find the right medical diagnosis code for 80 percent of the claims. The customer service database would be current, reducing the costs of conducting a customer satisfaction survey. And this was only one instance of use of the customer service customer information. Consider how many other processes failed trying to use this information. Or worse, how many private customer databases were spawned because knowledge workers who needed vital customer contact information could not trust it from the official and supposedly authoritative source?

Consider the economics of quotas that have the effect of decreasing information quality. Because others cannot use the poor-quality information in a common sharable database, or in managed replicated databases, they *will* be forced to:

Not use the data, because it lacks quality. The result is suboptimization of the process or decision due to "missing" (actually unusable) information. This is the equivalent of manufacturing "scrap." Lacking the necessary quality, and too costly to rework, it is "thrown away."

Look for an alternative source (supplier) of the information. Creating their own private databases, possibly by extracting the data from the original source, they clean it up for their use. This is the equivalent of manufacturing "rework." The further tragedy of this "solution" is that the newly cleaned data is not available to other knowledge workers because it is being maintained in a private, proprietary, and inaccessible database.

One newly appointed information quality staff person who came from one of the business areas confided to me that she had been "guilty" of developing her own proprietary database when she was in the business area. She was not able to use the data from the official corporate database because it lacked quality. The financial company's business drivers happened to be speed of work. Never mind the quality or the costs. The company must capitalize on new business opportunities quickly due to the competition. A high degree of redundant databases exist in this company because speed of product delivery to the marketplace superseded the "luxury" of quality, shared databases. But at what cost? Even as I write these words, this company is under pressure to reduce its costs of operations, and has postponed some vital projects that could mitigate the costs of the redundant databases and unintegrated applications.

When information producers are forced to make a choice between information quality that others can use, and quotas for which they are measured to receive their pay raises, the choice is already made. Only management can change the performance measures. When management recognizes it cannot afford the high costs of poor information quality, it will change the performance measures.

How to Replace Quotas with the Right Measures

Information producers will do a good job if they have the resources and right measures. Quotas cause poor information quality, and poor quality causes excessive scrap and rework downstream. The solution is straightforward:

1. Reallocate resources required to do information scrap and rework to the front end where information is produced.

2. Develop contracts and service levels between downstream beneficiaries and upstream information producers for quality levels.

3. Fund additional resources for upstream to provide the required information quality levels *from* the money and people squandered on the information scrap and rework activities.

4. Provide training and support resources for the upstream information producers to provide the required information quality.

Because the costs of information scrap and rework are more than the costs of defect prevention by a factor of from 5 or 10 to 1, the additional savings from the downstream budgets can be applied to value-adding initiatives, cost reduction, or profit.

Point 12: Remove Barriers to Pride of Workmanship

A major pitfall of the Industrial Age was to take pride out of workmanship. During the Agricultural Age, a cottage industry craftsman made his products from start to finish. This is "*my* work." But the principle of specialization of labor forced workers to see only part of the work product, removing the feeling of accomplishment. When Volvo reengineered its manufacturing process, rather than have each person perform a small set of tedious tasks, such as bolting the left-hand doors to the car, a team of workers would follow an automobile down the assembly line and as a team perform all of the assembly. Three things happened. Morale went up—"I built *this* car!" Productivity went up due to less absenteeism and higher enjoyment of work. And quality went up—the pride of workmanship was back. When a person identifies with the work product in its whole, there is a sense of ownership and a desire to do quality work. The result is that both quality and productivity go up.

How can one have pride of workmanship with assembly-line barriers that allowed one U.S. auto manufacturer to produce a three-door car? Workers on one side installed a two-door assembly on the chassis while a one-door unit was installed by the workers on the other side!

The essence of Deming's Point 12, "Remove barriers that rob people of pride of workmanship," is simple. Allow people to feel good about their work, and they will do good work. Period. Barriers and other obstacles in organization structure, lack of training, and lack of feedback rob the worker of "his birthright, the right to be proud of his work, the right to do a good job."[45]

Information Age technology gives knowledge workers a way to overcome the separation and disjointed work environment caused by specialization of labor. By collaborating in their work products through shared databases, information producers and knowledge workers do not just do *their* isolated job, they share in the entire process and the finished product.

At the same time, however, because information technology enables fewer people to do more work, management must not view people as expendable commodities. People are, and will always be, the most important asset in an organization. And while money is important, what really motivates employees "to perform—and to perform at higher levels—is the thoughtful, personal kind of recognition that signifies true appreciation for a job well done," Bob Nelson asserts with confirmation by numerous studies.[46]

How to Remove Barriers of Quality Information Production

Information producers, by and large, want to do a good job. Give them an opportunity to "work with pride, and the 3 percent that apparently don't care will erode itself by peer pressure."[47]

Guidelines for removing information production barriers:

1. Train information producers how to capture information accurately.

2. Let information producers know who uses the information they create and the processes that require it, and therefore the importance of their information products. Have knowledge workers swap jobs with the information

---

[45]Deming, *Out of the Crisis*, p. 77.
[46]Bob Nelson, *1001 Ways to Reward Employees*, New York: Workman Publishing, 1994, p. xv.
[47]Deming, *Out of the Crisis*, p. 85.

producers who create the information they use. Likewise, have the information producers go to the knowledge worker areas to observe what is done with the data. Have the information producers perform the exception processes if data is missing or inaccurate. This lets them feel the pain of poor-quality data.

3. Hold periodic "value chain" meetings with all stakeholders to discuss and resolve issues and participate in the success. This allows information producers to see and participate in the end product and result of their work.

4. Remove quotas or incentives based on speed or volume of data created. "Money and time spent for training will be ineffective unless inhibitors to good work are removed."[48]

5. Prototype human-factors design of applications *with* information producers so they provide feedback as to its intuitiveness and ergonomics and ease of use. Minimize unnecessary keystrokes and hand and eye movements.

6. Implement business rules and reasonability tests that prevent inadvertent errors. Minimize data entry of data that can better be selected from a list of values or that the application can access and provide.

7. Do *not* implement business rules that force errors. For example, if an edit requires a birth date when the information producers have no way to get it, they will have to "make one up." Rather, allow for a value of "unknown." If that field is a required field for the next process, mark the data as being in an incomplete state until it can be provided.

8. Eliminate redundant data creation and private, proprietary databases. If data cannot be physically shared from one database, provide for managed replication of the data, and control its synchronization based on knowledge workers' real requirements.

9. Identify where information producers must do workarounds to capture required data, because of poor database design, and unacceptable costs or time to modify the database and application. Eliminate unmanaged redundant databases and applications to free up information systems professionals to perform value-adding work on sharable databases and reusable applications.

10. Encourage information producers to identify problems in the application or data design or in data create and update procedures. Accompany this with fast response and feedback as to their suggestions.

11. Involve information producers in application design and data definition, so they can "own" the definition and design.

12. Develop clear and complete data definition including complete lists of valid domain values and business rules.

---

[48]Deming, *Out of the Crisis*, p. 53.

13. Have management perform the data production work so they know the data production job and the working conditions. When salaried workers took over production during a strike, the managers found horrible working conditions that included machines out of order and badly in need of maintenance. After the strike, they instituted a system that enabled employees to easily report problems with machines and materials, and other problems, along with mechanisms for responding to the reports.[49]

14. Assure that the information producers are the *natural* point of data production for the data being created or maintained. If not, move the data production process to the best place in the enterprise. The right "place" is the first business process that comes to know the data.

15. Develop processes that automatically capture data electronically, rather than have it entered by hand. For example, use barcode readers, optical scanners, and chips that electronically sense and capture data. This frees the information producers to have time to capture data that cannot be automatically captured.

16. Provide feedback frequently to information producers, not just when data is bad, but also when the data enables significant business success.

17. Recognize and reward information producers for improving information quality that eliminates the costs of poor-quality information downstream.

Point 13: Encourage Education and Self-Improvement

So important is education and training in quality that it constitutes two of Deming's 14 Points. While Point 6 addresses job training, Point 13 addresses people development. "What an organization needs is not just good people; it needs people who are improving with education."[50] Point 13 reads, "Institute a vigorous program of education and self-improvement."[51] Not just a program for the exceptional staff, or just an optional program, or a program considered expendable when profits are down, but a "vigorous" program for "everybody" for improvement in *tomorrow's* skills. Investment in training in vacuum tube and transistor technology represents an investment in 1940's and 1950's success, but that will not create competitive advantage in the twenty-first century.

Optical Fibres, a Northern Wales manufacturer of some of today's information technology, has a strong people-centric focus. While they—like other enterprises—can no longer guarantee lifetime employment, they can—and

---

[49]Deming, *Out of the Crisis*, p. 85.
[50]Ibid., p. 86.
[51]Ibid., p. 24.

do—guarantee their people the opportunity for self-development and self-improvement. Every person in the company has the opportunity to undergo extensive quality improvement training, as well as other development and education opportunities. The payback? Loyalty with low employee turnover, high morale, strong sense of teamwork, and commitment to continuous improvement and innovation.

Point 13 places the right priority on the resources of the enterprise—its people resources. But how do you know tomorrow's skills today? You don't. You develop people's knowledge, and let them apply their knowledge to create tomorrow's new technologies, techniques, and processes that add new value. If *you* change the paradigm of how and what work is done, then everyone else must catch up to you. If your competitor changes the paradigm of how work is done, then you must catch up to them—if you can.

But it may not be in the best interest of your organization to "create" change. That's okay. You must, however, develop your people so they are prepared to make the paradigm shift when it is feasibly right for your enterprise. Management must determine which change orientation is right. Appropriate organizational change orientation strategies include experimenter (create change), early adopter (make change work), or pragmatist (change when stable).[52] Change strategies of late adopter (change only when forced to), or resister (*attempt* to avoid change), risk organization failure.

Ramifications of Self-Improvement on Information Quality

Point 13 brings to full focus the requirement for understanding and education in the principles of the Information Age paradigm. Joel Barker, a Futurist, describes a crucial and profound truth when paradigms change. He calls it the "Going Back to Zero Rule." This rule says, "When a paradigm shifts, everyone goes back to zero. It doesn't matter how big your market share is, or how strong your reputation. Or how good you are at the old paradigm. Your past success guarantees nothing."[53] Barker illustrates this truth with the following lesson.

In 1969, Switzerland, renowned for more than a hundred years for its watch-making excellence, dominated the market for watch-making with 65 percent of world market share and with expert estimates of over 80 percent of the profits.[54] Yet, 10 years later—less than a tenth of the time they dominated the market—their market share slid to less than 10 percent, causing layoffs of 50,000 of the 65,000 (over 75 percent!) watch-makers during the next 3 years. Why? The introduction of the quartz watch, invented by the Swiss themselves, changed

---

[52]James Martin, *Reskilling the IT Professional*, New York: Prentice Hall Computer Books, 1993.

[53]Joel Barker, Video: *Discovering the Future: The Business of Paradigms*, Burnsville, MN: Charthouse International Learning Corporation, Master trainer's manual, p. 79.

[54]Ibid., p. 80.

the paradigm of watches. In fact, the Swiss watch manufacturers were so convinced the quartz watch would not succeed that they did not patent it. However, when it was displayed at the annual watch conference in 1967, Texas Instruments and Seiko saw the potential of the new paradigm. The demise of the Swiss watchmaking industry demonstrates the power of paradigm shifts. The new invention did not fit the paradigm of that era's watch-making management. Even though the quartz watch concept was first presented to the Swiss watch manufacturers, the idea was so counter to their paradigm of watches with bearings, gears, and a mainspring that they dismissed it. They were blinded by their paradigm to the future of a totally electronic and versatile watch that could be a thousand times more accurate than the then-current technology.

This is not an isolated incidence. Many of the world's successful organizations have gone through paradigm shifts, and come through them only after some traumatic reinventing of themselves, and with significant loss of market share. IBM, General Motors, Sears Roebuck and Company, and Kodak are just some examples. But many do not make the shift. Fifty percent of the companies on previous Fortune 500 lists are missing 10 years later. They failed or were gobbled up by the competition. The rate of "missing-in-action" is accelerating in today's Realized Information Age.

Today's future belongs to those who understand the paradigm of the information resource and who implement the principles of managing *and* maximizing its information resources. Management principles similar to those applied to every other business resource must be applied to the information resource. However, the use that can be made of managed information enables—and requires—fundamental organization and relationship changes.

The management and organization characteristics of the Information Age enterprise are counter to those of the Industrial Age enterprise. These characteristics are contrasted in Table 11.2.

Organizations that have a vision to thrive will invest in their people resources so they are prepared for the new paradigms of the Realized Information Age.

Point 14: Accomplish the Transformation for Information and Business Quality

Every information quality initiative will struggle with the first 13 of Deming's Points of Quality. The long-term success of an information quality initiative depends on this final point. Management must organize itself to make the first 13 points happen. Point 14 states: "Put everybody in the company to work to accomplish the transformation. The transformation is everybody's job."[55] An information quality team will be overwhelmed by the apparent enormity of the task of information quality improvement alone. The good news is the information quality

[55]Deming, *Out of the Crisis*, p. 24.

Table 11.2 Industrial Age versus Information Age Enterprise Characteristics

INDUSTRIAL AGE CHARACTERISTICS:	INFORMATION AGE CHARACTERISTICS:
Hierarchical and bureaucratic	Horizontal team configuration
Organized around functions	Organized around processes and results
Static and traditional	Dynamic and entrepreneurial
Product focus	Customer-supplier focus
Profit driver and measure	Customer-satisfaction driver and measure
Centralized concentration	Distributed: "close" to customers
Disconnected: interface-based	Connected: integrated, cooperative relationships relationships
Individual rewards	Team rewards
Specialized labor	Empowered, informed, trained knowledge workers
Financial currency and resource	Information currency and resource

team is not alone in the mandate to make information quality happen. Information quality improvement is *everybody's* job. Top management is where the quality starts and continues. This is true for quality of the *information* products as well as the business products.

Management must take action to make the transformation of the organization to an Information Age enterprise. Those actions include:

- Agreeing to carry out the new philosophy of information quality for improved customer satisfaction and reduced costs of business operation.

- "The courage to break with tradition, even to the point of exile among their peers."[56]

- Providing leadership and communicating through seminars and other means to a "critical mass" of people in the organization why change is necessary, and that the change will involve everyone. *Everyone* means from information producers and data intermediaries to knowledge workers; from design to production to marketing to sales personnel; from operations to support personnel, from top management to the most junior clerk. *Everyone* also means from application developers, to data resource management staff to information systems management.

The premises of Point 14 are:

[56]Deming, *Out of the Crisis*, p. 86.

- Every activity and every job is a part of a process. Any activity or job that involves information is within the scope of information quality improvement. Every process can be improved in an economically feasible way to accomplish one or more of the following:

  - Decrease costs
  - Decrease time-to-market
  - Increase business opportunity
  - Increase ease-of-use
  - Increase customer satisfaction
  - Result in increased profit and increased shareholder or stakeholder value

The fundamental technique for accomplishing information quality through process improvement was laid out by Walter A. Shewhart in the 1930s. Dr. Shewhart proposed that the traditional, linear approach to quality control of specification, production, and inspection was wrong. The steps must be circular, with the inspection step providing continuous feedback to the specification step to provide continual improvement to the process to reduce variability, and thereby reduce costs. Process operations viewed in this way makes up a "continuing and self-corrective method" of production.[57]

This self-corrective method was adopted by Deming and called the "Shewhart cycle."[58] It has been popularized as the "PDCA" or "Plan, Do, Check, Act" cycle as a technique for process improvement. It is described in Chapter 9 as applied to information quality improvement. The steps are simple, yet effective:

Plan. Develop a plan for improving a process that produces data with unacceptable quality.

Do. Implement the improvement in a controlled environment.

Check. Assess the results to see if it has achieved the desired results and level of information quality.

Act. If so, roll out the improvement to provide consistent results.

- Management must move forward now, with deliberate speed, to create the environment and organization to guide continual information quality improvement. Every day's delay is a day of lost time, cost of defective

---

[57]Walter A. Shewhart, *Statistical Method from the Viewpoint of Quality Control*. Original publisher: Washington: Graduate School, Department of Agriculture, 1939. Unabridged republication: New York: Dover Publications, 1986, pp. 44-45.

[58]Deming, *Out of the Crisis*, p. 88.

data scrap and rework, and missed opportunity as a result of poor-quality information.

- Everyone can participate in an information quality improvement team, whose goal is to improve the input and output of any step in the information value chain.

- Management must create an effective organization structure for information quality improvement. The information quality organization and its evolution are described in Chapter 13, "Implementing an Information Quality Improvement Environment."

How to Make the Transformation Happen

You can make things happen by doing the following:

1. Quantify the costs of nonquality information. Management has no incentive to change the status quo until they understand and feel the pain of the costs of nonquality information. Those costs include lost time due to data cleanup, wasted time and resources due to unnecessary redundancy, and customer dissatisfaction with its missed opportunity and lost customer lifetime value due to nonquality information. See Chapter 7 for how to quantify these costs. Management has enormous competing priorities. Management will embrace information quality improvement when they understand four things:

   Many of the obstacles to accomplishing their objectives are the result of not having quality information.

   The cause of nonquality information is defective processes for managing information, as well as for creating and maintaining it.

   The direct costs of nonquality information may be 15 to 25 percent of revenue or operating budget, and yet they are entirely preventable at a fraction of the costs of information scrap and rework.

   Management themselves must take action to change. The status quo is what has caused the problem.

2. Do not focus blame—focus on defective processes and fix them. People are the most valuable resource. They are only part of the system. Exploit their strengths. Seek out the root cause of defects and eliminate the cause.

3. Exploit the value of a trained, qualified consultant to advise management. When people are too close to a problem, sometimes they cannot see it. When people have a vested interest in a process, they may be blind to the obvious solution. However, hiring a quality consultant with the right qualifications is more difficult than it sounds,[59] according to Rafael Aguayo, a

---

[59]Aguayo, *Dr. Deming*, p. 215.

consultant in quality and management who worked with Deming for seven years. Making sustainable organizational culture change is not a task for contract consulting personnel. It requires multifaceted expertise and experience in working with people at all levels, understanding the new paradigms, and thoroughly understanding the principles and methods of information quality improvement.

4. Train an internal consultant. The proper use of consultants is for knowledge transfer. The organization must develop internal competencies in how to conduct information quality assessments and facilitate information quality process improvement.

5. Simply do it. Be proactive. Take responsibility for yourself. Know your information customers and information suppliers. Find out the needs of your customers and strive to meet them. Help your suppliers understand your requirements and listen to them to find out how you can provide benefit to them in return. Quantify the value of the benefits you create as a result. Then publish them, so others can learn by your example.

Conclusion

There are those who contend quality improvement does not work. And there are studies that indicate that many organizations that have initiated "quality improvement" programs have failed to achieve significant gains. Those who reject information quality improvement may shrug it off as unnecessary cost and effort. The question is this, Was the concept faulty? Or was the process implemented or performed incorrectly? Did the organization perform a root-cause analysis on the results?

Those organizations that do not address and achieve the 14 Points of Information Quality face the threat of extinction as their competitors start achieving the benefits from quality managed information. Those who do will redefine the economics of conducting business in the Information Age.

Information Stewardship: Accountability for Information Quality

"Who then is the faithful and wise steward, whom his master will put in charge of his household."

–BIBLE, LUKE 12:42

Implementing automated edit and validation routines in application programs can guarantee roughly *zero* percent of information quality. Edit and validation routines can prevent gross errors such as creating a date of "December 32, 1999," or the fact that someone has 97 children. Only people can create accurate information.

Information stewardship is an essential element in an information quality environment. Kaizen, or continuous process improvement, means everyone in the organization takes responsibility for the process to continually improve *everything* in the business.

In this chapter we describe what information stewardship is and why it is required for information quality. We then identify and describe business and information systems roles in their accountability for their respective roles in information development, production, and use. We conclude with a description of the kinds of support resources required for empowering and sustaining information stewardship.

Information Quality and Accountability

Information producers will create information only to the quality level for which they are trained, measured, and held accountable. Real and sustainable information quality improvement can only be achieved by implementing *management* accountability for information like accountability for other business products and resources. If managers have no accountability for information quality, there is no incentive for removing barriers that prevent information producers from creating correct, complete, and timely information.

Without information stewardship, it is virtually impossible to foster trust in sharable databases. Organizations routinely discover operational data that satisfactorily supports departmental processes but is woefully inadequate for cross-functional information or data warehousing needs.

Quality for any business product requires:

- Understanding customer expectations

- Training in how to produce products that meet customer expectations

- Implementing performance measures and incentives that motivate

- Taking measurement of quality to assure process effectiveness

- Creating an effective process for process improvement

- Encouraging empowerment of all employees to improve their work processes

- Placing accountability for all work products, including information products

Information is a business product in the same way as manufactured products and delivered services; therefore, information quality requires the same ingredients. Information quality *improvement* requires changes in training, performance measures, and accountability. That's the formula for information stewardship.

What Is Information Stewardship?

Peter Block defines stewardship as "the willingness to be accountable for the well-being of the larger organization by operating in service of, rather than in control of those around us."[1] People are good "stewards" when they perform their work in a way that benefits their internal and external "customers" (the larger organization), not just themselves or their department. Valuable workers understand how others depend on their work products, and work to provide customer service.

Information stewardship is "the willingness to be accountable for a set of business information for the well-being of the larger organization by operating in service, rather than in control of those around us."

Stewardship is not ownership. An owner possesses the rights to something. The historical use of the term *steward* refers to one who has accountability for managing something that belongs to someone else. Shareholders who own the tangible assets of the corporation also *own* the information assets. *All* employees, then, are stewards of the information assets.

---

[1]Peter Block, *Stewardship: Choosing Service over Self-Interest*, San Francisco: Berett-Koehler, 1993, p. xx.

The term *data ownership* is problematic. True ownership of information, like other assets, belongs to the shareholders of the enterprise or to the stakeholders of public entities. Laws governing information may actual specify that certain personal information is the property of the individuals themselves. Other registered information, such as trademarks and copyrighted information, is the property of the trademark or copyright holder. The enterprise itself is a steward of its information resources. Neither information producers, nor process "owners," nor departments "own" the information they may create. Rather, they are stewards of that information for other stakeholders who depend on it.

The objectives of information stewards are reflected in Table 12.1.

Information Stewardship Roles

Seven major business roles and nine major information systems roles comprise information stewardship. Everyone in the organization has a stewardship responsibility for their role in creating, defining, or using information.

The following discussion will use the name *steward* for various roles of information accountability. This does not imply a *title*. Many organizations do use the term *steward* in the role name. Other organizations use terms such as *trustee*, *custodian*, or *pilot*.

Business Stewardship Roles

The business roles are listed in Table 12.2 with a brief statement of information accountabilities. The roles are described afterward. Most people will play more than one role. For example, an information producer who creates some information will also be a knowledge worker who uses other information to do so.

Table 12.1   Information Stewardship Objectives

INTERMEDIATE OBJECTIVES	ULTIMATE OBJECTIVES: IN ORDER TO:
Business accountability for information quality	Improve the value and quality of information, and decrease the costs of nonquality information
Business "ownership" of data definition	*Increase business communication, understanding and productivity* through data as a common business language
Data conflict resolution mechanism	*Maximize data value* through quality shared data with common definition, and *minimize data costs* through eliminated nonshared or redundant databases, interfaces, and applications
Improve business and information systems partnership	Improve customer satisfaction and team effectiveness

Table 12.2   Business Information Stewardship Roles and Accountabilities

BUSINESS ROLE	STEWARDSHIP ROLE	ACCOUNTABILITY
Knowledge worker	Knowledge steward	Accountable for their work outcomes. Also accountable for use of information, including upholding any policies or regulations governing its use.
Information producer	Operational information steward	Accountable for the quality of information I produce. The producer creates the actual information content.
Data intermediary	Information transcription steward	Accountable for transcription of data from one form to another; e.g., from a paper form to a computer record. Not accountable for content, but for completeness and accuracy of transcription.
Process owner or manager	Managerial information steward	Accountable for the integrity of the processes performed under their charge and for the quality of any produced information.
Process (definition) owner	Process steward	Accountable for the integrity of the definition of a business process or business value chain.
Executive manager	Strategic information steward	Accountable for establishing information policy and performance measures for resource management.
Business subject matter expert	Business information steward	"Accountable" for validation of the definition of data, including specification of valid values and business rules.

Knowledge Workers and Knowledge Stewardship

Knowledge workers who use information to perform work are information "consumers"—they use information to do their jobs. They are knowledge stewards, accountable for their work outcomes. This accountability is the most generally understood and applied. People are accountable for their work outcomes, regardless of whether they use information as input or not.

However, knowledge workers are also accountable for *how* they use information, including upholding all internal policies that specify protection and use of the information as well as any external regulations and laws that govern the information and its use. For example, "insider trading" in the form of buying or selling shares of stock on the basis of proprietary or confidential information not available to the general investor is illegal in the United States and other countries.

Knowledge workers are supported by business information stewards who must understand knowledge workers' information requirements and assure clear, accurate definitions of the information and any policies and regulations affecting it. Operational information stewards support knowledge workers by providing complete, accurate, and timely information to meet their needs.

Information Producers and Operational Information Stewardship

Information producers, whose work processes create or update data, are information "suppliers." They produce knowledge or information content, whether electronically into a database, on paper, in a report, or for a Web page. Information producers are operational information stewards, accountable for the completeness, accuracy, and timeliness of information products to meet both *intra*departmental *and inter*departmental knowledge workers' needs. Knowledge workers depend on information producers to become good stewards when they create data that benefits their internal and external information customers.

Information producers may create information or they may update it. If I am responsible for product prices and raise or lower them, I am the producer of product price information.

Information producers are supported by business information stewards who assure clear and accurate data definition and business rules. Information producers need to know what knowledge workers use their information. They need feedback from them to know how well they are meeting their information customers' needs.

Data Intermediaries and Information Transcription Stewardship

Data intermediaries are those who take information in one format, as in data on a completed order form or medical history form, and transcribe the information into another format, such as into a database. Data intermediaries are like translators who translate speech or written text from one language to another. The result should have the same meaning in the translated speech or text. Intermediaries do not produce content; they translate content from one form to another, without losing information or introducing error. As such, data intermediaries are accountable for accuracy, completeness, and timeliness of the transcribed information.

Much of the time, data intermediary work does not add value. It only adds the cost and time of an additional step in the value chain. However, there are times when the cost is economical relative to the value of the information produced. Consider the following: A consulting company "automated" the project time reporting process to eliminate paper. Time data was entered electronically by each consultant, rather than on paper forms submitted to a clerk. What used to take the consultants from 30 seconds to a couple of minutes each week, took from 5 to 10 minutes per *day*, or about one half to one hour per week, to enter into the new graphical system.

Intermediaries can add value, however. Intermediaries may become experts in the subject matter. As such, they may be able to identify and correct errors in the original information, or complete missing data and enter it faster than the originating information producer. In doing so, they add value to an otherwise cost-adding activity.

Intermediaries depend on the information producers for their input, and the business information stewards for the definition of the data. They should also know all knowledge workers who depend on their work and what processes use it. In this way, they can have a sense of value knowing how their information is used.

Managers and Managerial Information Stewardship

Process (production) owners and business managers are managerial information stewards accountable for integrity of the performed process. They have ultimate accountability for the quality of their processes' information products. This accountability includes information quality to meet the downstream knowledge workers' needs, not just their own department or business area.

Managerial information stewards are responsible for:

- Quality of information produced by their processes or in their business area
- Implementing information policy and assuring compliance
- Providing resources and training to information producers to assure quality standards are met
- Developing plans consistent with information sharing to maximize reuse value of information and minimize information costs

The mechanics of operational and managerial information stewardship are easy—there is historical precedence for it. Accountability, or stewardship, is a fundamental principle of resource management. One must take care of resources in their charge to assure they are maintained, protected, and used wisely. Industrial Age organizations have written accountability for financial and people resources into managers' job descriptions and hold them accountable.

Information Age organizations write information accountability into managers' job description and hold managers and information producers accountable for their information products. Why? Processes in one business area depend on information created in other business areas. Managerial and operational information stewardship is *not* optional. Every business manager is accountable for assuring that information created or updated within their processes is accurate and complete to satisfy all knowledge workers. Cominco Ltd., a mining company, has accountability for information not only written into its managers' and miners' job descriptions, but also written into the collective agreement with its contract miners. Figure 12.1 is a sample manager job description that contains a statement of information accountability. Without information stewardship, no enterprise can successfully reengineer cross-functional processes or effectively achieve sharable databases and integrated applications.

Process (Definition) Owners and Process Stewardship

Process (definition) owners are senior managers who have accountability for the definition of key business processes or business value chains that may span multiple business units or functional areas. They are not accountable for performing the processes. Line management is responsible for performing all or some of the activities of the processes. These line managers are the ones

---

Position Description: Manager, . . .

Position Purpose / Summary:
    Overall responsibility for all activities of the department including
    financial, safety, security, education and training . . .
Responsible to / authority relationship: Director, . . .

Responsibilities / Accountabilities:
1.   Responsible for management and control of fiscal resources.
    Develop budgets and manage expenses within approved guidelines.
2.   Responsible for personnel management of the department. Provide
    employee development. Uphold policies, schedule, oversee salary
    administration of staff, resolve staff problems.
3.   *Responsible for management, control, and use of information.*
    Maintain integrity of data created within the process or department.
    Implement and enforce information policy. Provide training of
    personnel in information quality principles and standards and
    provide resources to accomplish information quality goals.

. . .
Education: . . .
Experience: . . .   * Italics denote process owner accountability
Skills / Abilities: . . .

Figure 12.1   Information Age manager job description with information accountability.

responsible for the quality of both information and tangible products produced. The process definition owners are responsible for defining the process specification to insure process integrity and consistency, where required, among all line managers who oversee process production.

Business Experts and Business Information Stewardship

Consider the following entity type definition: "Customer: 'a person who has a record in the Customer table.'" Or consider the following attribute domain value set: "gender-code domain: '1 = male; 2 = female; 3 = initials; 4 = unrecognizable; 5 = ambiguous.'" Both of these definitions are incredible, incredulous, and fail miserably at the first data definition quality test—does the data represent object, event, or fact? How will the business respond if its data mining tool discovers a trend that "small widgets" tend to be the predominant choice of the "ambiguous" customers, and recommends a marketing campaign to that segment? These definitions did not come from the Dark Ages "data processing" shops in backward organizations. These definitions actually came from respected businesses that have sophisticated and relatively large data administration functions.

The problem with the gender-code domain stems from the fact that the attribute is used for two purposes. On the one hand, gender-code here is used to mean the sex of a person. The second—and inappropriate—use of the attribute is to indicate why a gender-code value cannot be "assigned" to a person based on first-name value. That reason is because the name is "initials" only, "unrecognizable," not able to be associated with one sex over the other, "ambiguous," or a name that is characteristic of either a woman or a man. This violates the principle that one fact should mean only one thing. This discussion of gender does not seek to oversimplify the realities of sex transformation or sexual orientation. Some organizations, in fact, must know these attributes. These attributes are separate attributes, if these characteristics should be known by the enterprise. The problem of unknown gender is solved by using a single domain value of "unknown."

What is the problem here? The problem is that both of these definitions were defined from a technical or functional perspective. Business subject experts were not responsible for these definitions. Both definitions came from well-intentioned information systems personnel who were looking at the data through "data processing" eyes.

What is the solution? Involve business subject matter experts as stewards or champions of the definition of business data. Here's why and how.

"Operational" and "managerial" information stewardship is business accountability for information (content) quality. Data *definition* quality or business "accountability" for assuring the accuracy of data definition is business information stewardship. There are also two levels of accountability for data definition quality: "strategic" and "business" information stewardship. Every senior manager in the enterprise is a "strategic information steward" accountable for enterprise resources and business performance. Business information stewards are subject matter experts *appointed* because of their knowledge of a given set of data and for their ability to see the impact of that data across the enterprise.

If data is a strategic enterprise resource, then the enterprise *must* apply the same principles of resource management as it applies to other strategic resources, such as human and financial resources. One of these principles is clear, accurate, and agreed-upon and consensus definition. Job positions are accurately defined so that anyone in the organization knows what is expected of one holding a given job position. General ledger account codes are accurately defined so that anyone working with a budget or financial report knows exactly what kinds of revenue or expenses are included in a specific account code. Product specifications and bill-of-materials are precisely defined in order to control the product manufacturing processes. So information must be clearly and precisely defined to assure effective communication across the enterprise.

Without clear, accurate, and common data definition, knowledge workers can only "assume" the meaning of the data they use. Information producers, who create the data, will not know the right values to create.

Business information stewards either define or validate data definition, domain values, and business rules for a discrete and specific set of entity types or subtypes and attributes. Their role is to assure that data definition meets the needs not just of their own business area, but also for all other business personnel who require that data to perform their business processes. Business information stewards generally establish the information quality standard for the data in their information group. They may also participate in the actual information quality assessments. They work with the data resource management group to assure the quality of data definition and to approve any definition changes to production databases.

Business information steward "accountabilities" include one or more of the following:

- Definition of, or review and approval of data definition, domain value specification, and business rule specification for a set of business data to meet all information customers' needs.

- Resolution of data definition among the stakeholders of that information.

- Establishment of information quality standards.

- Establishment of data access security. Most information should be open for *read* purposes to all employees. The only data that should be restricted is data that requires training for understanding its meaning or legal responsibilities and confidentiality.

- Access approval to classified data.

- Identification and documentation of regulatory or legal restrictions, including retention, governing the data.

- Championing the use of the "official" set of enterprise data.

- May work with information quality team for the assessment and reporting of information quality.

It is important to note that the term *accountability* for data *definition* is very much a voluntary responsibility in business personnel. I know of no precedent for a formal, written-in-the-job-description accountability like accountability for information content in business managers and information producers. Any business information stewardship program must seek ways to minimize the time element of persons who take on this role. Guidelines for success include:

- Keep the size of the stewardship information groups small, from 20 to 80 entity types and attributes.

- Focus first on only the high-priority data, that data with a high degree of data sharing and where errors have high costs.

- Use facilitated data definition workshops to define data initially.

- Rotate business information stewards from time to time.

- Provide training, documentation, and other resources to minimize steward time.

In global or multidivisional enterprises, one single steward may not be able to validate data definition requirements for data common to many countries or business units. In multidivisional enterprises, one information group may have several business stewards, each of whom represents one or more countries or business units, with one steward serving as a team leader for that information group.

Characteristics of effective business information stewards:

- ❏ Predominant stakeholder and customer of the information group. Business information stewards who will be assuring definition quality should be a major customer of the data.

- ❏ Knowledgeable in business subject.

- ❏ Authority to resolve business issues concerning the information. This comes from both their standing in the enterprise and the appointment from senior management.

- ❏ Decision-making ability. They must weigh differing viewpoints and come to a win-win decision when necessary.

- ❏ Credibility with peers. They have the respect of others.

❑ Understands enterprise as a whole. They have the ability to see the big picture and how the data in their charge impacts the whole of the enterprise.

❑ Awareness of the impact of shared data on other knowledge workers. Stewardship means the willingness to be accountable for the larger organization. They look out for the needs of others.

❑ Diplomat with people skills. They can create a win-win among people with differing viewpoints.

❑ Visionary. They solve tomorrow's problems. They know what information is not known today, but should be for effectiveness in the global economy.

Executive Management and Strategic Information Stewardship

The executive or senior management team members who are responsible for the performance of the enterprise are, in fact, strategic information stewards. They establish information policy, like other policy, and establish performance measures related to information quality and management and use of information to accomplish the enterprise mission and goals. Senior management sponsors the change required to transform an organization's treating data as merely a *byproduct* of business processes to treating information as a primary and strategic product—and business resource—of business processes. Each senior manager has accountability for one or more key business processes that tend to be associated with one or more key business information subjects, such as customer information (Marketing and Sales), product information (Production or Operations), financial information (Finance), or human resource information (Human Resources). Each senior manager will be naturally associated with one or more major information subjects, and therefore becomes the strategic information steward of that subject.

Each strategic information steward appoints or gives authority to selected business information stewards to be accountable for specific subsets of information. This authority provides the business information steward the authority to bring resolution to data name, definition, and business rule issues. Senior management becomes the ultimate point of resolving conflict related to the data definition and business rules, should the business information steward not be able to achieve consensus for critical shared or potentially sharable data.

Information Systems Stewardship Roles

Business personnel alone are not the only ones who have accountability for the information resources. Information systems personnel have accountability for the role in the resource (see Table 12.3).

Table 12.3 Information Systems Stewardship Roles and Accountabilities

SYSTEMS ROLE	STEWARDSHIP ROLE	ACCOUNTABILITY
Chief Information Officer	Strategic information and systems steward	Accountable for information strategy and for integrity of information technology, sharable database, and integrated application implementation.
Information manager or data administrator	Information architecture steward	Accountable for the "structural" quality of information infrastructure and data models. Accountable for effective data standards and repository for data definition. They facilitate data definition.
Database administrator	Database steward	Accountable for the "structural" integrity of physical databases. Not accountable for content, but for fidelity to information architecture, physical security, recoverability, and performance of *sharable* databases to meet multiple needs.
Systems analyst	Application requirements steward	Accountable for the integrity of application requirements specification as a component in a business process or business value chain and to meet knowledge workers' and information producers' information needs.
Systems developer	Application steward	Accountable for the integrity of applications to implement specifications and to meet knowledge workers' and information producers' information needs.
Information technology manager	Information technology steward	Accountable for information technology architecture and infrastructure implementation.
Data warehouse manager	Strategic information architecture steward	Accountable for the "structural" quality of the data warehouse information model and database design. Accountable for facilitating data definition to support strategic and tactical business processes.
Internet and intranet information manager	Virtual information architecture steward	Accountable for the "structural" quality of the Internet and intranet information model and database design. Not accountable for content,

Table 12.3   *(Continued)*

SYSTEMS ROLE	STEWARDSHIP ROLE	ACCOUNTABILITY
		but for facilitating information content that is integrated with existing data and to meet external and internal information customer knowledge needs.
Computer operations manager	Data operations steward	Accountable for the operational integrity of computer operations to support the business processes.

Information Stewardship Teams

The "structure" of information stewardship is informal and ad hoc to accomplish the objectives, but not to become another layer of bureaucracy. There are two key stewardship teams: the business information stewardship team and the executive information steering team. The relationships of these teams can be seen in Figure 12.2. The steering team either appoints business information stewards or gives authority to the selected stewards to carry out the responsibilities they have. This authority includes making the time available from the stewards' schedules to provide the business validation for data definition. The responsibilities of the teams are described later in the chapter.

Figure 12.3 is a variation of Figure 12.2 and is a model for large or global enterprises. Where there are multiple divisions and it is not feasible for a single business expert to be able to represent all stakeholders of the information, there may be multiple business information stewards for a single information group, such as common Product information. A local information stewardship team is made up of two or more subject matter experts for a single information group, each steward representing a geographic or business unit or division stake in the data. One steward serves as the team leader.

Business Information Stewardship Team

This team or council consists of all or a subset of the business information stewards. This team generally is chaired or facilitated by the information or data resource manager. Typical responsibilities of this team include:

- Resolve information-related issues across information groups or issues that cannot be resolved by a business information steward or local stewardship team.

- Provide support and knowledge transfer among business information stewards.

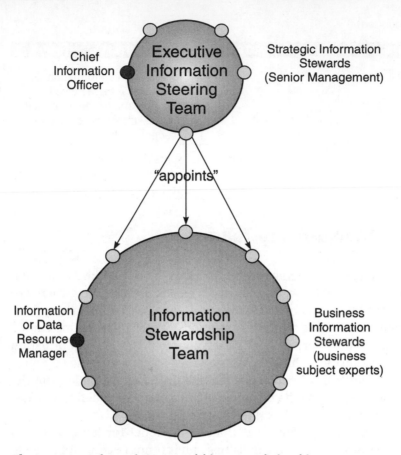

Figure 12.2 Information stewardship team relationships.

- Provide or recommend education for stewards at all levels.
- Identify or recommend information policies.
- Identify, recommend, or approve data standards.

Executive Information Steering Team

This team or governance council is made up of the senior management team, and may be facilitated by the Chief Information Officer or other executive. Some large organizations may have an information steering team appointed by and accountable to senior management for the steering committee role.

As a steering team, responsibilities include:

- Establishing enterprise vision, mission, values, and strategies that address information as a business resource
- Being accountable to the information stakeholders, such as customers, shareholders, employees, communities, and external regulatory entities

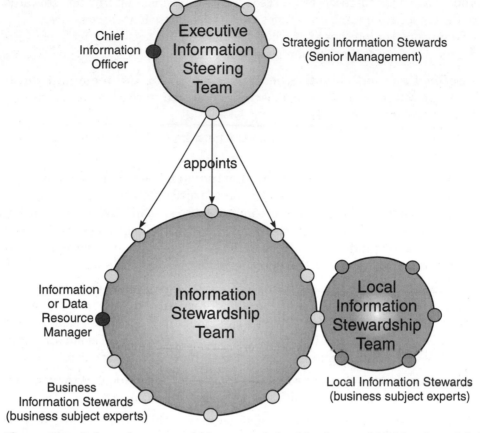

Figure 12.3   Information stewardship team relationships in a multidivisional or global environment.

- Establishing and issuing information policy, like financial and human resource policies
- Resolving major information-related issues that cannot be resolved by the business information stewardship team
- Establishing performance measures for information
- Effecting culture change for information accountability and information quality as a management tool

Data Definition Team

The most effective way to establish common and consensus data definition is to conduct facilitated data definition sessions involving representatives of all business areas that have a stake in a business subject or common collection of information. Business subjects are information groups centered around the business resources, such as human resources, financial resources, customer resources, product and material resources, and so forth. The business information stewards for the respective information groups would participate in these sessions.

Some organizations have not utilized data modeling sessions effectively. Critical success factors that are often overlooked include:

Defined and authoritative business charter for the team and workshop outcomes. The team must be empowered to reach a consensus definition for the enterprise.

Clear objectives and scope. The team must know the scope for the modeling session.

Involvement of the right business personnel. They must be knowledgeable in the subject, and the collection of participants must represent both the breadth and depth of the enterprise. *Breadth* means all information views or stakeholders are represented, including knowledge worker and information producer. *Depth* means both high-level or strategic and tactical information views as well as operational information views are represented.

Strong facilitator. The facilitator must be results oriented and time driven. The goal is the essence of the definitions without unnecessary wordsmithing or laboring over the "perfect" definition. This can be accomplished later by the business information steward, if necessary. Facilitators must have diplomatic people skills as well as technical modeling skills.

Clear guidelines for name and definition. Having guidelines for data definition minimizes the tedium and increases consistency.

Rapid data definition and model support. The team must be able to rapidly capture electronically the information created and turn it around quickly for immediate feedback.

An effective process for data definition conflict and issue resolution. Figure 12.4 illustrates an appeals process and the relationship of these ad hoc data modeling teams to the information stewardship teams. Simply having an appeal process empowers the team to achieve consensus. Organizations using such "appeal" mechanisms have rarely had to take issues up-line. Only truly significant issues affecting business policy tend to be taken to the executive steering team.

Data model teams create data definition. They provide the basic definition of data. This minimizes the time requirements for the business information stewards.

Support Tools for Information Stewards

Information stewardship does not just happen. Training and support tools are required for effective guidance and for sustaining a "volunteer" group in an environment of competing demands. Support tools include:

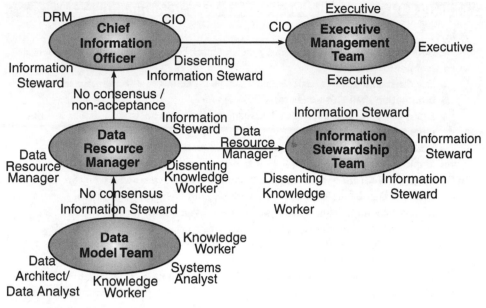

Figure 12.4   Data definition conflict resolution process.

Information policy. See the sample information policy that follows.

Training. An extensive list of training for information stewardship is found in Table 11.1 in the previous chapter under *Point 6 Institute Training on Information Quality.*

Information stewardship guidelines. This is often handled in the form of an information stewardship handbook or manual. This is best maintained online in an intranet document or other sharable resource. This resource should contain illustrated guidelines for all tasks that stewards will perform. Topics should include an introduction to the definition and purpose of stewardship, role and responsibility descriptions, support resources available, guidelines for data definition, information quality standard setting, data access classifications, and other tasks.

EXAMPLE INFORMATION POLICY STATEMENT

Purpose: **The purpose of this policy is to maximize the effectiveness of the enterprise to continually satisfy our customers through applying management principles to information as a strategic business resource.**

Premise:

- **Information and data are business resources owned by the enterprise.**
- **Management of information and data is critical to the success and profitability of the business.**

Continues

EXAMPLE INFORMATION POLICY STATEMENT *(Continued)*

Policies:

- Data shall be classified as to enterprise essential; business unit (area) essential; and nonessential.
- Enterprise and business unit (area) data shall be managed as enterprise resources.
- Information shall be shared across business units.
- Enterprise data shall be modeled, named, and defined consistently across business units.
- Data shall be created and maintained as close to the source as feasible.
- Employees who discover corrections to erroneous or missing facts shall update them in the record of reference or communicate to the personnel who can.
- Data shall not be maintained redundantly without business justification.
- Data quality shall be managed actively to approved quality levels.
- Data cleanup costs will be charged back to business units that created the data.
- Data in all forms shall be safeguarded and secured based upon requirements.
- Data shall be readily accessible to all, except as determined to be restricted.
- Information technology will be selected according to enterprise evaluation procedure.

Goals:

- To manage information as a strategic resource to improve the profitability and competitive advantages of both our customers and ourselves.
- To create databases that are flexible, dependable, and accessible to meet all enterprise requirements.
- To maximize business process effectiveness through quality information management across all business units.

Accountabilities: Every *manager* is an information steward accountable for:

- Implementing and ensuring compliance with information policy.
- Establishing objectives and action plans to implement this information policy and monitor progress.
- Developing plans that drive application and data development that are consistent with enterprise business and information architecture.
- Assuring and maintaining the quality of data created and maintained in the business unit.
- Authorizing access to secured data.
- Communicating this policy and providing education and training in data management principles to employees.

Every *employee* is an information steward accountable for:

- Assuring the accuracy and completeness of any and all data they create or update, because others depend on it.
- Using information wisely to support our customers and stakeholders, and to protect our customers and their trust.

Issued by: Senior management and CIO.

Conclusion

All the edit routines in the world can be embedded in applications, but the resulting information quality can still be abysmal. Sustainable information quality requires stewardship of information; in other words, the willingness to be accountable for the information I produce that you need to meet your needs. I am willing to do this because I know you and others are willing to be accountable for the information you produce that I need.

Implementing an Information Quality Improvement Environment

"We cannot solve problems with the same thinking we had when we created the problems."

—ALBERT EINSTEIN

Shortcuts taken to produce information fast without attention to quality are paid for multiple times over in the costs to find and correct the data and to recover from the process failure. Why do organizations continue to do this? Pure and simple: The management systems and performance measures reinforce nonquality information production and tolerate the costs of information scrap and rework.

To solve the information quality problems, we must change the way we think about information and the way we manage—or should I say, mismanage—it. Information is not "documentation" or "clerical" output; it is a strategic business resource. Information is not a "byproduct" of business processes; it is a true "product" created by one process and required for successful performance of others. When that data is bad, processes fail.

To implement sustainable information quality improvement requires breaking those things that motivate nonquality behavior. This requires culture change. Quick wins can be achieved without culture change to be sure. However, to sustain an environment of business performance excellence you must cut through the barriers that prevent people from doing a good job. Any organization with a culture of speed or productivity or reducing costs as a means of increasing profits will not thrive in the Information Age; in fact, many will not even survive. The thriving, intelligent learning organization in the twenty-first century will create speed, productivity, and cost reduction through a culture of improving product, service, and *information* quality to continually delight its customers.

This chapter is divided into four sections. The first section establishes the critical success factors for a sustainable information quality environment, including a discussion of why quality improvement initiatives fail.

The second section, the heart of the chapter, provides a practical step-by-step process for how to start. It refers you to processes in Part Two, "Processes for Improving Information Quality," for how to implement various steps. It begins by describing how you can assess the maturity of your organization with respect to information quality as a management tool. Based upon where its maturity is, it outlines what information management ingredients must be in place in order to move to the next stage of maturity.

The third section provides some practical tips on how to sustain momentum for your information quality initiative once you get started.

The final section describes the organizational aspects and potential job or role functions for the information quality team.

Critical Success Factors for Sustainable Information Quality

As with any endeavor of significance, there are key ingredients required for creating and sustaining a successful information quality environment. I use the term *environment*, because information quality is not a project or a program or a function. You may begin with a *project* and information quality may become a *program* or *function*, but you must see to it that it evolves to permeate the very fabric and culture of the enterprise. Information quality is a *value system* that understands that information is an integral component required for the success of the enterprise. It is a *mind-set* of accountability for my information products and customer service to my information customers. It is a *habit* of improvement; that is, being persistently impatient with faulty processes that produce nonquality information and patiently improving the processes to eliminate the cause.

As you seek to implement information quality improvement, you will be confronted by resistance, skepticism, and rejection. Do not despair; no idea that has created benefit to the human experience was adopted without the same resistance, skepticism, and rejection. So you must expect this fact, accept it, and find ways to overcome it. The first step is to understand why similar quality improvement initiatives fail.

Why Quality Improvement, Business Process Reengineering, and Data Cleansing Initiatives Fail

There is a high mortality rate among various business transformation and quality improvement initiatives. Why?

When a quality improvement initiative fails, is the failure due to some flaw in the concept itself? No. Improvement is a concept that has been demonstrated to work time and again. This is true whether the improvement is to our personal growth and development, organizational growth and development, manufactured product improvement, business process improvement, or information quality improvement.

Why then, do quality improvement initiatives fail? There are many different reasons, but they all stem from two causes: faulty implementation or systemic and cultural barriers. These reasons for failure are common to any endeavor that seeks to change the status quo. These include:

- Failure to fully understand the concept
- Failure to implement the concept effectively
- Implementing the concept on the wrong problem
- Lack of training
- Systemic factors, such as:
  - Lack of incentives
  - Lack of management understanding and active involvement
  - Failure to manage change

Brown, Hitchcock, and Willard have compiled an extensive list of reasons why Total Quality Management initiatives fail, along with ways to prevent failure.[1] They include the following reasons for failure during startup:

Lack of management commitment. Management may be attracted to quality initiatives for the wrong reasons.

Poor timing and pacing. Quality initiatives must be implemented with timing to provide resources, and to meet business objectives.

Wasted education and training. Training is a significant component of quality improvement. Sometimes the wrong training is implemented, or the right training is implemented incorrectly.

Lack of short-term, bottom-line results. While quality is a long-term organizational strategy, it must produce results quickly.

Reasons for failure during roll-out into the enterprise:

Divergent strategies. Quality is not separate from work or the quality organization's responsibility. It is part of *my* work.

Inappropriate measures. You get what you measure. It is easier to measure what is easier to count than what is important.

---

[1]Mark G. Brown, Hitchcock, and Willard, *Why TQM Fails and What to Do About It*, Chicago: Irwin Professional Publishing, 1994, pp. 2, 70, 138–9.

Outdated appraisal methods. Performance measures must incent quality.

Inappropriate rewards. Most compensation systems focus on individual performance, resulting in competition rather than teamwork and cooperation.

Reasons for failure during culture change and integration:

Failing to transfer true power to employees. Integrating quality into the fabric of the culture means transferring power to self-direction and self-managed teams. While these concepts "strike terror in the hearts of many mid-managers," they are required to survive in a knowledge-based economy.

Maintaining outmoded management practices. Inconsistencies in management behavior are quite visible to employees. Failure to "walk the talk" leads to failure of employees to "walk."

Poor organization and job design. Stovepipe communication systems must be dismantled and replaced with horizontal, networked communications. Jobs must be redesigned to allow for empowering employees.

Outdated business systems. Business processes must be reinvented. Most planning systems do not have mechanisms for those closest to the customer to provide input into the business strategies.

Failing to manage learning and innovation diffusion. Most organizations fail to share learning and innovative solutions to quality problems with others. Learning from experiences of both success *and* failure must be shared broadly across the enterprise in order to create a "learning organization."

After Deming took his quality message to Japan, he learned an important message as he observed quality improvement initiatives decline and fail in American companies. The reasons became apparent. Professionals who implement quality improvement know its importance. However, if management does not have a clear understanding of the direct correlation between quality and business effectiveness and does not communicate the importance of quality or take a personal role in it, there will be a lack of motivation to continue the quality initiatives. Those initiatives, however effective, will subsequently wither away.

Recognizing this, Deming sought always to help top management understand their personal obligation in making quality happen. In fact, he insisted on active management involvement and participation as a starting point in the quality improvement process. This is why his 14 Points of Quality are 14 Points of "Management Transformation," and not just 14 points in a program.

Masaki Imai, founder of the Kaizen Institute, reinforces the absolute responsibility of management in quality: "I would say there were three important words to make business work. They are: first, senior management commitment; second, senior management commitment; and third, senior management commitment."[2]

---

[2]Masaaki Imai, *Quality in Practice: BS 5750 and Kaizen*, BBC Training Videos, London, 1993, p. 47.

INFORMATION FRAUD: THE CRIME OF INFORMATION HOARDING

When internal politics cause people to hoard information for their own benefit rather than for that of the enterprise, its customers, and its shareholders, it is tantamount to fraud. It forces others to spend money and time to re-acquire information that is already known, thereby decreasing the current profits of the company as well as future profits and robbing the shareholders.

Critical Success Factors

Overcoming cultural barriers is neither easy nor automatic. You must understand the problems and the nature of the solution. To succeed in implementing an environment that embraces information quality as a management tool, you must:

Understand fully what information quality improvement is and why you are doing it. The end result must include increased customer satisfaction, reduced costs of information scrap and rework, and increased profits. Use of information quality improvement as a tool must be to make the business perform better and to accomplish its mission successfully. Information quality improvement for any other reason will fail.

Implement information quality improvement effectively. Information quality improvement cannot be implemented like application or business projects; it must be implemented as a culture change and habit. There are no shortcuts to sustainable information quality improvement.

Implementing information quality improvement on the right problem. Improving trivial information will cause the initiative to fail. *Do not improve processes that should never have been performed in the first place*. This wastes money. Eliminate those non-value-adding processes. Focus energy at the business problems that, if not solved, can cause enterprise failure. These will involve problems at the organizational boundaries.

Training and communication. With culture change, it is most important to keep frequent, open, and honest communication. Training, including both awareness raising and skills development, is paramount. Feedback is most important. Discover the concerns of people whose procedures may be changing. Get feedback, and improve the information quality improvement processes themselves, as they are being performed.

Address the systemic factors, such as:

Incentives for information quality. The incentives and performance measures in effect today reinforce the habits of the status quo. Permanent change to behavior requires changes to incentives to encourage and incent the *new* behavior. From psychology we know that in order for a people to stop bad habits, they must replace them with something at least as gratifying.

Otherwise, the new behavior will be short lived. In order to implement sustainable information quality improvements, management must replace the performance measures that encourage the creation of nonquality information with performance measures that encourage creation of quality information. Management must learn that quotas and other "productivity" measures actually increase costs.

Management commitment to information quality improvement as a management tool. You will obtain *tentative* management commitment when you raise awareness to the costs of nonquality information. You will obtain *permanent* management commitment when your information quality improvement initiatives help management achieve and sustain their business objectives. However, you will only sustain that management commitment when management fully *comprehends* the relationship between information quality improvement and the accomplishment of their business objectives. This requires continued education, communication, and active participation of management.

Managing change. Change in behavior at its best disrupts enterprise function, and at its worst threatens enterprise survival. You must assure that change is "managed." This means you must plan, organize, lead, and control for change. Utilize internal or external organizational change management resources, if necessary.

Implementing Information Quality: Where to Start

If you have no formal information quality program currently in place, here is an action plan. The steps listed here are described later.

1. Conduct an information quality management maturity assessment to discover the organization's level of maturity.

2. Revisit and revise, or create a vision, mission, and objectives for information management and information quality improvement to describe the possible future state of the enterprise and what problems are to be solved.

3. Identify and empower an information quality leader to take some action and get started.

4. Conduct a customer satisfaction survey of the information stakeholders to find out their frustrations and barriers as a result of nonquality information.

5. Identify other business transformation or improvement initiatives or external resources to learn from and to leverage. You may be able to join these initiatives in process and increase their likelihood of success.

6. Select a small, manageable, and high-payoff area to conduct a pilot project.

7. Define the business problem to be solved, and the measures for the information quality improvement project success.

8. Define the information value chain and develop an inventory of a small, select set of critical information.

9. Perform a baseline information quality assessment of that critical information.

10. Calculate customer lifetime value, if you can, to estimate missed and lost opportunity resulting from nonquality information.

11. Analyze customer complaints and attrition due to information-related complaints.

12. Quantify the costs due to quality problems in the pilot set of critical information.

13. Identify and develop personal rapport and communication with change sponsor and provide awareness orientation.

14. Define information stewardship and quality roles.

15. Define information quality principles, processes, and objectives.

16. Analyze the systemic barriers to information quality and recommend changes.

17. Conduct an information quality management maturity assessment with senior management and provide formal education.

18. Conduct an information quality *improvement* project and quantify the benefits achieved, as compared with the original state.

19. Establish a regular mechanism of communication and education with senior management to sustain their involvement and commitment.

20. Keep improving the information quality improvement processes as you go.

Step 1: Conduct an Information Quality Management Maturity Assessment

Where you start your information quality initiative depends on where you are. First conduct an Information Quality Management Maturity Assessment and gap analysis. Select interested business and information systems personnel and have them each provide their individual assessment of the enterprise's maturity as to information quality as a management tool.

I have adapted Philip Crosby's quality management maturity grid for assessment of information quality management maturity. It is illustrated in Figure 13.1.

Measurement Categories	Stage 1: Uncertainty (Ad hoc)	Stage 2: Awakening (Repeatable)	Stage 3: Enlightenment (Defined)	Stage 4: Wisdom (Managed)	Stage 5: Certainty (Optimizing)
Management understanding and attitude	No comprehension of information quality as a management tool. Tend to blame data administration or I/S org for "information quality problems" or vice versa.	Recognizing that information quality management may be of value but not willing to provide money or time to make it all happen.	While going through information quality improvement program learn more about quality management; becoming supportive and helpful.	Participating. Understand absolutes of information quality management. Recognize their personal role in continuing emphasis.	Consider information quality management an essential part of company system.
Information quality organization status	"Data" quality is hidden in application development departments. Data audits probably not part of organization. Emphasis on correcting bad data.	A stronger information quality role is "appointed" but main emphasis is still on correcting bad data.	Information quality organization exists, all assessment is incorporated and manager has role in development of applications.	Information quality manager reports to CIO; effective status reporting and preventive action. Involved with business areas.	Information quality manager is part of management team. Prevention is main focus. Information quality is a thought leader.
Information quality problem handling	Problems are fought as they occur; no resolution; inadequate definition; lots of yelling and accusations.	Teams are set up to attack major problems. Long-range solutions are not solicited.	Corrective action communication established. Problems are faced openly and resolved in orderly way.	Problems are identified early in their development. All functions are open to suggestion and improvement.	Except in the most unusual cases, information quality problems are prevented.
Cost of information quality as percent of revenue	Reported: unknown Actual: 20%	Reported: 5% Actual: 18%	Reported: 10% Actual: 15%	Reported: 8% Actual: 10%	Reported: 5% Actual: 5%
Information quality improvement actions	No organized activities. No understanding of such activities.	Trying obvious "motivational" short-range efforts.	Implementation of the 14-point program with thorough understanding and establishment of each step.	Continuing the 14-point program and starting to optimize.	Information quality improvement is a normal and continued activity.
Summation of company information quality posture	"We don't know why we have problems with information quality."	"Is it absolutely necessary to always have problems with information quality?"	"Through management commitment and information quality improvement we are identifying and resolving our problems."	"Information quality problem prevention is a routine part of our operation."	"We know why we do not have problems with information quality."

Figure 13.1 Information quality management maturity grid.

Source: Adapted from Philip Crosby.

There are similarities to the five stages of maturity in the Capability Maturity Model, developed by the Software Engineering Institute.

There are five stages of maturity:

Stage 1: Uncertainty (Initial).[3] This stage is the least mature. The Uncertain organization is characterized by the phrase, "We do not know why we have a problem with information quality," or "Do we have a problem with information quality?" The Uncertain organization is highly reactive. Blame and fire fighting characterize the organization. Nothing is done to solve long-term problems.

Stage 2: Awakening (Repeatable). The organization has become aware that there is an information quality problem, usually because of some catastrophic result, such as the failure of the data warehouse, or public embarrassment resulting from an information quality incident. However, the organization is not sure how much of a problem it has, nor what to do about it. The Awakening organization is characterized by the phrase, "Is it absolutely necessary to always have problems with data quality?" Management says they want to do something about quality but are afraid to commit funds. They are unsure of the business case. Teams may be set up to deal with problems, but the emphasis is on data cleanup, rather than defect prevention. The "educational" mechanisms tend to be slogans and motivational efforts to get the information producers to improve. Here there is minimal change to the processes or management systems.

Stage 3: Enlightenment (Defined). In this stage, a major corner has been turned. Attitudes are noticeably different. Rather than blame, the Enlightened organization has begun openly assessing itself and is seeking to make permanent improvements. The organization is characterized by the phrase, "Through management commitment and quality improvement we are identifying and solving our problems." Funding is committed. Management is learning information quality principles and processes, and these are being implemented in parts of the enterprise. The results of improvement yield sizable economic benefits, and there is improved teamwork within the business areas and with information systems.

Stage 4: Wisdom (Managed). The organization in the Wisdom stage sees significant benefits from its information quality initiatives. The impact on the bottom line is dramatic, and all people in the organization are participating in improvement projects, some formally, most informally. The *Wise* organization is continuing to implement and mature its information quality improvement processes. It is characterized by the phrase, "Data error prevention is a routine part of our operation." People have incorporated a true

---

[3] The Maturity Stage names are those of Philip Crosby, and are described in *Quality Is Free,* New York: Penguin Group, 1979, pp. 32–33. The names listed in parentheses are those of the Capability Maturity Model. See Mark Paulk, Weber, Curtis, and Chrissis, *The Capability Maturity Model,* New York: Addison-Wesley, 1995, p. 16.

customer service attitude to their fellow employees who depend on the information they produce. Information systems and business personnel form partnerships in their projects. Not only do they like each other, they would not consider a project without integral participation by the other.

IMPLEMENTING AN EFFECTIVE INFORMATION QUALITY METHODOLOGY AT HEWLETT-PACKARD

Until developing an information quality and value methodology, Hewlett-Packard (HP) could not measure the value of accurate customer information or the cost of bad information. Problems faced included decisions regarding:

- What was the business's information quality—where to make information quality improvements.
- What was the value of information—where to invest to manage information effectively.

HP developed and implemented a methodology for assessing both the quality and value of information and for improving quality. In place for over three years, the methodology has been used in many successful projects across the company. HP's information quality program consists of internal consulting, training, and services to help the business units solve information quality and value problems.

The approach HP used was to bring in an external information quality consultant to teach them and help develop the methodology. The methodology was then applied on a manageable proof-of-concept project. Danette Taggart McGilvray, now the Program Manager, was assigned full-time to the project to gain knowledge transfer in the methodology development and to customize it to HP.

Benefits from the individual projects are varied. A few examples:

- One project quantified the impact of a previously known quality. Because the extent of the problem was then visible, changes to a central company system were implemented.
- Another project showed how data quality was impacting one product line's marketing programs. This resulted not only in making fixes to data quality that were "quick wins," but also solved one problem which was previously thought to "take a small miracle."
- Ongoing data quality management processes have been implemented, and funded, and metrics are available on a Web site for another system. Duplicates have decreased as a result. A data quality forum meets on a regular basis to solve quality issues uncovered. Finding and correcting a flaw in the update logic is just one example of other improvements made.
- Currently, data quality is being designed into a new system. All data sources will go through a quality analysis before linking to the system. Source data is cleaned or correctly filtered prior to loading, thus addressing quality from the beginning. Source systems receive specific actionable recommendations for improving their data quality long term.
- A favorite quote from one project member, "The business sponsor stated many times that she appreciated the methodology and the project itself for guiding her funding decisions. Forty-four percent of the recommendations were quick wins—cost little but

Management is removing the obstacles to information quality that in the past made error-free information impossible.

Stage 5: Certainty (Optimizing). The highest degree of maturity, the Certain organization has reaped huge gains in profits by reducing the costs of

made definite improvements. Instead of embarking on a cleanup project, it helped her prioritize and know where to spend her money."

All of the benefits listed earlier show *how* the data quality was improved and a few of the resulting benefits. Always remember, the real benefit from data quality comes when the improved data quality then provides *value* to the company. Some examples of how data quality can bring value to any company:

Increased revenue. Current and complete customer profile information allows the business to target the audience that can best benefit from mailing promotions and marketing seminars. Customer requests are funneled to the right sales reps, thus resulting in increased sales.

Increased productivity. Accurate orders and shipments result in fewer returns.

Increased customer satisfaction. A call center agent has accurate information when answering support calls, thus reducing time on the phone and satisfying customer needs.

Decreased costs. Quality information results in better product forecasts, further resulting in the right inventory needed to support demand. Less time is spent fixing incorrect invoices.

Decreased credit risk. Where credit limits are assigned to each customer record, decreasing the number of duplicate records also decreases the chance that a customer has an inflated credit limit.

Tips for Others:

■ Understand how information is supporting your business. Don't get lost in data quality for data quality's sake. Keep your business needs in the forefront and understand how the quality affects the value.

■ Tie your information quality efforts into current, visible issues and "burning platforms" at your company.

■ Be flexible to change the scope as needed. When HP realized the work was bigger than one project, an ongoing program and resources were funded. Always implement measures appropriate to the need.

■ Plan on a long-term investment. Find advocates and funding sponsors within the company who are willing to invest in data quality.

■ Start building a resource pool of people with needed skill sets (consultants, data management, quality concepts, statistics, project management, data quality, data modeling, process analysis, etc.). Collaborate and use their expertise.

■ Educate, market, and communicate! Collect and document project results and the subsequent benefits. Raise the awareness of the information quality and value generally throughout the company. Marketing and communications is a continual task. Spend the time to find out how best to get the attention of your audience. Use successes to further market the value of information quality.

■ Get started, take action, and don't give up. Your efforts will pay off!

"information scrap and rework" and through increased customer lifetime value as a result of increased customer satisfaction. The organization has reached a stage of virtually complete data defect prevention and is characterized by "We know why we do not have problems with information quality." When information quality problems do occur, the Certain organization swarms over them like the National Air Safety Transport Board does an airplane crash. They want to find out the cause and put preventive measures to assure it never happens again. Furthermore, the habit of employees is to look for potential problems *before* errors occur.

As you rate your organization, the following characteristics will help you determine your organization's stage of maturity. There are five areas to assess: management understanding and attitude; information quality organization status; information quality problem handling; cost of information quality as a percent of revenue or operating budget; and information quality improvement actions. Within each of these I discuss the general characterization.

Management Understanding and Attitude

This row measures management's comprehension of information quality management as a tool for managing and improving the business. The attitude management has toward information quality will translate in actions, positive or negative.

Stage 1: Uncertainty. In this stage management has no awareness that information quality improvement can help them solve business problems. In fact, they may not even be aware that there is an information quality problem. It is not uncommon for the most senior manager to estimate the costs of nonquality information to be lower than all others in the group— and by a considerable margin. One such manager even "boasted" to another that the lowest rating was his. Management may be unaware of the real costs because they have been shielded from the facts, or because they believe information and information quality are being "handled"—generally by the information systems group. They blame information systems for problems that are brought to their attention. On the other hand, the information systems management in the Uncertain organization blames the business for problems actually created by applications themselves.

Stage 2: Awakening. In the Awakening stage, management has realized information quality is a problem and that an information quality improvement program may have some value, but they are not willing to put resources into it. They will give you the charge to "go do it," but within your existing budget. Management here may even know some of the costs of nonquality information, but need to work some problems out before they can pay attention to this.

Stage 3: Enlightenment. The Enlightenment stage signals the true beginning of the enterprise transformation. They understand that everyone in the enterprise is accountable for their role in information quality. They are providing funding. They are sponsoring the information quality improvement initiatives to implement information quality processes and make systemic changes. Management has begun to see the correlation between information quality problems and business success.

Stage 4: Wisdom. In Wisdom, management recognizes and accepts their own accountability in information quality, and are sponsoring systemic changes in the performance measures of the enterprise to include information quality measures and employee satisfaction measures. Wise management sees absolutely that when information quality goes down, so do customer satisfaction and profits.

Stage 5: Certainty. Management would not consider managing the business without having an information quality management system in place.

Information Quality Organization Status

This row assesses the maturity of the information quality organizational maturity of the enterprise. This does not mean size. This means whether or not the enterprise is organized in a way to lead the enterprise to make quality information happen.

Stage 1: Uncertainty. If there is any kind of information quality organization it will be invisible to the business, possibly in a software development group. What measures that will be in place will not include measures that are truly important to the business. They may include "systems" quality measures, such as "uptime" or "system response time," but will not include measures of business information quality or the relationship of information quality and business performance. If information quality measures are in place, they will be used for cleanup only.

Stage 2: Awakening. In the Awakening organization, an information quality leader will be appointed or even an organization formed, but the emphasis and goals of the group will mostly be on data cleanup, rather than preventive actions.

Stage 3: Enlightenment. The Enlightened organization has a formal information quality organization whose role is to assess information quality for the purpose of identifying root cause of problems and to facilitate information process improvement initiatives. The information quality organization may be part of the data resource management unit or in a business area. A business information stewardship team consisting of business subject matter experts has begun to attack problems in data definition across disparate organization units and information systems.

Stage 4: Wisdom. The Wisdom stage sees the information quality organization reporting directly to the Chief Information Officer (CIO) or into an enterprise business area. The CIO is accountable for the technical side of information management, and not just information technology management. Applications are not viewed as the end deliverables of information systems. They are seen as the intermediate deliverables to support processes that create, update information products from business information producers, and deliver information products to knowledge workers. There is strong involvement with the information stewardship team, the business community in general, and with the application and data development organizations.

Stage 5: Certainty. The Certain organization considers the information quality organization an essential part of the management team. Information quality is a part of any business reengineering or business quality improvement project. The information quality organization does not oversee or correct information quality problems—those problems do not exist. Their role is to assure that new processes and systems are designed in such a way as to eliminate or reduce to nearly zero the possibility for error. The information quality organization has a strong relationship to the business information stewardship team that guides the business roles in information quality.

Information Quality Problem Handling

Problem handling addresses how the organization acts or reacts to information quality problems. Does the organization ignore them, react as they occur, or does it anticipate and prevent them.

Stage 1: Uncertainty. The Uncertain organization attacks problems as they occur—if they cannot cover them up. Problems tend to be "solved" by finding blame. Work relationships tend to be combative, with teamwork coming only out of necessity. There is a lot of backbiting, and criticism made about others, but not to them face-to-face.

Stage 2: Awakening. The Awakening organization recognizes problems and sets up teams to solve them. The predominant approach is to react to information quality problems by cleansing or correcting them. Software tools tend to be seen as the answer and "solution."

Stage 3: Enlightenment. Enlightened organizations analyze causes of information quality problems and attack the causes in order to prevent them. Information quality problems across organizational boundaries are addressed openly by cross-functional teams. Long-term solutions are sought and implemented. The enterprise is changing the organizational and systemic barriers to information quality.

Stage 4: Wisdom. The Wisdom organization has optimized its application and data development processes and its business processes to design in quality, and to identify potential problems early in the cycle. Defect prevention is the norm. All organizations are open to suggestions for improvement even when they come from outside organizational groups.

Stage 5: Certainty. The Certain organization has all but eliminated problems from happening. Only in causes outside their control do problems occur, and when they do, the Certain organization jumps on them immediately to analyze the root cause with the goal to never allow it to happen again.

Cost of Information Quality as a Percent of Revenue or Operating Budget

How can an organization manage its resources without knowing its costs? How can a manufacturing firm manage its production without knowing its costs of nonquality? How then, can the Information Age organization manage and control its information products without knowing its cost of information and its cost of information scrap and rework? It cannot.

There are three categories of costs of quality:

- Costs of information scrap and rework, and process failure
- Costs of information quality assessments
- Costs of information process quality improvement and data-defect prevention

Organizations that seek to cost justify categories 2 and 3 without understanding the costs of 1 will miss the boat.

Stage 1: Uncertainty. The Uncertain organization does not have any scientific measure of the costs of poor information quality. It has never considered measuring it. After all, information is simply "documentation." Attempts to guess will produce estimates all over the board. Only the knowledge workers suffering from poor-quality information will be close in their guessing. Based on numerous cost analyses, the typical organization may see from 15 to 25 percent of its revenue go to pay the costs of information scrap and rework. Furthermore, 40 to 50 percent or more of the information systems budget is spent in information processing scrap and rework. This includes the costs of redundant data handling in multiple databases and systems, and in the interfaces that do not add value, but simply add costs of moving data from one proprietary database to another proprietary database. One organization discovered that the equivalent of over one half of their application developers were spending their time on maintaining interface programs. They had become full-time "data movers," rather than business problem-solvers. The organization to date has made no effort to change its habits. It is an Uncertain organization.

Stage 2: Awakening. Organizations here have discovered some of the costs of poor-quality information; usually they are the costs of data cleanup initiatives. They do not know clearly the extent of the information quality problems nor the true costs of scrap and rework and process failure. By cleaning up data, they now have reduced some scrap and rework costs, those of the downstream processes using the cleaned data. They are still incurring the scrap and rework costs in the upstream processes.

Stage 3: Enlightenment. By focusing on implementing information quality principles and processes, including measuring the costs of nonquality information and implementing information quality defect prevention, the organization has a better, although incomplete, picture. It is gaining more dramatic cost reductions through data defect prevention. There are more architected databases and a higher degree of data sharing, reducing the costs of application development, and increasing the speed of application delivery against the shared databases. There is some reduction in private databases in the departments, as knowledge workers can trust the "production" data sources more. Data correction actions are made to the sharable databases.

Stage 4: Wisdom. Wisdom organizations are reaping significant cost reductions through widespread information-process quality improvement initiatives. There is much less data redundancy, and what redundancy exists has high control to assure consistency. There are fewer private databases in the enterprise. The production databases are highly reliable.

Stage 5: Certainty. The costs of quality consists, almost exclusively, of costs of regular assessment of critical data to assure control, and in information quality improvement at the business process and application planning and design phases.

Information Quality Improvement Actions

How mature is the enterprise in implementing improvement initiatives and changes to the culture to make information quality routine?

Stage 1: Uncertainty. The Uncertain organization takes no organized actions for information quality improvement, nor does it understand what kinds of actions should be taken. It just reacts from problem to problem, accepting this and the information scrap and rework activities as the normal costs of doing business.

Stage 2: Awakening. The Awakening organization may be heard to say, "We want to get the low-hanging fruit," meaning we will be content to get the big wins. Motivational efforts to get people to improve and do the right thing characterize this stage. Nobody here bothers to change the incentives for people to "improve and do the right thing," however. There is a real danger in this stage of giving up and falling right back into the old habits and continue the defective processes. Once you are in this stage, the information quality leaders must quantify the costs of nonquality information and continually communicate this to management and provide the education for management to understand its personal involvement and responsibility and information quality actions it must take.

Stage 3: Enlightenment. The Enlightened organization is formally implementing the information quality components described in Chapter 11, "The 14 Points of Information Quality." These are implemented as formal systems and processes that improve information processes and incent information quality. These ingredients are understood completely as they are implemented.

Stage 4: Wisdom. The Wisdom organization continues its implementation of the 14 Points of Information Quality, and is *improving* them. These points are becoming ingrained in the culture of the enterprise.

Stage 5: Certainty. Contrary to popular convention, the Certain organization does not sit back and rest on its laurels. The 14 Points are routine. Information quality improvement is a normal and regular habit. Customers are happy. Market share is increasing. Information is used to create new opportunities. Things never conceived in the past as possibilities are now happening with regular frequency.

Once you know the maturity state of your organization, you will know how to progress.

Step 2: Create a Vision, Mission, and Objectives

Every person and organization in the enterprise needs to know its purpose and how that relates to the enterprise mission and objectives. The vision, mission, and objectives of information management and information quality improvement must describe how information quality improvement can enable the enterprise to fulfill its mission and solve its problems.

Revisit and revise your existing vision and mission, or develop one if you do not have one. Start with the enterprise vision mission and objectives. If you do not know them, find them. If your enterprise does not have them, look for another enterprise that knows where it is going. An enterprise without a mission will fail as described in Deming's First Point of Quality. For more information, see Chapter 11.

Once you have developed your vision and mission, start each day for a month by reading it and reflecting on it. Review the enterprise mission, and then your own personal mission. Visualize how this can permeate and influence your actions today. If your mission is important to the enterprise, this should be the driver in all that you do. By the time the month is up, this should become a habit.

Step 3: Identify and Empower an Information Quality Leader

Information quality does not just happen; it takes work. Someone must lead the enterprise to take some action and get started. You cannot wait for the blessing of senior management. If no one will "appoint" a leader, adopt that role yourself. The enterprise needs someone to awaken it before nonquality information causes its demise.

Step 4: Conduct an Information Customer Satisfaction Survey

Conduct this survey with both the knowledge workers and information producers who are trying to carry out the work of the enterprise. Find out their frustrations and barriers as a result of nonquality information.

Identify the high-priority problems. They may be related to a common information group, such as `Customer` or `Order`, or a common value chain, or one part of the business. Use this to identify a key problem to solve in your pilot project.

Step 5: Identify Other Business Transformation, Improvement Initiatives, or External Resources

Implementing information quality improvement requires culture change. Implementing an information quality environment is not simply a project. If your organization has undergone *successful* business transformation or quality improvement changes, you can gain knowledge transfer from those experiences. If your organization has not undertaken such culture change initiatives, or if the ones it has undertaken have failed, you may need outside consulting or training resources that have successfully guided organizations through the process to guide you.

Use Internal Business Transformation or Improvement Initiative Resources

Discover internal improvement initiatives for two reasons. The first is to learn from them, both positive and negative lessons.

The second is that everyone today has too much to do and too little time in which to do it. The key resources are already on many important projects. If you have other quality improvement initiatives or transformation initiatives, seek them out. You may be able to leverage those projects with information quality improvement components. Often these other initiatives will see information quality problems as part of what they need to help them attain their goals of cost reduction and customer satisfaction improvement. Develop your skills and become indispensable for their projects.

Use External Information Quality Improvement Consulting Resources

Should your organization not have internal expertise in implementing quality initiatives or in culture change, or if you do not feel comfortable in attacking this by your own internal resources, do not hesitate to seek outside guidance. Because information quality improvement is a relatively new discipline, there will emerge a lot of potentially unqualified consultants who offer services in this area. Select consultants carefully who will guide you through this transformation.

Here are the questions to ask when selecting information quality consulting resources:

Have they successfully implemented information quality improvement initiatives with other clients?

What kinds of benefits did those organizations achieve?

How long have they been providing information quality services? While length of time is not the major factor, do they have broad experience they can bring to your organization? If they do not have much experience in information quality improvement services, does your organization have a relationship of positive experience and trust with the firm? Every consultant has to have a "first" client. You may be willing to use a consultant whom you trust to learn with you.

Does the consultant understand the principles of quality from other disciplines? What is his or her experience with Deming, Juran, Crosby, ISO 9000, Baldrige Award, Kaizen, or other quality programs? Knowledge from other quality disciplines is transferable.

Is this their primary consulting service or is this an add-on service? If this is an add-on service, are the primary services focused on information management or business process management? Again, this is not a major issue, but be aware of whether the firm may bring a hidden agenda to the table. For example, will a firm whose primary service is systems integration offer information quality improvement with the objective of selling its systems integration services?

Do they offer a complete methodology or set of services to meet your organization's needs? Do the services address all aspects of information quality improvement, or do the methods or services address only part of the information quality improvement life cycle? Some organizations may specialize in data cleansing, and this may meet your immediate needs. Later you may need to focus on information defect prevention. You may need to bring in other external resources for this.

Do they sell an information quality software product? If the services are from a software product provider, will the information quality improvement consulting be geared to selling their tool, or only contain a methodology geared to the use of the features of that tool? You must be sure that any information quality improvement processes you implement meet your enterprise objectives, and not just those of the software tool supplier. The optimum enterprise benefit may be derived from a combination of training that includes both independent consulting and training in information quality improvement methods, and specific tools-based consulting and training in the application of the tools. Principles precede products.

Do the services include training or only consulting? Information quality improvement is a culture change, and it must include a high degree of knowledge transfer.

Is the consultant able to develop rapport with both senior management and professionals who are implementing the information quality improvement initiatives? Quality initiatives involve all levels in the enterprise.

Is the consultant able to develop rapport with both business and information systems professionals? Quality requires teamwork and partnership of everyone in the enterprise.

Step 6: Select a Small, Manageable Pilot Project

Focus on an area that is small enough to manage for success, and yet delivers a big payoff as a proof-of-concept project. Critical success factors include having a high-level sponsor that is suffering the pain of poor-quality information and where nonquality in the information is creating significant enterprise costs and problems.

Do not include more than 10 or 15 data elements. Focus on the "Zero-defect" class of data.

Step 7: Define the Business Problem and Measures for Success

Be sure you understand the problem you are solving. State it in business terms and in terms of the relationship to preventing accomplishment of enterprise objectives. If this project problem is not hampering enterprise goals, any improvement will be inconsequential. Avoid this and look for another project.

Define clearly how you will determine that the project has been successful. Seek your sponsor and other management "expectations" for success. Again, these measures should be directly related to the enterprise measures. See Chapter 7, "Measuring Nonquality Information Costs," step 1, *Identify Business Performance Measures*, to define the measures of success for your information quality initiative.

Step 8: Define the Information Value Chain and Develop a Data Inventory

Identify all database files containing this information along with the information value and cost chain. This will tell you all the processes that can create, update, interface, and transform the data. See Chapter 6, "Information Quality Assessment," step 3, *Identify the Information Value and Cost Chain*, for how to do this.

Step 9: Perform an Information Quality Assessment

Assess the critical information to find out its quality level. You may assess the state of the database itself or the state of the current processes, depending on your project objectives. See Chapter 6 for guidance.

Step 10: Calculate Customer Lifetime Value

If you can, calculate customer lifetime value so you can estimate missed and lost opportunity as a result of nonquality information. See Chapter 7, step 5, *Calculate Customer Lifetime Value*. If calculating customer lifetime value is too costly to do in detail, ask marketing and sales for an educated estimate to use.

Step 11: Analyze Customer Complaints

This is an important step to understand what percent of complaints are information-related. See your customer service group. See Chapter 7, step 6, *Calculate Information Value*.

Step 12: Quantify the Costs of Nonquality Information

Based on the assessment of the critical information, calculate the costs of information scrap and rework. See Chapter 7, step 3, *Calculate Nonquality Information Costs*.

Step 13: Develop Personal Rapport with Your Change Sponsor

You must develop personal relationships with those who can make change happen. If you are not at a level to do that personally, find someone who is, someone who has suffered pain from information quality problems. Listen carefully to the sponsor and understand carefully the stated problems and the underlying problems.

Develop and provide awareness orientation to the change sponsor. The first awareness must include concrete evidence of the problems and how they impact the objectives of the management audience. Be sure the pilot addresses problems that are on the change sponsor's agenda. Find ways to communicate regularly with the change sponsor, whether directly or indirectly.

Step 14: Define Information Stewardship and Quality Roles

This will have both a short-term and a long-term plan. Your initial quality initiative may involve roles and no formal organization structure. As it evolves there may even be a temporary "organization structure." As it matures, the formal organization will emerge. Be sure that you focus your pilot project on *results* and not on an organization structure. The best way to kill a project is to appear to recommend new bureaucracy and staff. See Chapter 12, "Information Stewardship: Accountability for Information Quality," and the section, *Organizing for Information Quality*, later in this chapter.

Step 15: Define Information Quality Principles, Processes, and Objectives

You must develop your own objectives for the information quality initiative. They must be based not on the theory or on the ideal, but on the practical and real need to accomplish your enterprise mission and objectives. See Part Two for the processes and Chapter 11 for the principles. A brief discussion of information quality principles is found in the last section of Chapter 3, "Applying Quality Management Principles to Information."

Step 16: Analyze the Systemic Barriers

Identify the cultural ingredients that incent poor information quality. You may not be able to change the incentives, performance measures, or counterproductive objectives personally, but you can certainly be proactive and challenge them. Do not just complain. Suggest alternatives. Identify the contradiction of existing incentives and quantify the counterproductive results.

Systemic barriers include:

- Management solely by financial performance, or the quarterly statement syndrome

- Employee incentives, quotas, and objectives that measure and reward "productivity" or speed over quality

- Management objectives that are departmentally aligned

- Funding of applications that are departmentally or functionally aligned

- Management salary based on size of budget and number of employees

- Performance measures based on individual performance rather than team performance

Alternative performance measures include:

- Balanced scorecard that includes customer satisfaction, employee satisfaction, and quality measures as well as financial performance. The first three actually drive the last.

- Eliminate arbitrary "productivity" measures such as how many claims are processed or calls handled. Instead, measure how many claims are processed without errors, or how many calls answered result in satisfied customers. Any measure of speed should be balanced with errors produced and costs of the resulting problems.

- Management objectives that include internal customer satisfaction of downstream departments using the information produced.

- Funding applications as described in Table 3.1 in which you:

    - Fund the reusable information infrastructure as a capitalized enterprise expense.

    - Charge back the value delivery components to the sponsor.

    - Charge a penalty for redundant development, including the costs of maintenance to redundant data and costs to maintain consistency, and resolve information quality problem costs as a result.

- Management salary based on value delivery, elimination of cost-adding processes, and contribution to meeting *enterprise* objectives.

- Performance measures based on team performance. The teams share in their success or failure. This incents the skilled to share their knowledge to help others develop theirs. New performance appraisal techniques such as 360 degree or multisource evaluations are important to bring about horizontal thinking and acting rather than vertical thinking. If part of my performance appraisal has as input, "feedback from downstream knowledge workers as to how well my work meets their needs," I will focus more on customer service to those who depend on the information

I produce. This type of measure applies first to process owners and managers, then to information producers.

Step 17: Conduct an Information Quality Management Maturity Assessment and Provide Formal Education for Top Management

Conduct the information quality management maturity assessment with top management. Compare the results with the perceptions of the others in step 1. This is especially illuminating if there is a perception mismatch. This can become a discussion point.

Develop formal education for management based on connecting information quality principles to business performance measures. Develop short modules. Get on the agenda frequently.

The first awareness training must include costs of nonquality information to your organization. Address the high-level principles comparing them to the principles applied to other resources. If you have other quality improvement programs, relate the similarities to those quality programs.

Your goal in top management education is to get invited back. Make sure your message addresses their concerns and offers them a way to meet their objectives and answer to their stakeholders.

Step 18: Conduct an Information Quality Improvement Project

This project goal is to improve a process that has been producing poor-quality data. Quantify the benefits derived from the improvement. Assessing information quality raises awareness, and cleaning up data makes a database usable; however, an information quality improvement project attacks and solves the root cause of the problem. Nothing succeeds like success. And nothing succeeds like success that solves real business problems.

Step 19: Establish a Regular Mechanism of Communication, Education, and Involvement with Top Management

To sustain management's involvement and commitment, keep on their agenda. Keep identifying the problems you find, and the solutions and their cost benefits you deliver. It is easy to slip back into complacency if we do not stay apprised of the benefits that continued hard work and good habits bring.

Step 20: Keep Improving the Information Quality Improvement Processes—Next Steps

Getting to information quality maturity goes well beyond implementing data quality analysis and data cleansing software, and measuring data quality and cleansing data. It requires implementing the 14 Points of Information Quality (see Chapter 11). Develop a plan to assure that each of these elements is implemented and sustained.

MAKING INFORMATION QUALITY HAPPEN AT A LARGE BANK

When it started its data quality initiative in January 1996, the bank had many problems with its customer data. Examples included a five-year-old girl with a marital status of "divorced" and a title of "Mrs.," a woman with 97 children, several people with a gender code of "female" and a salutation of "Mr.," 40 percent of business customers had no address to trade from, and an *open* account for a customer who had died more than 30 years earlier.

Customer data quality was so bad employees could not do their jobs. Frustrated by this, one senior analyst took the initiative to improve the information quality out of a desire to do her job properly. She is now the Data Quality Manager.

Conducting an information quality assessment resulted in eye-opening discoveries that led to several actions. The bank

- Identified critical customer fields.
- Designed a customer survey form to capture the data fields needed, which was sent to customers with a letter explaining why the data was needed, along with a self-addressed, postage-paid envelope for returning the data form. An incentive program of a drawing for a £500 (@$850) gift certificate to a local department store for customers who returned the forms was included. The response rate was nearly 40 percent.
- Established measurable objectives for benchmarking data quality scores of branches and regions. The scores ranged from 50 percent to 100 percent. Each branch had a target of 90 percent to achieve over a 1-year period. At the beginning of the program 47.5 percent of the data was less than 50 percent accurate!
- Created a logo, to help create awareness and communication. Also created were standardized stationery, rulers, satchels, etc., to assist with improving the standardization of forms and instructions, and to keep the idea of the data quality initiative in front of everyone.

Also, training sessions and meetings were set up for people who collected the data, and for middle managers. They measured how many training sessions and presentations were given. Regular update meetings provided branch managers updates of their branch's progress. They measured and reported

- How many customers responded to surveys
- How many data items were corrected
- Time spent

Continues

MAKING INFORMATION QUALITY HAPPEN AT A LARGE BANK (CONTINUED)

- How many assessments were given
- The number of records cleaned
- The level of data duplication
- How much mail was returned due to bad addresses

Monthly meetings were held with regional directors to compare the data quality performance of the banks within regions and the regions themselves.

Updates on the key initiatives were communicated in the company newsletter.

Benefits Achieved

- Now the bank has good information for marketing and strategic business decisions (2.5 years earlier the actual number of customers was unknown).
- Increased customer satisfaction, as measured by a significant reduction in complaints.
- Increased awareness of tellers and other bank employees as to the need for quality information.
- A significant decrease in the number of customer data errors.
- Eighty-seven percent reduction of data duplication, from 7 percent to 1 percent.
- Fifty percent reduction in the amount of returned mail due to bad addresses.
- By the end of the 1-year improvement program, the percent of customer data quality that met its target quality level of 90 percent or greater accuracy increased from only 10.5 percent to 79.7 percent, an improvement of nearly eight-fold. The percent of data that had less than 70 percent accuracy decreased from 70.2 percent to 0.

Tips for Others

- Make sure the program is continuous. Quality will not be achieved if it is not a regular program.
- The program must be a full business solution. Information quality is not just cleansing; it must treat the *cause* of the problem.
- Sponsorship from high-level people is mandatory. They must believe in the cause so you do not constantly have to answer questions such as, "Why should we do this?"

Based on the assessment of your organization's information quality management maturity, this section identifies the next steps for you to take. These are foundational and require you to have them in place as a solid foundation to move to the next level of maturity.

Moving from Stage 1 to Stage 2: Awakening

To move from stage 1 to stage 2, you must:

- Break the gridlock of the status quo. You must help management feel the pain. Here you must identify the problems with poor-quality information and quantify the direct out-of-pocket costs and, to the extent possible, the missed and lost opportunity.

- Appoint an information quality leader.

In stage 2, these components must be put into place:

❑ Enterprisewide data resource management function.

❑ Enterprisewide data standards must exist and be followed. These standards must be quality standards. See Chapter 5, "Assessing Data Definition and Information Architecture Quality."

❑ Data is being defined. All new application development and data development must be defining data from a shared, cross-functional perspective.

❑ Information quality of critical information is being assessed.

❑ Costs of poor-information quality are being quantified.

❑ Data is being cleaned up so it can be trusted and used.

Moving from Stage 2 to Stage 3: Enlightenment

To move from stage 2 to stage 3 requires:

- Developing personal relationships with management sponsors.

- Developing and providing formal education to senior management in information quality principles.

- Assuring the quality of data standards.

- Continuously assessing information quality of the next most important data.

- Continuously assessing costs of nonquality information to heighten the urgency of the problem.

- Identifying and quantifying the costs of redundant application and database development.

In stage 3 these components must be put in place:

❑ Value-centric application and data development methodologies. Applications and databases must be developed around the business value chains for shared information, not for *interfaced* information.

❑ Information policy implemented by senior management.

❑ Information modeling tools are used *effectively*.

❑ Data definition and information architectures are maintained in *shared* information repositories or dictionaries, and data definition is available to knowledge workers and information producers.

❑ Some data sharing is occurring.

❑ Enterprise information models govern development and database design.

❑ The 14 Points of Information Quality are being implemented.

❑ Information quality organization is being formalized.

❑ Information quality training is available for all levels of staff.

❑ Information quality improvement process is implemented and performed.

❑ Information stewardship is being started.

Moving from Stage 3 to Stage 4: Wisdom

To move from stage 3 to stage 4 requires:

- Conducting continuing education for management.

- Implementing information stewardship formally.

- Measuring the results of the information quality improvement process and projects.

- Improving application and data development processes to reuse architected data and reusable components.

- Changing funding for application and data development.

- Introduction of new incentives and performance measures for information quality.

- Capturing data electronically at the source and eliminating major unnecessary intermediary steps.

In stage 4 these components must be put in place:

❑ The 14 Points of Information Quality are fully implemented and are maturing.

❑ All major processes are controlled and information quality levels are maintained.

❑ There is significant data sharing and reuse.

❑ There is significant reduction of redundant data.

❑ Information stewardship exists for most important data.

❑ Information quality training exists for all staff.

❑ Education and self-development of all employees, because there is some elimination of unnecessary intermediary steps.

❑ Data defect prevention is routine.

❑ Application and data design defect prevention is routine.

❑ Business rule and data integrity processes are removed from applications and implemented around the data types.

Moving from Stage 4 to Stage 5: Certainty

To move from stage 4 to stage 5 requires:

- Improving and optimizing the information quality improvement processes.
- Eliminating all unnecessary redundant data and application processes.
- Implementing information stewardship for all data.

In stage 5 these components must be put in place:

- ❑ Process optimization feedback applied to all information processes, both development and business processes. Feedback mechanisms must be in place immediately—electronically if possible—to the source, so minimal errors of a given kind occur.
- ❑ Application and data development are being implemented from an "assemble to order" approach.
- ❑ Information stewardship exists for all information.
- ❑ Information quality defect prevention is routine.

Staying in Stage 5: Certainty

Reaching stage 5 is not the end. More than one organization has reached the top of their market, only to be blinded by their "success" into a fatal complacence and lose their advantage when the competition redefined the competitive rules. To stay in stage 5 requires:

- Continual and immediate feedback.
- Immediately attacking data quality problems when they occur.
- Not forgetting the costs of nonquality information as discovered and eliminated in stages 2, 3, and 4.
- "Looking the customer ahead" to discover tomorrow's information requirements.

Sustaining Information Quality: How to Keep It Going

As you begin implementing information quality initiatives, you will have achieved tentative management commitment. The goal now is to keep it sustained. Here is how:

Always quantify the costs of the status quo before the quality initiative begins. Be sure the measures are business measures. You must have the baseline from which to measure the success of your project.

Quantify the benefits derived from the improvement process. Even if this is a cleansing project, measure the benefits in business economic measures, not just percent of data cleansed or defects prevented. Management does not care that the quality of the database is now 95 percent when it used to be 88 percent. It cares about how much cost is reduced, profit gained, or customer satisfaction increased.

Analyze the cause of any information quality initiative "failure." Nothing will kill the movement faster than a failure that can be used by those who would defend the status quo to challenge the concept. You must be able understand the cause of the failure and communicate why the next initiative will not fail. Remember: There is no such thing as a "failure" if you are trying to solve the right problems and you (and others) learn from the experience.

Create a lessons-learned document. Conduct an assessment of each information quality initiative, especially at the beginning, and analyze both positive and negative aspects. The positive aspects can be used to encourage others to take the information quality "first steps" and convince the skeptics. Get customer satisfaction surveys from those who are benefiting from the increased information quality soon after the initiative, while the pain of the former status quo is fresh on their minds. If information quality levels subsequently fall later, this information will be valuable for reestablishing the improvements. If this was a data cleansing effort, this becomes the business case for information process quality improvement.

Communicate your successes with everyone. Use your internal newsletters, put your experiences on the company bulletin boards, both physically and electronically, and put the experiences on your intranet so everyone can both see the results and learn ideas for their own areas.

Communicate your successes with top management. This is key to sustainable success. Do not hesitate to communicate the failures along with the analyzed reasons why.

Organizing for Information Quality

The organization for information quality will evolve over time. How it evolves depends on the value delivered by the information quality initiatives. The information quality organization will begin where the business first realizes the importance and "inherits" a sponsor.

We have seen this happen in three general ways. The first is within information systems in the data resource management area, as an extension of the "improve data integrity" objective. The second is within the data warehousing initiative to provide data cleanup as a result of trying to integrate and consolidate basically unintegrated and disparate data. The third way that information quality organizations happen is from a business area that is suffering significant pain and costs as a result of poor-quality information, such as marketing, claims processing, or order fulfillment.

It matters less where you establish the formal information quality organization than in the principles and processes it implements, and how it communicates its message.

Information Quality Job Functions and Descriptions

The following are some key roles or jobs within information quality.

Information Quality Manager or Leader

The information quality manager must be a leader, visionary, and change agent. The information quality manager is accountable for implementing processes to assure and improve information quality.

Responsibilities include:

- Raising awareness of the costs of nonquality information.
- Developing and implementing information quality assessment and improvement programs.
- Overseeing or coordinating data cleanup initiatives.
- Measuring and analyzing data definition, information architecture, and information quality.
- Providing analysis and feedback of information quality assessments.
- Facilitating analysis of information quality problem causes.
- Recommending improvements to development and business processes.
- Providing support to process owners to improve processes or facilitating process improvement projects.
- Facilitating information quality standards.
- Developing and coordinating information quality training.

Information Architecture Quality Analyst

This role is responsible for analyzing and assuring quality of the data definition and data model processes. The Information Architecture Quality Analyst is accountable for assessing data definition and data architecture quality, and recommending changes to the application and data development processes.

Responsibilities include:

- Measuring and analyzing data definition and information architecture quality.
- Providing analysis and feedback of information architecture assessments.
- Recommending improvements to application and data development processes.
- Providing support to data analysts and data architects in quality concepts.

Data Cleanup Coordinator, Data Quality Coordinator, or Data Warehouse Quality Coordinator

This is, or should be, a relatively temporary role. It exists only for the duration of cleanup initiatives. The role generally exists for data warehousing initiatives, data conversion projects, or cleanup of major databases. Once this is accomplished, the role migrates to Information Quality Analyst or one of the other quality roles.

The Data Cleanup Coordinator is responsible for overseeing the data acquisition and cleansing activities of a data warehousing initiative, conversion, or cleanup initiatives.

Responsibilities include:

- Identifying authoritative data sources requiring cleanup.
- Identifying business rules in existing databases.
- Discovering and facilitating the definition of the formal business rules for the cleaned and transformed data.
- Developing data transformation rules.
- Overseeing cleanup activities.
- Recommending improvements to source data capture processes.

Information Quality Analyst

The Information Quality Analyst is responsible for assessing and measuring information quality and providing feedback.

Responsibilities include:

- Developing information quality assessment processes for business data.
- Conducting automated and physical information quality assessments and report to source areas and knowledge worker areas.
- Recommending quality controls to information processes.

Information Quality Process Improvement Facilitator

This role facilitates improvements in information processes.
Responsibilities include:

- Facilitating root cause analysis workshops of information quality problems.
- Facilitating information process quality improvement planning.
- Recommending best practices in information quality.
- Providing consulting to application and data development teams in quality principles.
- Conducting (possibly) information quality training.

Information Quality Training Coordinator

This role is responsible for overseeing the development and delivery of education, training, or awareness raising in information quality to all levels of personnel in the enterprise.
Responsibilities include:

- Identifying different audiences for information quality training.
- Identifying training needs of different audiences and establishing learning objectives. See Table 11.1 for a sample of training.
- Developing or securing information quality training and education.
- Delivering, or coordinating delivery of, information quality training.

The Information Quality Organization Evolution

As the information quality organization matures it tends to rise in the organization. Figure 13.2 represents an evolution path for the information quality organization. It may begin within the information or data resource management (DRM) area, or in a business area.

Notice how the Information systems organization has matured in the third maturation level. Here its vision and role is that of information management as opposed to simply delivering application systems. Note that the information quality improvement organization may in fact begin outside of information systems.

It is most important to reinforce two concepts. The first is that the goal of information quality improvement is not to create an organization or bureaucracy, but to create a culture of information quality improvement. The second is that the Information Quality Improvement Organization *is not responsible*

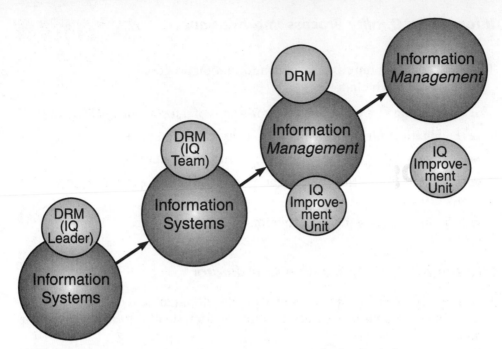

Figure 13.2   An information quality improvement organization evolution.

for information quality, *but for facilitating* the enterprise to be responsible for information quality.

Conclusion

Implementing information quality is not the responsibility of the information quality team; it is the responsibility of everyone in the enterprise. Someone must lead and get the information quality movement started. The implementation must include the growth and development of all groups, from top management to clerical data intermediaries, and from information producers to knowledge workers, and from data administrators to application developers.

The journey is long, but it is a journey of small steps at a time. The key is to know where you are, know where you ultimately want to be, and take the next step and do not try to leap over the required stages. If you create value in what you do, you will be noticed and given resources to accomplish what needs to be done next.

CHAPTER 14

Epilogue: Reaping the Benefits of Quality Information

"A journey of a thousand miles must begin with a single step."

–CHINESE PROVERB

If you are reading this, you have either read through this book and are already benefiting from improved information quality, or you have been skimming the book to put it into perspective. I leave you with some thoughts.

You Get There by Beginning

There is no finish to a race not begun; but the real reward is not in "finishing," but in improving and achieving results. The plain truth is, you will never finish. Even organizations reaching the highest stage of maturity cannot stop, because they become the "target."

When the road looks tough, keep reminding yourself of the following:

Information quality is a journey, not a destination. While the task looks huge, and the challenges great, you will never reap the tremendous benefits without getting started. Do something; do anything! Sitting back in the complacency of the status quo will only allow the information quality crisis to get worse, costing more than if you start now.

Improvement does not just happen—someone must take the initiative. Every event or initiative that led to changing the course of history was started by someone who dared to challenge the status quo. Never before has it been more important to challenge the status quo of current information (mis)management practices in business and government. The waste that occurs as a result of nonquality information squanders valuable people and financial resources at best, and is enterprise threatening at worst. Who will lead the way?

Do not be overwhelmed—quality is achieved one step at a time. Yes, getting to the stage of "certain" quality is monumental, but you will never reach it without taking the first step. The second step will be easier than the first. To be sure, you will encounter resistance. No challenge to the status quo was every embraced by those who had a vested interest in it. But the victory of the first success weakens the resistance, and as the benefits of quality information increase business performance, the opposition will turn to embrace them.

Information quality improvement is not the responsibility of the information quality department or leader—it is the responsibility of everyone in the enterprise. The burden of making information quality certain is not the responsibility of one individual, or team, or even department or division. Information quality is the responsibility of everyone in the enterprise. When we all do our part, quality becomes easy.

Information quality improvement is not a program—it is a habit. While there must ultimately be some "organization" structure around the information quality "function," it must never become the objective to create an organizational empire. The information quality "team" or "unit" or "group" must be a facilitator and catalyst for an information quality mind set within the enterprise.

Perfection is not the objective—customer satisfaction is. Zero-defect data may be a required goal for some data, but not all. The real objective is to consistently meet all customer expectations in our information products and services. This means satisfying both internal and external information customers' needs with the information on which they depend. It is this customer satisfaction that makes it all worthwhile.

Quality Information: Differentiator for Business Success

The Information Age resources are information and people. Information is in fact a *strategic* business resource. As a strategic resource, information may be employed strategically in operational processes, such as to eliminate unnecessary intermediary activities. Or, it may be employed in data warehouses to identify trends and patterns of customer behavior in which new opportunities simply present themselves to take advantage of.

In a competitive environment, the winner will always be the organization with the best (quality) people resources, including visionary leadership and empowered staff. This is true even when an organization has the best information. But who wins when two competitors have equivalent quality people resources? The one with the highest-quality information.

So who will invest in quality information? The organization with visionary leadership. Peter Drucker is right on target when he admonishes organizations to "put your resources on tomorrow's breadwinners, where the results are, and not on yesterday's breadwinners, where the memories are." Investing in the status quo is the surest way to fail in the Information Age.

The Bottom Line: Information Quality Improvement Reduces Costs and Improves Business Effectiveness

If there is any truth in what I write, it is that information quality improvement results in improved business performance, reduced costs of doing business, and increased customer satisfaction. What Ed Deming, Joseph Juran, and Philip Crosby have demonstrated in business product and service quality is true in information quality. Quality information reduces the costs of doing business. Quality information increases business effectiveness. Quality information increases customer satisfaction. And, as a direct result, quality information increases business profits and stakeholder value. Period.

Let me refresh the observation of Crosby:

"Quality is free. It's not a gift, but it is free. What costs money are the unquality things—all the actions that involve not doing jobs right the first time.

"Quality is not only free, it is an honest-to-everything profit-maker. Every penny you don't spend on doing things wrong, over, or instead of, becomes half a penny right on the bottom line... If you concentrate on making quality certain you can probably increase your profit by an amount equal to 5 to 10 percent of your sales. That is a lot of money for free." [2]

Let me state that another way:

The Visible Value of Quality Information

Every hour or dollar you *don't* spend:

- Doing something over,
- Working around data problems,
- Fixing problems caused, or
- Correcting bad data

---

[2]Philip B. Crosby, *Quality Is Free*, New York: Penguin Group, 1979, p. 1.

—because you create and maintain quality information—is an hour or dollar you *can spend* doing something worthwhile and adding value.

But even more value-adding is the fact that you will be delighting valuable customers, and in so doing, increasing their customer lifetime profits as well as the potential profits of those they influence.

Please share with me your experiences as you apply the principles and processes of information quality improvement by e-mailing me at Larry.English@ infoimpact.com.

PART

Four

Appendixes

Glossary

6 Sigma (6σ or 6s): Six standard deviations used to describe a level of quality in which six standard deviations of the population fall within the upper and lower control limits of quality and in which the defect rate approaches zero, allowing no more than 3.4 defects per million parts.

Accessibility: The characteristic of being able to access data when it is required.

Accuracy to reality: A characteristic of information quality measuring the degree to which a data value (or set of data values) correctly represents the attributes of the real-world object or event.

Accuracy to surrogate source: A measure of the degree to which data agrees with an original, acknowledged authoritative source of data about a real world object or event, such as a form, document, or unaltered electronic data received from outside the organization.

Aggregation: The process of associating objects of different types together in a meaningful whole. Also called *composition*.

Algorithm: A set of statements or a formula to calculate a result or solve a problem in a defined set of steps.

Alias: A secondary and nonstandard synonym or alternate name of an enterprise standard business term, entity type or attribute name, used only for cross-reference of an official name to legacy or software package data name.

ANSI: Acronym for *American National Standards Institute*, the U.S. body that sets standards.

Application: A collection of computer hardware, computer programs, databases, procedures, and knowledge workers that work together to perform a related group of services or business processes.

Application architecture: A graphic representation of a system showing the process, data, hardware, software, and communications components of the system across a business value chain.

Archival database: A copy of a database saved in its exact state for historical purposes, recovery, or restoration.

Artificial Intelligence (AI): The capability of a system to perform functions normally associated with human intelligence, such as reasoning, learning, and self-improvement.

Association: See *Relationship*.

Associative entity type: An entity type that describes the relationship of a pair of entity types that have a many-to-many relationship or cardinality. For example, COURSE COMPLETION DATE has meaning only in the context of the relationship of a STUDENT and COURSE OFFERING entity types.

Asynchronous replication: Replication in which a primary data copy is considered complete once the update transaction completes, and secondary replicated data copies are queued to be updated as soon as possible or on a predefined schedule.

Atomic value: An individual data value representing the lowest level of meaningful fact.

Attribute: An inherent property, characteristic, or fact that describes an entity or object. A fact that has the same format, interpretation, and domain for all occurrences of an entity type. An attribute is a conceptual representation of a type of fact that is implemented as a field in a record or data element in a database file.

Attributive entity type: An entity type that cannot exist on its own and contains attributes describing another entity. An attributive entity type resolves a one-to-many relationship between an entity type and a descriptive attribute that may contain multiple values. Also called *characteristic* or *dependent* entity type.

Audit trail: Data that can be used to trace activity such as database transactions.

Authentication: The process of verifying that a person requesting a resource, such as data or a transaction, has authority or permission to access that resource.

Availability: A percentage measure of the reliability of a system indicating the percentage of time the system or data is accessible or usable, compared to the amount of time the system or data should be accessible or usable.

Backup: To restore a database to its state at a previous point in time. Backup is achieved: (1) from an archived or a snapshot copy of the database at a specified time; or (2) from an archived copy of a database and applying the logged update activity of changes since that archived copy was made.

Benchmarking: The process of analyzing and comparing an organization's processes to that of other organizations to identify *Best practices*.

Best practice: A process, standard or component, that is generally recognized to produce superior results when compared with similar processes, standards or components.

Bias: A vested interest, or strongly held paradigm or condition, that may skew the results of sampling, measuring, or reporting the findings of a quality assessment. For example, if information producers audit their own data quality, they will have a bias to overstate its quality. If data is sampled in such a way that it does not reflect the entire population sampled, the sample result will be biased.

Bounds: See *Confidence interval*.

Business application model: A graphic illustration of the conceptual application systems, both manual and automated, including their dependencies, required to perform the processes of an organization.

Business information steward: A business subject-matter expert designated and accountable for overseeing some parts of data definition for a collection of data for the enterprise, such as data definition integrity, legal restriction compliance standards, data quality standards, and authorization security.

Business process: A synonym for *value chain*, the term is used to differentiate a value chain of activities from a functional process or functional set of activities.

Business process model: A graphic and descriptive representation of business processes or value chains that cut across functions and organizations. The model may be expressed in different levels of detail, including decomposition into successive lower levels of activities.

Business process reengineering: the process of analyzing, redefining, and redesigning business activities to eliminate or minimize activities that add cost and to maximize activities that add value.

Business resource category: A business classification of data about a resource the enterprise must manage across business functions and organizations, used as a basis for high-level information modeling. The internal resource categories are human resource, financial, materials and products, facilities and tangible assets, and information. External resources include business partners, such as suppliers and distributors; customers; and external environment, such as regulation and economic factors. Also called *subject area*.

Business rule: A statement expressing a policy or condition that governs business actions and establishes data integrity guidelines.

Business rule conformance: See *Validity*.

Business term: A word, phrase, or expression that has a particular meaning to the enterprise.

Business value chain: See *Value chain*.

Candidate key: A key that can serve to uniquely identify occurrences of an entity type. A candidate key must have two properties: (1) Each occurrence or record must have a different value of the key, so that a key value identifies only one occurrence; and (2) No attribute in the key can be eliminated without nullifying the first property.

Cardinality: The number of occurrences that may exist between occurrences of two related entity types. The cardinalities between a pair of related entity types are: one to one, one to many, or many to many. See *Relationship*.

CASE: Acronym for *Computer-Aided Systems Engineering*. The application of automated technologies to business and information modeling and software engineering.

Catalog: The component of a Database Management System (DBMS) where physical characteristics about the database are stored, such as its schema, table or file names, primary keys, foreign key relationships, and other data required for the DBMS to manage the data.

Cause-and-effect diagram: A chart in the shape of a "fishbone" used to analyze the relationship between error cause and error effect. The diagram, invented by Ishikawa, shows a specific effect and possible causes or error. The errors are drawn in four categories, each a bone on the fish. The categories are: (1) Human (Ishikawa called this *manpower*), (2) Methods, (3) Machines, and (4) Materials.

Central tendency: The phenomenon that data measured from a process generally aggregates around a value somewhere between the high and low values.

Checklist: A technique for quality improvement to identify steps to perform or items to check before work is complete.

Class word: See *Domain type*.

Cleansing: See *Data cleansing.*

Cluster sampling: Sampling a population by taking samples from a smaller number of subgroups (such as geographic areas) of the population. The subsamples from each cluster are combined to make up the final sample. For example, in sampling sales data for a chain of stores, one may choose to take a subsample of a representative subset of stores (each a cluster) into a cluster sample rather than randomly select sales data from every store.

Code: (1) To represent data in a form that can be accepted by an application program. (2) A shorthand representation or abbreviation of a specific value of an attribute.

Column: The vertical component or field of a table. An attribute of an entity type. A column has a name and a particular data type, such as date, character, number, and a domain of valid values.

Commit: A DML command that signals a successful end of a transaction and confirms that a record(s) inserted, updated, or deleted in the database is complete.

Common cause: A source of unacceptable variation or defect caused by the process or system itself. See also *Special cause.*

Completeness: A characteristic of information quality measuring the degree to which all required data is known. (1) *Fact* completeness is a measure of data definition quality expressed as a percentage of the attributes about an entity type that need to be known to assure that they are defined in the model and implemented in a database. For example, "80 percent of the attributes required to be known about customers have fields in a database to store the attribute values." (2) *Value* completeness is a measure of data content quality expressed as a percentage of the columns or fields of a table or file that should have values in them, in fact do so. For example, "95 percent of the columns for the customer table have a value in them." Also referred to as *coverage.*

Conceptual data model: See *Data model.*

Concurrency: (1) A characteristic of information quality measuring the degree to which the timing of equivalence of data is stored in redundant or distributed database files. The measure data concurrency may describe the minimum, maximum, and average information float time from when data is available in one data source and when it becomes available in another data source. Or it may consist of the relative percent of data from a data source that is propagated to the target within a specified time frame.

Concurrency assessment: An audit of the timing of equivalence of data stored in redundant or distributed database files. See *Equivalence.*

Concurrency control: A DBMS mechanism of locking records used to manage multiple transactions access to shared data.

Conditional relationship: An association that is optional depending on the nature of the related entities or on the rules of the business environment.

Confidence interval, or **confidence interval of the mean:** The upper and lower limits or values, or bounds on either side of a sample mean for which a *confidence level* is valid.

Confidence level: The degree of certainty, expressed as a percentage, of being sure that the value for the mean of a population is within a specific range of values around the mean of a sample. For example, a 95 percent confidence level indicates that one is 95 percent sure that the estimate of the mean is within a desired precision or range of values called a *confidence interval.* Stated another way, a 95 percent confidence level means that out of 100 samples from the same population, the mean of the population is expected to be contained within the confidence interval in 95 of the 100 samples.

Confidence limits: See *Confidence interval.*

Configuration management: The process of identifying and defining configurable items in an environment by controlling their release and any subsequent changes throughout the development life cycle; recording and reporting the status of those items and change requests; and verifying the completeness and correctness of configurable items.

Consensus: The agreement of a group with a judgment, decision, or data definition in which the stakeholders have participated and can say, "I can live with it."

Consistency: A measure of information quality expressed as the degree to which a set of data is equivalent in redundant or distributed databases.

Constraint: A business rule that places a restriction on business actions and therefore restrictions the resulting data. For example, "only wholesale customers may place wholesale orders."

Control: The mechanisms used to manage processes to maintain acceptable performance.

Control chart: A graphical device for reporting process performance over time for monitoring process quality performance.

Control group: A selected set of people, objects, or processes to be observed to record behavior or performance characteristics. Used to compare behavior and performance to another group in which changes or improvements have been made.

Conversion: The process of preparing, reengineering, cleansing and transforming data, and loading it into a new target data architecture.

Corporate data: See *Enterprise data*.

Correlation: A predictive relationship that exists between two factors, such that when one of the factors changes, you can predict the nature of change in the other factor. For example, if information quality goes up, the costs of information scrap and rework go down.

Cost of acquisition: (1) The cost of acquiring a new customer, including identifying, marketing and presales activities to get the first sale. (2) The costs of acquiring products, such as software packages, and services. This should be weighed against the *cost of ownership*.

Cost of ownership: The total costs of ownership of products, such as software packages, and services, including planning, acquiring, process redesign, implementation, and support required for the successful use of the product or service.

Cost of retention: The cost of managing customer relationships that result in subsequent sales to existing customers.

Coverage: See *Completeness*.

Critical information: Information that if missing or wrong can cause enterprise-threatening loss of money, life, or liability, such as failure to properly calculate pension withholding, not setting the airplane flaps correctly for takeoff, or prescribing the wrong drug.

Cross-functional: The characteristic of data or process that is of interest to more than one business or functional area.

Currency: A characteristic of information quality measuring the degree to which data represents reality from the required point in time. For example, one information view may require data currency to be the most up-to-date point, such as stock prices for stock trades, while another may require data to be the last stock price of the day, for stock price running average.

Customer: The persons or organizations whose needs the enterprise must meet, and whose satisfaction with its products and services, including information, determines enterprise success or failure.

Customer life cycle: The states of existence and relative time periods of a typical customer from being a prospect to becoming an active customer, to becoming nonactive and a "former" customer.

Customer lifetime revenue: The net present value of the average customer revenue over the life of relationship with the enterprise.

Customer lifetime value (LTV): The net present value of the average profit of a typical customer over the life of relationship with the enterprise.

Customer segment: A meaningful aggregation of customers for the purpose of marketing or determining customer lifetime value.

Customer-supplier relationship: See *Information customer-supplier relationship*.

CUSUM: Abbreviation for Cumulative Summation, a more sensitive method for detecting out-of-control measurements than a simple control chart. The CUSUM indicates when a process has been off aim for too long a period of time.

Cycle time: The time required for a process (or subprocess) to execute from start to completion.

***d*:** A symbol representing the set of deviations of a set of items from the mean of the set of items, expressed as d = x-x bar for each value of x.

Data: The representation of facts. The raw material from which information is produced when it is put in a context that gives it meaning.

Data administration: See *Data management*.

Data administrator: One who manages or provides *data administration* functions.

Data analyst: One who identifies data requirements, defines data, and synthesizes it into data models.

Data architect: One who is responsible for the development of data models.

Data audit: See *Information quality assessment*.

Data cleansing: An information scrap-and-rework process to correct data errors in a collection of data in order to bring the level of quality to an acceptable level to meet the information customers' needs.

Data cleanup: See *Data cleansing*.

Data consistency assessment: The process of measuring data equivalence and information float or timeliness in an interface-based information value chain.

Data content quality: The subset of information quality referring to the quality of data values.

Data defect prevention: The process of *information process improvement* to eliminate or minimize the possibility of data errors from getting into an information product or database.

Data definition: The specification of the meaning, domain values, and business integrity rules for an entity type or attribute. Data definition includes name, definition, and relationships, as well as domain value definition and business rules that govern business actions that are reflected in data. This term is synonymous with the term *metadata*.

Data Definition Language (DDL): The language used to describe database schemas or designs.

Data definition quality: A component of information quality measuring the degree to which data definition accurately, completely, and understandably defines what the information producers and knowledge workers should know in order to perform their job processes effectively. Data definition quality is a measure of the quality of the information product specification.

Data dictionary: A repository of information (metadata) defining and describing the data resource. A repository containing metadata. An *active* data dictionary, such as a catalog, is one that is capable of interacting with and controlling the environment about which it stores information or metadata. An *integrated* data dictionary is one that is capable of controlling the data and process environments. A *passive* data dictionary is one that is capable of storing metadata or data about the data resource, but is not capable of interacting with or controlling the computerized environment external to the data dictionary. See also *Repository*.

Data-driven development: See *Value-centric development*.

Data element: The smallest unit of named data that has meaning to a knowledge worker. A data element is the implementation of an attribute. Synonymous with data item and *field*.

Data flow diagram: A graphic representation of the "flow" of data through business functions or processes. It illustrates the processes, data stores, external entities, data flows, and their relationships.

Data independence: The property of being able to change the overall logical or physical structure of the data without changing the application program's view of the data.

Data intermediary: A role in which individuals transform data from one form, not created by them, to another form; for example, a data entry clerk entering data from a manual form into a database.

Data intermediation: The design of and performance of processes in which the actual creator or originator of knowledge does not capture that knowledge electronically, but gives it in paper or other form to be entered into a database by someone else.

Data management: The management and control of data as an enterprise asset. It includes strategic information planning, establishing data-related standards, policies, and procedures, and data modeling and information architecture. Also called *data administration*.

Data Manipulation Language (DML): The language used to access data in one or more databases.

Data mart: A subset of enterprise data along with software to extract data from a data warehouse or operational data store, summarize and store it, and to analyze and present information to support trend analysis and tactical decisions and processes. The scope can be that of a complete data subject such as Customer or Product Sales, or of a particular business area or line of business, such as Retail Sales. A data mart architecture, whether subject or business area, must be an enterprise-consistent architecture.

Data mining: The process of analyzing large volumes of data using pattern recognition or knowledge discovery techniques to identify meaningful trends and relationships represented in data in large databases.

Data model: A logical map or representation of real-world objects and events that represents the inherent properties of the data independently of software, hardware, or machine performance considerations. The model shows data attributes grouped into third normal form entities, and the relationships among those entities.

Data presentation quality: A component of information quality measuring the degree to which information-bearing mechanisms, such as screens, reports, and other communication media, are easy to understand, efficient to use, and minimize the possibility of mistakes in its use.

Data quality: See *Information quality*.

Data quality assessment: See *Information quality assessment*.

Data reengineering: The process of analyzing, standardizing, and transforming data from unarchitected or nonstandardized files or databases into an enterprise-standardized information architecture.

Data replication: The controlled process of propagating equivalent data values from a source database to one or more duplicate copies in other databases.

Data resource management: See *Information Resource Management*.

Data store: Any place in a system where data is stored. This includes manual files, machine-readable files, data tables, and databases. A data store on a logical data flow diagram is related to one or more entities in the data model.

Data transformation: The process of defining and applying algorithms to change data from one form or domain value set to another form or domain value set in a target data architecture to improve its value and usability for the information stakeholders.

Data type: An attribute of a data element or field that specifies the DBMS type of physical values, such as numeric, alphanumeric, packed decimal, floating point, or datetime.

Data value: A specific representation of a fact for an attribute at a point in time.

Data visualization: Graphical presentation of patterns and trends represented by data relationships.

Data warehouse: A collection of software and data organized to collect, cleanse, transform, and store data from a variety of sources, and analyze and present information to support decision-making, tactical and strategic business processes.

Data warehouse audits and controls: A collection of checks and balances to assure the extract, cleansing, transformation, summarization, and load processes are in control and operate properly. The controls must assure the right data is extracted from the right sources, transformed, cleansed, summarized correctly, and loaded to the right target files.

Database administration: The function of managing the physical aspects of the data resource, including physical database design to implement the conceptual data model; and database integrity, performance, and security.

Database integrity: The characteristic of data in a database in which the data conforms to the physical integrity constraints, such as referential integrity and primary key uniqueness, and is able to be secured and recovered in the event of an application, software, or hardware failure. Database integrity does not imply data accuracy or other information quality characteristics not able to be provided by the DBMS functions.

Database marketing: The use of collected and managed information about one's customers and prospects to provide better service and establish long-term relationships with them. Database marketing involves analyzing and designing pertinent customer information needs, collecting, maintaining, and analyzing that data to support mass customization of marketing campaigns to decrease costs, improve response, and to build customer loyalty, reduce attrition, and increase customer satisfaction.

Database server: The distributed implementation of a set of database management functions in which one dedicated collection of database management functions, accessing one or more databases on that mode, serves multiple knowledge workers or clients that provide a human-machine interface for the requesting of a creation of data.

DDL: Acronym for *Data Definition Language.*

Decision Support System (DSS): Applications that use data in a free-form fashion to support managerial decisions by applying ad hoc query, summarization, trend analysis, exception identification, and "what-if" questions.

Defect: An item that does not conform to its quality standard or customer expectation.

Defect rate: See *Error rate.*

Definition conformance: The characteristic of data, such that the data values represent a fact consistent with the agreed-upon definition of the attribute. For example, a value of "6/7/1997" actually represents the "Order

Date: the date an order is placed by the customer," and not the system date created when the order is entered into the system.

Delphi approach: An approach, used to achieve consensus, that involves individual judgments made independently, group discussion of the rationales for disparate judgments, and a consensus judgment being agreed upon by the participants.

Derived data: Data that is created or calculated from other data within the database or system.

Deviation (d): The difference in value of an item in a set of items and the mean (x bar) of the set as expressed in the formula $d = x\text{-}x\ bar$, where $d =$ deviation, x = the value of an item in a set, and $x\ bar$ is the mean or average of all items in the set.

DFD: Acronym for *Data Flow Diagram*.

DIF: Acronym for *Data Interchange Format*.

Dimension: A category for summarizing or viewing data (e.g., time period, product, product line, geographic area, and organization).

Directory: A table, block, index, or folder containing addresses and locations or relationships of data or files and used as a way of organizing files.

Discount rate: The market rate of interest representing the cost to borrow money. This rate may be applied to future income to calculate its net present value.

DML: Acronym for *Data Manipulation Language*.

Domain: (1) Set or range of valid values for a given attribute or field, or the specification of business rules for determining the valid values. (2) The area or field of reference of an application or problem set.

Domain chaos: A dysfunctional characteristic of an attribute or field in which multiple types of facts are represented by more. For example, unit of measure code for one product has a domain value of "doz," to represent a unit of measure of "one dozen," while for another product, the unit of measure code has a value of "150," to represent a the reorder point quantity.

Domain type: A general classification that characterizes the kind of values that may be values of a specific attribute, such as a number, date, currency amount, or percent. The domain type name may be used as a component of an attribute name. Also called a *class word*.

Domain value redundancy: A dysfunctional characteristic of an attribute or field in which the same fact of information is represented by more than one value. For example, unit of measure code having domain values of "doz," "dz," and "12" may all represent the fact that the unit of measure is "one dozen."

Drill down: The process of accessing more detailed data from summary data to identify exceptions and trends. May be multitier.

Drill through: The process of accessing the original source data from a replicated or transformed copy to verify equivalence to the record-of-origin data.

DSS: Acronym for *Decision Support Systems*.

E-commerce: Acronym for electronic commerce, the conducting of business transactions over the Internet (I-Net).

EDI: Acronym for *Electronic Data Interchange*.

Edit and validation: The process of assuring data being created conforms to the governing business rules and is correct. Database integrity controls and software routines can edit and validate conformance to business rules. Information producers must validate correctness of data.

EIS: Acronym for *Executive Information System*.

Enterprise data: The data of an organization or corporation that is owned by the enterprise and managed by a business area. Characteristics of corporate data are that it is essential to run the business and/or it is shared by more than one organizational unit within the enterprise.

Entity integrity: The assurance that a primary key value will identify no more than one occurrence of an entity type, and that no attribute of the primary key may contain a null value. Based on this premise, the real-world entities are uniquely distinguishable from all other entities.

Entity life cycle: The phases, or distinct states, through which an occurrence of an object moves over a definable period of time. The subtypes of an entity that are mutually exclusive over a given time frame. Also referred to as entity life history and state transition diagram.

Entity Relationship Diagram (ERD): See *Entity relationship model*.

Entity relationship model: A graphical representation illustrating the entity types and the relationships of those entity types of interest to the enterprise.

Entity subtype: A specialized subset of occurrences of a more general entity type, having one or more different attributes or relationships not inherent in the other occurrences of the generalized entity type. For example, an hourly employee will have different attributes from a salaried employee, such as hourly pay rate and monthly salary.

Entity supertype: A generalized entity in which some occurrences belong to a distinct, more specialized subtype.

Entity type: A classification of the types of real-world objects (such as person, place, thing, concept, or events of interest to the enterprise) that have common characteristics. Sometimes the term *entity* is used as a short name.

Entity/process matrix: A matrix that shows the relationships of the processes, identified in the business process model, with the entity types identified in the information model. The model illustrates which processes create, update, or reference the entity types.

Equivalence: A characteristic of information quality that measures the degree to which data stored in multiple places is conceptually equal. Equivalence indicates the data has equal values or is in essence the same. For example, a value of "F" for Gender Code for J. J. Jones in database A and a value of "1" for Sex Code for J. J. Jones in database B mean the same thing: J. J. Jones is female. The *measure* equivalence is the percent of fields in records within one data collection that are semantically equivalent to their corresponding fields within another data collection or database. Also called *semantic equivalence*.

ERD: Acronym for *Entity Relationship Diagram*.

Error rate: A measure of the frequency that errors occur in a process. Also called *failure rate* (in manufactured products), or *defect rate*.

Event: An occurrence of something that happens that is of interest to the enterprise.

Executive Information System (EIS): A graphical application that supports executive processes, decisions, and information requirements. Presents highly summarized data with drill-down capability, and access to key external data.

Expert system: (1) A specific class of knowledge base system in which the knowledge, or rules, are based on the skills and experience of a specific expert or group of experts in a given field. (2) A branch of artificial intelligence. An expert system attempts to represent and use knowledge in the same way a human expert does. Expert systems simulate the human trait of thinking.

Export: The function of extracting information from a repository or database and packaging it to an export/import file.

Extensibility: The ability to dynamically augment a database (or data dictionary) schema with knowledge worker-defined data types. This includes addition of new data types and class definitions for representation and manipulation of unconventional data such as text data, audio data, image data, and data associated with artificial intelligence applications.

Fact completeness: See *Completeness*.

Failure rate: A measure of the frequency that defective items are produced by a process; hence, the frequency with which the process fails. See also *Error rate*.

Feedback loop: A formal mechanism for communicating information about process performance and information quality to the process owner and information producers.

Field: A *data element* or data item in a data structure or *record*.

File integrity: The degree to which documents in a file retain their original form and utility (i.e., no misfiled or torn documents).

Filter: See *Information quality measure*.

Flexibility: A characteristic of information quality measuring the degree to which the information architecture or database is able to support organizational or process reengineering changes with minimal modification of the existing objects and relationships, only adding new objects and relationships.

Focus group: A facilitated group of customers that evaluates a product or service against those of competitors, in order to clearly define customer preferences and quality expectations.

Foolproofing: Building edit and validation routines in application programs or procedures to reduce inadvertent human error.

Foreign key: A data element in one entity (or relation) that is the primary key of another entity that serves to implement a relationship between the entities.

Frequency distribution: The relation number of occurrences of values of an attribute, including a graphic representation of that "distribution" of values.

Functional dependence: The degree to which an attribute is an inherent characteristic of an entity type. If an attribute is an inherent characteristic of an entity type, that attribute is fully functionally dependent on any candidate key of that entity type. See *Normal form*.

Gemba Kaizen: From Gemba, the Japanese word meaning "real place," and Kaizen, "continuous improvement," Gemba Kaizen means focusing on continuous improvement in the workplace where products are developed and services are provided.

Generalization: The process of aggregating similar types of objects together in a less specialized type based upon common attributes and behaviors. The identification of a common supertype of two or more specialized (sub)types. See also *Specialization*.

Heuristics: A method or rule of thumb for obtaining a solution through inference or trial-and-error using approximate methods while evaluating progress toward a goal.

Highly summarized: Data that is summarized to more than two hierarchies of summarization from the base detail data. Highly summarized data may have lightly summarized data as its source.

Homonym: A word or phrase that has the same spelling or sounds the same, but has a different meaning.

Hoshin Kanri: An enterprise vision that drives the deployment of initiatives to achieve a few critical improvements for the enterprise.

House of quality: A mapping of customer quality expectations in product or service to the quality measures of the product or service to summarize all expectations and the work to meet them.

Human factors: Static constraints related to human ergonomic and cognitive limitations.

Hypermedia: The convergence of hypertext and multimedia.

Hypertext: The ability to organize text data in logical chunks or documents that can be accessed randomly via links as well as sequentially.

Hypothetical reasoning: Hypothetical reasoning is a problem-solving approach that explores several different alternative solutions in parallel to determine which approach or series of steps best solves a particular problem. It is useful in business planning or optimization problems, where solutions vary according to cost or where numerous solutions may be feasible.

Identifier: One or more attributes that uniquely locate an occurrence of an entity type. Conceptually synonymous with *primary key*.

Inadvertent error: Error introduced unconsciously; for example, when a data intermediary unwittingly transposes values or skips a line in data entry. See also *Intentional error*.

In control: The state of a process characterized by the absence of special causes of variation. Processes in control produce consistent results within acceptable limits of variation.

Incremental load: The propagation of changed data to a target database or data warehouse in which only the data that has been changed since the last load is loaded or updated in the target.

Informate: A term coined by Shoshona Zuboff in *The Age of The Smart Machine* to described the benefit of information technology when used to capture knowledge about business events so that the knowledge can "informate" other knowledge workers to more intelligently perform their jobs.

Information: Data in context. The meaning given to data or the interpretation of data based on its context. The finished product as a result of the interpretation of data.

Information architecture: A "blueprint" of an enterprise expressed in terms of a business process model, showing what the enterprise does; an enterprise information model, showing what information resources are required; and a business information model, showing the relationships of the processes and information.

Information architecture quality: A component of information quality measuring the degree to which data models and database design are stable, flexible, and reusable, and implement principles of data structure integrity.

Information assessment: See *Information quality assessment.*

Information chaos: A state of the dysfunctional learning organization in which there are unmanaged, inconsistent, and redundant databases that contain data about a single type of thing or fact. The information chaos quotient is the number of unmanaged, inconsistent, and redundant databases containing data about a single type of thing or fact.

Information chaos quotient: The count of the number of unmanaged, inconsistent, and redundant databases containing data about a single type of thing or fact.

Information customer-supplier relationship: The information stakeholder partnerships between the information producers who create information and the knowledge workers who depend on it.

Information directory: A repository or dictionary of the information stored in a data warehouse, including technical and business metadata, that supports all warehouse customers. The technical metadata describes the transformation rules and replication schedules for source data. The business metadata supports the definition and domain specification of the data.

Information float: The length of the delay in the time a fact becomes known in an organization to the time in which an interested knowledge worker is able to know that fact. Information float has two components: Manual float is the length of the delay in the time a fact becomes known to when it is first captured electronically in a potentially sharable database. Electronic float is the length in time from when a fact is captured in its electronic form in a potentially sharable database, to the time it is "moved" to a database that makes it accessible to an interested knowledge worker.

Information group: A relatively small and cohesive collection of information, consisting of 20–50 attributes and entity types, grouped around a single subject or subset of a major subject. An information group will generally have one or more subject matter experts and several business roles that use the information.

Information life cycle: See *Information value/cost chain.*

Information Management (IM): The function of managing information as an enterprise resource, including planning, organizing and staffing, leading and directing, and controlling information. Information management includes managing data as the enterprise knowledge infrastructure and information technology as the enterprise technical infrastructure, and managing applications across business value chains.

Information model: A high-level graphical representation of the information resource requirements of an organization showing the information classes and their relationships.

Information myopia: A disease that occurs when knowledge workers can see *only part* of the information they need, caused by not defining data relationships correctly or not having access to data that is logically related because it exists in multiple nonintegrated databases.

Information policy: A statement of important principles and guidelines required to effectively manage and exploit the enterprise information resources.

Information preventive maintenance: Establishing processes to control the creation and *maintenance* of volatile and critical data to keep it maintained at the highest level feasible, possibly including validating volatile data on an appropriate schedule and assessment of that data *before* critical processes use it.

Information process improvement: The process of improving processes to eliminate data errors and defects. This is one component of *data defect prevention*. Information process improvement is *proactive* information quality.

Information producer: The role of individuals in which they originate, capture, create, or maintain data or knowledge as a part of their job function or as part of the process they perform. Information producers create the actual information content and are accountable for its accuracy and completeness to meet all information stakeholders' needs. See also *Data intermediary*.

Information product improvement: The process of data cleansing, reengineering, and transformation required to improve existing defective data up to an acceptable level of quality. This is one component of *information scrap and rework*. See also *Data cleansing*, *Data reengineering*, and *Data transformation*. Information product improvement is *reactive* information quality.

Information quality: The degree to which information consistently meets the requirements and expectations of the knowledge workers in performing their jobs.

Information quality assessment: The random sampling of a collection of data and testing it against its valid data values to determine its accuracy and reliability. Also called *data quality assessment* or *data audit*.

Information quality contamination: The creation of inaccurate derived data by combining accurate data with inaccurate data.

Information quality decay: The characteristic of a collection of data such that its quality (accuracy) will diminish over time if no updates are applied.

Information quality decay factor: The rate, usually expressed as a percent per year, at which the data quality of a data collection will deteriorate over time if no data updates are applied (e.g., person age decay rate is 100 percent; if 17 percent of a population moves annually, the decay rate of address is 17 percent).

Information quality management: The function that leads the organization to improve information quality by implementing processes to measure, asses costs of, improve and control information quality, and by providing guidelines, policies, and education for information quality improvement.

Information quality measure(s): A specific quality measure or test (set of measures or tests) to assess information quality. For example, Product ID will be tested for uniqueness, Customer records will be tested for duplicate occurrences, Customer address will be tested to assure it is the correct address, Product Unit of Measure will be tested to be a valid Unit of Measure domain code, and Order Total Price Amount will be tested to assure it has been calculated correctly. Quality measures will be assessed using business rule tests in automated quality analysis software, coded routines in internally developed quality assessment programs, or in physical quality assessment procedures. Some call information quality measures *filters* or *metrics*.

Information Resource Management (IRM): (1) The application of generally accepted management principles to data as a strategic business asset. (2) The function of managing data as an enterprise resource. This generally includes *data management* or data administration, *repository management*, and *database administration*.

Information scrap and rework: The activities and costs required to cleanse or correct nonquality information, to recover from process failure caused by nonquality information, or to rework or work around problems caused by missing or nonquality information. Analogous to manufacturing *scrap and rework*.

Information stakeholder: Any individual who has an interest in and dependence on a set of data or information. Stakeholders may include information producers, knowledge workers, external customers, and regulatory bodies, as well as various information systems roles such as database designers, application developers, and maintenance personnel.

Information steward: The role of people with respect to their accountability for the integrity of some part of the information resource.

Information stewardship: Accountability for the integrity of some part of the information resource for the good of the larger organization. See

Strategic information steward, Managerial information steward, and *Operational information steward.*

Information value: The measure of importance of information expressed in tangible metrics. Information has *realized* and *potential* value. Realized value is the actual value derived from information applied by knowledge workers in the accomplishment of the business processes. Potential value is the future value of information that could be realized if applied to business processes in which the information is not currently used.

Information value/cost chain: The end-to-end set of processes and data stores, electronic and otherwise, involved in creating, updating, interfacing, and propagating data of a type from its origination to its ultimate data store, including independent data entry processes, if any.

Information view: A knowledge worker's perceived relationship of the data elements needed to perform a process, showing the structure and data elements required. A process activity has one and only one information view.

Information view model: A local data model derived from an enterprise model to reflect the specific information required for one business area or function, one organization unit, one application or system, or one business process.

Intentional error: Error introduced consciously. For example, an information producer required to enter an unknown fact like birthdate, enters his or her own or some "coded" birthdate used to mean "unknown." See also *Inadvertent error.*

Interface program: An application that extracts data from one database, transforms it, and loads it into a noncontrolled redundant database. Interface programs represent one cost of information scrap and rework in that the information in the first database is not "able" to be used from that source and must be "reworked" for another process or knowledge worker to use.

Internal view: The physical database design or schema in the ANSI 3-schema architecture.

IRM: Acronym for *Information Resource Management.*

ISO: Acronym for *International Organization for Standardization.* A European body founded in 1946 to set international standards in all engineering disciplines, including information technology. Its members are national standards bodies; for example, BSI (British Standards Institute). ISO approves standards, including OSI communications protocols and ISO 9000 standards.

ISO 9000: International standards for quality management specifying guidelines and procedures for documenting and managing business processes and providing a system for third-party certification to verify those procedures are followed in actual practice.

Kaizen: A Japanese word meaning "continuous improvement," including continuous improvement in all aspects of life: personal, social, professional, and in work. In work, Kaizen means continuous improvement involving everyone in the organization, both managers and workers.

Knowledge: Information context; understanding of the significance of information.

Knowledge base: (1) That part of a knowledge base system in which the rules and definitions used to build the application are stored. The knowledge base may also include a fact or object storage facility. (2) A database where the codification of knowledge is kept; usually a set of rules specified in an if . . . then format.

Knowledge base system: A software system whose application-specific information is programmed in the form of rules and stored in a specific facility, known as the knowledge base. The system uses Artificial Intelligence (AI) procedures to mimic human problem-solving techniques, applying the rules stored in the knowledge base and facts supplied to the system to solve a particular business problem.

Knowledge error: Information quality error introduced as a result of lack of training or expertise

Knowledge worker: The role of individuals in which they use information in any form as part of their job function or in the course of performing a process, whether operational or strategic. Also referred to as an *information consumer* or *customer*. Accountable for work results created as a result of the use of information and for adhering to any policies governing the security, privacy, and confidentiality of the information used.

Legacy data: Data that comes from files and/or databases developed without using an enterprise data architecture approach.

Legacy system: Systems that were developed without using an enterprise data architecture approach.

Lifetime value (LTV): See *Customer lifetime value.*

Lightly summarized: Data that is summarized only one or two levels of hierarchy of summary from the base detailed data.

Load: To sequentially add a set of records into a database or data warehouse. See also *Incremental load.*

Lock: A means of serializing events or preventing access to data while an application or information producer may be updating that data.

Log: A collection of records that describe the events that occur during DBMS execution and their sequence. The information thus recorded is used for recovery in the event of a failure during DBMS execution.

Lower control limit: The lowest acceptable value or characteristic in a set of items deemed to be of acceptable quality. Together with the *upper control limit*, it specifies the boundaries of acceptable variability in an item to meet quality specifications.

LTV: Acronym for Customer *Lifetime Value*.

Managerial information steward: The role of accountability a business manager or process owner has for the quality of data produced by his or her processes.

Managerial information stewardship: The fact that a business manager or process owner who has accountability for one or more business processes also has accountability for the integrity of the data produced by those processes.

MDDB: Acronym for *Multidimensional Database*.

Mean: The average of a set of values, usually calculated to one place of decimals more than the original data.

Measure: A metric or characteristic of information quality, such as percent of accuracy or average information float, to be assessed.

Measurement system: A collection of processes, procedures, software, and databases used to assess and report information quality.

Median: The middle value in an ordered set of values. If the set contains an even number of values, the median is calculated by adding the middle two values and dividing by 2.

Metadata: A term used to mean data that describes or specifies other data. The term *metadata* is used to define all of the characteristics that need to be known about data in order to build databases and applications and to support knowledge workers and information producers. The term has not made its way into either *Webster's Unabridged Dictionary* or the *Oxford English Dictionary*. The closest term is *meta language*, defined as "a language used to describe other languages." This book uses the term *data definition* to refer to all aspects others call *metadata*.

Methodology: A formalized collection of tools, procedures, and techniques to solve a specific problem or perform a given function.

Metric: (1) See *Measure*. (2) A fact type in data warehousing, generally numeric (such as sales, budget, and inventory) that is analyzed in different ways or dimensions in decision support analysis.

Misinterpretation: Human error resulting from poor information presentation quality.

Modal interval: The range interval used to group continuous data values in order to determine a mode.

Mode: The most frequently occurring value in a set of values.

Monte Carlo: A problem-solving technique that uses statistical methods and random sampling to solve mathematical or physical problems.

Muda: The Japanese word for "waste." Muda elimination is the elimination of non-value adding activities of all kinds in the workplace.

Multidimensional Database (MDDB): A database designed around arrays of data that support many dimensions or views of data (such as product sales by time period, geographic location, and organization) to support decision analysis.

***n*:** Algebraic symbol representing the number of items in a set.

Net Present Value (NPV): The value of a sum of future money expressed in terms of its worth in today's currency. NPV is calculated by discounting the amount by the discount rate compounded by the number of years between the present and the future date the money is anticipated.

NIST: Acronym for *National Institute of Standards and Technology*. The U.S. government agency that maintains *Federal Information Processing Standards* (FIPS). NIST is responsible for administering the Baldrige Quality Award program.

Nonduplication: A characteristic of information quality measuring the degree to which there are no redundant occurrences of data.

Nonquality data: Data that is incorrect, incomplete, or does not conform to the data definition specification or meet knowledge workers' expectations.

Nonrepudiation: The ability to provide proof of transmission and receipt of electronic communication.

Normal form: A level of normalization that characterizes a group of attributes or data elements.

    First Normal Form (1NF): (1) A relation R is in first normal form (1NF) if and only if all underlying domains contain atomic values only. (2) A table is in 1NF if it can be represented as a two-dimensional table, and for every attribute there exists one single meaningful and atomic value, never a repeating group of values.

    Second Normal Form (2NF): (1) A relation R is in second normal form (2NF) if and only if it is in 1NF and every nonkey attribute is fully functionally dependent on the primary key. (2) A table is in 2NF if each non-identified attribute provides a fact that describes the entity identified by the entire primary key and not part of it. See *Functional dependence*.

    Third Normal Form (3NF): (1) A relation R is in third normal form (3NF) if and only if it is in 2NF and every nonkey attribute is nontransitively dependent upon the primary key. (2) A table is in 3NF if each nonkey column provides a fact that is dependent only on the entire key of the table.

Boyce/Codd Normal Form (BCNF): (1) A relation R is in Boyce/Codd normal form (BCNF) if and only if every determinant is a candidate key. (2) A table is in BCNF if every attribute that is a unique identify of attributes describing an entity is a candidate key of that entity.

Fourth Normal Form (4NF): (1) A relation R is in fourth normal form (4NF) if and only if, whenever there exists an MVD in R, say A ->-> B, then all attributes of R are also functionally dependent upon A. In other words, the only dependencies (FDs or MVDs) in R are of the form K -> X (i.e., a functional dependency from a candidate K to some other attribute X). Equivalently, R is in 4NF if it is in BCNF and all MVDs in R are in fact FDs. (2) A table is in 4NF if no row of the table contains two or more independent multivalued facts about an entity.

Fifth Normal Form (5NF): (1) A relation R is in fifth normal form (5NF) (also called Projection Join Normal Form [PJ/NF]) if and only if every join dependency in R is a consequence of the candidate keys of R. (2) A table is in 5NF if a relation or record in which all elements within a concatenated key are independent of each other and cannot be derived from the remainder of the key.

Normalization: The process of associating attributes with the entity types for which they are inherent characteristics. The decomposition of data structures according to a set of dependency rules, designed to give simpler, more stable structures in which certain forms of redundancy are eliminated. A step-by-step process to remove anomalies in data integrity caused by add, delete, and update actions. Also called *non-loss decomposition*.

NPV: Acronym for *Net Present Value*.

Null: The absence of a data value in a field or data element.

Occurrence: A specific instance of an entity type. For example, "customer" is an entity type. "John Doe" is an occurrence of the customer entity type.

Occurrence of record: A specific record selected from a group of duplicate records as the authoritative record, and into which data from the other records may be consolidated. Related records from the other duplicate records are re-related to this occurrence of record.

OCR: Acronym for *Optical Character Recognition*.

ODS: Acronym for *Operational Data Store*.

On-Line Analytical Processing (OLAP): Software technology that transforms data into multidimensional views and that supports multidimensional data interaction, exploration, and analysis.

Operational data: Data at a detailed level used to support daily activities of an enterprise.

Operational Data Store (ODS): A collection of operation or bases data that is extracted from operation databases and standardized, cleansed, consolidated, transformed, and loaded into a enterprise data architecture. An ODS is used to support data mining of operational data, or as the store for base data that is summarized for a data warehouse. The ODS may also be used to audit the data warehouse to assure the summarized and derived data is calculated properly. The ODS may further become the enterprise shared operational database, allowing operational systems that are being reengineered to use the ODS as their operations databases.

Operational information steward: An information producer accountable for the data created or updated as a result of the processes he or she performs.

Optical Character Recognition (OCR): The technique by which printed, digitized, or photographed characters can be recognized and converted into ASCII or a similar format.

Optimum: As applied to a quality goal, that which meets the needs of both customer and supplier at the same time, minimizing their combined costs.

Paradigm: An example or pattern that represents an acquired way of thinking about something that shapes thought and action in ways that are both conscious and unconscious. Paradigms are essential because they provide a culturally shared model for how to think and act, but they can present major obstacles to adopting newer, better approaches.

Pareto diagram: A specialized column chart in which the bars represent defect types and are ordered by frequency, percentage, or impact with the cumulative percentage plotted. This is used to identify the areas needing improvement, from greatest to least.

Pareto principle: The phenomenon that a few factors are responsible for the majority of the result.

Partnership: The relationship of business personnel and information systems personnel in the planning, requirements analysis, design, and development of applications and databases.

PDCA: Acronym for *Plan-Do-Check-Act*.

Perceived needs: The requirements that motivate customer action, based upon their perceptions. For example, a perceived need of a car purchaser is that a convertible will enhance his or her attractiveness. See also *Real needs* and *Stated needs*.

Personal data: Data that is of interest to only one organization component of an enterprise, (e.g., task schedule for a department project). Contrasted with *Enterprise data*.

Physical database design: Mapping of the conceptual or logical database design data groupings into the physical database areas, files, records, elements, fields, and keys while adhering to the physical constraints of the hardware, DBMS software, and communications network to provide physical data integrity while meeting the performance and security constraints of the services to be performed against the database.

Plan-Do-Check-Act (PDCA) cycle: A closed-loop process for planning to solve a problem, implementing suggested improvements, analyzing the results, and standardizing the improvements. Also called a *Shewhart cycle* after its developer, W. A. Shewhart.

Population: An entire group of items or data that comes from an entire group of items that we wish to measure.

Postcondition: A data integrity mechanism in object orientation that specifies an assertion, condition, business rule or guaranteed result that will be true upon completion of an operation or method; else, the operation or method fails.

Potential information value: See *Information value.*

Precision: A characteristic of information quality measuring the degree to which data is known to the right level of granularity. For example, a percentage value with two decimal points (00.00%) discriminates to the closest 1/100th of a percent.

Precondition: A data integrity mechanism in object orientation that specifies an assertion, condition or business rule that must be true before invoking an operation or method; else, the operation or method cannot be performed.

Presentation format: The specification of how an attribute value or collection of data is to be displayed.

Primary key: The attribute(s) that are used to uniquely identify a specific occurrence of an entity, relation, or file. A primary key that consists of more than one attribute is called a *composite* (or *concatenated*) primary key.

Prime word: A component of an attribute name that identifies the entity type the attribute describes.

Procedural error: Error introduced as a result of failure to follow the defined process.

Process: A defined set of activities to achieve a goal or end result. An activity that computes, manipulates, transforms, and/or presents data. A process has identifiable begin and end points. See *Business process.*

Process control: The systematic evaluation of performance of a process, taking corrective action if performance is not acceptable according to defined standards.

Process management cycle: A set of repeatable tasks for understanding customer needs, defining a process, establishing control, and improving the process.

Process management team: A team, including a process owner and staff, to carry out process ownership obligations.

Process owner: The person responsible for the process definition and/or process execution. The process owner is the managerial information steward for the data created or updated by the process, and is accountable for process performance integrity and the quality of information produced.

Product: The output or result of a process.

Product satisfaction: The measure of customer happiness with a product.

QFD: Acronym for *Quality Function Deployment*.

Quality: Consistently meeting or exceeding customers' expectations.

Quality assessment: An independent measurement of product's or service's quality.

Quality circle: An ad hoc group formed to correct problems in or to improve a shared process. The goal is an improved work environment and productivity and quality

Quality Function Deployment (QFD): The involvement of customers in the design of products and services for the purpose of better understanding customer requirements, and the subsequent design of products and services that better meet their needs on initial product delivery.

Quality goal: See *Quality standard*.

Quality improvement: A measurable and noticeable improvement in the level of quality of a process and its resulting product.

Quality standard: A mandated or required quality goal, reliability level, or quality model to be met and maintained.

r: Algebraic symbol represented in the coefficient of correlation.

Rapid Application Development (RAD): The set of tools, techniques, and methods that results in at least one-order-of-magnitude acceleration in the time to develop an application with no loss in quality compared to using conventional techniques.

Rapid Data Development (RADD): An intensive group process to rapidly develop and define sharable subject area data models involving a facilitator, knowledge workers, and data resource management personnel, using compression planning techniques.

Random number generator: A software routine that selects a number from a range of values in such a way that any number within the range has an equal likelihood of being selected. This may be used to identify which records from a database to select for assessment.

Random sampling: The sampling of a *population* in which every item in the population is likely to be selected with equal probability. This is also called *statistical sampling*. See also *Cluster sampling*, *Stratified sampling*, and *Systematic sampling*.

Real needs: The fundamental requirements that motivate customer decisions. For example, a real need of a car customer is the kind of transportation it provides. See also *Stated needs* and *Perceived needs*.

Realized information value: See *Information value*.

Record: A collection of related fields representing an occurrence of an entity type.

Record of origin: The first electronic file in which an occurrence of an entity type is created.

Record-of-reference: The single, authoritative database file for a collection of fields for occurrences of an entity type. This file represents the most reliable source of operational data for these attributes or fields. In a fragmented data environment, a single occurrence may have different collections of fields whose record of reference is in different files.

Recovery: Restoring a database to some previous condition or state after system, or device, or program failure. See also *Commit*.

Recovery log: A collection of records that describe the events that occur during DBMS execution and their sequence. The information thus recorded is used for recovery in the event of a failure during DBMS execution.

Recursive relationship: A relationship or association that exists between entity occurrences of the same type. For example, an organization can be related to another organization as a Department manages a Unit.

Reengineering: A method for radical transformation of business processes to achieve breakthrough improvements in performance.

Reference data: A term used to classify data that is, or should be, standardized, common to and shared by multiple application systems, such as Customer, Supplier, Product, Country, or Postal Code. Reference data tends to be data about permanent entity types and domain value sets to be stored in tables or files, as opposed to business event entity types.

Referential integrity: Integrity constraints that govern the relationship of an occurrence of one entity type or file to one or more occurrences of another entity type or file, such as the relationship of a customer to the orders that customer may place. Referential integrity defines constraints for creating, updating, or deleting occurrences of either or both files.

Relationship: The manner in which two entity or object types are associated with each other. Relationships may be one to one, one to many, or many to many, as determined by the meaning of the participating entities and by business rules. Synonymous with *association*. Relationships can express *cardinality* (the number of occurrences of one entity related to an occurrence of the second entity) and/or *optionality* (whether an occurrence of one entity is a requirement given an occurrence of the second entity).

Replication: See *Data replication*.

Repository: A database for storing information about objects of interest to the enterprise, especially those required in all phases of database and application development. A repository can contain all objects related to the building of systems including code, objects, pictures, definitions, etc. Acts as a basis for documentation and code generation specifications that will be used further in the systems development life cycle. Also referred to as *design dictionary, encyclopedia, object-oriented dictionary*, and *knowledge base*.

Requirements: Customer expectations of a product or service. May be formal or informal, or they may be stated, required or perceived needs.

Return on Investment (ROI): A statement of the relative profitability generated as a result of a given investment.

Reverse engineering: The process of taking a complete system or database and decomposing it to its source definitions, for the purpose of redesign.

ROI: Acronym for *Return on Investment*.

Role type: A classification of the different roles occurrences of an entity type may play, such as an organization may play the role of a customer, supplier, and/or competitor.

Rollback: The process of restoring data in a database to the state at its last commit point.

Root cause: The underlying cause of a problem or factor resulting in a problem, as opposed to its precipitating or immediate cause.

Rule: A knowledge representation formalism containing knowledge about how to address a particular business problem. Simple rules are often stated in the form: "If <antecedent> then <consequent>, where <antecedent> is a condition (a test or comparison) and <consequent> is an action (a conclusion or invocation of another rule)." An example of a rule would be "If the temperature of any closed valve is greater than or equal to 100°F, then open the valve."

Sample: An item or subset of items, or data about an item or a subset of items that comes from a *sampling frame* or a *population*. A sample is used for the purpose of acquiring knowledge about the entire population.

Sampling: The technique of extracting a small number of items or data about those items from a larger population of items in order to analyze and draw conclusions about the whole population. See *Cluster sampling*, *Random sample*, *Stratified sampling*, and *Systematic sampling*.

Sampling frame: A subset of items, or data about a subset of items of a *population* from which a *sample* is to be taken.

SC21: Acronym for *ISO/IEC JTCI* Sub-Committee for OSI data management and distributed transaction processing.

Schema: The complete description of a database in terms of its entity types, attributes and relationships or structure, or of an object base in terms of the definitions of types classes, attributes, operations and interfaces, or protocols.

Scrap and rework: The activities and costs required to correct or dispose of defective manufactured products. See *Information scrap and rework*.

SDLC: Acronym for *Systems Development Life Cycle*.

Seamless integration: True seamless integration is integration of applications through commonly defined and shared information, with managed, replication of any redundant data. False "seamless" integration is use of interface programs to transform data from one application's databases to another application's databases.

Security: The prevention of unauthorized access to a database and/or its contents for updating, retrieving, or deleting the database; or the prevention of unauthorized access to applications that have authorized access to databases.

Semantic equivalence: See *Equivalence*.

Sensor: An instrument that can measure, capture information about or receive input directly from external objects or events.

Shewhart cycle: See *Plan-Do-Check-Act cycle*.

sigma (σ or s): Lowercase Greek letter that stands for *standard deviation*. The symbol "σ" refers to the standard deviation of an entire population of items. The symbol "s" refers to the standard deviation of a sample of items.

Sigma ($\sum$): Uppercase Greek letter that stands for the summation of a group of numbers.

Six Sigma (6σ): See *6 Sigma*.

SME: Acronym for *Subject Matter Expert*.

Source information producer: The point of origination or creation of data or knowledge within the organization.

SPC: Acronym for *Statistical Process Control*.

Special cause: A source of unacceptable variation or defect that comes from outside the process or system.

Specialization: The process of aggregating subsets of objects of a type, based upon differing attributes and behaviors. The resulting subtypes specialization inherits characteristics from the more generalized type.

Spread: Describes how much variation there is in a set of items.

SQC: Acronym for *Statistical Quality Control.*

Stability: A characteristic of information quality measuring the degree to which information architecture or a database is able to have new applications developed to use it with minimal modification of the existing objects and relationships, only adding new objects and relationships.

Standard deviation (σ or s): A widely used measure of variability that expresses the measure of spread in a set of items. The standard deviation is a value such that approximately 68 percent of the items in a set fall within a range of the mean plus or minus the standard deviation. For data from a large sample of a population of items, the standard deviation σ (standard deviation of a population) or s (standard deviation of a sample) is expressed as:

$$s = \sqrt{\Sigma d^2}$$

$s\ (\sigma)$ = standard deviation of a sample (population)
d = the deviation of any item from the mean or average
n = the number of items in the sample
Σ = "the sum of."

Standard deviation calculation: A measure of dispersion of a frequency distribution that is the square root of the arithmetic mean of the squares of the derivation of each of the class frequencies from the arithmetic mean of the frequency distribution. Also a similar quantity found by dividing by one less than the number of squares in the sum of squares instead of taking the arithmetic mean.

State: A stage in a life cycle of an object class in which an entity occurrence or object may exist at a point in time. Transition to a state is triggered by an event. The state of an object is represented by the values of its attributes at a point in time and determines future behavior of the object.

Stated needs: Requirements as seen from the customers' viewpoint, and as stated in their language. These needs may or may not be the real requirements. See also *Perceived needs* and *Real needs.*

State transition diagram: A representation of the various states of an entity or object along with the triggering events. See also *Entity life cycle.*

Statistical control chart: See *Control chart*.

Statistical Process Control (SPC): See *Statistical quality control*.

Statistical Quality Control (SQC): Processes and methods for measuring process performance, identifying unacceptable variance, and applying corrective actions to maintain acceptable process control. Also called *statistical process control*.

Stored procedure: A precompiled routine of code stored as part of a database and callable by name.

Strategic information steward: The role a senior manager holds as being accountable for a major information resource of subject, authorizes business information stewards and resolves business rule issues.

Stratified sampling: Sampling a population that has two or more distinct groupings, or strata, in which random samples are taken from each stratum to assure the strata are proportionately represented in the final sample.

Subject area: See *Business resource category*.

Subject database: A physical database built around a subject area.

Subject Matter Expert (SME): A business person who has significant experience and knowledge of a given business subject or function.

Suboptimization: The phenomenon such that the accomplishment of departmental goals minimizes the ability to accomplish the enterprise goals.

Subtype: See *Entity subtype*.

Supertype: See *Entity supertype*.

Synchronization: The process of making data equivalent in two or more redundant databases.

Synchronous replication: Replication in which all copies of data must be updated before the update transaction is considered complete. This requires two-phase commit.

Systematic sampling: Sampling of a population using a technique such as selecting every eleventh item, to ensure an even spread of representation in the sample.

System log: Audit trail of events occurring within a system (e.g., transactions requested, started, ended, accessed, inspected, and updated).

System of record: See *Record of reference*. The term *system of record* is meaningless when defining the authoritative record in an integrated, shared data environment where data may be updated by many different application systems within a single database.

Systems approach: The philosophy of developing applications as vertical functional projects independent of how they fit within the larger business value chain. This approach carves out an application development project into a standalone project and does not attempt to define data to be shared across the business value chain or to meet all information stakeholder needs.

Systems Development Life Cycle (SDLC): The methodology of processes for developing new application systems. The phases change from methodology to methodology, but generically break down into the phases of requirements definition, analysis, design, testing, implementation, and maintenance. If data definition quality is lacking, this process requires improvement.

Systems thinking: The fifth discipline of the learning organization, this sees problems in the context of the whole. Applications developed with systems thinking see the application scope within the context of its value chain and the enterprise as a whole, defining data as a sharable and reusable resource.

Taguchi Loss Function: The principle (for which Dr. Genichi Taguchi won the Japanese Deming Prize in 1960) that deviations from the ideal cause different degrees of loss in quality and economic loss. Small deviations in some critical characteristics can cause significantly more economic loss than even large deviations in other characteristics. Some data quality problems are likewise critical and cause significantly more economic loss than others, and become the higher priority for process improvement and cleanup.

Teamwork: The cooperation of many within different processes or business areas to increase the quality or output of the whole.

Third normal form: See *Normal form*.

Timeliness: A characteristic of information quality measuring the degree to which data is available when knowledge workers or processes require it.

Total Quality Management (TQM): Techniques, methods, and management principles that provide for continuous improvement to the processes of an enterprise.

TPCP: Acronym for *Two-Phase Commit Protocol*.

TQM: Acronym for *Total Quality Management*.

Transaction consistency: The highest isolation level that allows an application to read only committed data and guarantees that the transaction has a consistent view of the database, as though no other transactions were active. All read locks are kept until the transaction ends. Also known as *serializable*.

Transformation: See *Data transformation*.

Trigger: A software device that monitors the values of one or more data elements to detect critical events. A trigger consists of three components: a procedure to check data whenever it changes, a set or range of criterion values or code to determine data integrity or whether a response in called for, and one or more procedures that produce the appropriate response.

Trusted database: Data that has been secured and protected from unauthorized access.

Two-phase commit: In multithreaded processing systems it is necessary to prevent more than one transaction from updating the same record at the same time. Where each transaction may need to update more than one record or file, the *two-phase commit* protocol is often used. Each transaction first checks that all the necessary records are available and contain the required data, simultaneously locking each one. Once it is confirmed that all records are ready and locked, the updates are applied and the locks freed. If any record is not available, the whole transaction is aborted and all other records are unlocked and left in their original state.

Two-stage sampling: Sampling a population in two steps. The first step extracts sample items from a lot of common groupings of items such as sales orders by order taker. The second stage takes a second sample from the items in the primary or first stage samples.

Uncommitted read: The lowest isolation level that allows an application to read both committed and uncommitted data. Should be used only when one does not need an exact answer, or if one is highly assured the data is not being updated by someone else. (Also known as *read uncommitted, read through,* or *dirty read).*

Undo: A state of a unit of recovery that indicates that the unit of recovery's changes to recoverable database resources must be backed out.

Unit of recovery: A sequence of operations within a unit of work between points of consistency.

Unit of work: A self-contained set of instructions performing a logical outcome in which all changes are performed successfully or none of them is performed.

Update: Causing to change values in one or more selected occurrences, groups, or data elements stored in a database. May include the notion of adding or deleting data occurrences.

Upper control limit: The highest acceptable value or characteristic in a set of items deemed to be of acceptable quality. Together with the *lower control limit,* it specifies the boundaries of acceptable variability in an item to meet quality specifications.

User: An unfortunate term used by many to refer to the role of people to information technology, computer systems, or data. The term implies dependence on something, or one who has no choice, or one who is inactively involved in the use of something. The term is inappropriate to describe the role of information producers and knowledge workers who perform the work of the enterprise, and for whom information technology should enable them to transform their work, and for whom information is a necessary and vital resource. With respect to information technology, applications, and data, the role of business personnel is that of information producers and knowledge workers. The relationship of business personnel to information systems personnel is not as users, but as partners who together solve the information and work problems of the enterprise.

Validity: A characteristic of information quality measuring the degree to which the data conforms to defined business rules. Validity is not synonymous with *accuracy*, which means the values are the correct values. A value may be a valid value, but still be incorrect. For example, a customer date of first service can be a *valid* date (within the correct range) and yet not be an *accurate* date.

Value: (1) Relative worth, utility, or importance. (2) An abstraction with a single attribute or characteristic that can be compared with other values, and may be represented by an encoding of the value.

Value-centric development: A method of application development that focuses on data as an enterprise resource and automates activities as a part of an integrated business value chain. Value-centric development incorporates "systems thinking," which sees an application as a component within its larger value chain, as opposed to a "systems approach," which isolates the application as a part of a functional or departmental view of activity and data.

Value chain: An end-to-end set of activities that begins with a request from a customer and ends with specific benefit or benefits for a customer, either internal or external. Also called a *business process* or *value stream*.

Value completeness: See *Completeness*.

Value stream: See *Value chain*.

Variance (vσ): The mean of the squared deviations of a set of values, expressed as:

$$v = \frac{\sum d^2}{n - 1}$$

View: A presentation of data from one or more tables. A view can include all or some of the columns contained in the table or tables on which it is defined. See also *Information view*.

Wisdom: *Knowledge* in context. Knowledge applied in the course of actions.

$\bar{x}$ (x bar): The algebraic symbol representing the mean, or average, of a set of values.

x: The algebraic symbol representing a set of values.

Xσ*ₙ* (***X*** **Sigma** ***n***): Formula to find the standard deviation(s) of the X values. Sometimes written as σ$_n$.

Zero defects: A state of quality characterized by defect-free products or 6-Sigma level quality. See *6 Sigma*.

Information Quality Recommended Reading and Bibliography

Recommended Reading

Bracket, M. *The Data Warehouse Challenge: Taming Data Chaos*. New York: John Wiley & Sons, 1996.

Buckland, J., R. Fowinkle, L. Shroyer, and F. Rice. *Total Quality Management in Information Services*. New York: Wiley Interscience, 1997.

Crosby, P. B. *Quality Is Free: The Art of Making Quality Certain*. New York: Penguin Group, 1979.

Deming, W. E. *Out of the Crisis*. Cambridge: Massachusetts Institute of Technology Center for Advanced Engineering Study, 1986.

English, L. P. "Data Quality: Meeting Customer Needs." *DM Review*. November 1996.

English, L. P. "Data Stewardship: A Human Solution to Data Integrity." *Database Programming & Design*. April 1993.

English, L. P. "Plain English on Data Quality." *DM Review*. Monthly column, Jan. 1997–present.

Huang, K-T, Yang Lee & Richard Wang. *Quality Information and Knowledge*. Upper Saddle River: Prentice-Hall, 1999.

Ishikawa, K., trans. David Lu. *What Is Total Quality Control?—The Japanese Way*. New York: Prentice-Hall, 1985.

Redman, T. *Data Quality for the Information Age*. Boston: Artech House, 1996.

Reingruber, M. C., and William W. Gregory. *The Data Modeling Handbook: A Best-Practice Approach to Building Quality Data Models*. New York: John Wiley & Sons, 1994.

Walton, M. *The Deming Management Method*. New York: Putnam Publishing Group, 1986.

Wang, R., Lee Yang, Leo Pipino, and Diane Strong. "Manage Your Information as a Product." *MIT Sloan Management Review*. Boston, 1998: 95–105.

Bibliography

"Acquisition Issues: Dealing with Massive 'Data Chunks'." *Health Management Technology*. v. 18. no. 10. September 1997: 20.

Aguayo, R. *Dr. Deming: The American Who Taught the Japanese about Quality*. New York: Simon & Schuster, 1990.

Aiken P. H. *Data Reverse Engineering: Slaying the Legacy Dragon*. New York: McGraw Hill, 1996. Alesandrini, K. *Survive Information Overload*. Homewood: Business One Irwin, 1992.

Alexander, C., S. Ishikawa, and M. Silverstein. *A Pattern Language*. Oxford: Oxford UP, 1977.

Alt, V. J. "Do You Know If Your Colleagues Like Your Standards: If You Don't Know, Conduct a Survey!" *Quality Data Processing*. no. 3. October 1989: 22–27.

Aragon, L. "Down With Dirt." *PC Week*. v. 14. no. 45. October 27, 1997: 83-85.

Aragon, L. "The Lowdown on Dust Bustin' Tools." *PC Week*. v. 14. no. 45. October 27, 1997: 84.

Arthur, L. *Improving Software Quality: An Insider's Guide to TQM*. New York: John Wiley & Sons, 1992.

Ashkenas, R., D. Ulrich, T. Jick, and S. Kerr. *The Boundaryless Organization*. San Fransisco: Jossey-Bass, Inc., 1995.

Baer, T. "The Data Cleansing Payback: Garbage Out, Value In." *Computer Finance*. Computerwire Inc., 928 Broadway, New York, NY 10010. Phone: (212) 677-0409.

Bailey, R. W. *Human Error in Computer Systems*. Englewood Cliffs: Prentice-Hall, 1983.

Bailey, R. W. *Human Performance Engineering: Using Human Factors/Ergonomics to Achieve Computer System Usability*. Englewood Cliffs: Prentice-Hall, 1989.

Barker, J. *Discovering the Future Series: The Business of Paradigms*. Burnsville: Charthouse International, 1991. (Video)

Barker, J. *Future Edge: Discovering the New Paradigms of Success*. New York: William Morrow and Company, 1991.

Barquin, R., and H. Edelstein. *Building, Using, and Managing the Data Warehouse*. Upper Saddle River: Prentice-Hall, 1997.

Barrett, E. *Text, ConText, and HyperText*. Cambridge: MIT Press, 1988.

Bartholomew, D. " The Price Is Wrong." *Information Week*. September 14, 1992.

Belasco, J. A. *Teaching the Elephant to Dance*. New York: Crown, Inc., 1990.

Bender, P. S. *Resource Management: An Alternative View of the Management Process*. New York: John Wiley & Sons, 1983.

Bertino, E., et al. "Integration of Heterogeneous Database Applications through an OO Interface." *Information Systems*. v. 14. no. 5. 1989: 407–420.

Bischoff, J., and Tex Alexander. *Data Warehouse: Practical Advice from the Experts*. Upper Saddle River: Prentice-Hall, 1997.

Block, P. *Stewardship: Choosing Service Over Self Interest*. San Francisco: Berret-Koehler, 1993.

Bohn, K. "Converting Data for Warehouses." *DBMS*. v. 10. no 7. June 1997: 61.

Booker, E. "Quality in I/S: Managing with Facts, Not Intuition." *Computerworld*. no. 23. December 11, 1989: 97.

Borsodi, R. *The Definition of Definition*. Boston: F. Porter Sargent, 1967.

Bracket, M. *The Data Warehouse Challenge: Taming Data Chaos*. New York: John Wiley & Sons, 1996.

Branscomb, A. W. *Who Owns Information?* New York: HarperCollins, 1994.

Brodie, M. L. *Specification and Verification of Database Semantic Integrity*. Ph.D. Thesis, Department of Computer Science, Toronto: University of Toronto, 1978.

Brown, M. G., D. Hitchcock, and M. Willard. *Why TQM Fails and What To Do About It*. Burr Ridge: Richard D. Irwin, Inc., 1994.

Bruce, T. *Designing Quality Databases with IDEF1X Information Models*. New York: Dorset House, 1992.

Bryce, T. "Building Quality into Systems." *Systems Development*. no. 8. September 1988: 3–6.

Buchanan, L. "Cultivating and Information Culture." *CIO*. v. 7, no. 6, December 15, 1994/January 1, 1995: 47–51.

Buckland, J., R. Fowinkle, L. Shroyer, and F. Rice. *Total Quality Management in Information Services*. New York: John Wiley & Sons, 1997.

Bulkeley, W. M. "Databases Are Plagued by Rein of Error." *The Wall Street Journal*. May 26, 1992: B6.

Camp, R. *Benchmarking: The Search for Industry Best Practices that Lead to Superior Performance*. New York: Quality Press, 1989.

Campbell, R. "Create Reports that Get Rave Reviews." *Data Based Advisor*. April 1996.

Capezio, P., and Debra Morehouse. *Taking the Mystery Out of TQM*. Franklin Lakes: Career Press, 1995.

Carpenter, S. L., and W. J. D. Kennedy. *Managing Public Disputes*. San Francisco: Jossey-Bass, Inc., 1989.

Celko, J. "Don't Warehouse Dirty Data." *Datamation*. October 15, 1995: 42–52.

Chaudhuri, A., and Horst Stenger. *Survey Sampling*. New York: Marcel Dekker, 1992.

Cohen, A., and David L. Bradford. *Influence Without Authority*. New York: John Wiley & Sons, 1990.

Connor, P.E., and Linda Lake. *Managing Organizational Change*. 2nd ed. New York: Praeger, 1994.

Conrad, R. "The Design of Information." *Occupational Psychology*. July 1962: 36.

Constantine, L. *Constantine on Peopleware*. Englewood Cliffs: Prentice Hall, 1995.

Covey, S. R. *The 7 Habits of Highly Effective People: Powerful Lessons in Personal Change*. New York: Simon & Schuster, 1989.

Crosby, P. B. *Completeness Quality for the 21st Century*. New York: Penguin Group, 1992.

Crosby, P. B. *Quality Is Free: The Art of Making Quality Certain*. New York: Penguin Group, 1979.

Date, C. J. *An Introduction to Data Base Systems*. 6th ed. Reading: Addison-Wesley, 1995.

Davenport, T., and Laurence Prusak. *Information Ecology: Mastering the Information and Knowledge Environment*. New York: Oxford University Press, 1997.

Davenport, T., R, Eccles, and L. Prusak. "Information Politics." *Sloan Management Review*. Fall 1992: 53–65.

Davidow, W., and B. Uttal. *Total Customer Service: The Ultimate Weapon*. New York: Harper & Row, 1989.

DeBono, E. *I Am Right—You Are Wrong*. London: Penguin Books, 1990.

DeBono, E. *Lateral Thinking: Creativity Step by Step*. New York: Harper & Row, 1970.

Deming, W. E. *Out of the Crisis*. Cambridge: Massachusetts Institute of Technology Center for Advanced Engineering Study, 1986.

Deming, W. E. *Quality, Productivity, and Competitive Position*. Cambridge: Massachusetts Institute of Technology Center for Advanced Engineering Study, 1982.

Dhar, V., and Roger Stein. *Seven Methods for Transforming Corporate Data into Business Intelligence*. Upper Saddle River: Prentice Hall, 1997.

Doyle, L. *Information Users as Information Custodians. Handbook of Data Management*. Boston: Warren Gorham Lamont, 1993.

Drucker, P. *The New Realities*. New York: Harper & Row, 1989.

Edwards, Mark R., and Ann J. Ewen. *360° Feedback: The Powerful New Model for Employee Assessment & Performance Improvement*. New York: AMACOM, 1996.

English, L. P. "Data Quality: Meeting Customer Needs." *DM Review*. November 1996.

English, L. P. "Data Stewardship: A Human Solution to Data Integrity." *Database Programming & Design*. April 1993.

English, L. P. "DRM Today, DRM Tomorrow." *Database Programming & Design*. November 1993.

English, L. P. "Help for Data-Quality Problems." *Information Week*. October 7, 1996, pp. 53–62.

English, L. P. "The Information-Age Organization: A Profile." *FMI Journal*. vol 3. no. 4. Winter 1993.

English, L. P. "Plain English on Data Quality." *DM Review*. Monthly column, Jan 1997–present.

English, L. P. "Redefining Information Management: IM as an Effective Business Enabler." *Information Systems Management*. Winter 1996.

English, L. P. "Transforming Information Management." *Handbook of IS Management, Fifth Edition*. Boston: Auerbach, 1997.

Farrand, A. B. "Common Elements in Today's Graphical User Interfaces: the Good, the Bad, and the Ugly." *INTERCHI '93*, 470–473.

Feigenbaum, A. V. *Total Quality Control*. 3rd rev. ed. New York: McGraw-Hill, 1983.

Fenick, S. "Implementing Management Metrics: An Army Program." *IEEE Software*. no. 19. March 1990: 219–221.

Fenton, N. *Software Metrics: A Rigorous Approach*. New York: Van Nostrand Reinhold, 1991.

Freiser, T. J. "Quality Assurance: The I/S Achilles' Heel." *CIO Journal*. no. 1. Winter 1989: 18–21.

Fry, A., and David Paul. *How to Publish on the Internet*. New York: Warner Books, 1995.

Fumas, G. W., et al. "The Vocabulary Problem in Human-System Communication." *Communications of the ACM*. v. 30. no. 11. November 1987: 964–971.

Galitz, W. O. *User-Interface Screen Design*. New York: John Wiley & Sons, 1993.

Gause, D., and Gerald Weinberg. *Exploring Requirements Quality Before Design*. New York: Dorset House Publishing, 1989.

Gellman, R. "Don't Fear Privacy Protection—Arm Yourself with Fairness Checks." *Government Computer News*. v. 17 no. 12. May 4, 1998: 26.

George, S., and Arnold Weimerskirch. *Total Quality Management: Strategies and Techniques Proven at Today's Most Successful Companies*. New York: John Wiley & Sons, 1994.

Gilbert, K. C., J.M. Reeves, and Richard A. Wannemacher. "Improving Information System Efficiency Through Statistical Process Control." *Journal of Information Systems Management*. no. 7. Spring 1990: 8–14.

Giles, J. "Is Data Warehousing Only First Aid?" *Database Programming & Design*. v. 11. no 7. July 1998: 34–40.

Gitlow, H. S., and Shelly Gitlow. *The Deming Guide to Quality and Competitive Position*. Englewood Cliffs: Prentice Hall, 1987.

Glazer, R. "Measuring the Value of Information: The Information-Intensive Organization." *IBM Systems Journal*. v. 32, no. 1, 1993.

Govoni, S. J. "License to Kill." *Information Week*. January 6, 1992.

Graham, A. *Teach Yourself Statistics*. Chicago: NTC Publishing, 1993.

Grant, E.L., and R.S. Leavenworth. *Statistical Quality Control*. New York: McGraw-Hill, 1996.

Guy, D., D. R. Carmichael, and O. Ray Whittington. *Audit Sampling: An Introduction, 4th ed*. New York: John Wiley & Sons, 1997.

Guy, D., D. R. Carmichael, and O. Ray Whittington. *Practitioner's Guide to Audit Sampling*. New York: John Wiley & Sons, 1998.

Haebich, W. "Data Quality in the Real World." *Database Programming & Design*. v. 11. no 2. February 1998: 50–58.

Hammer, M. "Reengineering Work: Don't Automate, Obliterate." *Harvard Business Review*. July/August 1990: 104–112.

Hammer, M., and James Champy. *Reengineering the Corporation: A Manifesto for Business Revolution*. New York: HarperBusiness, 1993.

Hammer, M., and Steven Stanton. *The Reengineering Revolution: A Handbook*. New York: HarperCollins, 1995.

Hammond, M. "Y2K Worries for DSS." *PC Week*. v. 15. no. 22. June 1, 1998: 14.

Hansen, M. D. "Data Quality: What Data Base Managers Need to Know." *Data Base Management*. v. 2. no. 10. October 1992: 28–30.

Hansen, M. D. "Managing Data Quality in DB2." *DB2 Journal*. v. 1. no. 3. November 1992: 18–22.

Hansen, M. D. "Zero Defect Data." MIT Alfred P. Sloan School of Management master's thesis. 1991.

Harrington, H. J., and Dwayne D. Mathers. *ISO 9000 and Beyond: From Compliance to Performance Improvement*. New York: McGraw-Hill, 1997.

Hayslett, H. T., Jr. *Statistics Made Simple*. New York: Doubleday, 1968.

Hix, D., and H. Rex Hartson. *Developing User Interfaces: Ensuring Usability Through Product and Process*. New York: John Wiley & Sons, 1993.

Horch, J. W. "Quality Makes Sense." *Systems Development*. no. 8. September 1988: 1–2+.

Horn, R. E. *How Desktop Publishing Is Changing How We Present the Information Mapping Method*. Waltham: Information Mapping, Inc., 1987.

Horn, R. E. "Recent Perspectives on the Information Mapping Method." Waltham: Information Mapping, Inc., 1985.

Horten, O. "Datakvalitet (Data Quality)." Norwegian School of Economics and Business Administration master's thesis, 1996.

Houston, J. "A Quality Product Takes Quality Data." *Automation*. no 37. March 1990: 18+.

"HTML Bad Style Page: A Collection of DON'Ts for HTML." www.earth.com/bad-style/.

Huang, K-T, Yang Lee & Richard Wang. *Quality Information and Knowledge*. Upper Saddle River: Prentice-Hall, 1999.

Hughes, A. M. *Strategic Database Marketing*. Chicago: Probus Publishing Co., 1994.

Huh, Y. U., et al. "Data Quality." *Information and Software Technology*. v. 32. no. 8. 1990: 559–564.

"IDU's Principles for Good Web Sites." www.idu.co.uk/idu/www_prin.html.

Imai, M. *Gemba Kaizen: A Commonsense, Low Cost Approach to Management*. New York: McGraw-Hill, 1997.

Imai, M. *Kaizen: The Key to Japan's Competitive Success*. New York: Random House, 1989.

Inmon, W. H. "Referential Integrity in the Data Warehouse." *Enterprise Systems Journal*. v. 13. no. 8. August 1998: 46–48.

Ishikawa, K. *Guide to Quality Control*. Tokyo: Asian Productivity Organization, 1994.

Ishikawa, K., trans. David Lu. *What Is Total Quality Control?—The Japanese Way*. Englewood Cliffs: Prentice-Hall, 1988.

Jackson, R., and Paul Wang. *Strategic Database Marketing.* Lincolnwood: NTC Business Books, 1994.

Japan Human Relations Association, ed. *Kaizen Teian 2: Guiding Continuous Improvement Through Employee Suggestions.* Productivity Press, 1997.

Juon, S. "Clean-Cut Warehousing: HP Comes Clean on their Reseller Database." *HP Professional.* v. 12. no. 7. July 1998: 22–24.

Juran, J. M. *Managerial Breakthrough.* New York: McGraw-Hill, 1964.

Juran, J. M. *Juran on Planning For Quality.* New York: Macmillan Free Press, 1988.

Juran, J. M. Frank M. Gryna, ed. *Juran's Quality Control Handbook, 4th ed.* New York: McGraw-Hill, 1988.

Kan, S. *Metrics and Models in Software Quality Engineering.* Reading: Addison-Wesley, 1995.

Kanter, R. M. *The Change Masters.* New York: Simon & Schuster, 1985.

Katzenbach, J., and D. Smith. *The Wisdom of Teams.* Boston: Harvard Business School Press, 1993.

Keen, P. *Competing in Time: Using Telecommunications for Competitive Advantage.* Cambridge: Ballinger, 1988.

Kent, W. *Data and Reality.* Amsterdam: Elsevier Science, Ltd., 1978.

Kiely, T. "Her Majesty's Data Guardians." *CIO.* October 15, 1992. 48–49.

Kiely, T. "Keeping Your Info Honest." *CIO.* October 15, 1992. 42–46.

Knapp, T. *Data Quality Engineering Handbook.* Ft. Belvoir: Defense Logistics Agency, 1994.

Knight, B. "The Data Pollution Problem." *Computerworld.* September 28, 1992: 81–84.

Knowles, A. "Dump Your Dirty Data for Added Profits." *Datamation.* v. 43. no. 9. September 1997: 80–85.

Krill, P. "Data Warehouses Have Need for Clean Data." *InfoWorld.* v. 20. no. 11. March 16, 1998: 27.

Latzko, W., and David Saunders. *Four Days with Dr. Deming.* Reading: Addison-Wesley, 1995.

Laudon, K. C. "Data Quality and Due Process in Large Interorganizational Record Systems." *Communications of the ACM.* v. 29. no. 1. January 1986.

Laurel, B. *The Art of Human-Computer Interface Design.* Reading: Addison-Wesley, 1990.

Levine, S. *Getting to Resolution.* San Francisco: Berrett-Koehler, 1998.

Levitin, A. V., and Thomas C. Redman. "Data as a Resource: Properties, Implications, and Prescriptions." *MIT Sloan Management Review.* Boston, 1998: 95–105.

Liepens, G. E. "Sound Data Are a Sound Investment." *Quality Progress.* v. 22. no. 9. September 1989: 61–64.

Linkemer, B. *How to Run a Meeting.* New York: American Management Association, 1987.

Little, R. J., and P. J. Smith. "Editing and Imputation for Quantitative Survey Data." *Journal of the American Statistical Association.* v. 82. 1987: 58–68.

Lock, D., ed. *Handbook of Quality Management.* Aldershot: Gower, 1990.

Loebl, A. S. "Accuracy and Relevance and the Quality of Data." In G.E. Liepins and V.R.R. Uppuluri, eds., *Data Quality Control: Theory and Pragmatics.* New York: Marcel Dekker, 1990: 105–143.

Louderback, J. "Moving Closer to the Goal of Zero-Defect Data." *PC Week.* v. 9. no. 31. August 3, 1992.

Lynch, P. J. and Sarah Horton. *Web Style Guide.* New Haven: Yale University Press, 1999.

Madnick, S. "Database in the Internet Age." *Database Programming & Design.* v. 10. no 1. January 1997: 28–33.

Madron, B. B. "Cost of Quality." *Quality Data Processing.* no. 3. October 1989: 14–16.

Main, J. *Quality Wars: The Triumphs and Defeats of American Business.* New York: Juran Institute, 1994.

Marchand, D. "Managing Information Quality. In I. Wormell ed." *Information Quality Definitions and Dimensions.* London: Taylor Graham, 1990.

Melrose, K. *Making the Grass Greener on Your Side.* San Francisco: Berrett-Koehler, 1995.

Miley, M. "Preparing Data on the Back End—In Stocking, Updating, Managing, and Otherwise Controlling an Ever-Growing Data Warehouse, IS Managers Need Helpful Tools." *LAN Times.* v. 15. no. 14. July 6, 1998: 26.

Miller, G. A. "The Magical Number Seven Plus or Minus Two: Some Limits on Our Capacity for Processing Information." *The Psychological Review.* v. 63. 1956: 84–97.

Miller, M. "Building Quality into the Data Management Infrastructure." *Data Resource Management.* v. 4. no. 1. Winter 1993: 14–25.

Mintzberg, H. "Covert Leadership: Notes on Managing Professionals." *Harvard Business Review.* November–December 1998: 140–147.

"MIS Quality Survey." *Quality Data Processing.* no. 3. January 1, 1989: 34–36.

Monks, R. A. G. *The Emperor's Nightingale.* Reading: Addison-Wesley: 1998.

Monks, R. A. G., and Nell Minow. *Power and Accountability.* New York: Harper-Business, 1991.

Montgomery, D. C. *Introduction to Statistical Quality Control.* New York: John Wiley & Sons, 1996.

Moody, D., and G. Shanks. "What Makes a Good Data Model—Evaluating the Quality of Entity-Relationship Models." *Proceedings of the 13th International Conference on the Entity-Relationship Approach.* Manchester, 1994.

Morey, R. C. "Estimating and Improving the Quality of Information in a MIS." *Communications of the ACM.* v. 25. no. 5. May 1982: 337–342.

Moriarty, T. "A Metadata Management How-To." *Database Programming & Design.* v. 10. no 2. February 1997: 57–61.

Moriarty, T., and Suzi Hellwege. "Data Migration." *Database Programming & Design.* v. 11. no 1. January 1998: 11–13.

Mullet, K., and Darrell Sano. *Designing Visual Interfaces: Communication Oriented Techniques.* Englewood Cliffs: Prentice Hall, 1995.

Mullins, C. "Data Warehousing Guidelines for DB2." *Enterprise Systems Journal.* v. 13. no. 8. August 1998: 18–21.

Murphy, J. "Real Risks and Virtual Rewards." *Computer Weekly.* May 14, 1998: V1.

Naisbitt, J., and Patricia Aburdene. *Re-Inventing the Corporation.* New York: Warner Books, 1985.

Nelson, B. *1001 Ways to Reward Employees.* New York: Workman Pub Co., 1994.

Nelson, M. *Guide to Worldwide Postal-Code and Address Formats.* New York: Nelson Intersearch Company, 1997.

Neuhauser, P. C. *Tribal Warfare in Organizations.* New York: Harper & Row, 1988.

Neuman, P. G. "Risks To the Public In Computers and Related Systems." *Software Engineering Notes.* no. 13. October 1988: 3–20.

Nielsen, J. *Usability Engineering.* Boston: Academic Press, 1994.

Nielson, J., and D. Sano. *SunWeb: User Interface Design for Sun Microsystem's Internal Web.* Sun Microsystems Inc., 1996. (www.sun.com/sun-on-net/uidesign/sunweb/)

Nissenbaum, H. "Computing and Accountability." *Communications of the ACM.* January, 1994.

Nunn, H., ed. *The Value of Information to the Intelligent Organization.* Hertfordshire: University of Hertfordshire Press, 1994.

Oman, R. C., and Tyrone B. Ayers. "Improving Data Quality." *Journal of Systems Management.* no. 39. May 1988: 31–35.

Osborne, D. and Ted Gaebler. *Reinventing Government:How the Entrepreneurial Spirit is Transforming the Public Sector.* New York: Plume, 1993.

O'Shea, J., and Charles Madigan. *Dangerous Company: The Consulting Powerhouses and the Businesses They Save and Ruin.* New York: Times Books, 1997.

Parker, G. M. *Cross-Functional Teams.* San Francisco: Jossey-Bass, Inc., 1994.

Parker, G. M. *Team Players and Teamwork.* San Francisco: Jossey-Bass, Inc., 1990.

Parkes, C. H. "The Long Road from Data to Wisdom." *DBMS.* v. 11. no. 3. March 1998: 72.

Parsaye, K., and Mark Chignell. *Intelligent Databases: Object-Oriented, Decutive Hypermedia Technologies.* New York: John Wiley & Sons, 1989.

Parsaye, K., Mark Chignell, et al. *Intelligent Database Tools & Applications: Hyperinformation Access, Data Quality, Visualization, Automatic Discovery.* New York: John Wiley & Sons, 1993.

Paulk, M., et al. *The Capability Maturity Model: Guidelines for Improving the Software Process.* Reading: Addison-Wesley, 1995.

Pautke, R. W., and T. C. Redman. "Techniques to Improve Quality of Data in Large Databases." *Proceedings of Statistics Canada Symposium 90: Data Quality.* 319–333.

Pinchot, G. *Intrapreneuring.* New York: Harper & Row, 1985.

Porter, M. *Competitive Advantage: Creating and Sustaining Superior Performance.* New York: The Free Press, 1985.

"Presenting the 1989 National Quality Award Winners and Why They Won." *Quality Data Processing.* no. 4. January 1990: 6–10.

Pritchett, P. *New Work Habits for a Radically Changing World*. Dallas: Pritchett & Associates, Inc., 1994.

"Quality in Practice: BS 5750 and Kaizen." *BBC Training Videos*. Wadworth: David Hall Partnership Ltd., 1993. +44 (0302) 852–932.

Redman, T. *Data Quality for the Information Age*. Boston: Artech House, 1996.

Redman, T. *Data Quality Management and Technology*. New York: Bantam Books, 1992.

Reingruber, M. C., and William W. Gregory. *The Data Modeling Handbook: A Best-Practice Approach to Building Quality Data Models*. New York: John Wiley & Sons, 1994.

Rhind, Graham. *Building and Maintaining a European Direct Marketing Database*. Aldershot: Ashgate Press, 1994.

Robbins, H., and M. Finley. *Why Teams Don't Work*. Princeton: Peterson's/Pacsetter Books, 1995.

Rodgers, T. J., W. Taylor, and R. Foreman. *No-Excuses Management*. New York: Doubleday Currency, 1992.

Rosenthal, S. "Improving the Quality of Data Descriptions." *DM Review*. April 1993.

Rubenstein, R., and H. Hersch. *The Human Factor: Designing Computer Systems for People*. Digital Equipment Corporation, 1984.

Rust, R., Anthony Zahorik, and Timothy Keiningham. *Return On Quality*. Chicago: Irwin Professional Publishing, 1994.

Ryan, A. J. "Where Quality Takes Command." *Computerworld*. no. 23. December 11, 1989: 1+.

Ryan, T. P. *Statistical Methods for Quality Improvement*. New York: John Wiley & Sons, 1989.

Scherkenbach, W. "Performance Appraisal and Quality: Ford's New Philosophy." *Quality Progress*. April 1985.

Schonberger, R. *Building a Chain of Customers*. New York: Free Press, 1990.

Schwadel, F. "Revised Recipe." *The Wall Street Journal*. August 14, 1985.

Senge, P. *The Fifth Discipline: The Art and Practice of the Learning Organization*. New York: Bantam Doubleday Dell Group, 1990.

Senge, P. (ed.), et al. *The Fifth Discipline Fieldbook: Strategies and Tools for Building a Learning Organization*. New York: Currency/Doubleday, 1994.

Shepperd, M. *Foundations of Software Measurement*. Englewood Cliffs: Prentice-Hall, 1995.

Shewart, W. *Statistical Method from the Viewpoint of Quality Control*. New York: Dover Publications, 1986.

Simon, A. "The Watchful Enterprise." *Database Programming & Design*. v. 10. no 13. December 15, 1997: 26–32.

Slaikeu, K. A. *When Push Comes to Shove: A Practical Guide to Meditating Disputes*. San Francisco: Jossey-Bass, Inc., 1995.

Small, J. E. *ISO 9000 for Executives*. Sunnyvale: Lanchester Press, 1997.

Smith, J. *Reusability & Software Construction: C & C++*. New York: John Wiley & Sons, 1990.

Smith, W. "A Challenge From the Chairman of the Editorial Board." *Quality Data Processing*. no. 2. January 1988: 12+.

Spewak, S. H. "The DRM Mission: Quality Data." *Data Resource Management*. v. 2. no. 1. Winter 1991: 6–10.

Stalk, G., and Tom Hout. *Competing Against Time*. New York: Free Press, 1990.

Stewart, T. *Intellectual Capital: The New Wealth of Organizations*. New York: Doubleday, 1997.

Strassmann, P. A. *The Politics of Information Management: Policy Guidelines*. New York: Information Economics Press, 1994.

Strassmann, P. A. *Squandered Computer*. New Canaan: Information Economics Press, 1997.

Strassmann, P. A. *Information Payoff: The Transformation of Work in the Electronic Age*. New York: The Free Press, 1985.

Sullivan, L. P. "Quality Funtion Deployment." *Quality Progress*. v. 19, no. 6. June 1986: 39–50.

Svanks, M. I. "Integrity Analysis." *Information and Software Technology*. v. 30. no. 10. December 1988: 595-605.

Tapscott, D. *The Digital Economy: Promise & Peril in the Age of Networked Intelligence*. New York: McGraw Hill, 1996.

Tasker, D. "Domains and Data Validation." *DataBase Newsletter*. May/June 1987.

Tasker, D. *Fourth Generation Data: A Guide to Data Analysis for New and Old Systems*. New York: Prentice Hall, 1989.

Te'eni, D. "Data Feeding/Data Consuming: Problems and Solutions." *Journal of Information Systems Management*. v. 7. no. 2. 1990: 23–32.

Terninko, J. *Step-By-Step QFD: Customer-Driven Product Design*. Boca Raton: St. Lucie Press, 1997.

Thorbeck, J. "The Turnaround Value of Values." *Harvard Business Review*. January/February 1991: 52–62.

The 3M Meeting Management Team, J. Drew, and M. Jewitt, *Mastering Meetings: Discovering the Hidden Potential of Effective Business Meetings*. New York: McGraw-Hill, 1994.

Tilton, E., C. Steadman, and T. Jones. *Web Weaving: Designing and Managing an Effective Web Site*. Reading: Addison-Wesley, 1996.

"Top Ten Things NOT to do on a Web Page." http://cast.stanford.edu/cast/www/donts.html.

Townsend, P., and Joan E. Gebhardt. *Quality in Action: 93 Lessons in Leadership, Participation, and Measurement*. New York: John Wiley & Sons, 1992.

"TQM Comes to Information Quality." *The Information Advisor*. v. 4. no. 6. June 1992.

"TRW Sued Over Credit Reports." *Asbury Park Press*. v. 112. no. 161. July 10, 1991: D7.

Tufte, E. *Envisioning Information*. Cheshire: Graphics Press, 1990.

Tufte, E. *The Visual Display of Quantitative Information*. Cheshire: Graphics Press, 1983.

Vavra, T. G. *After Marketing: How to Keep Customers For Life Through Relationship Marketing*. New York: Irwin Prof Publishers, 1992.

Vincent, D. *The Information-Based Corporation*. Homewood: Richard D. Irwin, Inc., 1990.

Wagner, S. F. *Introduction to Statistics*. New York: HarperPerennial, 1992.

Walton, M. *The Deming Management Method*. New York: Putnam Publishing Group, 1986.

Wang, R., and D. M. Strong. "Beyond Accuracy: What Data Quality Means to Consumers." *Journal of Management Information Systems*. v. 4, 1996: 5–34.

Wang, R., Lee Yang, Leo Pipino, and Diane Strong. "Manage Your Information as a Product." *MIT Sloan Management Review* Boston, 1998: 95–105.

Watson, G. H. *Strategic Benchmarking: How to Rate Your Company's Performance Against the World's Best*. New York: John Wiley & Sons, 1993.

Weaver, R., and John D. Farrel. *Managers As Facilitators*. San Francisco: Berret-Koehler Publishers, 1997.

Weinberg, G. *Quality Software Management: Volume 1 Systems Thinking*. New York: Dorset House, 1992.

Weinman, L. *"Designing Web Graphics: How to Prepare Images and Media for the Web."* 11 (1). 1996. 40–45.

Weinman, L. "How to Spice Up Your Site." *The Net*. 11 (1). 1996. 40–45.

Weldon, J. L. "Who Owns the Data?" *Journal of Information Systems Management*. Winter 1986.

Wertz, C. J. *The Data Dictionary: Concepts and Uses*. Indianapolis: New Riders Publishing, 1996.

Wheatley, M. *Leadership and the New Science: Learning About Organization from an Orderly Universe*. San Francisco: Berrett-Koehler, 1994.

White, C. "Managing Data Transformations." *Byte*. v. 22. no. 12. December 1997: 53–54.

Williams, J. "Tools for Traveling Data." *DBMS*. v. 10. no. 7. June, 1997: 69.

Wilson, L. "Insurer Gets a Quality Check on Decision Support." *Computerworld*. v. 31. no. 33. August 18, 1997: 71–73.

Wilson, L. "The Devil in Your Data." *Information Week*. August, 1992: 48–54. *Computerworld*. August 31, 1992: 48–50.

Wilson, S. *World Wide Web Design Guide*. Indianapolis: Hayden Books, 1995.

Woodall, J., Deborah K. Rebuck, and Frank Voehl. *Total Quality in Information Systems and Technology*. Delray Beach: St. Lucie Press, 1997.

Zachman, J. A. "Enterprise Architecture: The Issue of the Century," Database programming and Design, March, 1997. pp. 44–53.

Zachman, J. A. "A Framework for Information System Architecture," IBM, Systems Journal, Vol. 26, No. 3, 1987, pp. 276–292.

Zuboff, S. *In The Age of The Smart Machine*. New York: Basic Books, 1988.

Index